D1241192

Bus Ride To Justice

Bus Ride To Justice

CHANGING THE SYSTEM BY THE SYSTEM

The Life and Works of Fred D. Gray

Preacher ▲ Attorney ▲ Politician

Lawyer for Rosa Parks, Martin Luther King, Jr.,
the Montgomery Bus Boycott, the Tuskegee
Syphilis Study, the Desegregation of Alabama
Schools, and the Selma March

FRED D. GRAY

The Black Belt Press

Montgomery

The Black Belt Press
P.O. Box 551
Montgomery, AL 36101

The Black Belt, defined by its dark, rich soil, stretches across central Alabama. It was the heart of the cotton belt. It was and is a place of great beauty, of extreme wealth and grinding poverty, of pain and joy. Here we take our stand, listening to the past, looking to the future.

Second Printing

Library Of Congress Cataloging-in-Publication Data
Gray, Fred D., 1930-
    Bus ride to justice : changing the system by the system, the life and work of Fred D. Gray, lawyer for Rosa Parks, Martin Luther King, Jr., and the Montgomery Bus Boycott / Fred D. Gray.
    p. cm.
    Includes index.
    ISBN 1-881320-23-5
    1. Gray, Fred D., 1930- . 2. Afro-American lawyers—Biography. 3. Civil rights workers—United States—Biography. 4. Afro-Americans—Legal status, laws, etc.—History—20th century.
I. Title.
KF373.G685A3 1994
342.73'085'092—dc20
[B]
[347.30285092]
[B]
                                                    94-41805
                                                    CIP

To my wife
BERNICE

And in loving memory of my mother
NANCY GRAY ARMS

Contents

Foreword

The surest way to determine whether an American society truly works and adheres to its stated values and declarations is to evaluate it from the perspective of a black civil rights lawyer. Fred D. Gray of Montgomery and Tuskegee, Alabama, is a veteran of the modern civil rights crusade. He was one of the chief architects of the strategies that sustained the Montgomery Bus Protest and represented Rosa Parks and Martin Luther King, Jr. as well as other Movement principals in those tumultuous early years. Fred and everyone involved viewed him as the "movement lawyer."

Though Gray largely operated behind the scenes, the white governing officials nevertheless knew with whom they were dealing. Ex-Alabama governor and ardent segregationist John Patterson confided in an interview that if any of the state-sanctioned maneuvers to remove Fred Gray from the city had worked then, the movement for desegregation perhaps could have been stalled or put on hold for a generation or more. He added that Gray just kept getting the people out of jail.

Gray is a modest, unassuming soft-spoken man; only the eyes reveal a steely determination. He never hated the white Southerners who fought so fervently to maintain racial segregation and discrimination. He never took their verbal attacks and manipulations personally, perhaps because he knew that the real culprit in the centuries-long war for justice, equality of opportunity, and freedom from oppression was the body of laws that littered the Southern judicial system.

Fred Gray returned from Case Western Reserve Law School in 1954 with a single-minded objective—to destroy segregation. Of course he had many strengths upon which to draw—a supportive family, a deep religious faith, a loving and loyal woman who would become his wife and secretary, and most important a personality and demeanor that even his worthiest adversary found non-threatening until they encountered him in the courtroom. Ever the archetype of the gracious and courteous Southern gentleman, Gray became someone else in court. His legal skill and dogged determination was a major factor in the Civil Rights Movement. It is fitting that the time has come to recognize and acknowledge his contributions to the Movement and to constitutional jurisprudence.

DARLENE CLARK HINE

JOHN A. HANNAH PROFESSOR OF HISTORY
MICHIGAN STATE UNIVERSITY

Acknowledgments

For more than eight years, my wife, Bernice, and I talked about and compiled information for use in this publication. She clipped and preserved many articles, read many books and generally assisted in the preparation of this manuscript. In the past three years, we have spent all of our vacation time and other free time in re-drafting this manuscript. I appreciate her dedication. Without her assistance, this publication would not be possible.

My sister Pearl Gray Daniels recognized the role I played in the civil rights field and wrote a book, *Portrait of Fred D. Gray*, which was published in 1975. I am grateful to her for that publication. She encouraged me to publish this work. Her research and preservation of documentation has been a great help.

My brother Hugh C. Gray has been a great source of encouragement and inspiration. He has worked behind the scenes in providing me the moral courage and fortitude to fight the system by the system.

Walter Stewart, professor at Mount Holyoke College in South Hardley, Massachusetts, encouraged me to commit my experiences to writing. For the past decade, he has been a one-man committee educating the nation about my role in the civil rights arena. He has contributed greatly toward the completion of this publication.

In January 1986, I met Darlene Hine, the John A. Hannah Professor of History at Michigan State University. I moderated a panel at the Smithsonian Institution and she was one of the panelists. I learned of her writings concerning civil rights, particularly in connection with "white primaries." We discussed the possibility of writing a book concerning my career. She made several visits to Alabama, interviewed scores of persons and generally assisted me and rendered valuable historical assistance in connection with the drafting of this manuscript. I am greatly indebted and appreciative to her for the assistance which she gave in connection with this publication.

Malcolm M. MacDonald, the director of the University of Alabama Press, discussed with me the importance of my writing about my experiences. He has continued to encourage and prod me every few months about completing the work. I am very grateful for his encouragement.

I am deeply appreciative to my editor, Randall Williams, at Black Belt Press. His personal knowledge of the Civil Rights Movement and of my career has contributed greatly to this work. His skill, insight, knowledge, experience and patience have extracted from me much more than I thought I could deliver.

My brother Abdullah H. Ghandistani assisted with the manuscript. He generally gave me valuable assistance in connection with the writing and publication of this manuscript. My brother Thomas Gray was not only familiar with my personal life history, but was a member of the board of directors of the Montgomery Improvement Association. He gave particularly valuable assistance in connection with the chapters dealing with the bus protest. He also edited the entire manuscript.

I am particularly appreciative to my oldest child, Deborah, for her assistance. After the more aged persons reviewed and edited the manuscript, she reviewed it with the view of a younger generation and made substantial editorial changes, many of which are included in the manuscript. Her assistance allowed me to view and write the manuscript in a fashion that will be readable and more appreciated by the younger generation.

My son Fred Jr. contributed greatly toward the editing of portions of this work. He used both his legal and writing skills in rendering valuable editorial services.

I met Thomas O. Jackson and his wife, Mattie, while I was a student at Case Western Reserve University. They assisted me in editing a portion of this publication.

I am also appreciative to my secretary Joanne Bibb who typed the initial draft of the manuscript and who has served as my assistant in retrieving, reviewing, and making available all of my court files of various cases and for generally assisting in the preparation of the manuscript.

I am also appreciative to the following persons who also assisted in the typing of the manuscript: Alberta Magruder, Trudy B. Powell, Vanessa Gray Taylor, Harriet Gilbreath, and Patsy Smith.

Finally, I am appreciative to the hundreds of clients who had faith and confidence in me and entrusted their legal matters to me for resolution. Without them, none of what is written here would have been possible.

Last, but not least, I am indebted to my mother, Nancy Gray Arms, for the sacrifices she made for all of her children. She passed in October 1992 at the age of ninety-eight years, but she lives through this publication and the work of others whose lives she touched. A portion of the proceeds from my book will go toward a scholarship in her name at Southwestern Christian College in Terrell, Texas.

Introduction

By Congressman John Lewis

I came of age during the Civil Rights Movement of the 1950s and 1960s. It was an era during which I found my own courage to try and make a difference in this society. I am convinced that the lessons of those years are still relevant today. The difficult experiences that many of us went through should remind people of the long struggle that was necessary to strengthen freedom and democracy in the post-World War II era.

As a young man, I had my first brush with the law when I met Dr. Martin Luther King, Jr., and his attorney, Fred Gray, in 1958. I sought their advice because I wanted to go to Troy State College, an all-white state college in Troy, Alabama. After writing Dr. King to inform him of my plans to desegregate Troy State, I received a round-trip bus ticket from him that would take me from my hometown of Troy to Montgomery, Alabama. When I arrived at the bus station in Montgomery, Fred Gray stood waiting to take me to meet Dr. King and Reverend Ralph Abernathy at Reverend Abernathy's church. Fred Gray was the first African-American attorney I had ever met and he impressed me tremendously.

In 1961, Fred Gray defended me and other participants of the Freedom Rides as we attempted to exercise our rights to travel on interstate buses without being segregated. Later, in 1965, Fred Gray would come to the defense of me and others as we attempted to march peacefully from Selma, Alabama, to Montgomery, in an effort to demonstrate the need for voting rights. Fred Gray eloquently defended our constitutional rights in court.

In his own right, Fred Gray has been a pioneer in the Civil Rights Movement of this nation. He has been a protector of civil rights, civil liberties, our Constitution, our nation, and the freedom and democracy for which our nation stands.

During the Movement, I would be arrested and jailed more than forty times. Each time, a civil rights attorney such as attorney Gray would come to my assistance and get me out of jail. As my colleagues and I protested what we considered unfair laws, we depended upon individuals like Gray to make sure that we received equal treatment under the law.

We worked closely with our attorneys to challenge unjust laws and practices. Members of the legal profession led the way in making our laws more fair, more colorblind, and more gender-blind. We depended on their wisdom and their wise counsel. They have firmly defended the Constitution and the Bill of Rights and people like me, stepping out in faith during the Civil Rights Movement. Where would we be without people such as Fred Gray, Oliver Hill, Justice Thurgood Marshall, Judge Frank Johnson, Jr., Burke Marshall, Nick Katzenbach, Bobby Kennedy, and John Doar?

Men and women of the bar, fighting the good and important fight, secured our civil liberties, our civil rights, and our freedom. Without them, the world would be a different place. I deeply feel that Fred Gray and others like him fulfilled a role in the legal phase of the Civil Rights Movement as critical as the role Dr. King fulfilled in the mass movement phase.

I consider individuals such as Mr. Gray to be the Founding Fathers of modern America. They represented the very best of the American tradition. They were champions of justice, and a source of inspiration to millions of Americans. These men and women had a vision of a new America, a better America. They had a dream of what America could become. Their eyes were on the prize.

Under the rule of law, our nation has witnessed a nonviolent revolution, a revolution of values and ideas, demonstrating to the world that America was ready to live up to the ideals on which it was founded. We began a journey down that long road to racial justice and equality. In turn, during the past thirty years, the nonviolent revolution in America has inspired freedom movements all over the world.

We have seen people in Africa, Europe, South America, and Asia moving towards democracy using the philosophy of nonviolence. They were not inspired by bullets, guns, and bombs. They were inspired by nonviolent revolution.

The drama in the United States to create a plural and just society continues to unfold. Looking back on the Civil Rights Movement, on the quest for justice and equality in this nation, we should recognize that the struggle has not ended. We must restore sanity and sensitivity to a nation which tolerates widespread hunger, poverty, injustice, and growing polarization among its people.

Prejudice and ignorance still divide many of us. We are still a society divided by race and class. I fear that many Americans have forgotten how vital the battle against racism is to the overall health of the nation's democracy. There is a feeling that race is no longer a central issue, that we got over the big hurdles and it's not something we should spend a great deal of time thinking about. Yet so many of the problems we're facing in America are based on deep-seated racial feelings. As a nation and as a people, we must continue to lay down the burden of race. We must continue our efforts to tear down all barriers which keep us from our full potential as human beings.

We must recognize the role that Fred Gray played in history. We must never forget his contribution to American society. He is an individual who truly helped America live up to its creed and philosophy. We are blessed to have the story of his life. We can learn much from this courageous man.

Bus Ride To Justice

1

The Making of a Lawyer

The nine old men inside were not waiting on me as I walked up the white marble steps of the United States Supreme Court on a warm May morning in 1959. But I was waiting for them. I—and those I represented—had been waiting for several centuries.

Across the top of the building were the famous words, "Equal Justice Under Law." As I passed beneath the chiseled phrase I recalled the constitutional law teachings of Professor Oliver Schroeder, and thought to myself, "We shall see."

I had my briefcase in one hand. Tucked under the other arm was a map of Tuskegee, Alabama. The map depicted one of the oddest municipal jurisdictions in recorded history, courtesy of the Alabama Legislature, which in drafting the document had exceeded even its own substantial creativity at keeping black citizens *in their place.*

I really wanted to use this map, but my complaint in the case at hand had been dismissed in a lower court before I got the chance. It was a fine map, made for me by Mr. William P. Mitchell, executive director of the Tuskegee Civic Association, and it cut to the heart of my case.

Mr. Mitchell's map showed the square shape of the Tuskegee city boundaries before black citizens there began a voter registration campaign in 1956. Superimposed over the original map was the twenty-five-sided shape of the boundaries after the Legislature had "improved" them. Coincidentally, the new boundaries managed to *in*clude virtually every white in the town, while *ex*cluding virtually every black.

I entered the hallway and took the map to the marshal's office for transfer to the courtroom at the proper time. I was then ready to argue *Gomillion v. Lightfoot*, challenging the Alabama Legislature's gerrymandering of Tuskegee for the purpose of denying blacks the right to vote. The case is recognized today as one of the landmarks in U.S. voting rights law. Ironically, as I write these words more than thirty years later, the gerrymandering of black voters is again an issue before the Supreme Court.

Gomillion was not my first experience with the nation's highest court. In 1956, I had won an appeal in which the Supreme Court had affirmed a lower court's ruling in my favor that segregated seating on Montgomery's city buses was unconstitutional. That was the famous Montgomery Bus Boycott case, which I had filed when I was only twenty-five years old. But this was my first time to appear in person before the Court.

I entered the courtroom as another case was being argued. As I sat and listened, I felt weak with apprehension. I remembered my childhood in Montgomery. How could I, a black man, born in an Alabama ghetto, whose father died when I was two years old and whose mother had only a sixth-grade education, argue a case before the United States Supreme Court?

When I was a boy, I never dreamed of visiting the United States Supreme Court. Now I was ready to speak before that Court. This was the opportunity of a lifetime. I sat patiently, and when the case was called, I trembled with fear.

But I stood and addressed the court, "Mr. Chief Justice, may it please the Court, I am Fred Gray from Montgomery, Alabama, and along with Robert Carter, I represent the petitioners, Dr. Gomillion and others, in this case."

Before I could get started, Justice Frankfurter, who we feared would rule against us in this case because of one of his earlier cases, asked me to explain the map. I did.

He then asked, "Where is Tuskegee Institute?"

I replied, "Tuskegee Institute is not on the city map."

He said, "You mean to tell me that Tuskegee Institute is not located in the City of Tuskegee?"

I said, "No sir, your Honor. It was in, but they have excluded it."

"Tuskegee Institute is excluded from the City of Tuskegee?"

"Yes sir, your Honor."

I think that satisfied Mr. Justice Frankfurter. I reasoned from his questions that if Tuskegee Institute was excluded from the City of Tuskegee, then my clients were entitled to relief. It was just a question as to how the Court would write the opinion to justify its conclusion.

As you can imagine, I felt that it was a good day's work.

However, my life and work did not begin in Washington, D.C., before the United States Supreme Court, but in Montgomery, Alabama. My desire to become a lawyer did not occur in Washington, D.C., but in Montgomery, Alabama, while I was a student at Alabama State College. My secret desire "to destroy everything segregated I could find" did not originate in Washington, D.C., but on a bus in Montgomery, Alabama.

I was always on and off the buses in Montgomery. Like most African-Americans in Montgomery in the late 1940s and early 1950s, I did not have an automobile. My only means of transportation was the public buses. I was on and off the bus several times a day. I would leave home on the west side of Montgomery in the morning and catch the South Jackson Street bus which would take me through town and then to the college. In the afternoon I would use the bus a second time, catching the Washington Park bus and getting off downtown to check in for my newspaper delivery job at the Advertiser Company. My third bus ride took me from the Advertiser Company back out to my delivery district on the east side of town. A fourth ride returned me downtown to check out. Frequently a fifth ride took me from the Advertiser back to the campus to the library. Finally, the sixth bus ride, this time on the Washington Park bus, carried me back home on the west side. In short, I used the bus as often as six times a day, seven days a week.

All of the bus drivers were white. Discourteous treatment of African-American riders was more the rule than the exception. The buses were segregated. Even on the South Jackson-Washington Park bus route, which served a 90 percent African-American clientele, the bus drivers refused to allow African-Americans to sit in the first ten seats, which included the cross seats.

The bus situation, especially the discourteous treatment by the drivers, grated on African-Americans in Montgomery. Frequently, when the bus was crowded the driver would collect your money in the front and tell you to enter through the back door. Sometimes the drivers would close the door before patrons got to the back. One African-American man was killed by a bus driver. Virtually every African-American person in Montgomery had some negative experience with the buses. But, we had no choice. We had to use the buses for transportation. As Jo Ann Robinson points out in her book, *The Montgomery Bus Boycott and the Women Who Started It*, working African-American women were especially dependent on the buses. My own dissatisfaction with the bus situation grew more acute as my college years ensued.

My Early Childhood

I was born on December 14, 1930, in Montgomery, Alabama. My mother was Nancy Jones Gray Arms (August 19, 1894–October 3, 1992) and my father was Abraham Gray (July 15, 1874–December 23, 1932). Mom worked as a domestic, particularly a cook, in several white homes in Montgomery. My father was a carpenter who received his training at Tuskegee Institute. He died when I was two.

I was born in a shotgun house at 135 Hercules Street in the Washington Park section of Montgomery. A shotgun house was one with all of the rooms built directly behind each other. It probably was so called because if a person fired a shotgun through the front door the shot would travel through each of the rooms and out the back door. In 1930, Washington Park was a typical black community in Montgomery, with no paved streets, no running

My eighth-grade
picture, 1942.

Mom (seated) with
my Aunt Sarah
McWright, 1982.

My
maternal
grandfather,
Thomas
Jones,
visiting us
on West
Jeff Davis
Avenue in
1945.

water, and no inside sanitary facilities. There were no hospitals for African-American children to be born. They, like me, were delivered by a midwife.

My parents were members of the Church of Christ. My father became a member in 1925 and my mother in 1928. Religion and the church played a major role in my family life. My father was a faithful member of the Holt Street Church of Christ until his death. He helped to build the first church building. He would canvass our neighborhood and take all the children to Sunday School. After his death, Mom would take us to Sunday School and church. The church was the center of our early childhood.

Mom wanted all of her children to obtain an education, become good Christians and make something of themselves. She taught us that we could be anything we wanted to be, and then gave us the necessary shoves to fulfill that prophecy.

I was the youngest of five children and after my father's death my mother had to support us. Finding someone to keep me before I started school was a problem for her, which led to my starting school early. The usual age for beginning school then was six years, but I would not turn six until December 14th. My mother and her sister, Sarah Jones McWright, a first-grade teacher at Loveless School, devised a plan where my aunt enrolled me in her class when I was five. They did this so my mother could work and because Aunt Sarah believed I was ready for first-grade work. So, my aunt and mother initiated, in 1935, a "head start" program for me. This was my first head start.

Loveless School was located on West Jeff Davis Avenue approximately two miles from home. I attended that school from the first through the seventh grades. Of course, all of the schools in Montgomery at that time were segregated.

After I finished the seventh grade, in 1943, Mom arranged to send me to the Nashville Christian Institute (NCI), an African-American boarding school in Nashville, Tennessee, operated by members of the Church of Christ. The Bible was taught daily, along with chapel programs, and emphasis was placed on teaching young men to become preachers and church leaders. From my childhood, Mom had wanted me to pursue the ministry. This school was a part of her plan.

The public schools in Montgomery opened in September, but the Nashville school did not open until October. So, when I did

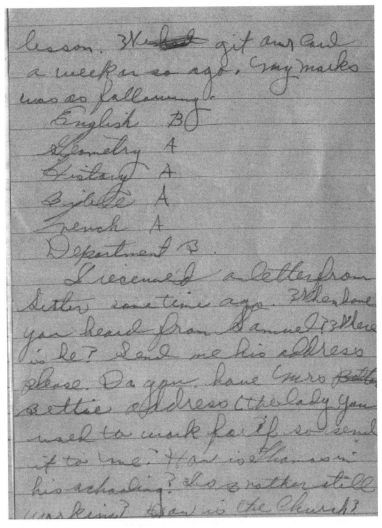

A page from one of my frequent letters home to Mom while I was away at high school in Nashville. This one, on October 18, 1946, reported my grades for the period.

Brother Marshall Keeble, teaching Richard Cooper and me.

not enroll in Montgomery, one of my friends, Howard McCall, began to tease me, saying, "Fred is not going to school," and implied that I was a dropout.

I was not a dropout. I was a twelve-year-old on a mission for God. My mother packed me up and sent me by our minister, Brother Sutton Johnson, to Nashville. At the time NCI was the only African-American Church of Christ-supported high school. It was a coeducational boarding school with on-campus living facilities for boys; girl students who did not live in Nashville were boarded with individual members of the church in various homes throughout the city.

NCI's principal was Professor E. Frank N. Tharpe. He was a graduate of Tennessee A&I State University with a major in history. He would brag that he taught our students at the Nashville Christian Institute history from the same book—*Civilization Past and Present*—that freshmen studied at Tennessee A&I.

NCI was a small high school. We had approximately three hundred students from about twenty-five states. Our facilities were meager, but we had dedicated faculty members who were genu-

In September 1994 I had a great time attending a reunion of my NCI high school. This photo includes many of my schoolmates and some of their spouses.

Front row, from left: Essie Battle, Jack Wooden, Barbara Thompson, Harry Kellam, Obie Elie, Annie DeGrafenaried, Fred Gray, Geraldine Johnson, Mary Brown, and Paul English.

Middle row: Alvin Hinkle, Mrs. Jack Wooden, Mrs. Freeman Wyche, Lovie Huddleston, Eugene Carter, JoAnne Harris, Aline Lewis, Jean Harris, Carl Taylor, Mrs. Ralph Payne, Ralph Payne, Mrs. William English, Vilen Shelton, and John Smiley.

Back row: Freeman Wyche, Vanderbilt Lewis, Collier James, Mrs. Eugene Carter, Nath Braden, David Jones, Frank Brown, Charles Spicer, J. R. Crum, William McDerris, Robert Woods, Arthur Fulson, and Billy English.

inely interested in the growth and development of its students. They gave us a good college preparatory education, and many of the graduates of NCI are leaders across the country and preachers in the Church of Christ throughout the nation. During my stay at NCI we all developed very close ties and friendships that have lasted a lifetime. When I arrived at the Nashville Christian Institute, I met Robert Woods, who now preaches for the Monroe Street Church of Christ in Chicago, Illinois. Later Obie Elie became my classmate and he is now my best friend and lives in Cleveland, Ohio.

Also while at NCI, I was selected by the president of the school, Brother Marshall Keeble, one of the pioneer African-American preachers in the Church of Christ, to travel with him all over the country as a "boy preacher," and as a school representative on his fund-raising trips. It was on one such trip that I met Brother J. S. Winston, whom I would get to know much better during my law school years. My NCI experiences and contacts have served me well.

In order to graduate early, I attended summer school during the summer of 1947. I was scheduled to finish during the Christmas break of 1947. I wanted to return to Montgomery and enroll at Alabama State College for the winter quarter, which began on December 1st. I was accepted at Alabama State subject to completing my high school work; however, this work would not be completed until the latter part of December. I went to my principal, told him I wanted to enroll in Alabama State, and asked if I could leave high school early. He said that if my teachers would give me the final examinations and, of course, if I passed, he would

My high school graduating class, in 1948 at the Jefferson Street Church of Christ, where our commencement service was held. I'm the third from the left on the first row. Brother Keeble is in the center front.

have no objections to my leaving early. My teachers were elated about my acceptance at Alabama State and were willing to give me my examinations early.

I passed the exams, left the Nashville Christian Institute during the Thanksgiving break, and enrolled in Alabama State College. I returned to Nashville for graduation ceremonies with my NCI class in May 1948.

You can see that education was serious business in the Gray household, and it had been true as well for the other children of Abraham and Nancy Gray, he a carpenter and she a domestic.

Let me take a moment to tell you about my older siblings.

My oldest brother, Samuel A. Gray, now Hassan Ghandhistani, graduated from high school in Montgomery in 1938. He attempted to take advantage of one of the New Deal programs launched during President Franklin D. Roosevelt's administration. These were federal programs that put high school graduates to work. White graduates were given office jobs. My brother was given a pick and shovel to work in a ditch. He resented this discriminatory treatment and did not return the next day. He left Alabama and went to Pennsylvania and lived with our aunt, Adella Steele. He later earned several degrees, including the Ph.D., and served in the United States Army Intelligence Corps. He speaks five languages fluently and is a psychologist and private tutor in Philadelphia.

Thomas, my next oldest brother, graduated from Alabama State College with honors and was a businessman in Montgomery during the Bus Protest. He was also an original member of the Board of Directors of the Montgomery Improvement Association, the organization which sponsored the Montgomery Bus Protest and was one of the ninety-eight persons arrested and charged with violating the Alabama anti-boycott law. He later became a lawyer and practiced in Cleveland, Ohio, for over twenty years. He has returned to Alabama and is now an administrative law judge in the Office of Hearings and Appeals with the Social Security Administration in Montgomery.

My sister, Pearl Gray Daniels, graduated from Stillman College

Our last picture of Mom, on her 98th birthday, August 19, 1992.
Clockwise from left: Tom, Fred, Hugh, Hassan, and Pearl.

(Tuscaloosa, Alabama), Alabama State College, and Tuskegee
University. She left Alabama to go to Washington, D.C., where she
taught for many years at the Paul Lawrence Dunbar High School.
She is the author of several books, including *Portrait of Fred Gray*
(1975), and is now back in Alabama and on the staff at Alabama
State University.

Brother Hugh, except for a period of time in the Army,
remained in Montgomery. For over thirty years, he has been a
businessman and is the owner of Gray's Flower Shop, which is
located in the community where we grew up.

A Student at Alabama State College, 1947-1951

I enrolled in Alabama State College for Negroes, now Alabama
State University, on December 1, 1947. All my life I had been
drawn to the ministry and when I entered Alabama State, I
envisioned becoming a social science teacher and a minister, as
those were the principal careers then open to college-educated

African-American males. You either preached or taught school. But my studies and associations at Alabama State began to change my goals.

Professor Thelma Glass taught history, geography, and English. She impressed upon me the recipe for success in college. She advised us to learn exactly what the teacher wanted, how the teacher wanted the material presented, and then to try to present it in that fashion. I have followed this advice ever since, not only in college, but in law school and law practice.

Another professor who made an indelible impression on me was J. E. Pierce, who taught political science and had done an extensive survey in the area of voter registration. Professor Pierce often talked about the importance of obtaining our civil rights. He noted my interest in civil rights and encouraged me to go to law school. The convergence of my bus riding experiences and his lectures helped me to decide, during my junior year, that I would attend law school and return to Montgomery to practice law. But I kept this goal to myself at that time.

I worked my way through Alabama State College as a district manager of the *Alabama Journal*, the afternoon paper in Montgomery. I was known on campus as the "newspaper boy." My delivery territory, District Six, encompassed the campus and all of the east side of Montgomery where African-Americans resided—African-American district managers supervised African-American areas, and white district managers supervised white areas. As a district manager, it was my responsibility to oversee the distribution of the newspaper for thirteen routes, to employ and manage newspaper carriers, and to increase circulation.

I reported to my substation before the papers and carriers arrived to make sure the carriers properly received and delivered the newspapers and that they paid their bills for them on time. In the evenings, I went back to the Advertiser Company in downtown Montgomery to complete my report for the number of papers we needed the next day for each route. I would submit names of any new subscribers—we used to call them starts—and discontinue persons—stops—who no longer wanted the newspaper.

A few of my Alabama State class-mates.

Professor Thelma Glass, 1949.

Although it seems that I was always working, always getting on and off the buses, my grades never suffered. I graduated with honors in the upper 10 percent of my class.

Alabama State College was altogether different from Alabama State University as it exists in 1994. During my time there, it was entirely segregated—faculty, students and staff. However, while we had an African-American president, the policy-making body was the all-white Alabama State Board of Education, with the governor of the state of Alabama serving as ex-officio chairman. These white men all believed in the "Southern way of life" and that included segregation and second-class status for blacks in every aspect of existence. This was just the way they believed and the way it was. Alabama State College, when compared to historically white institutions in Alabama, was woefully underfunded, with inferior buildings and inadequate resources. But, we had a dedicated faculty whose members were concerned about the students. They were concerned that we receive the best education the institution could give. They taught us that we were somebody, and that with hard work and dedication we could succeed.

Social life on the campus of Alabama State College was typical of social life on historically black institutions during that period of time. There were the usual student organizations, religious organizations, sororities and fraternities. The major African-American sororities and fraternities were located on the campus. The fraternities included Omega Psi Phi, Alpha Phi Alpha, Kappa Alpha Psi, and Phi Beta Sigma. The sororities were Delta Sigma Theta, Alpha Kappa Alpha, and Zeta Phi Beta. I became a member of Omega Psi Phi, primarily because my older brother Thomas was an upperclassman at Alabama State College at the time I entered and he was a member and Basileus of Omega Psi Phi. Not only did I later become a member, but I also became its Basileus.

The Greek letter organizations were important on and off-campus. In those days, Alabama State College was the center of cultural activities for African-Americans in Montgomery. Everything in the city of Montgomery, in those days, as was the case throughout the South and in many places across the nation, was totally segregated. Churches, schools, hospitals, public accommodations—everything was segregated. Whites and blacks were segregated from the time they were born until they were buried in segregated cemeteries.

Selection of a Law School

In my senior year of college, I applied to several law schools, including the University of Denver and Western Reserve University, now Case Western Reserve University in Cleveland. I selected schools in cities where job opportunities existed. As far as I could discern, Cleveland was a good place to both learn law and get a job. Another influential factor was Case Western Reserve University's schedule of classes. I could take classes from 8:30 in the morning until 12:30 in the afternoon and still have time to work a full-time job and study.

I did not apply to the University of Alabama Law School because I knew there was no chance I would be accepted. The state of Alabama, as did all of the Southern states at that time, had out-of-state-aid arrangements for African-American students who on their merits should have been admitted to white colleges, universities, and professional schools. Many Southern states inaugurated

With my mother at her store, 705 W. Jeff Davis Street on Montgomery's west side, about 1950.

these schemes to circumvent the 1938 United States Supreme Court decision, *Gaines v. Canada, ex rel.* The *Gaines* case held that states that have a segregated higher education system must provide African-Americans with equal educational facilities.

If an African-American student was interested in pursuing an advanced degree in a subject offered at the University of Alabama or Auburn University that was not offered at African-American institutions, including Alabama State, Tuskegee Institute, or Alabama A&M, then the student was required to file an application with the state superintendent of education for out-of-state aid. The application process included submission of proof that the student had been admitted to a school in another state. Then the Alabama superintendent of education would make available financial assistance. The state would pay the following expenses: 1) round-trip transportation once a year to the school; 2) the difference between tuition fees at the University of Alabama and the particular university chosen; and 3) the difference between room and board at the institution desired and the costs at Alabama State University. There was a specific formula to calculate expenses, but the funds were available only on a reimbursement basis. This was the catch. This policy proved especially difficult for poor African-American students to overcome because they did not have the money to make the initial payment. I applied for such aid and it was granted. The state superintendent at the time was Austin Meadows, a man who became a defendant in many subsequent lawsuits that I filed. After I began to practice law in Montgomery, Dr. Meadows once stated that he was proud of the fact that he, as state superintendent, had signed my papers so I could go to law school.

On one of the last few days of my employment at the Advertiser Company, one of the white district managers asked me what I was going to do after graduation. I told him I was going to law school. Another district manager asked me, "Well, where are you going to practice law?" I said, "Right across the street." There was a long silence. The Montgomery County Courthouse at that time was located across the street from the Advertiser Company.

Private Pledge to Destroy Segregation

Privately, I pledged that I would return to Montgomery and use the law to "destroy everything segregated that I could find."

I kept my plans secret. I did not want anything to interfere with my going to law school. I completed the applications without any discussion with family members.

After I was admitted to Western Reserve University Law School, I showed mother my acceptance letter. She said, "All right, Mr. Smarty, now that you have been admitted, where are you going to get the money from?" Of course I didn't have the money and she didn't have the money, but it was a rhetorical question because immediately she went to work and borrowed money to help me go to law school.

My brother, Thomas, was then in business in Montgomery. He and William Singleton operated Dozier's Radio Service, a repair shop and television and home appliances store. Thomas accompanied me to the First National Bank of Montgomery where I applied for a loan. I told the loan officer that I had been admitted to law school. I took with me the papers indicating that I would be reimbursed for a certain portion of the money once I had paid my fees and expenses. However, I did not have sufficient security, nor did my brother. Consequently, the loan was denied. My family, a few friends, and I continued to work and raised enough money to pay the first installment on my tuition, room and board, and transportation costs.

A Law Student At Western Reserve University, 1951-1954

In September of 1951, with barely enough money to cover expenses, I took the train to Cleveland to begin law studies at Western Reserve University. I was assigned housing at 1408 Bell Flower Road, known as the Hudson House. Western Reserve had several houses, each with its own housemother. I was on the second floor and my roommate was Pohlmann Bracewell, from Monrovia, Liberia, West Africa.

Of the approximately 120 students in my class, six were African-Americans, including a fellow Alabamian, Ishmael Childs, a former high school principal from Sylacauga, Alabama, who is now a lawyer in Cleveland. The other African-Americans were Carl Chancellor, now a retired senior attorney for the Cleveland Illuminating Company, Rudy Henderson, a government lawyer with the State Department in Washington, D.C., and Napoleon Bell, who practices in Columbus, Ohio. Pohlmann Bracewell returned to Liberia, rewrote his country's tax code, and for many years was the general counsel for Firestone Rubber Company in Liberia.

The few African-American upperclassmen were Edwin L. Davis, Sarah Harper, George Trumbo, James B. Simmons III, Robert Penn, Clarence Holmes, James R. Willis, and C. B. King. Edwin

Davis of Miami, Florida, became one of my law partners. He greatly assisted me in many cases in Montgomery and Tuskegee and recently retired as a member of my firm. Robert Penn is now a state court judge in Toledo, Ohio. James B. Simmons, III, now practices law in his hometown of Toledo, Ohio. Clarence Holmes and James Willis now practice in Cleveland. C. B. King was from Albany, Georgia, where he returned and practiced law for many years. He was an outstanding civil rights lawyer whose practice in Georgia paralleled mine in Alabama. He represented Dr. Martin Luther King, Jr., and the Southern Christian Leadership Conference in the Albany Crusade. C. B. passed away a few years ago. Sarah Harper Trumbo is a state court of appeals judge in Cleveland. Her husband, George Trumbo, is a municipal court judge in Cleveland.

From day one at Western Reserve, I reminded myself constantly that I would return to Alabama to practice. After all, that was the only reason I was there. As soon as I settled in at Western Reserve, I began to prepare to return to Alabama. I knew that the most difficult part of the Alabama law that differed from the general law of the other states was in the area of pleadings and practice. At that time, Title Seven of the Alabama Code was that part of the statute that I had to master. I asked the librarian if she would order for me Title Seven of the Alabama Code. I paid her, she ordered it, and in my spare time I typed and outlined that entire title of the Alabama Code.

I developed a systematic approach to studying and working. Immediately after class, one of the other African-American students and I would stop by the dining facility and have lunch. I would return to the house in the afternoon, review and type up my notes. I would ascertain for each point of law that we covered whether Alabama followed or departed from the same principle. If it differed, I found out what the Alabama rule was and committed it to memory. Then I would prepare for my next day's classes. As further preparation for returning to Alabama, whenever we had legal research papers, I would always do my paper on some facet of Alabama law. My adviser during my law school days was Samuel

Sonnenfield, professor of civil procedure. We had many conversations about my future plans. He told me on one occasion that he thought I could develop into a good lawyer, but that he did not believe this would happen if I returned to Alabama. He felt that because of my color I would not be given an opportunity to develop to my fullest potential. He urged me to seek employment in the Cleveland area, particularly with one of the many African-American lawyers there. I appreciated his concern, but the only reason I had gone to Cleveland to go to law school was to return to Alabama to practice. I was determined to do just that.

Professor Sonenfield did teach me something that has been one of the guiding principles of my law practice. He advised me always to seek assistance and never be afraid to share a fee with an older lawyer who has more experience. I really took that advice to heart. In all of my early cases, including the civil rights cases, I always involved some other experienced lawyer. Those other local African-American lawyers were usually Arthur Shores, sometimes Orzell Billingsley and Peter Hall, all of Birmingham, or Charles Langford of Montgomery, who later became one of my law partners. The white lawyer upon whom I depended most for advice was Clifford Durr.

My first year of law school was very difficult. I had to prove to myself that I could do the work. I had an inferiority complex about having graduated from Alabama State College for Negroes. I had never been in a white environment in which all of the professors and teachers were white. In fact, virtually everything around Reserve was white. I was under a lot of self-imposed pressure. Many of the white students had done their undergraduate work at Harvard, Yale, Princeton, and Western Reserve universities. I was anxious to see if I could compete with the white students in my class who came from prestigious universities.

There was neither money nor time to do much other than study and participate at church. The first Sunday I was in Cleveland, I went to the East 100th Street Church of Christ and met Thomas O. Jackson, a businessman who owned a downtown parking lot and garage. Socializing was limited to after-church dinners with

If I had not been set on returning to Montgomery to practice law, I might have settled in Cleveland. My brother Tom, shown above right with me receiving the key to the city from Cleveland Mayor Carl Stokes, did. And my best friend Obie Elie, shown on the left with Tom and me in the lower photo (about 1984 at Tom's house), is from Cleveland.

many people, including Thomas and his wife, Mattie, who was a registered nurse and a graduate of Hampton University. She did her practicum in psychiatric nursing at Tuskegee Institute. The Jacksons lived in a house behind the church. Thomas O. Jackson now serves as minister of the Goulds Church of Christ in Miami, Florida, and serves with me as member of the board of trustees of Southwestern Christian College in Terrell, Texas—a board which I chair.

I attended most church services on Sundays. When time permitted, I went to evening services and Bible Study during the week. Eventually, J. S. Winston, whom I met while I was a student at Nashville Christian Institute, became minister and I served as his assistant. Later, the East 100th Street Church built a beautiful new building near Western Reserve University and it is now known as University Church of Christ. I learned a lot about church work and human nature while working with Brother Winston. He has retired as a full-time local minister, but also serves with me as a member of the board of trustees of Southwestern Christian College.

There was always a money crisis. I managed to pay fees on installments, but still owed money when the time came to take final exams. Nevertheless, I was permitted to take the exams. I had applied for a $250 professional scholarship from my undergraduate fraternity, Omega Psi Phi.

I waited to see the results from my exams—the first substantial proof of my ability to do law school work—to see how I had done in comparison to the other students in my class. However, at the end of the first semester, the secretary to the dean of the law school informed me that my exam grades would not be posted until I had paid all of my tuition and fees. Of course, I knew the fees hadn't been paid. I was in agony. I had survived the first semester. I completed all of my exams. But I was not able to ascertain the results. It was a devastating blow.

As fate would have it, on the same day I arrived home from classes I found the letter from Omega Psi Phi containing a check for $250. It was more than enough to pay the balance due on my tuition. I ran over to the business office and paid my bill. The dean's office was notified and I received the results of my exams. I had passed and ranked in the top 15 percent of the class. This was the real pivotal point! I had proven to myself that I could do the quality of work that was expected of students at Western Reserve University. I did not graduate that high in my class, but being near the top after my first semester gave me the impetus and encouragement that I needed.

Now that I had paid my first semester's tuition, I obtained the necessary certification from the business office and finally received reimbursement from the State of Alabama. I had concentrated all my energies on courses during the first semester in order to be assured of the reimbursement money. The reimbursement money was used to pay tuition and fees for the second semester. I decided that I would work doubly hard during the summers to earn money. Unfortunately, I was unable to find employment in Cleveland, so I returned to Montgomery. The *Alabama Journal* needed a circulation manager for my old district and I readily agreed to work for them that summer. Of course, I still did not have a car, so I was back on the buses. One of the needs for the district was additional paper boys, particularly in the Tulane Court area.

While searching for a paper boy in that area one day, I saw a young lady, Bernice Hill, whom I had known for some time. She lived at 560 Smythe Curve and was sitting comfortably on her front porch. I knew she was a student majoring in commerce at Alabama State College. She was also a member of the Gail Street Church of Christ, where I had preached on occasion. I went up and talked with her and asked her about a possible paper boy. She suggested several names, one of whom I employed. From that point on Bernice and I started seeing each other and we eventually developed a relationship. Bernice describes me as the kind of person that just grows on you. I guess she means that it takes time to get to know and like me. She really was not interested in becoming involved with a preacher.

The next summer I remained in Cleveland, picking up and delivering clothes for a dry cleaning firm on Prospect Avenue. I was able to keep the job during the next school year. Actually, during the next summer I worked two jobs. One was at Republic Steel in the hot metal finishing department, on the 11 p.m. to 7 a.m. shift. From there I would go to the dry cleaners, pick up, and deliver dry cleaning in the company truck.

Despite constant money woes and the small number of African-Americans, Western Reserve was an excellent university from which to receive a legal education. During my tenure there, I never experienced any unpleasantness or any form of discrimination. It proved to be the right background to prepare me to sit for the bar and for an outstanding legal career.

By my senior year I was already studying for the Ohio and Alabama bar exams. I knew I could not take the bar review course in Alabama because of my race, but there was an Ohio bar review course being offered in Cleveland and I took it.

The secretary of the Alabama Bar Association suggested I contact Judge Walter B. Jones, who owned Jones Law School in Montgomery and offered a bar review course. I wrote to Judge Jones, who was unsure when he would be offering another course. He suggested that I study Title Seven of the Alabama Code and suggested that I read and study certain other articles in the *Alabama Lawyer*, the official publication of the Alabama Bar Association. Judge Jones was one of two state circuit court judges in Montgomery at that time. Judge Jones later enjoined the NAACP from doing business in Alabama. He was considered a staunch segregationist and wrote a weekly *Montgomery Advertiser* column entitled "Off the Bench." One of his articles, headlined "I Speak for the White Race," appeared in the March 4, 1957, edition. He begins the article by stating:

> I speak for the White Race, my race, because today it is being unjustly assailed all over the world. It is being subjected to assaults here by radical newspapers and magazines, Communists and the Federal Judiciary. Columnists and photographers have been sent to the South to take back to the people of the North untrue and slanted tales about the South.

He continued, "Their real and final goal is intermarriage and mongrelization of the American People." He concluded, "We shall never submit to the demands of integrationists. The white race shall forever remain white."

Becoming a Lawyer, 1954

At long last graduation day arrived. My mother and Bernice, who by that time was my fiancée, came for the commencement ceremony, then returned to Montgomery. I remained in Cleveland to concentrate on studying. I studied day and night. This was very necessary because I was preparing myself for two bar examinations, the Ohio and Alabama. The Ohio exam was given in June and the Alabama exam in July. For the past three years I had studied and attended law school. Now I was a law graduate, and all of the hard work would be to no avail if I did not pass the bar exams. The only way I would be able to practice law in any state would be, for the most part, to pass the bar examination of that state. While I was primarily interested in becoming a lawyer in Montgomery and carrying out my secret pledge, I was realistic enough to realize it was possible that the examiners in Alabama might discriminate against me, and regardless of what I did on the exam, they could say that I did not pass. I was taking the Ohio bar exam as a precaution.

Each segment of the Ohio bar exam, which was given over a three-day period, had six questions. Examinees were expected to answer five of the six. It was suggested that we read through all of the questions first and then answer the one that appeared easiest. I tried that strategy but it didn't work for me because as I read the second or third question, my mind would flash back to the first question. So, the technique that I used was to simply read the question, and if I understood it, I would answer it. If I did not understand the question or did not know the answer, I would proceed to the next one.

I remember the last day of the exams very well. By that time I was exhausted. I passed in my paper, said goodbye to a few of my classmates, and went to the train station. The train was actually scheduled to leave at 3:45 p.m. and the exam was not scheduled to end until 4:00 p.m., but I had written all that I knew. I boarded the train to Cincinnati, and transferred there to a train going to Montgomery.

The Alabama bar exam was scheduled for the fourth Tuesday in

July. I arrived home in late June. From the moment I arrived in Montgomery I had very little social contact with anyone. I just studied everything I could get my hands on.

Knowing enough to pass the Alabama bar exam was not the only obstacle. There were a couple of other hurdles that I had to get over before I could take the exam. Alabama required that one register as a law student by filing an application and submitting character affidavits from five lawyers who had been practicing for at least five years. I had filed the application when I enrolled in law school, but I did not know five lawyers at the time. I completed the application, admitted that I did not know five lawyers, and informed them I would submit the affidavits as soon as possible.

At this juncture, with my dream so close to becoming a reality, all that was left for me to do was to talk to Mr. E. D. Nixon. I had known his wife for many years because she and I attended the same church. Ed Nixon had been "Mr. Civil Rights" in Montgomery and in the state for many years. By occupation, he was a Pullman car porter, so he was frequently in and out of town. If anybody ever had problems with the city police or any matter where they thought their civil rights had been denied, they would always contact E. D. Nixon. For over fifty years, E. D. Nixon advocated the cause of African-Americans in Montgomery and central Alabama. He was president of the State Conference of Branches of the NAACP and president of the Montgomery Branch of the NAACP. He was a founding member of the Montgomery Progressive Democratic Club, which later became a charter member of the Alabama Democratic Conference. Mr. Nixon believed that African-Americans should have the same rights as other Americans. He believed that segregation was wrong and he dedicated his life, efforts, and resources to eradicating those wrongs. He was also to become one of the founders and leaders of the Montgomery Bus Boycott, which ended segregation in public transportation in the City of Montgomery. He was actively involved in getting persons registered to vote, and getting lawyers to defend African-Americans whose constitutional rights were violated, and he paved the way for many of us and was a role model in the field of civil rights.

So, like other African-Americans in Montgomery who had problems, I talked with Mr. Nixon about my need to have lawyers sign affidavits. There were only a handful of African-American lawyers in the state. The best known African-American lawyer was Arthur Shores of Birmingham. Charles V. Henley was Grand Master of the Masons; he didn't practice law, but he had a law license. At that time Oscar Adams, who later became the first African-American to serve as a justice on the Alabama Supreme Court, Orzell Billingsley, Peter Hall, Charles Langford, and David Hood were also practicing law, but none had yet practiced the requisite five years. I asked Mr. Nixon to help me to get the affidavits both to register as a law student and to take the Alabama bar exam. With Mr. Nixon's and Bernice's help, I soon had the necessary affidavits.

Bernice was working for the wife of Nesbitt Elmore, a white attorney. After she informed them about my predicament, a meeting was arranged. Bernice introduced me to Elmore who, in turn, introduced me to his uncle, Clifford Durr. Mr. Nixon also introduced me to Mr. Durr. The first time I met Mr. Durr he did not sign the affidavit. This was understandable. Mr. Durr did not know me at that time. The affidavit required that you know the applicant personally, that you know his character to be good, and you must state the facts and circumstances showing how you know the applicant. Later Nesbitt Elmore, Mrs. Elmore, and Mr. Nixon encouraged Mr. Durr to sign the affidavit. The lawyers who ultimately signed character affidavits for me included Arthur Shores, Nesbitt Elmore, Charles Henley, Clifford Durr, Woodley C. Campbell, Henry Heller, and Kenneth McGee. With the exception of Shores and Henley, the signers of my affidavits were white. Without their support I could not have taken the bar exam. I will always be grateful to them. Woodley C. Campbell still practices law in Montgomery.

℃

The long-awaited day of the Alabama bar exam was finally at hand—the fourth Tuesday in July 1954. I arrived before 8 a.m., and I remember that as I entered the building, I was thinking of my initial desire to practice law. Just for a moment I even remembered the reason I wanted to become a lawyer. And I realized that I had come a long way from where I was born, 135 Hercules Street, to go to Nashville to high school, to college at Alabama State, to Western Reserve University to law school, and even to take the Ohio bar, which I had done a few weeks earlier.

But this one was the real test. The passing of this exam was the final hurdle which stood between my initial desire to become a lawyer and my actually being sworn in as a member of the Alabama Bar. As I entered the room, I offered a little silent prayer and took my seat.

John B. Scott, a Montgomery City Judge and the secretary to the Alabama Bar Association, checked in the applicants. Meanwhile, I looked around the room. Some twenty-five others were also being tested that morning, although a number of other recent law school graduates would be admitted to the Alabama bar without taking the exam. In those days, if you were a graduate of the University of Alabama, you did not have to take the Alabama bar examination. You were admitted on a motion. If separate but equal had been a reality, I should have been admitted on a motion, too, because the State of Alabama had paid a portion of my tuition, room and board at Case Western in lieu of admitting me to the University of Alabama law school. So, if they had given me an equal education, I should have been given an equal bar entry. But, there I was at 8 a.m. with the other would-be Alabama lawyers.

Actually, I really didn't mind taking the exam. I felt that I had prepared myself well from the very first day I entered law school. I had always kept good notes, I had studied hard in the weeks leading up to the exam, and I was ready and eager.

Only one other African-American was taking the exam that day. I do not recall the man's name, but he lived in Louisville, Kentucky, and his intention was to return to Louisville to practice. I never knew whether he had succeeded or not.

In those days, as now, the Alabama bar exam covered three days. It was completely an essay-type examination. Each day's session was divided into a morning part and an afternoon part, covering some fifteen subjects in all.

The examinees received their exam booklets, and we began to work, each retreating into his—there were no women—own world, scarcely looking at or noticing his fellows. I approached this exam as I had the Ohio bar exam and my examinations during law school. I read the questions carefully, tried to analyze the issues, made a brief outline of my answer, and then proceeded to answer the question in the booklet. As I had anticipated, the major difference between the Alabama and Ohio examinations was in the areas of civil procedure and domestic relations. I found absolutely nothing in the examination that indicated any disparity in Alabama law toward the treatment of black and white citizens.

At the conclusion of the first day of the exam, I was completely exhausted and didn't even want to think about the next day. After a good night's rest, I was refreshed and went back the second day with the determination to give it my very best. At the conclusion, I felt comfortable that I had been reasonably familiar with the material. I believed if the examiners would grade the papers fairly, that I had written a good paper and should pass.

After having taken both the Ohio and Alabama bars, I was completely exhausted, frustrated and at wits' end. Where to begin? There was no place in Montgomery for an African-American lawyer in those days to get a job working in a legal office. I knew that the white lawyers would not employ me. There were no doors open in government, and black law clerks were unheard of.

The lone African-American lawyer in town then was Charles Langford, and his practice was still young and very limited. I simply had to wait it out. I hesitated to contact too many of the local residents out of fear that I may have failed the bar. If I didn't pass, I did not want to be placed in a position of having talked to people about being a lawyer and then not making it.

Not knowing the results of either of the two bar exams I had taken made me very restless. Unable to stand the inactivity, I told Mom that I was going back to Cleveland. On my way back north

I visited Robert Woods, a high school friend in Gallatin, Tennessee. I spent some days with Bob, and on the designated day made a call to Columbus, Ohio. I called from a pay station phone and was informed that I had passed the Ohio bar exam. I said goodbye to Bob and caught a bus to Cleveland to be sworn in on the appropriate day. Robert Woods, incidentally, went on to serve more than forty years as minister of Chicago's Monroe Street Church of Christ.

My First Client, August 1954

During that brief stay in Cleveland, I performed my first legal work. My high school classmate Obie Elie was in the demolition business in Cleveland. We had renewed our friendship while I was in law school. After I was sworn in as a member of the Ohio bar on August 26, 1954, I incorporated the Obie and Oliver Company as the first official piece of legal work of my career. I never billed for it and I was never paid. (Oliver was one of Obie's brothers and business partner.)

While still in Cleveland, I talked to Mom and she told me that I had a letter from the Alabama Bar Association. I had passed the Alabama bar! However, there was no swearing-in ceremony in Alabama at this time: the process simply entailed signing an oath before a notary public and returning it. As soon as I got back home to Montgomery from Cleveland, this was done and my license to practice law in Alabama is dated September 7, 1954. I had reached a long-sought goal. I was now a lawyer in the state of Alabama.

Upon settling back in Montgomery, I began preparations to open an office.

At first I talked with attorney Charles Langford about the possibility of sharing offices with him. He had an office then at 131^1/$_2$ Monroe Street, upstairs in the building next door to Dean Drug Store, a business on the northwest corner of Monroe and Lawrence streets that had served the African-American community since approximately 1888. I had nothing to offer Langford, so he wasn't too interested in my joining him at that time. Later he was to assist me in the legal work for the bus protest. We also became partners. He is still one of my law partners and a good friend. He is also a member of the Alabama State Senate from a district that includes part of Montgomery County.

The Opening of My Law Office, September 1954

As it turned out, Dr. Solomon S. Seay, Sr., a minister and the secretary-treasurer of the Home Mission Department of the African Methodist Episcopal Zion Church, came to my rescue. Dr. Seay occupied the upstairs offices of the building where Sears Auto Shop was located at 113 Monroe Street. He used only the front part of the building. The back part of the building was vacant. I talked with him and he agreed to sublease that space to me. Further, he stated that if I didn't have the rent every month he would understand. The rent was fifty dollars per month. It represented a substantial amount considering I had no financial resources.

Sharing offices next to Dr. Seay proved to be a significant asset. He was a man of great knowledge and wisdom. For the next few years he was to serve as my adviser, and, for all practical purposes, he was like a father to me. He gave sound advice, and referred many clients, including my first wrongful death case. Later, I invited his son, Solomon S. Seay, Jr., to practice law with me and we worked together for many years on many of our civil rights cases. Many years later, Dr. Seay wrote me a letter reflecting on our relationship during those early years. He said:

...Last night during the 10:00 clock news I was asleep until you spoke. I heard your voice in my sleep and it awakened me. I felt proud almost to tears. Perhaps this is hard to understand on your part. I say this because so many people so often never understand the kind of person I am.

I lay in bed reminiscing first concerning you and your wife before marriage and your youthful anxieties. I thought of the factors that had to do with your determination, therefore, your goals and ultimate achievements. I remembered some things I said to you, I am sure perhaps you have forgotten.

One day I said to you: "Fred if you will continue to work hard and trust God you will make it." Those were dark days. Another time I added the following: "As you work be sure to get your fees"! I remember this one mainly because I have been such a poor example of it.

There have been three things in your favor: (1) You were born with native qualities with which to face the disadvantages confronting you. (2) You were identified with the church of your choice. (3) You married the girl that loved you and was prepared in spirit to face life with you, whatever it was like.

Well, I am Solomon S. Seay Sr. I am 72 years old. I have been preaching 51 years. I have tried to light a candle for every person traveling the dark slippery road over which I also have had to travel. I have felt the urge to put a thorn in no person's bosom even those whom I have considered unfriendly. I have tried not to be a burden to those whom I have considered friendly. In the most trying times I have never begged an enemy for mercy. I have never felt ashamed to serve in what our cultural standards would consider to be small places, for to me stations in life never make real

July 6, 1955, receipt for a $5 fee from one of my early clients. I was glad to get it.

persons. Real persons are what they are wherever they are.
. . . I shall always remember you.

Dr. Seay was a great man and he greatly inspired me to be the best. Dr. Seay's autobiography, *I Was There By The Grace Of God,* was published in 1990.

Bernice played a major role in helping me to open my law office. I borrowed some of Nesbitt Elmore's books so that the office looked like a law office when I had open house. I invited church people, former teachers and classmates, and basically everybody that I could think of. One of my former college classmates, Mrs. Bennye Black Reasor, assisted with the selection of office stationery. She was a high school instructor, later an instructor at Trenholm State College and Alabama State University. Her daughter Joanne is now employed as a secretary in our Montgomery office. A nice group came to my open house. The next day I returned Mr. Elmore's books. I was now open and ready to do business. I was also ready to pursue my secret goal of "destroying everything segregated I could find."

2

The Bus Protest Begins

Bernice Hill, then my fiancée, recalls well the early days of my practice. "When Fred first graduated from law school, it was very difficult. He had a basic, bare-looking office, but he was very proud of it and so was I. Soon after he opened his office in 1954, he said to me, 'as soon as I make a little money we can get married,' but to me it seemed like a dream, far, far away."

Building a law practice takes time. It is slow, tedious, hard work. I had to get out among the people and make myself known to them. I had to establish contacts and earn their trust.

These were the days before advertising, but, even then, there were many ways to work oneself into a community. Since I was interested in civil rights and politics, I started attending the National Association for the Advancement of Colored People (NAACP) meetings. Rosa Parks was the secretary to the Montgomery Branch of the NAACP and also served as youth director. I worked with the youth and with Rosa Parks. In her capacity as youth director, and through my interest in the activities of the NAACP, we developed a very close relationship. Mrs. Parks was very kind, quiet, gentle, loving and would never hurt anyone. She was and is one of the kindest and loveliest persons that one would want to meet. She still maintains these qualities almost forty years later.

During the early months of my law practice, I had few clients and little to do. At lunch time Mrs. Parks often walked to my office, located one and a half blocks from the Montgomery Fair

Department Store where she worked as a seamstress. We became very good friends. She would walk to my office and we would sit down and share our lunches.

For almost a year, we met, shared our lunches, and discussed the problems in Montgomery. We had talked about the situation involving Claudette Colvin, a fifteen-year-old student at Booker Washington High School, who was arrested March 2, 1955, for refusing to get up and give her seat to a white woman on a Capital Heights bus in downtown Montgomery. We discussed the possibility of a boycott. I told Mrs. Parks, as I had told other leaders in Montgomery, that I thought the Claudette Colvin arrest was a good test case to end segregation on the buses. However, the black leadership in Montgomery at that time thought we should wait. Mrs. Parks shared my feelings that something had to be done to end segregation on the buses. There was a congruency in our thoughts and ideas that helped me understand her strong interest in me, a struggling young lawyer. She gave me the feeling that I was the Moses that God had sent to Pharaoh and commanded him to "Let My People Go." She saw that I was penniless and she wanted to help me get on my feet. More importantly, she wanted to help our people eradicate segregation and discrimination on the Montgomery buses.

December 1, 1955, was a typical day in Montgomery. It was late fall, but it had not begun to get cold. We had lunch together that day, just as we had done many times before. When 1:00 p.m. came and the lunch hour ended,

This photo was made about the time I began my law practice.

My first famous client—and a dear friend—Rosa Parks.

Mrs. Parks went back to her work as a seamstress. I continued my work and left the office in the early afternoon for an out-of-town engagement.

Upon my return to the city later that evening, I was shocked to learn that Mrs. Parks had been arrested in an incident involving the buses. I immediately began to return the numerous phone calls informing me of her arrest. Subsequently, I met with Rosa Parks, E. D. Nixon and Jo Ann Robinson.

That day was, for me, the beginning point of all the monumental events that soon began to unfold. My immediate little world began to change. And so did the larger world. I had pledged to myself that I would wage war on segregation. The opening shot had now been fired. With Mrs. Parks's arrest came the beginning of the Montgomery Bus Boycott. It changed the history of civil rights in Alabama, in the nation, and in the world. And it launched my legal career.

Jo Ann Robinson and the Women's Political Council

In private moments, I often thought about the buses and about segregation. Although I personally had never had any negative experiences on the buses, I knew that many people did, especially African-American women.

While a student at Alabama State, I had become acquainted with Jo Ann Robinson, a professor of English and a leader of the Women's Political Council. Mrs. Robinson had related to me her horrendous experience on a Montgomery City bus in December of 1949. She boarded an almost empty city bus, paid her fare and observed only two passengers on the bus—a white woman who sat in the third row from the front, and a black man in a seat near the back. She sat in a seat in the middle of the bus. The bus driver stopped, came back to where she was seated, told her she was sitting too near the front of the bus, and demanded that she move back or get off the bus. She was afraid he would hit her, so she got off the bus.

She was upset, fearful, in tears, humiliated, and embarrassed. I am confident that this was the beginning of Mrs. Robinson's determination to end racial discrimination on city buses in Montgomery. She vividly describes this incident in her book, *The Montgomery Bus Boycott And The Women Who Started It.*

Robinson was a member of the Ten Times One is Ten Club, the oldest African-American women's federated club in Montgomery. The members of that club were the pillars of African-American society in Montgomery. There were about eight or nine of these clubs in Montgomery at that time. I spoke to the women's clubs and helped them with their legal problems or with whatever they wanted to do. Indeed, one of my earliest speeches as a young lawyer was delivered to the Ten Times One is Ten Club on the occasion of its sixty-seventh anniversary on Sunday, October 30, 1955, in Tullibody Auditorium on the campus of Alabama State College. This was thirty-one days before Rosa Parks refused to give up her seat on December 1, 1955.

In my speech to the Ten Times One is Ten Club, I challenged

the members to bring an end to segregation in all areas of life in Montgomery. I said:

> We must be alert, we must be diligent, we must not accept anything less than full integration in public schools, public transportation, and in all other public facilities.
>
> Let us forever remember that segregated schools and segregation itself is inherently unequal; it creates an inferiority complex upon our children. We must be strong, and we must be financially able and willing to carry our cases to court if our officials will not voluntarily desegregate our schools, parks, transportation system and all other public facilities. During these crucial days; days of great decision, may the God of Heaven direct us, help us and may He through His divine guidance lead all men to realize that we were all made from one flesh, and that we are all God's children. May God bless us, assist us, and may He speed the day when all of our schools and all other public facilities will be completely integrated.

Can you imagine me, a young lawyer twenty-four years of age, telling these women, who were old enough to be my mother or grandmother, that they must do everything possible to end segregation? They were not critical of my speech. On the contrary, they accepted it and we became partners in destroying segregation in Alabama.

Jo Ann was definitely committed to ending segregation. Few realized how much Jo Ann did and the significant role she played in helping to improve conditions for African Americans in Montgomery until she published her memoirs. Little did many know that much activity that impacted on the Civil Rights Movement in Alabama occurred at Jo Ann Robinson's house.

After Claudette Colvin had been arrested and before the arrest of Mrs. Parks, Jo Ann and I had many discussions in her house and other places, with reference to what should be done in the event another incident occurred, and the bus company and the city

Jo Ann Robinson, left, and Portia Trenholm (wife of Alabama State College President H. Council Trenholm) were powerful players in the bus protest. For political reasons, both had to keep a low profile publicly.

officials did not live up to the commitments they made immediately following the Colvin incident. The night of Mrs. Parks's arrest, I went to Jo Ann's house. We discussed the strategy and what needed to be done to begin immediately a protest and make it successful.

Throughout the 381 days of the protest there was almost daily contact between the two of us, both by phone and at her residence. Jo Ann later recalled an occasion on which she had telephoned me late one evening when I was pretty tired. Jo Ann recalled that in the course of the conversation I cried, "Woman, what do you want? Go ahead and tell me what's on your mind." Those who know me will recognize that I don't usually respond like that. But, those were difficult days. In any case, the conversations and the plans made with Jo Ann helped to lay the ground work for the unfolding of the protest.

Community Involvement before the Bus Protest

My involvement with the NAACP and the Young Alabama Democrats brought me into close contact with E. D. Nixon and Rufus Lewis, leaders in the fight for African-American voter registration. They were very different men—one a Pullman porter with limited education, the other a military veteran and college coach—but they worked for similar goals. People often said, "Mr. Nixon had the masses and Coach Lewis had the classes."

E. D. Nixon was the key to the history of the African-American struggle for first-class citizenship and equal rights in Alabama. He was courageous and genuinely interested in civil rights. He was not concerned with private gain and never received anything personally as a result of his efforts to gain equal treatment for others. Mr. Nixon wanted to get a job done, and he was one of the few African Americans in the city whose employment was such that the white power structure could not bring any type of economic reprisals against him. Mr. Nixon was also a good friend of A. Philip Randolph, the founder of the Brotherhood of Sleeping Car Porters union, and thus enjoyed an excellent relationship with organized labor. In other words, Nixon could say what he wanted to about the whites, police brutality, civil rights and discrimination. He backed his words with actions.

E. D. Nixon not only had the ability to lead African Americans in Montgomery, but he could attract national figures to come to Montgomery and speak out in favor of voter registration. Several months before the beginning of the Montgomery Bus Boycott, New York Congressman Adam Clayton Powell came to Montgomery at Nixon's invitation to encourage African Americans to register to vote. Powell's speech was given in the gymnasium on the campus of Alabama State College, and he delivered a powerful message. Powell's visit to Montgomery was also notable because he was extended by then-Governor "Big Jim" Folsom all of the courtesies due a visiting congressman, including the lending of the governor's limousine and driver, Winston Craig. This Southern hospitality earned Folsom considerable criticism from other state officials and the media in what was becoming an increasingly polarized climate in the state. Powell was invited to the governor's mansion and had a widely publicized cocktail with Folsom. The idea of the Alabama governor drinking in the parlor of the official mansion with a black man—even if he was a U. S. Congressman—infuriated the state's rabid segregationists. The KKK even made a widely publicized demand for Folsom to fire Winston Craig, a demand ignored by the Governor but which led to an incident that was typical of the racial overtones which infused every aspect of life at that time.

It seems that the KKK, failing to get Craig fired, put out the word that on a given night they were going to Craig's home in the Mobile Heights community and "get him." Several of Craig's neighbors, including my brother Tom, formed an impromptu guard committee to keep an eye out. On the early evening of the expected Klan visit, Craig passed on the news that the governor was also sending an unmarked car of highway patrolmen to watch over him. However, this turned out to be not such a blessing. Tom had the second shift on the watch committee, and he woke up not to the expected phone call to come take his turn, but to William Singleton phoning for Tom to come to the city jail to get Singleton and another watcher out of jail.

As it turned out, Singleton and his partner were patrolling the neighborhood in their car, when they pulled into Singleton's driveway to get out for a cup of coffee. The unmarked patrol car was also driving around the neighborhood and when Singleton got out, the plainclothes officer stopped and called for Singleton to approach the patrol car. Singleton was expecting some casual conversation, but as he and his partner got out of their car, the interior lights came on, and through the open car door the officers could see the shotguns the two men had with them in the car. At this point, the patrolmen drew their guns, and ordered the two African Americans to assume the position, and frisked them. In addition to the hunting weapons in the car, Singleton had a loaded .45 in his overcoat pocket. So both men were charged with possessing concealed weapons. Some thought this was an odd

Gray, Congressman Adam Clayton Powell, E. D. Nixon, J. W.
King, and P. M. Blair, on the occasion of Powell's celebrated visit
to Montgomery in 1954.

arrest since at the time of the arrest Singleton was in his own yard,
and the hunting guns were inside the automobile, and both
arrested men had valid hunting licenses. Besides which, the reason
for their activity was that a KKK attack was anticipated in an
African-American community. Nevertheless, they were in jail.

Brother Tom was taking all this in during the phone call from
Singleton, who was basically asking him to round up bail money
and come to police headquarters. Tom said over the phone, "I'm a
property owner, do you think those birds will allow me to provide
a personal bond for you?" At which point another voice—to the
immense surprise of caller and callee—came on the line, saying,
"These birds ain't going to let you do nothing." Then, when Tom
got to the jail, and paid the bonds, and they were all getting ready
to leave, a very tall policeman came up and asked, "Which one of
y'all called us birds? That's a nasty expression, don't ever call us

birds, boy!" Tom says he kept quiet and expected a blow, though none came. When they were finally outside the jail, the other arrested man said to Tom, "I'll never let you get me out of jail again." They all laughed with relief, and, in retrospect it was a harmless incident. But it also shows how careful African-American men had to be about every little thing they did or said, and, I think, it helps explain why forty years later relations are still strained between the black community and law enforcement.

Anyway, I had had the opportunity of meeting Congressman Powell at his speech, and I accompanied him in the governor's limousine, chauffeured by Winston Craig, to his next engagement in Birmingham. Craig, incidentally, was very active in the community. His work with E. D. Nixon was an example of how Nixon was able to bring together African Americans of all callings—from congressmen like Powell to chauffeurs like Craig—in support of voter registration.

Rufus Lewis was a leader of the elite African Americans in Montgomery. He was educated and lived on the east side of town where Alabama State College is located and where more of the educated African Americans lived. I lived on the west side, the less-educated side of town. Coach Lewis was primarily concerned with one aspect of the civil rights field, voter registration. He was a very good friend of Professor J. E. Pierce, my old political science instructor. I think Professor Pierce may have influenced Coach Lewis a great deal. Coach Lewis had a night club called the Citizens Club. One had to be a registered voter to be admitted.

Ironically, Nixon probably did more to get folks out to vote and to become involved in civil rights issues than either Lewis or Pierce. Nixon was president of the Montgomery Progressive Democratic Club, the forerunner of the Alabama Democratic Conference. The ADC today is one of the state's two major African-American political action groups, but for most of the past thirty years it was *the* source of black political power in Alabama . Still, in those days, there were many, including some highly educated African Americans, who thought Nixon was a little too aggressive. After all, registering to vote is one thing, but getting lawyers to defend an

African-American fellow like Jeremiah Reeves, who was accused of raping a white woman, was another thing—and Nixon did this.

I was closer to Nixon than to Lewis. The point I made clear, however, was that I was willing to work for either and all sides. I would work with anyone who was trying to do something positive. Mr. Nixon encouraged me to organize African-American youth into an organization known as the Young Alabama Democrats (YAD) as a part of his Montgomery Progressive Democratic Club. YAD consisted of high school students, college students, and young adults. The purpose of this group was to get young people involved in the political process.

My work with youth made it possible for me to lecture in schools, churches, and throughout the communities. The YAD deserves a great deal of credit for being one of the first organizations to promote greater youth participation in the political process.

To be sure, YAD paralleled the youth group of the NAACP; the youth of the two organizations worked together. Ms. Inez J. Baskin was an inspiration to the YAD in the same way that Rosa Parks was to the NAACP youth organization. Ms. Baskin, an employee of the *Montgomery Advertiser* and *Alabama Journal,* reported on African-American social news in Montgomery. (At that time the Montgomery newspapers each dedicated a page to report the news for the "colored" community. It had its own "colored" editor, E. P. Wallace, and Inez Baskin served as his assistant. The colored paper was identified by stars on the front. Those papers were not delivered in the white community.)

The youth divisions of the NAACP were integral parts of each branch's activities. Their purpose was to develop young people to be good students, good citizens, and good Christians. The youth were instrumental in carrying out the objects and purposes of the NAACP.

I discussed youth involvement with Mr. Nixon and he thought it would be very important if we could get young people interested in registering to vote, to get them to encourage their parents to become registered voters, and generally, to assist in taking people to the polls on election day. I was primarily interested in developing contact with these young people, because as a young lawyer in the community, there wasn't too much difference in our ages. It would serve to encourage them and, at the same time, it would give me some contact with their parents. The primary goal of the YAD was political in nature, and to assist in the political process—to give these people at an early age an opportunity of learning and participating in political activities.

The Arrest of Claudette Colvin, March 2, 1955

Nine months before Rosa Parks refused to give up her seat I represented Claudette Colvin for a similar act of resistance. On March 2, 1955, Claudette, a fifteen-year-old high school student, refused to obey a bus driver's order that she relinquish her seat. She was already at the back of the bus and refused to make her seat available to a white person. When she remained seated, the bus driver called police officers who dragged her from the bus and arrested her. Claudette was a member of the NAACP Youth Council and was quite willing to follow any advice that Nixon or Robinson offered. Claudette lived in a community known as King Hill. I was fond of this community because I would visit and sometimes preach for one of our churches, known as the King Hill Church of Christ, which was located in that community. In addition, some of these young people were YAD members. One of the young ladies who was on the bus with Claudette at the time of her arrest, Annie Larkins, was crowned queen of YAD one year.

I readily agreed to represent Claudette, thinking that this well could be the chance I had been waiting on to challenge the constitutionality of Montgomery's segregation ordinances and Alabama's segregation statutes. One of the first things I did was to invite Clifford Durr to help me with the legal research. As a matter of course, I would always invite established African-American and white lawyers to join forces with me on civil rights cases. There was so much that I didn't know and the advice of my former law professor stayed in my mind. He recommended that I willingly share fees with an older lawyer who had more experience. Clifford Durr proved to be a great behind-the-scenes lawyer throughout the

Montgomery Bus Protest Movement and was very important to me through the balance of his life.

Not only did Clifford Durr assist me in civil rights cases, but in any number of cases of all types he personally would help me with drafting pleadings, briefs and other documents. He, more than any other person, taught me how to practice law. I will always be grateful to Clifford and his wife, Virginia, for assisting me in becoming a good lawyer. He provided this service without charge.

Durr, a member of a distinguished upper-middle-class white family in Montgomery, was a graduate of the University of Alabama and a Rhodes Scholar, who earned his law degree from Oxford University in 1922. His wife, Virginia Foster Durr, was the sister-in-law of Hugo L. Black, first a U.S. Senator from Alabama and later one of the nation's most distinguished justices of the Supreme Court. Clifford Durr had worked in the Roosevelt Administration and was credited with helping save the nation's banking system during the Great Depression. Then he had been appointed by Roosevelt as one of the first members of the new Federal Communications Commission, a position he resigned after Roosevelt's death when then-President Harry S Truman imposed a loyalty oath requirement on federal employees. Durr believed the oath was unconstitutional and he refused to sign it. The Durrs then moved home to Montgomery, where he faced an unsteady future, both because he and his wife were smeared by the anti-Communist hysteria of the day and because he did not go along with the segregationists who were gaining control of every aspect of official power in Alabama at the time.

Durr made a distinction between civil rights and civil liberties. He believed that the rights of African-American people had to be preserved and protected, not because they were African-American, but because the denial of liberties to one group of Americans was an open invitation to undermine the entire body of civil law upon which this country was founded. I respected the distinction he made; however, I was more determined to remove the very real shackles that circumscribed African-American freedom. He and his wife, Virginia Foster Durr, endured public scorn and social ostracism from prominent whites in the city for their sympathetic support and involvement in these lawsuits.

Immediately after Claudette was arrested, Jo Ann Robinson and members of the Women's Political Council arranged a meeting with Mayor Tacky Gayle, the two other members of the City Commission, Montgomery City Lines Manager Clantello Bagley, and others for the purpose of discussing the case. Of course, as Claudette's lawyer I was also invited. During the meeting, Jo Ann threatened to initiate a protest. The city officials and the bus company officials assured us they were sorry for this incident, it would not occur again, and that the bus drivers would be more courteous in the future.

As it turned out, the Colvin case proved a false start as far as giving me the opportunity to challenge Alabama's segregation laws. Even though I had developed and presented an excellent defense for Claudette, the juvenile court of Montgomery County convicted her on all charges. I appealed the decision and ultimately the Montgomery County Juvenile Court placed her on indefinite, unsupervised probation. Although the case did not result in a challenge to the segregation laws, there were some benefits. This was the first case in which I raised the issue of the constitutionality of the Montgomery city ordinances and Alabama state statutes that provided for segregation. The case gave me courage and a faith that there would be another opportunity to challenge Alabama's segregation laws.

Although I was disappointed by the result of the Colvin case, I learned some important lessons. It was evident that at least a small circle of people, most notably E. D. Nixon and Jo Ann Robinson, were ready to get behind a legal challenge to the city's segregation ordinances and to mobilize support to destroy segregation on buses. We knew that there would be another opportunity and we would be ready. We waited. Finally, everything fell into place.

The Arrest of Rosa Parks, December 1, 1955

On December 1, 1955, Mrs. Rosa Parks was arrested for disorderly conduct—not for violating the segregation laws. This was the first of several crucial mistakes made by the white authorities. Anyone who knew Mrs. Parks knew that she would never do anything disorderly. She was soft-spoken, trustworthy, and very reliable. Disorderly conduct was altogether inconsistent with her reputation and character. Rosa Parks had the right temperament to test the segregation laws.

It is always stated that she refused to give up her seat to a white man. Technically, what happened is that she refused a bus driver's order. She had boarded at one stop and sat in the first row of seats behind the white section. On Montgomery buses, this was an arbitrary line that was adjustable by the drivers to accommodate the number of white passengers on board at a given time. At the third stop after Mrs. Parks boarded, all the seats were filled and a white male passenger was left standing. The driver then ordered Mrs. Parks and the other three African-American passengers on the row with her to get up and stand in the aisle in the back. The others complied, but Mrs. Parks did not. The driver asked her again, and when she still would not move, he got off the bus and found two policemen, who came on board the bus, put Mrs. Parks under arrest, and took her off. A good description of the arrest, in Mrs. Parks's own words, is found in the book *My Soul Is Rested*.

As I related earlier, after my lunch with Mrs. Parks on December 1, I went out of town to keep an engagement. Upon my return in the early evening, I had many calls from Mrs. Parks, Mr. Nixon, Jo Ann Robinson, and just everybody, telling me that Mrs. Parks had been arrested. Of course, by the time of my return, Mr. Nixon, with the assistance of attorney Durr, had posted her bond and she had been released. In fact, she was never actually jailed. The normal procedure of the police department in such a case at that time would be to arrest her on the bus, place her in a police car, take her to the city jail (then located on North Ripley Street), fingerprint her, "book" her, and then give her an opportunity to make a phone

Rosa Parks,
Mother
of the
Movement

call so that bond could be arranged. All of this had already occurred by the time I arrived back into town that evening.

Bernice was one of the persons who had called me, and I returned her call. She explained to me what had happened, and I told her of the calls I had received and that I was going to follow through on those calls. She was very concerned about Mrs. Parks and her well-being.

Rosa and Raymond Parks lived in the Cleveland Court apartments, not far from downtown on Montgomery's west side. At Mrs. Parks's invitation, I immediately went over to her house. She told me what had happened and asked me to represent her, and I took it from there. I left her house in Cleveland Court and went a short distance to Mr. Nixon's house on Clinton Avenue, where he and I discussed the matter at length.

(Just for the record, you will notice that I was not riding the bus between these various stops. Not long after taking the Alabama Bar exam, I had bought my first car, a new tan 1954 two-door, stick shift Ford.)

Later that same evening, I went to Jo Ann Robinson's house and we discussed the incident. During the course of our discussion, we outlined a strategy for action. We concluded:

(1) If we were ever going to have a bus protest in Montgomery, Alabama, we must have it now.

(2) For the bus protest to be successful, the African-American community must support it. We must have the wholehearted support of the African-American preachers and both E. D. Nixon and Coach Lewis. We could not risk losing the support of either.

(3) A leader must be selected who would be able to organize, motivate, and keep the people together. Jo Ann believed that her pastor, a young newcomer to Montgomery, the Rev. Martin Luther King, Jr., could be that person.

So Jo Ann and I made the necessary phone calls and divided up some specific assignments. Recommendations were also made concerning who should do what in preparation for the protest.

It was a long, adrenaline-filled night, yet I enjoyed every minute of it because things were beginning to fall into place. We designed a road map to accomplish a successful protest and to accomplish my goal of ending everything segregated I could find. The buses were just the beginning.

Over the next four days, we made numerous phone calls and had frequent conversations and meetings with Montgomery's African-American leaders. It was all happening quickly. The mood was electric. This was the beginning of the Montgomery Bus Boycott. My days of having little to do in my fledgling law practice were over.

Need for New Organization—Formation of M.I.A.

Initially, the Women's Political Council (led by Mary Fair Burks and Jo Ann Robinson), E. D. Nixon, and Rufus Lewis were more interested in the Protest than were the ministers. This soon changed as the ministers' interest caught fire. Meanwhile, as the Protest gained momentum I could see that we would need a new, legal organization. Prior to the Protest, we had only one organization that had taken the lead in civil rights cases and that was the NAACP. Some people felt that the NAACP was not a viable organization and there were too many factions in the African-American community. I believed we needed one key organization that could involve everyone. The Protest was a new movement and there was no reason to get the older organization involved in it. We would run the risk of getting bogged down legally. (As it turned out, my concerns were well-founded, because on June 1, 1956, the State of Alabama sued and enjoined the NAACP from conducting business in the state.)

Selecting a leader or spokesman for the new organization required much diplomacy. If E. D. Nixon had been made the spokesman, some of Coach Lewis's followers would have been unhappy. If Lewis had been made the spokesman, Nixon's folks would have felt left out. Martin Luther King, Jr., was fresh, a newcomer, young, articulate, knowledgeable, highly educated, and had not identified himself with any community activities other than his church. It was generally agreed to arrange it so that Dr. King would be designated the spokesman.

In fact, the first official planning meeting for what was to be named the Montgomery Improvement Association was held at Dr. King's church, Dexter Avenue Baptist, on December 3, 1955. The Reverend Roy Bennett, pastor of Mt. Zion A.M.E. Zion and president of the Ministerial Alliance, presided. Bennett also presided at a second meeting held later at his own church. At that second meeting Reverend Ralph D. Abernathy nominated Dr. King, who was not present at the time, to lead the new organization. Abernathy was then himself nominated as vice president. My brother Thomas nominated E. D. Nixon for treasurer. These nominees were unanimously elected. Rufus Lewis was appointed chairman of the transportation committee. Jo Ann Robinson, as a professor at Alabama State College, was a state employee; for her to have any official position would have cost her job.

It was very important that two key positions be designated for Nixon and Lewis. Nixon as treasurer had the primary responsibility for raising funds to finance the boycott. Lewis as chairman of the transportation committee had the responsibility of designing and implementing an alternative transportation system for Montgomery's forty thousand African Americans. Martin King was the spokesman; Ralph Abernathy was his assistant.

I was chosen to handle the legal work. Whatever Dr. King was involved in legally, from then until he left Montgomery, was my responsibility. So, while I was to direct and coordinate the legal activities, Jo Ann Robinson performed other critical duties. Specifically, on December 4, 1955, Jo Ann went over to Alabama State College and, with the help of a couple of students, mimeographed thirty thousand leaflets calling for people to stay off the buses. The memo read:

> This is for Monday, December 5, 1955.
>
> Another Negro woman has been arrested and thrown into jail because she refused to get up out of her seat on the bus for a white person to sit down. It is the second time since Claudette Colvin (sic) Case that a Negro woman has been arrested for the same thing. Negroes have rights, too. They help to keep the buses rolling. If it were not for Negro riders the buses could not operate. So we must stop these arrests now. The next time may be you, or you, or you. The woman's case will come up Monday. We are, therefore asking every Negro to stay off the buses Monday in protest of the arrest and trial. Don't ride the buses to work, to town, to school, or anywhere on Monday. You can afford to stay out of school for one day if you have no other way to go except by bus. You can afford to stay out of town for one day. If you work, take a cab, or walk. But please, children and grown-ups, don't ride the bus Monday. Please stay off all buses on Monday.

At that time, very few Alabama lawyers handled civil rights cases. Notable exceptions included Arthur Shores, Orzell Billingsley, Peter Hall and David Hood, all of Birmingham.

Arthur Shores is the dean of African-American lawyers in Alabama. He handled civil rights cases throughout the state, from the Gulf of Mexico to the Tennessee line and from Mississippi to Georgia. In 1952, he represented Autherine Lucy in her efforts to integrate the University of Alabama. He is my mentor and assisted me in many civil rights cases. He also assisted me in successfully integrating the University of Alabama with the admission of Vivian Malone. Mr. Shores recently retired from the practice of law; his daughter now heads his law firm in Birmingham.

Most white lawyers, except Clifford Durr and one or two others, just would not handle these types of cases. A civil rights practice was precisely what I wanted to do and as a matter of principle I tried to involve as many of the African-American lawyers as possible in my civil rights cases.

December 5, 1955, *City of Montgomery v. Rosa Parks*

The beginning of the boycott was planned to coincide with the trial of Mrs. Parks on December 5, 1955. At the time I was living at 705 W. Jeff Davis Avenue, on the west side of the city. Mr. Nixon and Mrs. Parks also lived on the west side. Dr. King, Rev. Ralph Abernathy and Coach Lewis lived on the east side. I got up at 5 a.m. and drove all over the city to see if our people were riding the buses. They were not. I later met with E. D. Nixon, Dr. King and Jo Ann Robinson. We were all elated that our people were staying off the buses. Then, it was on to Montgomery's municipal court.

The trial of Mrs. Rosa Parks took all of thirty minutes. The drama leading up to the trial and the trial itself was a lifetime in the making. The case was scheduled to begin at 9 a.m. in the Recorders Court of the City of Montgomery. At 8 a.m. I met with Mrs. Parks, Mr. Nixon, Rev. Abernathy, Dr. King and other leaders at my office, which was a block and a half away from the court. After deciding on the final tactics, we walked from my office down Monroe Street, turned right on Perry Street, passed by the main City Hall entrance, turned left on Madison Avenue, and entered the Recorder's Court chambers. Police officers and people were gathered everywhere. Hundreds of African Americans were outside the courtroom and could not get in.

The courtroom, of course, was segregated. I walked up the aisle, white people sitting on one side and black people sitting on the other. Mrs. Parks took a seat on the front row. This was a momentous occasion for me. It was a very emotional experience because, not only was I representing Mrs. Parks as her attorney, but we were friends. In addition, this was my first case with a large audience. And I knew this case, if not necessarily this particular hearing, would allow me an opportunity not only to represent Mrs. Rosa Parks, but to raise legal issues which ultimately would be decided by the United States Supreme Court. Was I nervous? Maybe a little. Was I determined? You bet.

When the case was called, Mrs. Parks and I approached the bench. I identified myself and indicated that I represented her. The stage was set. Attorney D. Eugene Loe prosecuted the case for the City. I raised certain constitutional issues, which were summarily denied. I knew that this was not the forum to challenge the segregation ordinances. The only victory that we could hope for with this case was to get Mrs. Parks exonerated because she was charged with disorderly conduct and not with violating the City's segregation laws. We vigorously defended Mrs. Parks; however, Judge John B. Scott found her guilty and fined her ten dollars and costs. We appealed, but ultimately lost on a technicality.

This case was important because it triggered the Montgomery bus protest. Most scholars believe that this case ignited the civil rights movement of the fifties and sixties. This case and the Montgomery Bus Boycott also gave an opportunity for Dr. King to exhibit his leadership; thus, it paved the way for the development of one of the greatest leaders in modern history.

Some five hundred or more African Americans were in and around the courtroom that Monday morning. Once the trial was over, it was a sigh of relief for all. However, since this was the first day of the bus boycott, most of the five hundred people who came had to walk back to their respective homes. I walked back to my office with King, Abernathy, Nixon, and the other leaders, where we spent the day in conference and prepared for a mass meeting that had been announced for Holt Street Baptist Church that evening. Mrs. Parks went home.

According to earlier plans, I had prepared two resolutions for possible adoption at the mass meeting. Resolution One to be presented to the body acknowledged the fact that Mrs. Parks had been unfairly treated, tried, and convicted; that segregation on buses in Montgomery, Alabama, was wrong; that we have the capacity to conduct a boycott, but will not proceed at this time; and we will seek to resolve these matters with the city officials. If the first day's boycott had been unsuccessful, then we would present Resolution One and would call a protest at a later date.

Of course, the events of that day were such that Resolution One was not needed. The essence of Resolution Two was that we called upon the residents and all African Americans in the city of Montgomery to refrain from riding the buses until we could return to them in a nonsegregated manner.

I arrived at Holt Street Baptist Church about 6 p.m., an hour before time for the meeting, only to find that I could not get a parking space within three blocks of the church. People had been assembling since 3:00 that afternoon. This was to become typical of every mass meeting for the three hundred and eighty-one days that the boycott lasted. As I entered the rear entrance to the church, I immediately went to pastor A. W. Wilson's study, where the leaders were assembled to make last-minute plans for the meeting. Dr. King was set to give the first of what would become known as the pep-talk for each of the Monday night mass meetings.

These talks were for many their first glimpse of the genius that was within Martin Luther King, Jr. He was elected president of the MIA at a meeting at which he was not present, at Zion A.M.E. Church on South Holt and Stone streets. He presided over a cross section of preachers, three college professors (including one woman), two physicians, three housewives, a Pullman porter, and most of the rest being preachers. He soon became a favorite of all of them. He rose in stature to the point that many of the women who attended mass meeting after mass meeting could be heard to say,

"Just let me touch his garment." Yet Martin appeared to have never lost the common touch. He could calm the rivalries which arose among some of the ministers on occasions. Before MIA board meetings, Martin was always alert to congratulate someone for some deed of kindness. He was jovial, at a well-bred ease and aware of events in the neighborhood, or asking those present about matters which might have escaped him. But those were qualities which were generally not yet realized on the night of the first mass meeting.

Finally, the scheduled time came.

Not only were there thousands of African Americans crowded in and around Holt Street Baptist Church, but also a few whites. The local media and some national media were present. There was an electricity in the air. Such a feeling of unity, success and enthusiasm had never been before in the city of Montgomery, certainly never demonstrated by African Americans. The people were together. They were singing. They were praying. They were happy that Mrs. Parks had refused to give up her seat and they were happy that they were a part of a movement that ultimately would eradicate segregation on city buses and would set a precedent for the elimination of segregation in almost every other phase of American life. They clapped and shouted "Amen" as the boycott leaders entered the auditorium. They welcomed their leaders, and they welcomed Mrs. Parks, and as the lawyer I was included in this group.

The high point of the meeting was the speech by Dr. Martin Luther King. This was the first time he had spoken to so many people. It was the first speech of his career as a civil rights leader, later to become an internationally known figure. Each of us listened to his words and waited for his next phrase. My fiancée Bernice was in the audience. She later described how King's inspiring speech ignited the crowd and was the motivating factor that was needed to make the protest successful. It was his message and his encouragement and his speech that gave those thousands of African Americans the courage, the enthusiasm and the desire to stay off the buses.

This mass meeting reminded me of the day of Pentecost as recorded in Acts 2:1-2.

> . . . [T]hey were all with one accord in one place. And suddenly there came a sound from heaven as of a rushing mighty wind, and it filled all the house where they were sitting.

The second high point of the meeting, of course, was the adoption of the resolution to continue the boycott until we could obtain dignity and until our three demands were met. Pictures and accounts of the mass meeting were subsequently published and broadcast across the nation. The coverage of this event gave additional credibility to the movement and focused the nation's attention on the struggle of African Americans in Montgomery, Alabama, to end segregation on buses.

Hundreds of accounts have been written about the success of the Montgomery Bus Boycott. I believe that one major circumstance helped tremendously in spreading the news about the planned boycott. Initially, the leaders planned to spread the word throughout the African-American community, but not the white community. We realized that this was impossible. Then a front page story appeared in the *Montgomery Advertiser* on Sunday, December 4, 1955, under the byline of Joe Azbell, the newspaper's city editor. Azbell reported that there was a planned boycott and that a mass meeting was scheduled to be held that Monday evening, thus notifying thousands of African Americans who otherwise would never have known about the protest. Joe Azbell was a very good friend of E. D. Nixon. I feel confident that Mr. Nixon discussed our plans with him. Joe Azbell, being the good newspaper reporter that he was, of course, verified the information as best he could and wrote the story.

It was not unusual for leaders of the movement to develop good working relationships with the media. It helped them and it helped us. Early on in the movement, I established a similar working relationship with Frank McGhee, who was then the news director of WSFA-TV, the Montgomery NBC affiliate. As a result of his coverage of the bus boycott, he was later employed by NBC News and went on to become a host of the "Today Show" in New York.

Bus Protest in Progress, December 5, 1955

Five days after the arrest of Rosa Parks, the buses in Montgomery were empty. And for the next fourteen months African Americans stayed off the buses.

None of us realized then that this was the opening event of the modern American civil rights movement. Little did we know that we had set in motion a force that would ripple throughout Alabama, the South, the nation, and even the world. But from the vantage point of almost forty years later, there is a direct correlation between what we started in Montgomery and what has subsequently happened in China, eastern Europe, South Africa, and, even more recently, in Russia. While it is inaccurate to say that we all sat down and deliberately planned a movement that would echo and reverberate around the world, we did work around the clock, planning strategy and creating an atmosphere that gave strength, courage, faith and hope to people of all races, creeds, colors and religions around the world. And it all started on a bus in Montgomery, Alabama, with Rosa Parks on December 1, 1955.

Many African Americans expected that after Mrs. Parks's arrest and the first day of protest that the city officials and the bus company would negotiate a settlement. These expectations rested upon the fact that the three modest requests presented to them could have been granted with little difficulty or inconvenience to the bus system and the city establishment.

Personally, I never shared the view that a settlement could be reached. Knowing white Montgomerians at that time as I did, I knew they would not give in to any demands from African Americans for equal rights. They would reason that "if you give them an inch they will take a mile."

On the other hand, we did not know how the first day of the protest would go. We had high hopes, and as it turned out, the first day was a resounding success; the bus protest was off to a good start.

A good number of the leaders of the bus protest.

At this juncture I advised the leaders to use the second resolution, demanding three very small actions:

1) all drivers display more courtesy toward the "colored" riders;

2) the seating be arranged on a first-come first-serve basis;

3) the company hire "colored" bus drivers on buses running into areas heavily populated by "colored" people. The population of Montgomery was about one hundred thousand and of that number roughly 40 percent were African Americans.

The actions requested in the resolution were not designed to integrate the buses; rather they were intended as very reasonable reforms. The city officials could have given in to us but they simply refused. Considering the jobs African Americans held in Montgomery prior to the protest, we attempted to make the requests reasonable. White city officials simply dug in their heels and refused to propose an alternate plan. They refused to offer to concede or compromise on any point. We had no choice but to continue the protest. We would have settled for first-come, first-serve seating. Meanwhile, the bus company was losing approximately three thousand dollars a day in fares.

In my opinion, much of the resistance to accepting the resolution was the work of Jack Crenshaw, the attorney for the bus company. He was a product of the times. He simply could not accept the fact that African-American people were not demanding anything from the whites to which they were not entitled. I believe that Crenshaw let his personal feelings interfere with the best interests of his client, the bus company.

In any event, attorney Crenshaw flatly declared that the bus company had no intention of hiring colored bus drivers, and it could not accept the seating arrangement because it violated the law. Of course, I disagreed with him with reference to the seating arrangement. I prepared an exhaustive brief, which pointed out that the seating arrangement did not violate the Alabama segregation laws. The same bus company that owned the buses in Montgomery owned the buses in Mobile. The Mobile buses employed the same type of seating arrangement we were requesting in Montgomery. Thus, as a practical matter, there was no logical reason why the bus company should have rejected our seating proposal.

While attorney Crenshaw did not agree with any of our proposals, I doubt that he really was anti-African American. It is rather interesting that many years later in the case of *Pollard v. United States of America*, which is the Tuskegee Syphilis Case, attorney Crenshaw did me a personal favor. After we reached a settlement in the case and I filed a petition for attorney's fees, I was looking for lawyers to testify to substantiate my fee. To my surprise, every lawyer I contacted told me the best person to prove my fee would be Jack Crenshaw. Initially, I was hesitant to ask attorney Crenshaw to testify for me because of my experience with him in the bus protest. Finally I decided I had nothing to lose. To my surprise, he was willing, without hesitation, to testify. He testified in the United States District Court for the Middle District of Alabama before Judge Frank Johnson that I was entitled to a substantial fee in that case. While the Court did not award me as much as Mr.

Crenshaw testified that I was entitled to, the fee I received was substantial.

Conflicting and Similar Viewpoints

Over the course of the bus protest and other civil rights developments, I had many disagreements with my clients, Dr. Martin Luther King, Jr., and Ralph Abernathy, in my effort to keep them on a sound legal track. There were times when they would consult other attorneys because they did not agree with my advice. It seems as if each time they failed to heed my advice, either one of the two or some other person very important in the Movement would be arrested or end up in jail. Needless to say, they did not hesitate to call me to their rescue when arrested, nor did I hesitate to assist.

Ralph Abernathy once teasingly told me, "Fred, you keep me out of jail and I will keep you out of hell." Ralph, of course, was always getting in jail in connection with the Movement. Later, reflecting on Ralph's comment, I told Bernice, "My job certainly is a lot tougher than his."

In spite of our differences of opinion, Dr. King, Ralph and the other leaders expressed great confidence in my legal abilities and they knew that I was always available, day or night. There were times when Dr. King said, "Fred, I understand what you say the law is, but our conscience says that the law is unjust and we cannot obey it. So, if we are arrested we will be calling on you to defend us." Dr. King frequently introduced me to others saying, "my attorney." I liked that.

There were several similarities between myself and Martin King, even though he was twenty-three months older. He came to Montgomery on September 1, 1954, to begin his pastorship at Dexter Avenue Baptist Church, which was his first church. I was admitted to practice law in Alabama on September 14, 1954. As the young pastor of Dexter Avenue Baptist Church, and as a young lawyer returning home, we developed a close personal friendship. We both have four children, two girls and two boys. Their ages are close together.

It is difficult for persons who did not know Dr. King to understand Martin as I knew him. When I met him, his primary concern was to do a good job as pastor of Dexter Avenue Baptist Church. I had returned to Montgomery with a desire "to destroy everything segregated I could find." Martin was receptive to assisting me in that desire. We joined forces and worked against segregation in Alabama. We had a close friendship during the bus boycott. We were dealing with each other on a day-to-day basis. He was a very kind, compassionate, considerate, easygoing, easy-talking Baptist preacher. He was an easy conversationalist who could talk about anything. Behind his church work and his work with the Movement, there was another side of Martin Luther King Jr. In those quiet moments, you would never think of him as the articulate speaker that he was, with the persuasive power that was able to change people. You wouldn't really think about him in terms of his being a future Nobel Peace Prize winner. He would sit down like you, me, or anyone else in a group and just have a good time and enjoy the fellowship. He never monopolized a conversation. He always listened. He had a tremendous sense of humor and enjoyed telling jokes and listening to jokes. He never met a stranger. He was one of those rare individuals. Nothing you did would upset him. During all of our trials, tribulations, setbacks, and victories I never saw him upset. I never saw him angry. I never saw him display hostility, nor hate toward anyone.

This is even more remarkable when you consider that it is hard even for those of us who knew him and saw him on practically a daily basis to comprehend the pressure he was under. Richmond Smiley was one of Martin's parishioners and they became good friends. Richmond often drove Dr. King to meetings and appointments, because we all recognized that it was dangerous for him to be on the streets alone.

I knew several of those who rode around with Martin from time to time, including the late Cleveland Dennard, who had married Belle Brooks, daughter of the ASU registrar, Dr. J. T. Brooks. Cleveland was later president of a school in Washington, D.C., and still later of Atlanta University. Some thought that those who

With Martin, 1956 (Photo courtesy of *Ebony* Magazine)

rode with Martin were bodyguards, but I never knew of Martin saying so. If any of them were ever armed, I'm sure that Martin never knew it.

In addition to the constant danger, Martin's life was also complicated by the incredible weight of the demands on his time. As the Movement intensified and he became more and more famous, he could never really relax at the church or even in his home, the parsonage. He would sometimes escape to Richmond Smiley's house for a little relief from all those who wanted to see him, and sometimes even that did not help. Richmond relates how he answered the doorbell once to find Sander Vanocur of CBS News on his doorstep asking for Dr. King. "I tried to explain to this gentleman that he was not in," Richmond recalled. "He looked at me and asked, 'Is it that he is not here, or is he really not here.' With this I invited him in and said I would check to see if Dr. King was available. Mr. Vanocur was kind enough to wait in my living room until Dr. King got some rest, and then they met." That's the kind of pressure that existed all the time. But despite it all, Martin rarely seemed ruffled. Or at least he didn't let us see it.

Even when his home—the Dexter parsonage on South Jackson Street—was bombed at the height of the Protest, he was a model of restraint. While he was certainly concerned about the well-being of his wife and children, he still maintained his composure. He had been at one of the weekly mass meetings when the bomb went off. Coretta was at home with their infant child and a friend, Mrs. Roscoe Williams, but fortunately they were all in the back part of the house and were not hurt. Of course, this was not clear when Martin got the news. He calmly left the mass meeting and went home. There was already a large crowd gathered outside, and a number of police and city officials were present, trying to control the crowd. Many of the onlookers were very angry and some were armed. It was a volatile situation, and the authorities on the scene were visibly concerned about losing control. After assuring himself that Coretta and the baby were not injured, Martin went back out onto the front porch and gave calming words to the crowd. He told them that no one was hurt. Everything was all right. Don't be violent. Go home and continue to stay off the buses.

Reassured by his manner, his faith, and, I believe, by the hand of God, the crowd calmed and gradually dispersed. This was a dramatic example of Martin's ability to remain true to his faith and his principles, and of his ability to lead others. This does not mean that Martin was never afraid. We all, at certain times during those momentous days, were afraid. But we believed in our cause and we believed in God. Even if it meant death, we were determined to let nothing stop us from carrying out our various goals of ending segregation and discrimination. Martin's innate abilities enabled him to be a true advocate of nonviolence and social change. He talked it, slept it, preached it, and lived it.

Many who were active in the bus protest did not understand

when Martin first began to articulate the principle of non-violence. My own brother Tom was a member of the board of the Montgomery Improvement Association. This brought him into the circles of the protest leaders. On a morning after the *Montgomery Advertiser* had carried a story about Martin's recent espousal of the Ghandian and Christian philosophy of "turning the other cheek," Tom went up to him and declared that this was an effective ploy for the news media. "Oh no, Brother Gray, this is no ploy at all," Martin responded. "If we are to succeed, I am now convinced that an absolutely non-violent method must be ours amid the vast hostilities we face." Tom noted Martin's seriousness and decided to drop the subject, because my brother was not personally convinced that he could absolutely follow that doctrine.

Of course, the Movement did result in Martin's death at the hands of a violent person. Incidentally, no one was ever convicted or even arrested for bombing the Dexter parsonage.

At the first meeting of the Montgomery Improvement Association after the bombing, Martin's father, Martin Luther King, Sr., (often called Daddy King) was present, having come over from Atlanta to check on his son. Dr. King Sr. made a fervent plea to the board members, for them to encourage Martin to come home to Atlanta so his son and family could live more safely and more conventionally than in Montgomery. To a person, the board agreed. But Martin would have no part of it. He thanked his father and the rest of the board, but voiced a belief that God could keep him as safe in Montgomery as in any other place, and that he had to be about the business in which we were engaged. As it turned out, he stayed in Montgomery another three years before moving to Atlanta, and even then he was frequently back in Montgomery and Alabama during key periods, such as the Freedom Riders Riot in 1961 and the Selma-to-Montgomery March in 1965.

The latter occasion provided another example of Martin's great courage and faith, as related by Dr. Emmitt Smiley, a Montgomery dentist and a member of Dexter Avenue Baptist Church. Smiley recalls that at the conclusion of the march, following the mass meeting on the steps of the Alabama capitol, he drove Dr. King back out to the City of St. Jude Catholic complex, which had served as the Montgomery headquarters of the March. St. Jude also housed a hospital and infirmary. Dr. King's feet were hurting after walking fifty miles, and Dr. Smiley drove him to the St. Jude Infirmary. The infirmary was, however, under heavy guard by Alabama state troopers, who were not allowing anyone into the building. One of the troopers drew his weapon and threatened to shoot Dr. Smiley. Dr. King walked up to him, directly in front of the drawn weapon, and said, "Young man, do you know why you are here? You are here to protect us." The officer put up his weapon and Dr. King got treatment for his feet.

The MIA board was more successful in urging its only white member, the Reverend Robert Graetz, to leave town following two massive bombings of his home, the parsonage of Trinity Lutheran Church, on Cleveland (now Rosa Parks) Avenue at Mill Street. Graetz was equally willing to remain in Montgomery, but there appeared to be even more hostility toward him—if it was possible—than toward Dr. King at that point. It was thought that this was because Graetz, a white, had allied himself with the black cause, which simply infuriated the most violent of Montgomery's white supremacists. Graetz finally agreed to move to Columbus, Ohio, where he pastored another Lutheran church. Graetz and his famly now live in southeastern Ohio, near the town of Logan.

The Lawsuit to Integrate the Buses, February 1956

After Mrs. Parks was convicted of disorderly conduct and her case was for the moment basically over, the primary question on everyone's mind was "How long are we going to be able to get the people to stay off the buses?" People must have something to look forward to. Of course, the Parks conviction was on appeal, but that alone would not suffice. The logical thing was to stay off the buses until we could return to them on an integrated basis. Jo Ann Robinson was especially astounded that the city officials were not wise enough to resolve this situation, even on a halfway basis. I was not surprised.

The denial of such simple demands as we had made and the

refusal by the white authorities to yield an inch had the effect of unifying the African-American community. It became obvious to everyone that there was no hope of obtaining justice or fair play from the white power structure. I had never thought for a moment that the authorities were going to give in to our small requests. But it was necessary to go through the motions. In the back of my mind I always knew that the matter was going to be resolved in court, and not in an Alabama court, but in federal court. And I started early working in that direction. The shift from the first-come, first-serve seating demand raised in the Parks case, to the demand for full integration of the buses is seen in the next bus case that I handled, *Browder v. Gayle.*

Within two weeks after the Protest started, I began talking to the leadership of the MIA about a new case. I started the research, and talked with other lawyers including Clifford Durr, Robert Carter, and Thurgood Marshall. In *Browder v. Gayle* we asked the Court to declare the segregation statutes unconstitutional and to issue an injunction enjoining the officials from enforcing the segregation statutes. I did not include Rosa Parks as a plaintiff in this case because I feared a question would arise in the federal suit about whether we were trying to circumvent and enjoin the criminal prosecution of Mrs. Parks. Including her would have given the opposition an opportunity to introduce a side issue. I wanted the court to have only one issue to decide—the constitutionality of the laws requiring segregation on the buses in the city of Montgomery.

I had completed much of the advance preparation for the suit by the time Martin's home was bombed on January 30, 1956. We had been waiting for the right moment to file the suit. The Bus Protest was ongoing, but it was a hardship to many people. I knew that we had to give the people something to hang on to so they would continue to make the sacrifice of staying off the buses.

From the outset, I realized that the legal system was against our cause and against me. I knew that as an African-American attorney I had to try every case, whether it was a traffic violation or a matter of race, as if it were going to the United States Supreme Court. We expected to lose in all the local courts. Our only hope was to get our cases eventually to a federal court, where we believed we could get justice.

It was standard procedure in Alabama in those days that if a case could be decided on technicalities, it would never be decided on merit. This was especially true in the segregation cases. In Alabama practice there were many technicalities to trap attorneys, especially attorneys with limited experience. A case could be dismissed because it was not timely filed or because of failure to obtain an extension of time to file transcript, or failure to obtain an extension of time to file the record, failure to state on the record "assignment of errors individually," failure to argue assignment of errors, or even for arguing assignment of errors in bulk. Most of these were administrative or technical matters and had nothing at all to do with the merit of a case. As an African-American lawyer in Alabama, I looked forward to getting cases to the federal courts where the cases could be decided on merit. It was also desirable to be on the offense instead of the defense and thus better positioned to win.

On February 2, 1956, three days after the bombing of the Dexter parsonage, I filed *Browder v. Gayle*. Aurelia Browder was a housewife; W. A. ("Tacky") Gayle was mayor of the City of Montgomery. The case made headlines and provided the encouragement needed for the people to remain off the buses until they could return on an integrated basis.

The suit was filed to declare unconstitutional and a violation of the 14th Amendment to the United States Constitution, ordinances of the City of Montgomery and statutes of the State of Alabama which required segregation of the races on city buses. Joining Mrs. Browder as plaintiffs were Mrs. Susie McDonald, who was seventy-seven years old; Mrs. Jeanetta Reese; Claudette Colvin by Q. P. Colvin, her father; and Mary Louise Smith by Frank Smith, her father. The plaintiffs were selected by the leaders of the Protest. Each plaintiff came to my office and signed a written retainer employing me to file the suit.

In addition to Mayor Gayle, the defendants were Clyde Sellers and Frank Parks, individually and as members of the Board of

Commissioners of the City of Montgomery, and Goodwin J. Ruppenthal, individually and as Chief of Police of the City of Montgomery; and the Montgomery City Lines, Inc., as a corporation; James F. Blake and Robert Cleere, bus drivers; and C. C. "Jack" Owen, Jimmy Hitchcock, and Sibyl Pool, as members of the Alabama Public Service Commission. The defendants were represented by Walter Knabe, Drayton N. Hamilton, Herman H. Hamilton, Jr., and Jack Crenshaw.

Joining me as attorneys for the plaintiffs were Charles Langford, Arthur Shores, Peter Hall, Orzell Billingsley, Jr., Robert Carter, and Thurgood Marshall.

Prior to filing the lawsuit, and during the time I was preparing the suit and discussing it with the officials of MIA, I decided that it would be useful to go to New York and discuss this lawsuit with Thurgood Marshall, the director counsel of the NAACP Legal Defense Fund and Educational Fund, Inc., and Robert Carter, the general counsel for the NAACP. (The NAACP and the Inc. Fund, as it was popularly called, were separate organizations.)

I not only wanted an opportunity to discuss this case with them, but also all of the other legal ramifications involved in the bus boycott. This was the first time that I met Thurgood Marshall, who was later to become U.S. solicitor general and a justice on the United States Supreme Court. From that initial conference throughout the years, I established an excellent working, professional relationship with him and he assisted me in many of the civil rights cases which I filed. It was also during this meeting that I initially met Robert L. Carter. He was also a lawyer from New York. We were to work together on many other cases in years to come. He assisted me in *Browder v. Gayle* and generally gave advice throughout the movement. He later retained me to assist him in representing the NAACP when it was enjoined from doing business in Alabama, beginning on June 1, 1956. He also assisted me in the arguments in the United States Supreme Court in the case of *Gomillion v. Lightfoot*.

This conference with Thurgood Marshall and Robert Carter was the beginning of a long professional relationship with these men, the top lawyers of the two major civil rights organizations in the country, the NAACP Legal Defense and Educational Fund, Inc., and the NAACP itself. I was now in a position that whenever I needed professional assistance in civil rights cases, I had a direct line and the ears of the two major legal civil rights strategists in the nation. This gave me courage, determination and a ready access to all the legal assistance that I would need in connection with all of the subsequent civil rights cases that I've handled. I have maintained that relationship with the appropriate officials of those two organizations over the years.

Pressure to Drop the Lawsuit

Shortly after *Browder v. Gayle* was filed, many influential whites in the community contacted me directly and indirectly and attempted to persuade me to drop the case. Numerous local, county, state, and federal officials in all three branches of government attempted to prevail upon me not to pursue the case. Some suggested that I dismiss the case outright because it would only create problems in the community and give me the reputation of an agitator. Others suggested that I agree to let the court pass the case over for a period of time so there would be no ruling on the segregation laws at the time.

When pressed for an answer with respect to a dismissal or to have the case passed over, I did not immediately tell these high public officials "no," but I told them I would confer with my clients. After having conferred with my clients, I told the officials that there was nothing personal involved, but my clients insisted that I pursue the case vigorously.

Some of the officials suggested that if I would get my clients to agree to either dismiss the case or have it passed over, I would not have to worry and they would assure me that from that point forward, I would have all the legal cases I could handle. Of course, I would never have agreed to such an inducement even though those making the offers had the power to deliver. They were capable of referring clients that would enable me to build a substantial practice. Remember, these assurances were made at a time when I had nothing. I did not give them a second thought. Had I accepted their recommendation, I would never have been able to file another suit challenging the segregation laws of the state of Alabama, nor would I have been able to face myself, my family, or those who trusted me. To accept their offers would have been contrary to my goal of "destroying everything segregated I could find."

The Browder Trial

Since *Browder v. Gayle* challenged the constitutionality of a state statute, a three-judge federal court was convened. The panel consisted of Judge Richard T. Rives, Court of Appeals for the Fifth Circuit, who had practiced law in Montgomery for many years before he was appointed to the bench, and who was a great appeals court judge; Judge Frank M. Johnson, Jr., a November 1955 appointee as United States District Judge for the Middle District of Alabama; and Judge Seybourne Lynne, United States District Judge for the Northern District of Alabama, Birmingham. The case was tried and taken under advisement.

3

The City's Get-Tough Policy

As the Protest continued and began to broaden its base of support within as well as outside Montgomery, division in the white community became evident. Some whites were sympathetic to our cause and did not oppose equal treatment of whites and blacks in bus transportation. But the overall white resistance drowned out the moderate voices. Remember that the Protest began only eighteen months after the Supreme Court decision in *Brown v. Board of Education*, the momentous school desegregation ruling. Throughout the South, cracks were being seen in the facade of Jim Crow segregation; where no cracks were yet visible, they could be imagined. The segregationists and white supremacists were busily organizing and agitating against any real or perceived threat to the "Southern way of life." Those Southern whites who might have listened to voices of reason were already being intimidated, forced out of public office, threatened economically and sometimes even physically. The oppression of moderate and liberal whites was only a token of what African Americans had to contend with, but it was there and it did have an impact. Of course, the full fury of the resistance still lay ahead.

In Montgomery, Mayor Tacky Gayle led the resistance. He urged white Montgomerians to stop using their automobiles as taxi services for the maids and cooks who worked for them. An article in the January 25, 1956, *Montgomery Advertiser* records Mayor Gayle criticizing whites who did not side with him on the issue. He said the maids and cooks, by boycotting the Montgomery City

Lines, were "fighting to destroy our social fabric just as much as the Negro radicals that were leading them." He continued,

> The Negroes are laughing at white people behind their backs. They think it's very funny and amusing that whites who are opposed to the Negro boycott will act as chauffeurs to Negroes who are boycotting the buses. The City Commission urges the white people of Montgomery to cease the practice of paying Negro maids, cooks, or other employees blackmail transportation money in any shape, form, or fashion.

A few years ago, there was a movie in which Whoopi Goldberg played a domestic worker in the household of a white Montgomery woman (Sissy Spacek) during the time of the Bus Protest. This movie, *The Long Walk Home*, was written by John Cork, a white Montgomerian who is the nephew of the present Montgomery mayor, Emory Folmar. Although it is a fictional account, Mr. Cork's screenplay depicts the prevailing attitude and situations in the white community in 1956 quite succinctly.

Early in 1956, Mayor Gayle, other city officials, white business leaders, and white ministers in Montgomery began to publicly announce that they had become members of the White Citizens Council. This was an organization that had begun in Mississippi following the *Brown* decision and had spread rapidly through the South with the stated goal of maintaining racial segregation in both public and private life. White Citizens Council members generally did not approve of the violence of the Ku Klux Klan, yet they were as adamant as the KKK on racial segregation. They did not wear hoods or burn crosses, but they had other weapons. These were often persons of substantial political and economic power in the community. They were the politicians, the city councilmen, the legislators, and the businessmen who were, however, die-hard segregationists.

One of the reasons why the city was unwilling to accept our compromise and grant our three meager requests was the authorities' fear that this would be interpreted as giving in to African Americans, and, in some measure, would signal the beginning of the end of segregation. Therefore, they were determined not to give an inch. For if they gave an inch, they feared we would take a mile. There was no doubt that the City of Montgomery had taken a get-tough stand and had aligned itself with a group notorious for its opposition to the fair and equal treatment of black citizens.

On the other hand, African Americans in Montgomery and across the U.S. saw *Brown v. Board* as a panacea for solving the key racial issues in this nation. This case in effect reversed *Plessy v. Ferguson,* the 1896 Supreme Court decision which established the doctrine of "separate but equal." That doctrine has been plaguing us ever since. Things became separate all right, but there was little equality to be found. With the Supreme Court's decision in *Brown,* African Americans thought they could see coming not only the end of segregated education, but the beginning of the end of segregation in every phase of life.

As a matter of fact, we cited *Brown* as a precedent for *Browder v. Gayle.* The decision in *Brown* had resulted from the work of Thurgood Marshall and other lawyers who had worked with him in the companion cases that were consolidated into the 1954 *Brown* ruling. The architect of the doctrine surrounding *Brown v. Board of Education* was Charles Hamilton Houston, an African-American lawyer who was dean of Howard Law School. He had worked for years with the NAACP and formulated the doctrine which the court initially announced in *Brown v. Board of Education.* He was also one of the professors who taught Thurgood Marshall. Naturally, this legal background was a part of what I was seeking when I visited in New York with Marshall and Robert Carter to enlist their help in the *Browder* case.

New Draft Status

Meanwhile, as the segregationist attitudes of the Montgomery authorities were intensifying, so were my own problems as my role in the Bus Protest became more public. Like many activists in the Movement, I suffered my share of harassment, including bomb

This smear sheet was an indication of the white community's attitude toward my ministerial deferment.

threats, crank telephone calls, hate letters, and an attempted stabbing. Although I held a 4-D draft status because of my ministerial work, I was suddenly reclassified to 1-A immediately after I filed the lawsuit to integrate the buses. In accordance with the law, I had made periodic reports to the draft board ever since I first registered, stating my ministerial involvement.

My draft matter was presented to the local draft board in Montgomery. I presented evidence to show my past and present ministerial activities. At the time, I was assistant minister of the Holt Street Church of Christ. The elders of the church, Mr. Boise McQueen and Mr. Willard Billingsley, along with the church's secretary, Thomas Gray, testified. The board refused to reconsider. I appealed to higher authorities, and eventually General Lewis Hershey, director of the Selective Service System, blocked the efforts of the Montgomery draft board to send me to military service. Hershey interceded the night before I was to ship out. In protest, draft boards throughout Alabama refused to induct anyone else. Alabama Selective Service officials created a new classification called F-G, and said they would use this deferment for other draftees until Fred Gray was inducted into the service.

I love my country as well as anyone and I did not use my ministerial position for the purpose of evading the draft. I was fully prepared to serve my country immediately upon graduation from law school. But when I made my periodic report to the draft board after returning to Montgomery in 1954, the board was evidently satisfied with my ministerial duties. It was only after I became active in the Bus Protest, and particularly after filing the lawsuit to integrate the buses, that I was reclassified. I fought being drafted because I resented the injustice of using the Selective Service System solely to remove from the Movement the person who was basically responsible for conducting its legal activities.

White politicians probably felt that if they could stop the legal work that I was doing, then they would be in a position to end the Movement or, at least retard the African-American quest for civil rights in Alabama. The conflict and tension over my ministerial deferment continued until I turned twenty-six and thereby became ineligible for the draft.

State v. Fred D. Gray, March 1956

I was also the victim of a politically motivated criminal prosecution in the March 1956 case of *State of Alabama v. Fred D. Gray.* The Montgomery County Grand Jury indicted me for allegedly representing Jeanetta Reese in a federal desegregation lawsuit without her consent. She claimed she had not retained me, had no knowledge of the lawsuit, and that I had unlawfully and illegally listed her as a plaintiff in *Browder v. Gayle.* In fact, Mrs. Reese had retained me both orally and in writing. As a plaintiff in the case, she had posed in my office for pictures for *Jet Magazine.* I also had tape recordings of our conversations in which she expressed her desire to be a part of the lawsuit and to obtain justice.

I later discovered that Mrs. Reese had worked in the home of a high-ranking Montgomery police official. Her employer and other authorities interrogated her about her involvement in the legal activities, and under that pressure, she disavowed any knowledge of the lawsuit. Even more problematic for her, I later learned, Mrs. Reese had failed to inform her husband that she was a plaintiff in the lawsuit. He was very critical of her when the inevitable harassing calls and other intimidating events began.

Recalling the saying, a lawyer who defends himself has a fool for a client, I did not defend myself against this indictment. Instead, I was defended by a team of African-American Alabama lawyers, Arthur Shores, Orzell Billingsley, Peter Hall, and Charles Langford. This was serious business. The state statute under which I was indicted called for automatic disbarment upon conviction.

I was shocked that the Montgomery County Grand Jury indicted me. However, I should not have been. I knew the authorities would do everything possible to stop the bus boycott. Knowing that, I had been very careful at the time at the outset of the *Browder* case to document the fact that each plaintiff had retained me to represent them. I had been extra careful to be sure they understood the problems and the criticisms that would emerge once the lawsuit was filed. In addition, I knew about the earlier use of this statute against attorney Arthur A. Madison, an African-American lawyer who was originally from Montgomery but at the time was practicing law in New York. Madison had returned to Alabama to assist people in becoming registered voters. J. Clay Smith, Jr., in his book, *Emancipation, the Making of a Black Lawyer, 1844-1944* describes attorney Madison's situation.

> In 1944, while trying to help blacks register to vote, he was arrested under an Alabama statute that made it a misdemeanor to represent a person without his or her consent. Madison had taken appeals for eight blacks who had been denied the right to vote, but "five (of the eight blacks) made affidavits that they had not employed Madison or authorized him to take the appeals." Madison attempted to obtain a legal decision that the restrictive registration law in Alabama was unconstitutional, but the white power structure, led by United States Senator Lister Hill, was adamant that Madison's efforts to register black voters be stopped by whatever means necessary. As a result of Senator Hill's influence and the pressure brought to

bear on the Montgomery County Board of Registrars, Madison was disbarred on July 24, 1945. He relocated to New York City.

This is an example of what had occurred earlier in Montgomery, Alabama, for the purpose of stopping blacks from becoming voters. This type of retaliation was one of the risks that black lawyers encountered in Alabama and the South in representing African Americans in an effort to end racial discrimination. I realized the risks; I wanted to minimize them, but I was prepared to pay the price if it became necessary. However, I am happy it was not necessary.

Either prior to or shortly after filing *Browder v. Gayle,* I personally met attorney Arthur Madison. He was the brother-in-law to Reverend S. S. Seay, my office landlord and my friend and mentor, and thus the uncle of attorney Solomon S. Seay, Jr., who later became one of my law partners. We practiced law together for over thirty years.

After my indictment and prior to the time of my arraignment, I was in the office of U.S. District Judge Frank M. Johnson, Jr., on another matter. When we had completed that matter, Judge Johnson asked how things were going in connection with the prosecution against me.

I responded, "About as well as can be expected."

He parenthetically stated words to the effect of, "You know whatever offense there was, if any, was committed when the lawsuit was filed on the second floor of this courthouse, of which the United States government has exclusive jurisdiction."

I was appreciative to Judge Johnson for his comment. I viewed this as an interesting comment designed to give me a tip if this argument had not been thought of by my defense team. In fact, this very argument had been included by my defense team in a motion to dismiss the case against me. Solicitor William Thetford, at the opening of the hearing in state circuit court, recognized that he could not secure a conviction so he asked the court to dismiss the indictment on the ground that the court did not have jurisdiction and that he would refer the matter to the United States Attorney. I never heard anything else on this matter.

This was not the last of the attacks against me as I continued to provide legal services to the Movement.

Arrested at Airport

During the middle of the Protest, Dr. King asked me to make a speech in Boston in his place because of a conflict in his schedule. I agreed.

My brother Thomas drove me to the Montgomery airport. The plane was delayed, so we took the nearest seats available in the waiting area. Shortly thereafter, a shabbily dressed man asked us to move to the "colored" section of the airport. My brother returned to his automobile. I guess I felt like Mrs. Parks must have when she was asked to give up her bus seat. I was so astonished by such a request that it seemed as if I were paralyzed. I was physically unable to move to the "colored" section. Two police officers arrested me, took me to the city jail, booked and fingerprinted me. When my brother returned to his car, he watched the officers put me in their car. He followed us to the jail to be sure that I arrived safely.

At the jail, a bondsman whom I knew saw me and with great surprise said, "Fred, what are you here for?" He then agreed to sign my release bond. A newspaper reporter took me back to the airport. I caught the delayed plane to Boston and gave the speech. During my speech, I not only discussed what was happening in Montgomery with reference to the Bus Protest, but I also related to my audience my arrest for sitting in the "white" section of the Montgomery airport.

After I returned to Montgomery, I appeared and was tried in the Recorder's Court of the City of Montgomery before Judge D. Eugene Loe. This was the same court where Mrs. Parks was tried on December 5, 1955, and the same court where Martin was tried in 1956 on a charge of speeding as he transported people in the car pool during the Bus Protest. When the case of *City of Montgomery v. Fred Gray* was called, it was dismissed. The judge reasoned that if the plane had been on time there would not have been a problem.

Like all of the leaders in the Movement, I refused to be intimidated by attacks. These had their good side for the Movement, because publicity accompanying these attacks led to more speaking requests and this offered even more opportunity to spread word of the Protest to other parts of the country.

Ninety-eight Arrested for Boycotting, March 1956

The same grand jury that indicted me in March 1956 for allegedly representing Mrs. Jeanetta Reese without her consent in *Browder v. Gayle*, also returned indictments against ninety-eight participants in the Montgomery Bus Protest. These individuals were indicted for violating the Alabama Anti-Boycott Statute.

We were aware of the anti-boycott statute. The Code of Alabama, Title 14, Section 54 provided the following:

> Two or more persons who, without a just cause or legal excuse for so doing, enter into any combination, conspiracy, agreement, arrangement, or understanding for the purpose of hindering, delaying, or preventing any other persons, firms, corporation, or association of persons from carrying on any lawful business, shall be guilty of a misdemeanor.

It was because of this statute that we never referred to our activities against the buses as a boycott. We always referred to the activities as a Protest because we expected the City of Montgomery would use this statute for criminal prosecutions as well as to enjoin the operation of our car pool. Each of the ninety-eight was charged with violating this statute. They were indicted in small groups. As each person appeared before Judge Eugene Carter, the indictment was read. I entered a plea of "not guilty" on behalf of each.

The arrest process was very unusual. When the sheriff's deputies went to make the arrests, they were very considerate. My brother Thomas recalls that he was arrested at home but was allowed to go by his place of business and explain to his employees why he was being arrested. The deputy sheriff then stopped to arrest Reverend A. W. Wilson, the pastor of Holt Street Baptist Church. Reverend Wilson told the deputy he was busy, but he would go to the jail later and be booked. And he did.

When the indictments were returned, people went to the jail voluntarily and offered to be arrested. Some were disappointed because they had not been indicted.

Ironically, as the word spread that ninety-eight* persons were indicted, including many African-American preachers, it became a real honor to have been indicted and arrested. Soon, deputies did not have to go out to make arrests; protest leaders and ministers voluntarily went down to the jail to see if they had been indicted and offered to be arrested. Any number of persons who were not indicted were very disappointed because they knew they were involved as much as the ones who were indicted. They felt that they had been somewhat insulted by not having been arrested for exercising their constitutional rights. One of these persons was Richard Harris, one of the unsung heroes of the Protest.

Harris was the owner of Dean Drug Store, located on the corner of Monroe and Lawrence streets; his father had operated that store

---

*Those indicted included: R. D. Abernathy, Mrs. R. T. Adair, W. F. Alford, Burl Averhart, John Henry Baker, Roy Bennett, Arthur Bibbin, R. B. Binion, Mose Bishop, P. M. Blair, J. W. Bonner, Louis Boswell, Eddie Bradford, Ida Mae Caldwell, Albert Carlton, Osborne C. Chambliss, J. H. Cherry, Louis Christburg, M. C. Cleveland, P. E. Conley, Fred Lee Davis, Alfred Ellis, Isaiah Ferguson, E. N. French, Jimmie Gamble, John H. Garrison, R. James Glasco, Thomas Gray, Addie James Hamilton, J. W. Haynes, Sitveria Heard, George Henderson, George Hill, John Green Hill, Aaron Hoffman, Booker T. Holmes, Hillman H. Hubbard, Alberta Judkins James, H. H. Johnson, Mentha H. Johnson, Robert Johnson, William H. Johnson, Moses William Jones, Eli Judkins, Willie James Kemp, Matthew Kennedy, J. N. King, M. L. King, Jr., B. D. Lambert, Audrey Belle Langford, C. W. Lee, E. H. Ligon, Mrs. Jimmie Lowe, Simon Peter McBryde, Jimmie Roy McClain, August McHaney, Cora L. McHaney, Freddie Morris, Walter Moss, Arthur W. Murphy, E. D. Nixon, Huestis James Palmer, Rosa Parks, Tom Parks, J. E. Pierce, Charley Polk, Eddie Lee Posey, W. J. Powell, James Theodore Primus, Mose Whatley Richburg, Jo Ann Robinson, Solomon S. Seay, Sr., Benjamin James Simms, J. C. Smith, Walter S. Smith, Frank Leon Taylor, Wesley S. Tolbert, Calvin Varner, Lottie Green Varner, Lonnie Charles Walker, Mrs. A. W. West, Edward Martin Williams, Henry Williams, A. W. Wilson, and Ronald Young.

My law office was near the drug store operated by Rich Harris; here Rosa Parks and I visit with Rich and his employees, Annie Birch and Alberta Williams.

before him, and Dean Drug was a fixture in the African-American community. Harris and his wife, Vera, lived two doors from Dr. King on South Jackson Street. Richard Harris was one of the key persons behind-the-scenes, truly a "mover and shaker" during the Protest. His drug store had a lunch counter and was a gathering place for the leaders of the Movement. It was located half a block from my office. Richard Harris served as my personal adviser on many matters, from "Don't let your clients stop and talk to you on the street, take them to your office," to advising me as to how to invest my money once I made some, what type of automobiles to purchase, and the type of tires to put on them.

Richard Harris was also known as "Dr. Harris" or, for those closest to him, "Rich Harris." His major Protest role was to solve problems, particularly in the transportation system. As long as the transportation system worked well and everyone was being transported, Rich Harris felt good and felt there was nothing for him to do other than to keep communication flowing between the various parties. In a real sense, Rich Harris at Dean Drug Store was the nerve center for all major problems. Whenever a problem needed resolution, whether it was a problem with transportation, or someone had been arrested or harassed, or just to get a message from one person to another, we would always call Rich Harris at Dean Drug Store. He was always there and could always make the contact and get the problem solved. Rich Harris spread the news of my arrest and indictment for representing Jeanetta Reese without her consent. He was looking out his drug store window and saw a deputy's car pass with me in the back seat and he knew something was wrong. I was immediately released on bond, but if I had not been, help would have soon arrived. Harris would have seen to it. He had two dedicated employees, Annie Birch and Alberta "Peaches" Williams, who also assisted in the Movement.

Rich Harris was one of those disappointed because he was not indicted with the ninety-eight. Robert Nesbitt, an insurance company executive, was not indicted, but he contributed substantially to the Movement. He was responsible for recruiting Dr. King to Montgomery to become the pastor of Dexter Avenue Baptist Church. Another unsung hero who was indicted was Dr. Moses William Jones, a well-respected physician and a member of the MIA board, who attended all of the mass meetings. He, too, is one of the unsung heroes of the Movement. There were many.

The Judges and the Circuit Clerk

Judge Eugene Carter presided over the anti-boycott cases. Judge Carter and Judge W. B. Jones were the two state circuit court judges in Montgomery at that time. These courts were part of Alabama's statewide judicial system, though they operated at the county level. They were the next courts up from the local recorder's or municipal courts such as the one where Mrs. Parks had been convicted of disorderly conduct and where my airport seating case had been dismissed. Recorder's court cases could be appealed to the circuit courts. Above the circuit courts were the state courts of civil and criminal appeals, and above them was the Alabama Supreme Court. Appeals beyond the state level went to the federal courts.

Judge Carter has since retired and still lives in the Chisholm

Community in Montgomery. He and the former sheriff, Mac Sim Butler, still meet at the Courthouse for coffee with some of the old-time lawyers. Judge Jones died many years ago.

While Judge Jones and Judge Carter were the two circuit judges, the old-time lawyers around the courthouse knew that the person who really ran the Circuit Court of Montgomery County was the circuit clerk, John Matthews. Mr. Matthews was truly a Southern gentleman. Early in my practice, I established a very good working relationship with him. While I am of the opinion that he believed in segregation, as did most white people at that time, he went out of his way to be fair with me and to show me that he treated me with the same type of courtesy and dignity that he treated white lawyers. It is important that a lawyer, and particularly a young lawyer, establish and maintain a good working relationship with the clerks of the courts because clerks can tell you how to file your documents, where to file your documents, exactly what should be included in them, and offer valuable tips that are not found on the faces of the judges or in the state code and law books.

I talked with Mr. Matthews on many occasions about my cases. When I would get a new type case and I didn't know exactly how to prepare the papers, I would go to Mr. Matthews and tell him that I had a case and I wasn't sure how to draft the documents.

He would say, "Fred, what kind of case do you have?"

I would describe the case. He would go in the files and pull out a case with similar facts, and I would use that case as a guide. At various times during my practice, I have raised almost every conceivable issue involving discrimination and segregation based on race. I have always presented each issue in a professional manner and have always enjoyed the respect of the bench, the bar, and the persons with whom I came in contact.

The Trial

Charles Langford, Arthur Shores, Peter Hall, Orzell Billingsley and I represented those charged with violating the anti-boycott statute. The prosecutors were William Thetford, Robert B. Stewart, and Maury D. Smith. It was a challenge to plan strategy to defend ninety-eight persons indicted for allegedly violating the anti-boycott statute. Even though our clients were indicted in groups, there were still sixteen individual cases. Early on, the opposing counsel and the court agreed that only one case would be tried and that would be the case against Dr. King. The other cases would be resolved depending on the outcome of his case.

There had been no violation of the Alabama anti-boycott statute. The statute in effect said that if a person, without just cause or legal excuse, boycotted a business, then there was a violation. While we believed that the statute was unconstitutional on its face, according to *Thornhill v. Alabama*, a case in which the U.S. Supreme Court declared unconstitutional an Alabama anti-picketing statute similar to the one here, certainly it was unconstitutional as applied to our clients. We further believed that there was no violation because we had legal excuse and just cause for failing to ride segregated buses, particularly where we had been mistreated and humiliated.

In preparation for the trial, we filed a number of pretrial motions, namely a motion to dismiss, a motion to quash the indictment, and almost any other motion we could think of, including a motion to integrate the courtroom. As expected, all motions filed were denied. The motions were filed not so much because of the likelihood of success, but rather for the purpose of preserving the record. This is the manner in which African-American lawyers knew we had to conduct all cases, even misdemeanor traffic offenses.

The case was ultimately tried without a jury. Judge Carter, as we expected, found Dr. King guilty and fined him five hundred dollars. Our motion for a new trial was denied. We appealed. The case ultimately, like most of our other cases, was never decided on the merits, but was dismissed on a technicality.

Subsequently, all of the other cases were dismissed. No fine was ever paid and no one served any time as a result of these indictments.

The Boycott Wedding, June 1956

Amidst the trials, tribulations, and protests, there were good times. The high point for Bernice Hill and me was our marriage. Bernice and her friends sent out two thousand invitations. When people sent word that they had not received an invitation, we went around and retrieved invitations from our close relatives and friends for those people who indicated they wanted to be invited. We wanted anyone who wanted an invitation to have one. I was considered most everybody's lawyer in the local African-American community, so a lot of people wanted to come.

We were married June 17, 1956, in the Holt Street Baptist Church. Our own church, the Holt Street Church of Christ, was constructing a new building and was not large enough for the crowd we expected. The wedding was to be at 6 p.m. The church was filled by 3 p.m. It was just like a mass meeting. People came early so they could get a seat. In the mass meetings, the people would get off work and bring their dinner so that they could get a seat. That is what they did for our wedding. It must have been the largest wedding ever held in Montgomery up to that time. Maybe it still is.

It was a Protest wedding; that's what we called it. Everybody pitched in to help us because we surely did not have that kind of money. The baker, Mr. Shaw, made a huge cake and did not charge the regular price. For something borrowed, Bernice wore Dr. Hagalyn Seay Wilson's wedding dress. She was the daughter of Reverend Seay and the sister of attorney Seay. I purchased Bernice's ring from Mrs. Frances Burk's husband, the owner of Burk's Jewelry, with a special discount. The church was decorated by my brother, Hugh, who still owns a floral shop in Montgomery. My childhood friend, K. K. Mitchell, minister of Holt Street Church of Christ, performed the wedding ceremony. The reception was at the Derby Supper Club, owned by D. Caffey, who served as a personal bondsman for many of the ninety-eight who were honored by being arrested for allegedly conducting an illegal boycott. Caffey was also the uncle of attorney Calvin Pryor who later

Bernice and I were married in what we felt was a Movement wedding; we invited the entire community.

became one of my law partners and recently retired from his position as assistant U.S. Attorney. Another of Caffey's nephews was Dr. Julius Pryor, a noted surgeon, who was also my mother's surgeon. All of the arrangements for the wedding were done by African Americans.

The day after the wedding, Bernice and I left for a working

honeymoon. My step-brother Curtis Arms, and his wife, Minnie, accompanied us to Cleveland for a reception and then to San Francisco, where I was the Montgomery Branch delegate to the annual convention of the NAACP. Our honeymoon was cut short because the Alabama draft board ordered me to report for a physical examination in preparation for my induction into the army.

The Court's Decision—A Great Victory

Meanwhile, two days after our wedding, on June 19, 1956, the United States Court for the Middle District of Alabama ruled in *Browder v. Gayle* that the city ordinances and the state statute requiring segregation on Montgomery buses were unconstitutional. As you can imagine, this was quite a wedding gift.

This was a day of rejoicing for the Movement and a great day for African-American people in Alabama. The ruling provided the impetus needed to keep the protest alive. In a broader sense, this was a great day for all the people in America. For the first time, a court had declared unconstitutional city ordinances and state statutes requiring segregation on city buses. The court used *Brown v. Board of Education* (the school desegregation case) as precedent for declaring segregation laws on buses unconstitutional. *Browder v. Gayle* is a landmark case and has been used many, many times as precedent for declaring segregation in other areas unconstitutional. The case is also significant in that it is the first civil rights case handled by Judge Frank M. Johnson, Jr. It was also significant to me because it was the first civil rights case that I won, making the first step toward realization of my goal to "destroy everything segregated I could find."

However, the white power structure would not be outdone. They appealed to the U. S. Supreme Court. Therefore, our people still had to remain off the buses until the case was decided by the U. S. Supreme Court. The Bus Protest continued.

Montgomery's African Americans had been walking or car pooling for 192 days. There had been twenty-eight mass meetings and one mass wedding. The Montgomery City Lines had lost hundreds of thousands of fares. There had been a dozen bombings, any number of physical attacks by whites on blacks, untold incidents of petty harassment, firings, foreclosures, etc. Several hundred people had been arrested. The legal expenses on both sides must have been substantial.

We were not even tired.

Dark Before Dawn—Ending of Boycott

So, the legal work went on. Whites employed many schemes to break the protest, including the refusal of the white-owned insurance companies to insure automobiles operated by the car pool drivers and protesters. Money had poured in from throughout the United States to finance our transportation system. A number of station wagons had been purchased and Rufus Lewis and his assistants had organized what amounted to a private, city-wide transportation company. The sudden inability to get insurance on these vehicles was a big crisis. When no one else would or could help, Martin called upon Mr. T. M. Alexander, a successful African-American insurance businessman of Atlanta. Mr. Alexander placed insurance coverage for Dr. King and the Montgomery Movement with Lloyd's of London. Alexander was no stranger to Montgomery. He was born in Montgomery. His father had been a contractor whose company had relocated Jefferson Davis's Confederate White House to its present site adjacent to the Alabama State Capitol. Martin's ability to reach out to successful African Americans outside Montgomery was a testament to his growing national prominence and influence, but it was also a sign of how hungry African Americans were across the country to strike a blow in the heart of Jim Crow.

Alexander's connection with Lloyd's of London got us past that crisis, but there were others. In another attempt to end the Bus Protest, the City of Montgomery filed a lawsuit on November 5, 1956, against the Montgomery Improvement Association, in the Circuit Court of Montgomery County, to enjoin the operation of the car pool. The City was represented by Walter J. Knabe. Judge Eugene Carter presided in the case. The lawsuit was against Dr.

SMITH. BIGGS & CO. INC.

1180 RAYMOND BOULEVARD   NEWARK 2. NEW JERSEY

Certificate of Insurance

This is to Certify THAT THE UNDERSIGNED HAVE PROCURED INSURANCE AS HEREINAFTER SPECIFIED FROM SOURCES INDICATED BELOW, THROUGH L. HAMMOND & CO., LIMITED, LONDON, ENGLAND:

Assured: Christian Churches, as per Schedule to be agreed.

Location: Montgomery, Alabama

Coverage: Automobile Bodily Injury and Property Damage Insurance on nineteen(19) Station Wagons property of the Assured, as per Schedule, wording as per domestic policy.

Limit of
Liability: Bodily Injury: $5,000 any one person
                             $10,000 any one accident

            Property Damage: $5,000 any one accident

Rate: 150% of Manual Premium.

Minimum Premium:$2,000..

Advance
Premium: Based on 150% of Manual premium.

Period: September 18, 1956 to September 18, 1957, 12:01 a.m.
         Standard Time at location as to both dates.

ALL AS PER TERMS AND CONDITIONS OF THIS CERTIFICATE AND FORMS ATTACHED AND/OR POLICIES TO BE FURNISHED.
INSURED WITH: Lloyd's Underwriters.

COUNTERSIGNED AT NEWARK, N. J.
Date September 26,   19 56   By   SMITH. BIGGS & CO. INC.

When local insurance agents would not write a policy on our station wagons, T. M. Alexander secured coverage from Lloyd's of London.

King, the MIA, and the leaders of the Bus Protest. It is interesting that the city had not filed such a lawsuit earlier. If such a case had been filed in December 1955 or January 1956, the Bus Protest perhaps might never have garnered the necessary support, financial or otherwise, to sustain itself.

While this trial was in progress, on November 13, 1956, there was suddenly quite a stir and a lot of whispering in the courtroom. I was handed a note signed by WSFA-TV newsman Frank McGee, which stated "I need to see you immediately outside the courtroom." The case was in progress, but I excused myself. I went outside, and Frank said he had just received word over the wire service that the United States Supreme Court had just affirmed the local federal court in *Browder v. Gayle,* and he wanted me to comment on that decision. I told Frank I was very happy about the decision but I would have to go back into the courtroom, and after the session I would be glad to give him an on-camera reaction. I returned to the courtroom immediately.

Judge Carter immediately recessed court and never reconvened for the conclusion of the case against the car pool operators. I never received another notice from the clerk about this case. I assume Judge Carter entered an order of dismissal.

In any event, the battle was won. Segregated seating on city buses, at least, had been destroyed.

The news from the Supreme Court was not only music to my ears, but also to those of all the leaders—Mrs. Parks, Dr. King, E. D. Nixon, and others; we were all elated that the three-judge district court decision had been affirmed. We knew that segregated seating was wrong, and we believed that it was unconstitutional. Now the highest court in the land had upheld our position. It was sweet vindication.

At the time Frank handed me the note, all of the lawyers who were working with me on the case were present—Orzell Billingsley, Peter Hall, and Arthur Shores. When I returned to the courtroom, I whispered to them what Frank McGhee had told me. And of course we were all very happy. When Judge Carter recessed court he never indicated the reason for the recess, but naturally the news spread like wildfire.

The white court officials, the deputy sheriffs, and the white community, to put it mildly, were generally not pleased. The African-American community was ecstatic. We knew that we would be able to ride the buses on an integrated basis. Even more importantly, I think, our people realized that as we had won this battle involving segregation of the buses in Montgomery, there were other battles to fight, and we would also be successful in them.

Even though the Supreme Court had affirmed the decision of the three-judge federal district court panel declaring state segregation laws unconstitutional, it was thirty-seven more days before the official paperwork arrived in Montgomery. So the Bus Protest continued for a little longer. Finally, on December 20, 1956, the long-awaited day arrived. The MIA and the African-American residents of Montgomery ended their protest.

The three-judge district court entered an order acknowledging receipt of the mandate from the Supreme Court, officially ending the case of *Browder v. Gayle*. Not only did it end the case of *Browder v. Gayle*, but upon the arrival of the mandate, Dr. King, Mrs. Parks, and others boarded a bus in downtown Montgomery and rode it on an integrated basis. With the court decree in place and our people able to ride the bus as they elected, there was no longer any need for the Bus Protest, per se. Even though some of the meetings continued for a period of time, the Protest officially ended. The transportation system was dismantled, and the station wagons were donated to the various churches.

This was the end of one mighty struggle, but only the beginning of others. There were many more desegregation cases to come. Nevertheless, I had realized a personal milestone toward my goal to "destroy everything segregated I could find."

Accomplishments of the Protest

There were many outstanding accomplishments as a result of the Montgomery Bus Protest. Mrs. Rosa Parks triggered the Protest, and she became the heroine of the Movement because of the beauty of her character. Also, she brings to mind the words concerning the woman found in Mark 14:8, "She hath done what she could..." to restore dignity and command respect for African-American people. Mrs. Parks is a glowing figure who has earned a place in history because of what she started on a bus. Her resistance

A 1975 gathering of movement leaders on the occasion of the twentieth anniversary of the beginning of the bus boycott. Among the notables are, seated from left, Virginia Durr, E. D. Nixon, Ralph Abernathy, Rosa Parks, S. S. Seay Sr., Coretta King, and Johnnie Carr. I'm standing behind Mrs. King, Andy Young is behind Rev. Seay, and John Lewis is behind Rev. Abernathy. Rufus Lewis is just behind me next to the U.S. flag.

to dehumanization gave courage to the forty thousand African Americans who united to make the protest effective. Her example has empowered many other peoples throughout the world to stand against oppression and to overcome it.

The arrest of Mrs. Parks set in motion the modern-day civil rights movement and gave birth to a world leader, Dr. Martin Luther King, Jr., a future Nobel Peace Prize laureate. King was the type who attracted other leaders and potential leaders. Though King was never annointed a king, he was appointed one by the people of Montgomery, Atlanta, and later, America and the world.

As a result of *Browder v. Gayle*, the United States Supreme Court held that certain segregation laws in the City of Montgomery violated the due process and equal protection clauses of the 14th Amendment to the United States Constitution. This was the first case to establish such a precedent. And, in helping to keep the community together and motivated in Montgomery during the Bus Protest, *Browder v. Gayle* showed to the emerging civil rights movement the political usefulness of litigation strategies.

A young, newly appointed federal judge with only three months on the federal bench was given an opportunity to demonstrate to the world that justice could be obtained even in Montgomery, Alabama, the Cradle of the Confederacy. *Browder v. Gayle* was the first major civil rights case in the career of Judge Frank M. Johnson, Jr. He went on to preside over many, many others. There is little doubt that he was the most significant federal district judge in U.S. history on civil rights issues.

On a personal note, the Bus Protest and the related legal cases provided me an opportunity not only to begin fulfilling my ambition to "destroy everything segregated I could find," but the cases helped to establish my legal practice. The crowds attending the many trials which transpired during the Bus Protest saw my legal skills first-hand. Consequently, my case load became very demanding. The days when I could have a leisurely lunch with Rosa Parks and discuss youth work were long gone.

It is rather interesting to note that most of the high-profile participants in the Bus Protest were in Montgomery during that period for specific purposes or to some degree became involved in the bus boycott by coincidence. However, in my case, I had intentionally left Montgomery for the purpose of becoming a lawyer. I returned to Montgomery to attack segregation. My involvement in the Montgomery Bus Protest was but the beginning of my putting thoughts and dreams of this goal into actions. The Bus Protest marked the beginning of my forty-year career to "destroy everything segregated I could find." By the way, I'm still on the job.

One could say that Mrs. Parks's refusal to surrender her seat on a Montgomery bus created an ever-widening ripple of change throughout the world. Her quiet exemplification of courage, dignity, and determination mobilized persons of various philosophies:

Martin Luther King—non violence
Clifford Durr—civil liberties
Fred Gray—integrated society
Jo Ann Robinson—courtesy and fair play

E. D. Nixon—everybody is somebody

A pebble cast in the segregated waters of Montgomery, Alabama, created a human rights tidal wave that changed America and eventually washed up on the shores of such far away places as the Bahamas, China, South Africa, and the Soviet Union.

And it all started on a bus.

4

Black Justice, White Law in Selma

While I focused on the day-to-day legal activities related to the bus protest, African-American clients concerned with a variety of issues sought my services. Slowly my practice grew. I became involved in a number of interesting cases, including that of Sergeant Wesley Jones in Selma, Alabama. This case began in December 1955, two weeks after the beginning of the bus boycott.

Jones, a U.S. Air Force sergeant stationed at Craig Air Force Base, retained me to defend him in the recorder's court of the City of Selma. As Jones was driving home from the base, a white couple was traveling in a car in front of him near downtown Selma. They stopped at an intersection and although the light changed twice, they did not move. Sergeant Jones blew his horn—some words were exchanged, and Jones pulled around the white couple's vehicle and passed it. Some time later the police arrested him on charges of disorderly conduct. I agreed to represent him.

Although Selma is only fifty miles west of Montgomery, it was dangerous for an African-American man to travel alone. Accordingly, I always tried to have someone with me. Frank Massey, a disabled veteran who lived in Montgomery, accompanied me on many of these trips. Elbert Hill, Bernice's brother, also frequently joined us. Frank and Elbert drove me to Selma to represent Sergeant Jones at the trial.

In reviewing my office file on Sergeant Jones for this book, I found a copy of my license to practice law still in the file. In a number of instances in those days, before I tried a case, I would have to prove that I was a lawyer. All too often I was the first African-American lawyer to set foot in some of the courts I visited.

When we arrived at the recorder's court, on the second floor of the Selma City Hall, Frank took a seat on the African-American side of the courtroom. Of course, the courtrooms were segregated. Whites sat on one side and African Americans on the other. As I proceeded with the defense I noticed that Frank had taken a seat at the back near the center aisle. Although I did not see it happen, as he sat in the back of the section reserved for African Americans, he was called outside by a police officer.

The trial meanwhile provided a quick lesson in the etiquette of race relations in the South. At one point in the trial I referred to my client as "Mr. Jones."

The judge interrupted me, asking, "What did you say?" The judge then indicated to me, "You don't call him that in this court."

Initially, I didn't understand the import of the judge's objections. It then dawned on me that he objected to my referring to my client as "Mr." I remarked to the judge that my client was a sergeant in the U.S. Air Force and asked if I could refer to him as "Sergeant Jones."

He said, "Oh yes, sergeant is fine."

We tried the case. As occurred in a majority of these kinds of cases, Sergeant Jones was convicted.

While the decision did not surprise me, I was shocked by the events that followed. As I prepared to leave the courtroom after the disappointing judgment, I noticed that Frank was nowhere in sight. I went out into the hall. A tall, burly police officer (all of them were white in those days) who appeared to me at the time to have been seven feet tall (he probably was not really that tall) and to have weighed over three hundred pounds (or that heavy) looked down on me and said, "If you're looking for that nigger that drove you over here, we have him locked up in jail."

I was astonished and said to him, for lack of knowing what else to say, "I beg your pardon."

He repeated, "If you're looking for that nigger that drove you over here, we have him locked up in jail."

I asked, "What do you have him in jail for?"

He said, "He was drinking liquor in the courtroom."

Of course I knew better than that. But I went back to the jail, and sure enough Frank was in custody.

I told Frank that rather than discuss the matter at that time I would go ahead and arrange bond. The only person I knew in Selma that bond would be accepted from was Ed Moss, an influential African-American man who was president of the Federal Credit Union. It took some time for me to find him. When I found Mr. Moss and brought him down to sign the appearance bond for Frank Massey, the police had already lectured Frank and released him.* I thanked Mr. Moss, and he went back to work. Ed Moss would later become one of the key leaders in the civil rights movement in Selma and was a dynamic force behind the Selma-to-

---

*On the drive back to Montgomery, Frank filled me in on what happened. I later had him write an affidavit. This is from Frank's account:

'This is my story in my own words as to what happened on a visit to Selma, Alabama, in Dallas County, on Tuesday, December 27, 1955.

'Attorney Fred D. Gray, Mr. Elbert Hill, and I, Frank L. Massey, left Montgomery about 12:30 p.m. and arrived in Selma, Alabama, about an hour later. We had a Coca-Cola and there I left to visit a friend on a street around the corner from the City Hall. A few minutes later I returned to the City Court where Attorney Gray and Mr. Hill were. At this time all of the colored seats were just about taken. I found a seat near the rear of the courtroom. There I was seated until . . . I was called at a surprise by a police officer. I looked back and pointed to a young lady who was and who had been talking continuously throughout the court proceedings, I just knew they wanted her. But instead I was called and told to bring a bottle of gin with me that was under my seat. It was not my bottle, and I did not know it was under the seat. I had not seen it before the officer pointed it out and requested me to come out of the courtroom and bring it with me. Outside the courtroom I was searched, the notes which I had taken were taken away, and my money, $8.00, was also taken away from me.

'I was put in jail and detained for 20 minutes or more. I asked what was I charged with and the amount of the bond if charged. No answer was given me. The word Negro or colored was never used by the police officers; they referred to me and other Negroes as "niggers." Almost every other word used was "nigger." I did not know if anyone knew I was in jail, that is, Attorney Gray or Mr. Hill. Later, Attorney Gray came back to the cell where I was and asked me what happened? I said I don't know. Attorney Gray started to put his hands in my pocket and a police officer and another official of the Police Department said "don't give that nigger nothing, not even a

Montgomery March. He has since served as a member of the Selma City Council.

Bear in mind that the Jones trial and Frank's encounter with the Selma police occurred during the height of the Montgomery Bus Protest. The officers very explicitly instructed Frank to tell me that when I "cross that bridge don't ever come back to Selma anymore. We are not going to have any mess here like they have in Montgomery."

For understandable reasons I was loathe to return to Selma. In fact, I didn't return to Selma for quite some time. Frank continued to travel with me all over Alabama. He still lives in Montgomery.

---

nickel." Attorney Gray said "I am not giving him anything." I gave Attorney Gray a name of a friend to call and tell what had happened, he got the name and address and left me in the cell at the jail. In a discussion with some inmate, I was told of the whippings they received in jail. I was told when I attempted to knock on the window, "please don't do that because the (police officers) would give all of us a good whipping." Finally, I heard a voice saying, "you Montgomery nigger come out." I walked out into a small room or hallway. There I was lectured to. There was quite a bit said to me by the police officers. I was told to get out of Selma, me and that smart nigger lawyer, by sun down and never be caught there again. "You niggers got hell going on in Montgomery, but this is Selma in Dallas County and you are not going to start anything here. Tell all the niggers in Montgomery to stay over there, they don't have no business at all in Selma, get out and stay out, if you don't, the nigger undertakers are going to have a lot of business, including them nigger soldiers who testified in court today."

'There was a police captain, a police officer, and two other members of the Selma Police Department who were doing the lecturing. Throughout their lecture, they were cursing and threatening to beat me and even threatened to kill me. As they were talking, I told them I knew the Sergeant that was in the Court Room. They thought I was talking about the Negro airman, Sergeant Jones, Attorney Gray's client. This upset them and they began their entire lecture again. However, I was not referring to Sergeant Jones but to Sergeant Shirley, of the Education Safety Department of the Highway Patrol for the State of Alabama, who was also in court.

'They finally let me out of jail, and after Attorney Gray had made arrangements for his client's appeal bond, we left Selma about 6:00 p.m.

'This is my true story in my own words. I am making it voluntarily because I want others to know the injustice which is being done in Selma, Alabama. Not only the injustice which I received, but what has happened and is happening to many other Negroes, who in fear of great bodily harm or of death, are afraid to speak. I wish it were possible for the Justice Department of the United States to investigate the situation in Selma, Alabama.'

I appealed the Jones case to the Circuit Court of Dallas County. Because of the unjust decision in the Recorder's Court of the City of Selma, the NAACP agreed to finance the appeal. NAACP support for Sergeant Jones's case was confirmed in a letter to me dated February 10, 1956, by the Reverend John D. Hunter, then president of the Selma branch of the NAACP and the pastor of the Ramah Baptist Church in Lowndes County. The case was finally dismissed. Reverend Hunter continued to be a leader in Selma. He is one of the heroes of the Selma movement.

There were two principal items involved in this situation:

1) It was a common practice by court officials in the state courts not to address African Americans as "Mr." and that included African-American lawyers. Court records and transcripts, when referring to white lawyers, read "Mr." and the lawyer's last name. When referring to African-American lawyers, transcripts read "Lawyer" and the lawyer's last name. This was particularly true in Montgomery. The practice of refusing to address African-American men as "Mr." or African-American women as "Mrs." reflected the social customs of that day. It demonstrated lack of respect and insulted the dignity of African-American people. In my opinion, whites just felt that no African American was worthy of the title "Mr." It was also a tactic used to diminish and subordinate African-American people.

2) Although Selma is only fifty miles west of Montgomery, the white power structure there was determined to prevent any occurrence that could be interpreted as the beginning of a civil rights movement in their town. Therefore, they wanted me to know that Selma whites would not tolerate any African Americans who chose to assert their rights as citizens and human beings, as African Americans were doing in Montgomery at the time.

State of Alabama v. L. L. Anderson, 1959-1963

Eventually I did return to Selma, this time as an attorney for Lewis Lloyd Anderson. I, along with Peter Hall and Orzell Billingsley of Birmingham, defended Lewis Anderson in a case that was a thinly veiled attempt to silence a major voice in the Civil

Rights Movement. Anderson was pastor of Selma's Tabernacle Baptist Church and regularly used the pulpit to promote African-American civil rights activism. One day as he drove from his home to church, a short distance away, he had a tragic accident that resulted in the death of an African-American resident named Tom Reese. It was truly an accident, but because of his civil rights activities, the white power structure was determined to send Reverend Anderson off to prison. In 1959, he was charged, tried and convicted of manslaughter. Under normal circumstances, the law enforcement officials of Selma and other cities in Alabama were not very concerned about the death of an African-American person and certainly not one that was the result of an automobile accident. In this case, however, they were concerned because they wanted to get rid of Reverend Anderson. Hall, Billingsley, and I appealed the conviction.

On several occasions during the Anderson case there were suggestions that the State would dismiss the case if Reverend Anderson would agree to leave town. He refused to leave town and consequently the case was tried many times. We even appealed to the United States Supreme Court. The conviction was reversed and ultimately he was exonerated.

Reverend Anderson continued his civil rights work and became one of the principal leaders in the Selma movement, and was particularly effective in the Selma-to-Montgomery March. Today, Reverend Anderson continues to live in Selma and is still pastor of Tabernacle Baptist Church.

That was my second experience in Selma. I was to visit Selma many times in the future in connection with the Selma-to-Montgomery March but I never enjoyed practicing law there. My distaste undoubtedly stems from my first experience in representing Sergeant Jones. I like to think of Selma as an aberration.

I know for a fact that in some communities the few African-American lawyers who did exist enjoyed excellent rapport with the white power structure. Even in Selma, African-American attorney Peter Hall seemed to have fared well. Hall was an excellent civil rights lawyer and assisted me in many of my early cases. However he managed it, Hall had excellent rapport with the whites in Selma. If it could be done there, Peter Hall was the one African-American attorney who could do it. I am sure that Hall could have gotten the case against Reverend Anderson dismissed without a trial except for Anderson's active participation in the civil rights movement.

The Oscar Adams–Peter Hall Incident

African Americans attempting to practice law in Selma in the fifties could identify with what happened to Birmingham attorney Oscar Adams—later to become the first African American to serve on the Alabama Supreme Court—when he traveled to Selma to file a case. In those days Selma had a female circuit clerk, Marguerite Houston. When attorney Adams went to file the papers, the clerk initially would not allow him to file them because she said she did not know he was a lawyer. He pleaded with her and told her that he was a lawyer who practiced in Birmingham. He had taken the Alabama Bar. He was a member of the court and just needed to file some papers.

She said, "Now where do you say you're from?" He replied, Birmingham. She said, "I don't know you're a lawyer. Do you know Peter Hall in Birmingham?" He said, "Yes, ma'am." She said, "Now Peter Hall is a lawyer. If Peter Hall tells me that you are a lawyer, I will permit you to file these papers." Attorney Adams got on the phone, called Peter Hall and explained his predicament. Peter laughed and indicated he would not help Oscar but then told him to let him talk to Mrs. Houston.

Oscar gave the phone to Mrs. Houston. She said, "Hello." He said, "Hello." She said, "Is this lawyer Peter Hall?" He said, "Yes, Mrs. Houston this is Peter Hall." She said, "I have this man down here in my office, Oscar Adams. He says he is a lawyer, but I don't know if he is a lawyer or not. Is he really a lawyer?" Peter joked with the clerk for a while and said, "Yes ma'am, he's a lawyer, let him file the papers." She then permitted Oscar to file his case.

Adams's first experience in Selma was a fairly typical occurrence throughout the South. If a white person had a friendly relationship with an African-American person, the white person would allow that African-American person to make recommendations about other African Americans.

To avoid this problem, I always carried a copy of my law license issued by the Alabama Supreme Court. You just never knew when someone white would question your identity.

While I never enjoyed practicing law in Selma, other African-American lawyers have had significant law practices there and I am appreciative of their work. J. L. Chestnut, Jr., has practiced in Selma and in the Black Belt for many years. He is the author of *Black In Selma*, a book concerning his life and work. Chestnut's law partners, Henry and Rose Sanders, also practice law in Selma and in the Black Belt. They have worked in west Alabama handling cases similar to mine in central and east Alabama. Bruce Boynton, the son of Mrs. Amelia P. Boynton Robinson, who was one of the organizers of the Selma-to-Montgomery March, also practices in Selma. They are all to be commended for their work in Selma.

State of Alabama v. NAACP, 1956-1966

Outspoken African-American ministers like the Reverend L. L. Anderson in Selma and the African Americans who boycotted the buses in Montgomery were not the only targets of repression. While ultimately Reverend Anderson went free, and Montgomery's buses were integrated, the State of Alabama achieved greater success in its vendetta against the NAACP. Even so, justice eventually prevailed.

During the early stages of the Montgomery Bus Protest, I had recommended to the leadership that we not use the NAACP or any other existing organizations as the sponsoring organization for the protest. Many white Southerners were quite intimidated by the NAACP. The very name NAACP provoked hatred and overreaction. I wanted to avoid focusing the hostile glare of whites on any organization with assets that could be subjected to any type of civil penalties. Therefore, I recommended to the group heading the protest movement that we incorporate a new nonprofit organization, and let that organization serve as the legal vehicle through which the Protest was orchestrated, formed and incorporated.

Incorporating a new organization soon proved to have been the right move in light of attacks against the NAACP. Midway through the Montgomery Bus Protest, on June 1, 1956, without notice or warning, Alabama Attorney General John Patterson sued the NAACP. At the same time, he obtained a temporary restraining order from Judge Walter B. Jones enjoining the NAACP from doing business in the state of Alabama. Patterson based his attack on the legal theory that the NAACP was a foreign corporation, and it had never been qualified to do business in the state of Alabama.

I was retained to assist NAACP General Counsel Robert L. Carter. Arthur Shores from Birmingham also worked on this case.

The NAACP had been doing business in Alabama for many years and had never been required to register as a foreign corporation. There were many nonprofit foreign corporations doing business in Alabama. Very few had registered to do business as a foreign corporation in Alabama.

Patterson successfully enjoined the NAACP from operating in Alabama until such time as it became qualified to do business in the state. This was simply another maneuver on the part of Patterson to persecute African Americans who were exercising their constitutional rights. This attack on the NAACP was repeated in virtually every Southern state.

Undoubtedly, if Patterson's plan worked, then he would gain even greater allegiance from fearful whites who would make him the next governor of Alabama. His suit against the NAACP on June 1, 1956, and against the Tuskegee Civic Association on August 15, 1957, set the stage for his 1958 gubernatorial campaign. He conducted one of the most racist campaigns in modern Alabama history against a liberal-by-comparison George C. Wallace.

Simultaneously with the filing of the complaint, the motion for the temporary restraining order, and the issuance of the temporary restraining order, Attorney General Patterson also filed a motion to compel the NAACP to produce the names, addresses, and phone numbers of all its members. Of course, if the NAACP was required to produce such a list, all the members of the NAACP would have been harassed, fired from jobs, and generally subjected to a vast array of physical and economic reprisals. The NAACP held steadfast and refused to produce the membership list.

As expected, Judge Walter B. Jones cited the NAACP for contempt of court and fined the organization $100,000. He also enjoined it from qualifying to do business until such time as it purged itself by producing the list of its members and paying the $100,000.

This lawsuit set in motion a legal tug of war which continued for eight years. The case went to the U.S. Supreme Court on four separate occasions, twice through the state court system, and twice through the federal court system. Finally, after eight years of litigation, on October 9, 1964, the NAACP again was permitted to qualify to do business in Alabama, thus ending one of the longest struggles to preserve the integrity and autonomy of the nation's oldest civil rights organization. I was proud to work on this case because it established several legal principles.

An organization such as the NAACP has a legal right to assert and to protect the rights of its members and was justified in refusing to give the names and addresses of its members to the attorney general. It was important, particularly during the early days of the civil rights movement, that members of the NAACP not be disclosed in order to avoid harassment and intimidation. Many other membership corporations have subsequently used these cases as legal precedent to protect their membership lists.

The case is also very important for another reason. The NAACP had been actively involved in the protection of the rights of African Americans for many, many years and it was very important that this work continue, including the sponsoring of litigation that assists African Americans in obtaining their constitutional rights. If Alabama had been successful in barring the NAACP from doing business in Alabama, all of the other Southern states would have done likewise.

I have represented many individuals with the NAACP as the sponsoring organization. However, it was a great pleasure for me to represent the oldest civil rights organization in the nation and assist it in being able to organize and carry on its business of protecting

A 1960 meeting of the Southwest Bar Association, which was an affiliate of the National Bar Association. These were the major civil rights lawyers in the South at that time.

the rights of African-American people in Alabama. On a wall in my office is displayed a July 3, 1958, letter from Robert L. Carter, General Counsel for the NAACP, in which he stated:

> This note is to express for myself and for the Association gratitude and appreciation for your help in this case. While you have given indispensable assistance on other matters, without your aid in the instant case the N.A.A.C.P. would be finished in the South. There is, of course, a long fight ahead in Alabama before we are back in business there but, at least we are now free to make that effort.

Robert L. Carter later became a U.S. District Judge in New York City.

Subsequent to the NAACP resuming business in the state, it became a plaintiff in a suit to bring an end to racial discrimination in the hiring of state highway patrol officers in Alabama. In an order signed by Judge Johnson, the Alabama state troopers were integrated. Today, Alabama has more African American state troopers than any other state. I was not counsel in that case. However, if the injunction enjoining the NAACP from doing business were still outstanding, the state trooper case could not have been successfully litigated with the NAACP among the plaintiffs.

The NAACP assisted me in many of my civil rights cases. Now I had been able to assist it in not only being able to resume its operation in Alabama, but also in continuing its larger work of destroying segregation. I had now joined forces with a national civil rights organization that was as committed as I was to destroying everything segregated in Alabama.

5

Seeking the Ballot in Macon County

Macon County is located in east central Alabama. Approximately 85 percent of its population is African American. Tuskegee, the county seat located about forty miles northeast of Montgomery, is the home of the famous Tuskegee Institute, now Tuskegee University. The University was founded by Lewis Adams in 1881 and achieved its greatest recognition under the leadership of Booker T. Washington. Washington recruited Dr. George Washington Carver, who brought international fame to the institution because of his many discoveries of various uses of the peanut and the sweet potato.

Today, a portion of Tuskegee University's campus is a National Historic Site. It consists of The Oaks, the home of Booker T. Washington, and the Carver Museum, which houses much of Dr. Carver's work. Approximately three hundred thousand visitors tour the site every year. One of the largest Veterans Administration hospitals in the United States is also located in Tuskegee. The land for the construction of the hospital was donated by Tuskegee Institute during the early segregation years when African-American veterans had no hospital in the South where they could receive medical care. Therefore, the university gave this land to the government. The government constructed a Veterans Administration hospital that was managed by African-American managers and basically staffed by African Americans. Of course, now it is completely integrated.

The serene ambience of today's Tuskegee belies the tension and acrimony of the late 1950s and 1960s surrounding the gerrymandering controversy and *Gomillion v. Lightfoot* court case that placed the town on the civil rights map.

Notwithstanding the high level of African-American education and professionals both at Tuskegee Institute and the Veterans Administration hospital, there were very few African Americans registered to vote in Macon County prior to 1955—not because they were unqualified, and not because they had not applied for registration, but because Macon County was 85 percent African American and white political authorities were determined to keep African Americans from registering to vote. However, white politicians did permit a select few African Americans to vote, such as the President and individual professors at Tuskegee Institute, but not the general African-American population. This effective African-American disenfranchisement policy was in keeping with the laws of the state of Alabama, specifically the Boswell Amendment. Before World War II, fewer than one hundred of twenty thousand African Americans in Macon County were registered as voters.

The state legislature adopted the Boswell Amendment in 1945, requiring that applicants for voter registration be able to read, write, and interpret the Constitution. William P. Mitchell, the executive director of the Tuskegee Civic Association, and others filed a successful suit in federal court to have that amendment declared unconstitutional and to enjoin state enforcement. As a result of the Mitchell lawsuit, a few African Americans were registered. Later the government filed a suit and additional African Americans were registered.

For the most part, however, whites developed many strategies to keep the registration rolls as lily white as possible. For example, some members of the Board of Registrars would register all the white applicants and then hide. Other registrars would resign before registering African Americans in any significant numbers. The problem of African-American disenfranchisement was the subject of a hearing before the U.S. Senate Subcommittee on Constitutional Rights of the Committee on the Judiciary in February and March of 1957.

The Tuskegee Civic Association

The Tuskegee community was well organized with an active chapter of the NAACP and the Tuskegee Civic Association (TCA). Dr. Charles C. Gomillion, dean of students at Tuskegee Institute and a sociology professor, served as TCA president. Mr. William P. Mitchell served as its executive director. The TCA sponsored most of the civil rights litigation in Macon County.

The history of the Tuskegee Civic Association is detailed in *Crusade for Civic Democracy—The Story of the Tuskegee Civic Association, 1941-1970,* by Jessie P. Guzman, who in 1954 ran for a seat on the Macon County School Board. She was director of the Department of Records and Research at Tuskegee Institute. Her book describes the individual leaders, issues, and cases, including the litigation spearheaded by the government to end segregation and to increase African-American voter registration.

Soon after I opened my law practice in Montgomery, I began to receive many clients from Macon County. While Macon County had many African-American doctors and educators, it had no African-American lawyers. When my clientele in Macon County increased significantly, I opened an office in Tuskegee two days a week. My clients came from all walks of life—physicians, teachers, professors, laborers, and farmers. In other words, my practice became much more diverse and included cases that had nothing to do with civil rights but were essential to my survival as a lawyer. Sometimes I refer to them as my bread and butter cases. They were not as glamorous or as exciting as the desegregation cases, but they are every bit as important to members of the African-American community.

I remember, for example, Mr. and Mrs. James Jackson, a farmer and his wife, who came into my Montgomery office one Saturday morning. They were residents of Macon County. They wanted me to prepare their wills. They were neatly dressed, obviously a hard-working couple, and owned a substantial amount of land in Shorter, Alabama, which is located in Macon County. They requested similar wills and paid for them. I never saw the man

C. G. Gomillion was an exemplary civil rights leader.

again. Many years later, his wife, Mrs. Satiree Jackson, returned and told me her husband was dead. She further stated that prior to his death, he told her "take my will to the young lawyer in Montgomery, and he'll know what to do." I probated his will and for many years represented her. I later discovered that James Jackson was a participant in the Tuskegee Syphilis Study [see Chapter 17].

An Attorney General Seeking the Governorship

When African-American citizens began to refrain from shopping in downtown Tuskegee in retaliation for the Tuskegee gerrymandering act, Attorney General John Patterson and Assistant Attorney General Gordon Madison filed suit against the Tuskegee Civic Association to enjoin the TCA and its members from failing and refusing to trade with the white merchants downtown. In effect, they sought to compel African Americans to trade with the white businesses. TCA retained my services, and I, in turn, brought in attorney Arthur Shores of Birmingham. This case was presided over by Circuit Judge Will O. Walton of LaFayette.

John Patterson was very ambitious. His father, Albert Patterson, had been a Democratic nominee for attorney general of Alabama, and had pledged to clean up corruption in his hometown of Phenix City, Alabama. Albert Patterson won the nomination, but he met an untimely death. He was shot and killed outside his office in Phenix City. After brief deliberation, the Democratic Party leaders gave the nomination to his son, John, who did not camouflage his ambition to become governor of Alabama.

During the case against the Tuskegee Civic Association, more

At the trial of the Tuskegee Civic Association, from left, Arthur Shores, Fred Gray, William Mitchell, and Martin L. King, Jr.

citizens packed the county courthouse in Tuskegee than had attended any other trial in the history of Macon County. I called Attorney General Patterson to the stand for the purpose of showing that his primary concern was not the merchants in Tuskegee, but was to further his political ambition, to make headlines, and to use African Americans in Macon County as stepping stones in his climb towards the governor's mansion. While he did not admit that he would run for governor, he declared that he had no plans to announce from the witness stand his gubernatorial aspirations.

This case was tried during election time. After the case ended, Judge Walton took the matter under advisement. The judge did a great deal of politicking. After he was reelected, he entered an order denying John Patterson relief. He stated that the members of the Tuskegee Civic Association were within their constitutional rights to trade with whomever they pleased. This was a great victory. Judge Walton was the only state court judge that I tried this type of civil rights case before who had the courage of his convictions to rule in favor of African-American citizens and against the State of Alabama.

Gomillion v. Lightfoot: One Man, One Vote Theory

As the Bus Protest began to wind down in Montgomery, court action initiated by the U.S. government resulted in many African-American residents of Macon County becoming registered voters. Under the leadership of State Senator Sam Engelhardt, Jr., who was also the executive secretary of the White Citizens Councils of Alabama, local white authorities devised an ingenious plan to nullify the potential African-American vote, especially of those who lived in the city of Tuskegee.

The plan was simple. In 1957, State Senator Engelhardt introduced and had passed a bill in the Alabama Legislature to change the boundaries of the city of Tuskegee from a square to what I called, in my arguments before the U.S. Supreme Court, a *"28-sided sea dragon."* The state legislature passed Alabama Act 140 unanimously and without debate.

Prior to the enactment of the law, the City of Tuskegee was a square with sides one-and-one-half miles equal distance from the courthouse. As a result of the act, approximately four hundred African Americans were surreptitiously removed from the city limits. The lines were drawn in such a manner as to exclude substantially all African Americans while retaining all white voters. The few African-American voters that remained within the city were those who could not be eliminated without excluding some whites. As a result of this gerrymandering strategy, African-American residents of Macon County could vote in county, state, and federal elections, but could not vote in municipal elections. The advocates of this scheme insisted that the law did not discriminate against African Americans because of color. Rather, African Americans could not vote in municipal elections solely because they lived outside the city limits. Virtually no one bought this ridiculous subterfuge.

Under the leadership of Dr. C. G. Gomillion, the African-American community decided to retaliate by no longer trading with the white merchants in downtown Tuskegee. The Tuskegee Civic Association spearheaded hundreds of weekly "Crusades for Freedom Meetings" in various community churches. These were modeled after the weekly Monday night mass meetings of the Montgomery Bus Protest.

The Tuskegee Civic Association retained me to have Alabama Act 140 declared unconstitutional and to reestablish the old residential boundaries. In this case, unlike civil rights cases I had handled, I found it exceedingly difficult to locate co-counsel who believed the suit to have legal merit. The majority of the lawyers I talked with surmised that there was no legal merit, based on the Supreme Court's decision in *Colegrove v. Green*. In an opinion written by Justice Frankfurter concerning redistricting of congressional districts in Pennsylvania, the Court declared that the practice of drawing lines for political subdivisions was a political matter and not an issue for the court. In short, courts should stay out of that political "thicket."

Even NAACP General Counsel Robert Carter, who was working with me on the *NAACP v. Alabama* cases, gave me little

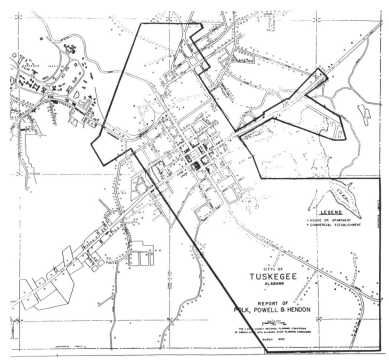

The entire area of the square comprised the city of Tuskegee prior to Act 140. The irregular black-bordered figure within the square represents the post-Act 140 city.

encouragement. Carter doubted that we could draft a complaint that would survive a motion to dismiss. He was especially concerned about who would be defendants and what my legal theory was. I told him I believed we could proceed in this lawsuit just as we had in the Bus Protest case: File a class action suit and request a declaratory judgment and injunctive relief alleging violations of plaintiffs' rights under the Fourteenth and Fifteenth Amendments.

A declaratory judgment would declare the gerrymandering act unconstitutional and enjoin those persons charged with the responsibility of enforcing it, the mayor and the city councilmen. Carter did not reject the idea, but informed me that the NAACP was having a meeting of its lawyers in Dallas, Texas, and that I should prepare a draft of a complaint and bring it over so that we could discuss the matter in person. I prepared such a draft and went to Texas to discuss the matter with him. Reluctantly, he agreed to work with me.

I was relieved considerably when in addition to Robert Carter, attorney Arthur Shores of Birmingham joined forces with me. Shores, by now a friend as well as an ally, had provided invaluable assistance in the boycott cases. I recall very vividly the way he tried civil rights cases all over Alabama long before I became a lawyer.

We prepared and filed the case in the federal court in Montgomery. It would take three-and-one-half years to work this case up to the United States Supreme Court.

The individual plaintiffs were: C. G. Gomillion, Celia B. Chambers, Alma R. Craig, Frank H. Bentley, Willie D. Bentley, Kenneth L. Buford, William J. White, Augustus O. Young, Jr., Nettie B. Jones, Detroit Lee, Della D. Sullins, and Lynnwood T. Dorsey, on behalf of themselves and others similarly situated.

The defendants were: Tuskegee Mayor Phil Lightfoot; G. B. Edwards, Jr., L. D. Gregory, Frank A. Oslin, W. Foy Thompson, and H. A. Vaughan, Jr., as members of the Tuskegee City Council; Tuskegee Police Chief O. L. Hodnett; E. C. Laslie, Charles Huddleston, J. T. Dyson, F. C. Thompson, and Virgil Guthrie, as members of the Board of Revenue of Macon County; Macon County Sheriff Preston Hornsby; and Macon County Probate Judge William Varner. The defense lawyers consisted of Harry Raymon of Tuskegee and James J. Carter of the law firm of Hill, Hill, Stovall & Carter in Montgomery. I was beginning to know attorney Carter pretty well; his firm had squared off with me on several of my earlier desegregation cases.

At the time I filed the lawsuit, I requested that William P. Mitchell order a large scale map showing the change in the boundaries of the City of Tuskegee. I wanted a map to graphically depict to the court the old city limits with the new city limits superimposed on it. Mitchell was the most efficient civil rights organization executive I had met. He would gather the facts and any information that was needed. I mentioned to him what I wanted and forgot about it. Several months later, he presented me with a beautiful, large map sufficiently drawn to scale, showing the old and new city limits. He, also, gave me smaller letter-sized copies which could be attached to papers filed in court.

As expected, the defense lawyers filed a motion to dismiss, claiming we had not stated a sufficient cause of action because the matters of which we complained were political and the African Americans of Tuskegee were neither denied their right to vote under the Fifteenth Amendment nor the equal protection or due process of law under the Fourteenth Amendment. They argued that under *Colegrove v. Green* the court should stay out of the "political thicket."

Judge Frank M. Johnson, Jr., accepted this argument and dismissed our complaint. This action was anticipated but not acceptable. I was disappointed that I did not get to use Mitchell's map.

We appealed to the U.S. Court of Appeals for the Fifth Circuit. The case was assigned to a three-judge panel—Warren Jones, John Brown, and John Minor Wisdom. By a two-to-one vote, Judge Johnson was affirmed. But when I read the opinion, I went home in a jubilant mood and reported to Bernice, "We have lost the case, but I believe we can win it in the Supreme Court."

She did not understand why I was rejoicing when I had lost the appeal. But I felt that if I could get one judge out of three in the Fifth Circuit, I could get five out of nine in the Supreme Court. Moreover, Judge Brown's dissenting opinion could serve as a road map for our argument in the Supreme Court. We filed the appeal.

Inarguably, this was a most important case, with many ramifications. I was aware that there were a number of lawyers who had pending cases dealing with redistricting of legislatures and Congressional reapportionment. The *Gomillion* case had attracted considerable attention all over the country. A favorable ruling would have a major impact on voting rights cases for years to come.

One of the major advantages of having Robert Carter serve as co-counsel was his wide-ranging network. Carter knew all the civil rights lawyers. He called upon some of the brightest to help us in the days before final arguments. In Philadelphia, Robert Carter convened a trial run of the arguments we would use in the United States Supreme Court. Robert Ming of Chicago, William Coleman of Philadelphia, and others assisted and interrogated us as part of our preparation for the argument before the High Court. I would open our argument and Robert Carter was to offer the closing argument.

The question arose during the trial run, or rehearsal, whether we would argue the Fourteenth Amendment questions of due process and equal protection, or the Fifteenth Amendment question dealing with the right to vote. Initially, the consensus appeared to be that we should argue only the Fourteenth Amendment question. The consensus reasoning was that African Americans in Tuskegee still had the right to vote in all elections except municipal elections, from which they were barred because, of course, they were no longer residents of the city.

I took a different position. I am what you might call a "shotgun lawyer"—have a complete arsenal of weapons, take aim, and shoot everything you have. At least one bullet is bound to hit. I prefer to argue as many theories as possible, and pray that the court will see fit to adopt one of them. I suggested that we argue a violation of both the Fourteenth and the Fifteenth amendments.

While my colleagues were saying there was no denial of the right to vote, my clients back home in Tuskegee, who formerly lived in the city, were being denied the right to vote for municipal officers. There was definitely a Fifteenth Amendment question.

I was the neophyte of the group and I'm not sure they gave much consideration to my views. However, later in the conference, Robert Ming said to Bob Carter, "I have changed my position and I agree with Fred. I think we should argue both." Finally, they all came around to my view.

Robert Carter and I argued for the plaintiffs in the Supreme Court. Dr. Gomillion, William P. Mitchell, and Mitchell's daughter, Peggy (now a newspaper reporter in St. Petersburg, Florida), my sister Pearl, and others were present. I had brought Mitchell's big map. I was excited. At last I would have an opportunity to use my map. I made arrangements with the marshal of the Court to display the map as soon as our case was called. The map was to be placed behind me so that it faced the nine justices during the entire argument.

I argued first.

As I began, the Chief Justice wanted to know the meaning of the map. I explained that behind me was a map of the City of Tuskegee showing the old city limits with the new city limits superimposed thereon. Justice Frankfurter immediately asked, "Where is Tuskegee Institute? I know it is still in the City of Tuskegee." I pointed out to Mr. Justice Frankfurter where Tuskegee Institute was on the map. I told him that Tuskegee Institute was gerrymandered outside the city limits.

He said, "You mean to tell me that Tuskegee Institute is outside the city limits of the City of Tuskegee?" I said, "Yes, sir, Mr. Justice Frankfurter." I believe that was the determining factor in getting Frankfurter's vote.

A reporter for *The New Yorker*, Bernard Taper, was in the court and he also thought the map had been important. He wrote in his book *Gomillion v. Lightfoot: Apartheid in Alabama* (1962): "It seemed to me that the map, which remained on view throughout the entire presentation of the case, raised and kept before the justices an essential question, one that was to be explored at some length; namely, what reasonable and constitutional purpose could the State of Alabama put forward for devising such a tortuous boundary?"

We were surprised and pleased when the opinion came down on November 14, 1960. It was not the five to four decision that I hoped for when we lost in the Fifth Circuit, but instead was a unanimous decision and it was written by Mr. Justice Frankfurter. In the opinion he noted that "When a legislature thus singles out a readily isolated segment of a racial minority for special discriminatory treatment, it violates the Fifteenth Amendment. In no case involving unequal weight in voting distribution that has come before the Court did the decision sanction a differentiation on racial lines whereby approval was given to unequivocal withdrawal of the vote solely from colored citizens. Apart from all else, these considerations lift this controversy out of the so-called 'political' arena and into the conventional sphere of constitutional litigation . . ." [See Appendix A-1] He then returned the case to U.S. District Judge Frank M. Johnson, Jr.

The mandate from the United States Supreme Court was received by the District Court on February 10, 1961, and on February 15, 1961, I filed a motion for judgment on the pleadings in favor of the plaintiffs as prayed for in the complaint. In February 1961, Judge Johnson granted the motion, declared Act 140 of the Alabama legislature to be unconstitutional, and permanently enjoined state and local officials from attempting to enforce it. The Tuskegee city boundaries were returned to their original position. [See Appendix A-2]

With the victory received in this case and the restoration of African Americans into the City of Tuskegee, African Americans ended their boycott of the white Tuskegee merchants. This was similar to what had happened in Montgomery when the United States Supreme Court affirmed the decision in *Browder v. Gayle*; African Americans then ended their protest against city buses.

As a direct result of this case, Johnny Ford became the first African American to serve as mayor of Tuskegee. He has held this position for more than twenty years and was recently reelected for a sixth term. All of the members of the Tuskegee City Council are now African Americans.

I sued the mayor and the city council of Tuskegee in the gerrymandering case of *Gomillion v. Lightfoot*. I now represent the mayor and city council as the Tuskegee City Attorney. I have done so for over twenty years. Times change.

The Importance of the Case

In many respects, *Gomillion v. Lightfoot* is perhaps the most important civil rights case that I have had the privilege of handling. In fact, this case was my "brainchild," and the one that I thought from the beginning we would win in spite of overwhelming odds.

This case had a number of implications. It was the first case involving racial gerrymandering that the High Court had ever considered. This case laid the foundation for the concept of "one man, one vote." The fact that white authorities could no longer dilute the African-American vote set the stage for later cases to hold that African Americans must be properly represented and single-member districts should be drawn in such a fashion that African Americans may be elected to public office. In the long run, as a result of this case and others which relied upon it, there are now thousands of African Americans and other minorities who are serving throughout the country as mayors, city council persons, members of the boards of education, county commissioners, state legislators, and in Congress using the concept of single-member districts.

Gomillion v. Lightfoot has been quoted at least 621 times by federal district courts, courts of appeals for the various circuits, state appellate courts, and the United States Supreme Court. I believe it is one of the most significant decisions in American jurisprudence. Interestingly, Judge John R. Brown, the circuit judge whose dissent made me feel we could win the case at the U.S. Supreme Court, believed *Gomillion* was his most important opinion. We have this on the authority of Judge John Minor Wisdom, himself a great judge on the old Fifth Circuit*, and one of the two judges who ruled against me. (In the Fifth Circuit, Judges Wisdom, who wrote the court's opinion, and Warren Jones ruled against me; Judge Brown ruled with me and wrote a dissenting opinion.) Writing in the *Texas Law Review* in 1993, Judge Wisdom said that Judge Brown "regarded his dissenting opinion in *Gomillion v. Lightfoot*, an early case in his judicial career, as his most important opinion. My concurring opinion in that case was painful for me to write, and it was probably my worst opinion." All law school students study *Gomillion v. Lightfoot* as a decision that

---

*The "old Fifth Circuit" included Texas, Louisiana, Mississippi, Alabama, Florida, and Georgia. In 1979, Alabama, Florida, and Georgia were split off to form a new circuit, the 11th.

prepared the way for the Supreme Court's rulings in later malapportionment cases. It has been the subject of many news articles and at least one book, the aforementioned *Gomillion v. Lightfoot: Apartheid in Alabama.*

The decision held that the Fourteenth and Fifteenth amendments prohibit sophisticated and ingenious forms of discrimination as well as simple-minded ones. As Judge Wisdom also points out so well in his law review article (71 *Texas Law Review* 913), the case paved the way for justices on the U.S. Supreme Court to travel from *Colegrove v. Green* to *Baker v. Carr.* The Court was not required to look at the intentions of the parties in order to find discrimination based on race, but instead could look at the outcome. If the result was discrimination against African Americans, then the Court would use its power to declare the law unconstitutional.

Finally, this case was a personal victory of another sort. Not only did I have the opportunity to appear and argue the case before the U.S. Supreme Court, but we won. I felt that I had come a long way from riding the buses in Montgomery, Alabama, and seeing injustice being done to African Americans, to standing before the highest Court in America. I had, to a great degree, accomplished my goal of "destroying everything segregated I could find." In this case, the Court announced a rule of law which would live on and be a mighty weapon for destroying racial discrimination.

Jury Discrimination in Civil and Criminal Cases Ended

Trial by jury is a precious, inalienable right which is guaranteed by the Constitution and laws of the United States of America and the various states, including Alabama. Along with this right, is the right of defendants to have a jury without having members of his race excluded from jury service because of their race and color. These rights are available both in criminal and civil cases. In Alabama and in most Southern states, in 1964, African Americans were excluded from serving on juries, in both criminal and civil cases, because of their race. The Tuskegee Civic Association retained me on behalf of African Americans in Macon County to file a suit against the Macon County Jury Commission in order to end jury discrimination in civil and criminal cases.

This was a case of first impression and was one of the first such cases to use this method of ending jury discrimination. This was a very important case. For many years, the United States Supreme Court held that a criminal defendant was entitled to a cross section of persons to serve on his jury, and that persons should not be discriminated against because of racial factors in juror selection. Jury selection challenges were usually made by a defendant in a criminal case or a party in a civil case by filing a motion to quash the venire (the pool of available jurors) on the grounds of systematic exclusion of African Americans. Another method was a motion to quash the indictment on the ground that African Americans were systematically excluded from serving on the grand jury that returned the indictments. I used this method of raising this issue in the *Eufaula Flake Hill* cases, before Judge George Wallace in 1957 [See Chapter 6]. We had also used this method in almost all criminal civil rights cases that I tried prior to 1964, including, but not limited to, the case of *Alabama v. Martin Luther King, Jr.*; the Alabama Anti-Boycott Statute cases, in 1957 [Chapter 3]; *Alabama v. Martin Luther King, Jr.*, Dr. King's tax case, in 1960 [Chapter 7]; and *Sullivan v. New York Times* in 1960 [Chapter 7]. This method of attacking jury discrimination in each individual case was ineffective. It had been used for decades and there still existed discrimination in jury selection throughout the country, including Macon County. A new method had to be found and used to eliminate racial discrimination in jury selection.

I believed that it was better to be on the offense than the defense. I wanted the entire procedure for guaranteeing the right of African Americans to serve on juries to be corrected by a federal court and use that case as precedent so that African Americans across the nation would have the benefit of a court ruling on this important matter. Therefore, I concluded we would use the same method that was used in other civil rights cases, including *Browder v. Gayle*, the bus desegregation case. We would bring a suit alleging violation of the Fourteenth Amendment, request a declaratory judgment declaring the acts of the defendants to be unconstitutional, and for injunctive relief, ask to have the court enjoin the jury commission from discriminating against African Americans. The case I filed for this purpose was one of the first for the purpose of ending such jury discrimination in both civil and criminal cases.

On June 3, 1964, I filed *Mitchell v. Johnston*. In addition to William P. Mitchell, the plaintiffs were Daniel L. Beasley, Otis Pinkard, Wright L. Lassiter, Jr., Lucius A. Hayden, and William C. Allen. The defendants were Edgar Johnson, E. P. Livingston, and H. P. Wilson, members of the Macon County Jury Commission; and Mrs. Grace P. Youngblood Hall, clerk of the Macon County Jury Commission. I represented the plaintiffs; the defendants were represented by Alabama Assistant Attorney General Leslie Hall and Circuit Solicitor Tom F. Young, the prosecutor for cases in the state judicial circuit which included Macon County.

The complaint was filed as a class action on behalf of the named plaintiffs and all other male African Americans who were qualified for jury duty in Macon County; in 1964, women were not eligible for jury service in Alabama. The complaint alleged that the defendants engaged in a practice of discriminating against African Americans in the selection of persons to serve as jurors in Macon County. It asked for a declaratory judgment that the acts of the defendants discriminating against African Americans were unconstitutional, in violation of the Fourteenth Amendment to the United States Constitution, and that a permanent injunction be issued enjoining the defendants from engaging in this type of conduct. On June 29, 1964, Judge Frank M. Johnson, Jr., designated the United States as a party and as amicus curiae ("friend of the court").

The evidence at the trial disclosed the following: During many terms of court, a panel of jurors would be selected to serve where there would be approximately one hundred male jurors, consisting of ninety to ninety-five whites and five to ten African Americans. According to the 1960 census, there were 1,365 white males twenty-one years of age and over in Macon County, and 6,234 African-American males in the same age group. There were 5,093

African-American males and 1,100 white males between the ages of twenty-one and sixty-five. Despite this population ratio, the number of African-American jurors called on civil or criminal panels in Macon County was never more than one to seven percent of the total jurors.

Each jury term, I would have cases to try in Macon County, and regardless of the merits of my case, I would seldom have even one African-American juror on a twelve-man jury, and I would always lose.

On January 18, 1966, Judge Johnson granted the relief requested. His order stated:

> *This case is one of the first civil actions brought to remedy systematic exclusion of Negroes from jury service generally.* There is no question that under Section 1983, Title 42, United States Code, these plaintiffs, under the evidence in this case, are entitled to the relief they seek and are entitled to have the defendants adopt procedures that will insure that they and all other qualified members of their class in Macon County serve on juries. (Emphasis added)

The Importance of the Case

This case is very important because, not only were we able to provide for African Americans to serve on juries in Macon County, but it also introduced a new method of attacking jury discrimination: that is, by filing a complaint in the United States District Court. Since that time, hundreds of lawsuits filed in Alabama and across the nation patterned after the *Mitchell* case have resulted in African Americans serving on juries in civil and criminal cases. As a result, where African Americans have been plaintiffs in meritorious cases, they have received the verdicts to which they were entitled.

The importance of this case was realized when twenty-five years later, the Alabama Supreme Court ruled in *Thomas v. Diversified Contractors, Inc.* that racial discrimination in civil jury selection is unconstitutional. Similarly, twenty-five years after *Mitchell*, the

United States Supreme Court in *Edmonson v. Louisville Concrete Company* held that racial discrimination in civil jury selection was unconstitutional, citing *Batson v. Kentucky.*

Discrimination in Administration of Farm Programs

In Macon County, Alabama, there was discrimination against African Americans in the administration of services provided by the Agricultural Stabilization & Conservation Services (ASCS). This program was established by Congress to administer federal crop acreage allotment, commodity price support and certain agricultural conservation programs. These programs are administered by the United States Department of Agriculture but operate through state, county, and community committees. The state committee, whose members are appointed by the U.S. Secretary of Agriculture, supervises the county and community committees. The primary responsibility of these committees is to determine which farmers receive conservation grants, additional allotments or release acreage, price support loans, and certain payments. The county and community committees are the key administrative organs in ASCS. Therefore, it was very important who served on the three-member county committee. There were no African Americans on the county committee in Macon County, nor in any other county in Alabama in 1967. However, there were many African-American farmers in Alabama who were entitled to share in farm programs under the control of the county committees. The exclusion of African Americans from the ASCS program meant that decisions which could cause economic disaster for small African-American farmers were left solely to the discretion of rural Southern whites.

The county committees are also responsible for conducting community committee elections, in accordance with regulations promulgated by the Secretary of Agriculture. Each community committee was comprised of three regular and two alternate members who were elected annually by eligible voters in the community. Candidates for the position of community committeemen were nominated in one or two ways. First, any persons satisfying the ASCS eligibility requirements could become a candidate by filing with the county committee a petition containing the signatures of a specified number of eligible voters. Secondly, community and county committee persons serving at the time were required to select at least six but not more than ten candidates in addition to those nominated by petition. There are detailed rules and regulations on conducting the elections.

The primary function of the community committee was to elect the county committee. They elected regular community committeemen to fill vacancies on the three-man county committee. In addition, the delegates elected one member of the county committee as chairman and one member as vice chairman.

Macon County was divided into five ASCS communities, each with its own three-member committee. In the 1967 community committee election, the three-member committee nominated a disproportionate number of African Americans, but nominated only a few whites. When that number was added to the nominees by petition, an unreasonable number of African Americans was running for the same position. African Americans' votes were therefore split and, consequently, African Americans were unable to elect a community committee person. For example, in community number one, African-American candidates received a total of 563 votes, 59.1 percent of the total votes counted. The votes were split such that none of the nine African-American candidates was elected to the three-member community committee. Similar situations arose in the communities two and four.

During the 1967 ASCS election, forty-three of the total fifty-nine candidates were African Americans. Communities one, two, three and four each had only three white candidates. Community five had four. Each community was to elect three candidates. While African-American candidates received 57.8 percent of the total votes tabulated, eleven of the fifteen community committeemen elected were white. Thus the African-American vote was diluted and they were denied the right to be elected to the three-member county committee, and ultimately the right to have an African American as chair of that committee.

I was retained for the purpose of filing a class action suit to correct these irregularities and illegal actions. The suit *Henderson v. ASCS* was filed in the familiar United States District Court for the Middle District of Alabama. The plaintiffs were James H. M. Henderson, Anthony T. Reid, Otis Pinkard, Lonnie Hooks, Oscar L. Downs, and R. V. Harris; and the Alabama Council on Human Relations, Inc. The defendants were the Macon County ASCS; B. L. Collins as state director of ASCS; Jack M. Bridges as chairman of the Alabama ASCS Committee; Jim Weldon as chairman of the Macon County ASCS Committee; B. M. Segrest as vice chairman of the Macon County ASCS Committee; T. R. Cunningham as a member of the Macon County ASCS Committee; Learly Whatley as office manager of the Macon County ASCS Committee; and Martha Terry, Marjorie Hornsby, Josephine Cole, Ann Simpson, Elizabeth Newman, and Bruce Bufford as staff members of the Macon County ASCS office. This was one of the first cases raising the issue of racial discrimination in providing farm services to African Americans under ASCS.

In representing the plaintiffs, I was assisted by Solomon S. Seay, Donald Ajelinek of the Southern Rural Research Project, Lee A. Albert, Lucy Vkatz, and Jack Greenberg of LDEF. The defendants were represented by U.S. Justice Department attorneys Ralph O. Howard, Robert Zener, Reed Johnston, Jr., and Ben Hardeman.

This was a class action suit challenging the validity of the Macon County ASCS Community and County Committee elections for the years 1967 and 1969. The plaintiffs, African-American farmers, owners, tenants and sharecroppers eligible to participate in ASCS elections in Macon County, alleged that the defendants violated their rights under the Fifth and Fifteenth amendments by manipulating the election procedures so as to assure the election of white committeemen. The suit sought a judgment declaring these acts to be unconstitutional, and requested a preliminary and permanent injunction ordering defendants to set aside the 1967 and 1969 community and county elections and to hold new elections under court supervision. The court granted defendants' motion to dismiss without prejudice because the U.S. Secretary of

Agriculture, without whom an adequate judgment could not be rendered, could not properly be served in the Middle District of Alabama.

We appealed to the Fifth Circuit. On August 4, 1969, the parties filed a joint motion to remand the case to the district court and the motion was granted on August 12, 1969. The Secretary of Agriculture, meanwhile, had consented to the suit being filed in Alabama.

After a full trial on the merits, the court found that the 1967 election was unlawful and unconstitutional. The court's memorandum opinion of August 31, 1970, stated "The evidence clearly reflects that defendants purpose in nominating a plethora of Negro candidates was to prevent the election of Negroes to membership on the community and county committees." [See Appendix A-3]

The court also concluded that "The evidence reflected other irregularities in the voter registration procedure that require a finding that the 1967 elections were conducted in a racially discriminatory manner."

It is interesting to note that when the cabinet appointments were made for the new Presidential administration in 1993, the Secretary of Agriculture was Michael Espy, an African American from Mississippi. We have made tremendous progress since 1967.

The Importance of This Case

Here the defendants involved were all persons who were employees of the United States government. They were local individuals, but charged with the responsibility of enforcing federal regulations. They permitted their personal beliefs with respect to segregation to enter into how they administered federally supported programs. The lawyers who defended the defendants were not white Alabama politicians, but white government lawyers, and some of them were from Washington. However, the federal district court was compelled to find that these federal employees violated the constitutional rights of African Americans.

As a direct result of this case, two African Americans were elected in 1970 to the Macon County ASCS Committee. They were Aldophus Hall and Otis Pinkard. Otis Pinkard was elected chairman. They were the first African Americans elected to such positions in the United States. The Macon County committee then employed the first African American to serve as county executive director, Homer Edwards. As a result of this suit, the Department of Agriculture has implemented policies nationwide to eliminate racial discrimination in the administration of the services under ASCS across the country.

Conclusion

It is abundantly clear from the cases discussed in this chapter that Macon County, Alabama, played a major role in ending racial discrimination in many areas, including but not limited to, the right to vote, the right not to be gerrymandered out of the city, the right not to have the African-American vote diluted, the right to serve on civil and criminal juries, the right to participate in and serve as county and community ASCS committee persons in the delivery of services to farm families, and the right to public education without regard to race and color.

6

George Wallace, Then and Now

Bullock County is just south of Macon County. The Bullock population is approximately 70 percent African American. African Americans there had the same difficulty in getting registered to vote as had African Americans in Macon County. Bullock County, however, did not have the substantial number of educated African Americans as in Macon County, although there were outstanding leaders in that county, including such men as Benjamin Jordan, Wilborn Thomas, and Aaron Sellers. Even in the fifties they were working to increase African-American voter registration. Dr. C. G. Gomillion and William P. Mitchell assisted the black leadership in Bullock County to become registered voters.

State v. Eddie Lee Jordan, 1957

I had been retained by Benjamin Jordan, one of the leading activists in Bullock County, to represent his seventeen-year-old son, Eddie Lee. The younger Jordan had been charged by the justice of the peace with speeding in connection with a confrontation with the circuit solicitor, Seymore Trammell. This was my first of many cases in Bullock County. Eddie had been driving on a country road in his father's truck and met a car going in the opposite direction. Eddie had a friend with him. When Eddie got to the pasture where he was going, his companion got out of the truck and opened the gate. About that time, a white man drove up, drew a gun on Eddie, cursed him and told him to slow the truck down. He told the man he was going within the speed limit. The man continued to talk to him. When Eddie's companion returned to the truck and closed the door, Eddie pulled off into the pasture leaving the white man holding the gun. Later, Eddie was arrested and charged with speeding. He did not know that the gun-wielding man was the circuit solicitor.

I tried this case as if I were trying a constitutional case. Nevertheless, Eddie Lee was convicted, fined twenty-five dollars, and sentenced to three months in jail. I appealed the case to the Circuit Court.

℘

On the morning set for the re-trial, I arrived in court in Union Springs. Circuit Judge George Corley Wallace was presiding. This was my first time to meet Wallace. He found my client guilty, but put off sentencing for a later date.

On the designated day for sentencing, March 1, 1957, I returned to Union Springs. I asked E. D. Nixon if he would ride down with me and I introduced Mr. Nixon to Judge Wallace. This probably was the first time the two of them met. The judge fined my client twenty-five dollars and sentenced him to three months in jail. This sentence was the same as given earlier by the justice of the peace. Judge Wallace, however, placed Eddie Lee on unsupervised probation and suspended the sentence.

I brought along an appeal bond and a notice of appeal. In the notice and in the bond, I indicated that Eddie Lee had been fined a blank amount and sentenced to a blank number of days in jail. When Judge Wallace looked at the filings, he said, "How did you know I was going to fine him and give him a jail sentence?"

I replied, "Your Honor, I didn't know, but I just wanted to be prepared." It was my custom in those days to be prepared to lose and always to have an appeal bond ready so I would be able to keep my clients out of jail.

While Judge Wallace ruled against us, he was very courteous in the manner in which he conducted the trial.

It is interesting to note that the case made the headlines in the

Union Springs Herald on March 7, 1957. Now I had met George C. Wallace for the first time, but we were to meet many times in the future.

The Eufaula Housing Case

In December 1957, I received a letter from a Reverend Holmes in Eufaula, Alabama. Eufaula is approximately ninety miles southeast of Montgomery, right on the Chattahoochee River, which forms the Alabama–Georgia border there. Eufaula is in Barbour County, the home county of George C. Wallace.

Reverend Holmes told me that he lived on Albert Street and he represented substantially all African-American property owners on Albert Street. He and representatives of a group called "The Albert Street Club" wanted to meet with me to discuss problems they were having concerning their property. Reverend Holmes, Mr. David Frost, Reverend Cummings, and Mr. Tate came to my office in Montgomery for an initial meeting.

Apparently the housing authority of the city of Eufaula wanted to purchase their property. But these African-American homeowners did not want to sell. That is why they were seeking my services. In the meeting, I learned that as early as 1955 letters had been written to U.S. Senator John Sparkman and to the U.S. Justice Department requesting assistance; a courtesy reply had been received, but no help was offered.

Members of the Albert Street Club and their parents had owned property on Albert Street since slavery time. Albert Street was located to the west of downtown Eufaula and was the only street where African Americans lived in that part of the city. Adjacent to and at the north end of Albert Street, the Eufaula Board of Education had recently constructed a modern white high school. At the time, whites lived on all sides of the African Americans on Albert Street.

The housing authority contacted each of the African-American Albert Street property owners and informed them that their houses were substandard. Since the authority had decided to redevelop the area, all of their homes would be taken. The housing authority promised the Albert Street homeowners that they would be paid for their houses and assured them that they could relocate to the southeast part of the city known as the Bluff, where most Eufaula African Americans lived.

Three years after the *Brown v. Board* decision, there was not one iota of integration in the public schools in the city of Eufaula, Barbour County, nor in any other school system in Alabama. The Eufaula City Board of Education had recently built a new high school for African Americans, McCoo High School, which was named after a local African-American doctor and was located on the Bluff.

It was quite clear that the housing authority was attempting to relocate the African-American residents of Albert Street to the side of town near the African-American school. The housing authority would then redevelop the properties near the white area for whites. When all of the African Americans lived in the community where McCoo High School was located, nothing could be said about discrimination based on race. It would just be that whites lived closer to the white school, African Americans lived closer to the African-American school, and both populations attended neighborhood schools.

One problem with the relocation plan was that the cost of new homes was out of the price range for my clients. My clients already owned their present homes. They had no interest in spending money to satisfy someone else's desire to have them live in another part of town. They were satisfied where they were, continuing to possess the property they already owned, which had passed from one generation to another.

Once I agreed to represent the African-American homeowners, I first considered the obvious. The housing authority had the power of condemnation if the homeowners rejected the authority's initial offer. If condemnation proceedings were to be initiated, three commissioners would be appointed to set the amount of compensation. If the homeowners accepted this amount, that would be the end of the problem. However, if they were not satisfied, they had the right of appealing to the circuit court of

Barbour County, where an all-white jury would decide the amount of compensation for their property. This was how matters would have normally proceeded, but I tried a different approach.

There was no question that the entire plan was racially motivated. It was designed to continue the pattern of racial discrimination in housing and in public schools in Eufaula. I saw an opportunity here to advance my goal of "destroying everything segregated that I could find" while accomplishing my clients' goal of keeping their property. My recommendation was to let me file a lawsuit on their behalf in the federal district court in Montgomery before the Eufaula Housing Authority could begin condemnation proceedings. My clients agreed. In the complaint I alleged, among other things, that our clients would be denied their constitutional rights of due process and equal protection under the Fourteenth Amendment, and I requested an injunction enjoining the housing authority from proceeding to take their property under the facts and circumstances of the case.

I hoped that Judge Frank M. Johnson, Jr., would rule with us as he had done in other integration cases. He had already struck down segregation on city buses in *Browder v. Gayle* and in public parks in *Gilmore v. Montgomery*.

This case was more difficult because there were a lot of "ifs" involved. I did presuppose that the Eufaula officials would not abide by the law and that they were doing what I alleged they were doing for racial purposes. At an NAACP meeting in Dallas, I discussed this matter with Constance Baker Motley, who was on the staff of the NAACP Legal Defense Fund. I asked for her assistance with the case. She agreed to help and sent me some information regarding a similar case that had been filed in Gadsden, Alabama. On June 9, 1958, Constance Motley and I filed the lawsuit *Stephen Tate v. City of Eufaula*. My clients were Stephen Tate, Clara Cochran, David Frost, Jr., Adolphus Cummings, Annie Bell Crews, Oscar Bouier, Gennie M. Griffin, Willie Griffin, Dan Walker, and Lula Young.

The defendants were the City of Eufaula, the Eufaula Housing Authority, and Harry Wrighton, its executive director. They were represented by James J. Carter of Hill, Stovall and Carter of Montgomery, and Archie Grubb and James LeMaistre, probably the most experienced lawyers in Eufaula. This was the same Carter who argued against me in *Gomillion v. Lightfoot*. The defendants filed a motion to dismiss in which they alleged twenty-six reasons why the complaint should be dismissed, including lack of jurisdiction, failure to state a claim, no permanent justiciable controversy exists; that is, prematurity of claim. Motley and I did not persuade Judge Johnson to retain jurisdiction. On August 5, 1958, he dismissed the action and stated in his opinion the following:

> In this complaint, before there is a genuine and presently existing justiciable controversy as required by the Declaratory Judgment Act, this Court must assume the redevelopment plan will be fully executed, the school board will acquire the land from the Housing Authority and construct thereon a public school, that qualified eligible Negroes will seek admission and that the school board will deny such applications solely on account of the fact that they are Negroes; that land for a public park will be acquired and a public park developed thereon, that Negroes will desire to use such park facilities and will be denied that use solely because they are Negroes; that those plaintiffs and/or others similarly situated will in good faith apply for public housing and if eligible will be discriminated against solely because of their color; and that the redevelopers will violate the binding covenants. This Court declines to declare or enjoin upon such future contingencies.

Meanwhile, the housing authority was proceeding with the condemnation proceedings in the Barbour County Probate Court, since a temporary restraining order was never issued. Three commissioners were appointed to determine the amount of compensation for my clients' property. In each of these hearings the commissioners gave what I thought were pretty good awards, and substantially more than what the housing authority had offered. Nevertheless, my clients' property was still being taken, so we appealed to the Circuit Court of Barbour County and requested a jury trial. The circuit judge of Barbour County was, of course, none other than George Corley Wallace. In 1958, Wallace was not widely known outside of Barbour and Bullock counties, the counties of his judicial circuit, although this was the year he first ran for governor, losing to a very racist John Patterson.

So Wallace and I were meeting for the second time. I filed a motion challenging the composition of the juries in Barbour County on the basis that African Americans were excluded from jury service. I put on testimony from lawyers and others that African Americans were not serving on juries in Barbour County. Judge Wallace denied my motions. This 1958 case was one of the first times that the question of systematically excluding African Americans from jury duty in civil cases was raised. This was eight years before I filed *Mitchell v. Johnson*, the jury case in Macon County. It was not until 1991 that the U.S. Supreme Court decided this issue in the *Edmonson v. Leesville Concrete Company, Inc.*, holding finally that a private litigant in a civil case may not use peremptory challenges to exclude jurors on account of race. The Alabama Supreme Court got around to adopting my argument in the 1991 case of *Thomas v. Diversified Contractors, Inc.* I was thirty years ahead of my time.

The condemnation cases were finally set for trial. I commuted from Montgomery to Eufaula over a two-week period and tried each of the cases separately. Bernice, my wife and secretary, and Frank Massey traveled with me and attended these trials.

I did not have co-counsel in these condemnation cases. By this time, I had gained more confidence and was satisfied that I could work alone. Even if I had had co-counsel, there probably would not have been sufficient money awarded to split fees with another attorney. I was not certain I would get enough to cover my expenses. I was the least experienced lawyer in the courtroom and I worked overtime on my cases. During the course of the trial, attorney Grubb referred to me as the "school boy lawyer." He was right. Most of what I knew about the practice of law, I had learned at Western Reserve University. But I knew where I wanted to go and how to get there.

On one occasion, attorney Grubb became a little excited when I demonstrated that I knew how to get certain evidence before the jury. The housing authority attorneys had denied my request for a copy of the authority's appraiser's report. My clients could not afford to have their own appraisals made; they had only their own testimony as to the value of their property. I had to build my case by cross-examining the housing authority's appraiser and I needed access to his written appraisal. I asked the appraiser whether or not he had made a report. He said he had. I asked if he were testifying based on information contained in his report. He said he was. I asked him then if I might see the report. Of course, he had to produce it. As the appraiser handed me a copy of his report, I looked at the authority's attorneys as if to say—you should have given me a copy. I got the report even though they didn't want me to see it. I used it to cross-examine the appraiser and made a good case for my clients.

I made a point of building good rapport with the jurors, the court, Circuit Clerk James Teal, and even with opposing counsel. We had a good time during the course of the trial. The courtroom developed into a very friendly atmosphere, with one notable exception:

During one of the recesses, Bernice left the courtroom to get a drink of water. She was drinking from one of the fountains—the "colored" fountain—which was beside the "white" water fountain. Separate water fountains in public buildings were one of the features of segregation that young people today simply cannot comprehend. Of course, they were a fact of life below the Mason-Dixon line until well into the 1960s. Even today if you look carefully in the small rural Southern courthouses you can see the evidence of where the separate fountains and restrooms were located. In this case, as Bernice was getting her drink, a big, burly white man came up to the white water fountain. He completely pushed her away from the colored fountain. Such incidents of open hostility toward African Americans were commonplace during the Movement years. I am happy that except in very rare cases today, Southern society has gotten past this type of behavior.

At the conclusion of each of the condemnation cases, which were tried one after the other, an all-white male jury in Barbour County, in 1958, returned verdicts that sometimes doubled and tripled the awards given by the commissioners.

I spoke afterwards with Judge Wallace and was appreciative to him for treating me as a professional, being generous, and as nice as any judge in whose courtroom I had tried a case. And that was the truth. I enjoyed trying the cases before Judge Wallace.

My clients had received substantially more money than they ever expected. When I talked to them about appealing the case, they said, "Well, lawyer, we appreciate everything you have done and we know you want to appeal it, but we are satisfied with the awards and we think we will take our money." They received their money and purchased new homes on the African-American side of town.

These were the first cases of my practice in which I received a reasonable fee. When I started the case, however, I did not know whether I would even be paid, because my clients had very little money. But I was willing to accept these cases because the Albert Street Club needed help. I was happy that I was able to serve, and the subsequent fees were icing on the cake.

While I appreciated the compensation, I was disappointed that I did not get an opportunity to appeal Judge Johnson's ruling in the federal case. All of the facts which I originally alleged in the complaint did, in fact, come to pass. Flake Hill became an all-white community. There are no African Americans living in the area near that white school today. You see, I had wanted not only to prevent the forced segregation of that residential area of Eufaula, but I wanted to get that school integrated. I had to wait to tackle that issue later. Eventually, I did develop a case to integrate the city schools of Eufaula as a part of the *Lee v. Macon* suit. I also filed *Franklin v. Barbour County Board of Education* to integrate the public schools in that county system.

The Importance of the Eufaula Cases

The *Eufaula Housing* and *State v. Eddie Lee Jordan* cases introduced me to George Corley Wallace, who was to dominate politics in Alabama for the next twenty years. He became a national figure. His influence for good and for bad has been and continues to be felt in Alabama.

The case was also important because in it I raised the issue of violation of the constitutional rights of African Americans due to exclusion from jury duty in civil cases because of their race. As I noted earlier, my legal reasoning was vindicated in 1964, when Judge Johnson accepted my argument in the Macon County jury case, *Mitchell v. Johnson*. And in 1991, the U.S. Supreme Court accepted that line of argument in the case of *Edmonson v. Leesville Concrete Company*, and in the same year, the Alabama Supreme Court accepted it in the case of *Thomas v. Diversified Contractors, Inc.*. Those latter two were not my cases, but the points in them were the same ones that I had raised thirty years earlier in a little country courthouse deep in the Black Belt of Alabama.

With the housing authority cases as my first legal experience in Eufaula and Barbour County, I developed a deep concern for the people there. In 1970 I was elected to serve Barbour, Bullock and Macon counties in the state legislature as one of the first African-American members of the House of Representatives in Alabama since reconstruction.

My law practice was growing and so was my reputation. I was continuously getting opportunities to strike at segregation, as I had now extended my practice one hundred miles southeast of my home in Montgomery. I had already been over to Selma, which is fifty miles west of Montgomery, and I had established a practice in Tuskegee, forty miles northeast. This was the little-known kudzu concept of civil rights law practice. Of course, that is a little joke, for all you non-Southerners who may be reading this book.

Even today Barbour County has never had a resident African-

American lawyer. Attorney James Baker from Birmingham commuted to Eufaula once a week over an extended period of time. He later became city attorney for Birmingham. Over the years there were offers to provide me with office space if I were to set up a branch office in Eufaula. I was unable to do so because of my schedule and the distance between Montgomery, Tuskegee, and Eufaula, plus I already had two offices at that time. As recently as October 1991, David Frost, a member of the Albert Street Club, wrote me a letter:

> We are very sorry that you cannot handle our case. The four of us, Mr. Tate, Reverend Holmes, Reverend Cummings and me who first went to your office in Montgomery to get you to come to Eufaula to work for us, I am the only one that is left alone alive. You said that our case was the first case that you made any money, and of course you slowed these white people down from taking black people's land. Now that they know that you are not going to work in Barbour County any more, they have started back.

I am hopeful that Barbour County will soon have a law practice established by an African American.

Other Meetings With George C. Wallace

My third meeting with George Corley Wallace was shortly after he became governor in January 1963. In his inaugural address on January 14, 1963, he stated, "I draw the line in the dust and toss the gauntlet before the feet of tyranny . . . and I say segregation now, . . . segregation tomorrow, . . . segregation forever." At that time we were preparing the cases of Vivian Malone and Jimmy Hood to integrate the University of Alabama. As a belated inaugural present to Governor Wallace, we filed the case of Vivian Malone to integrate the University of Alabama. This case ultimately led to Wallace's infamous "stand in the schoolhouse door." He was troubled because I filed that suit.

The first formal, scheduled, major meeting I had with Governor Wallace was at the conclusion of the Selma-to-Montgomery March in 1965. I represented participants in the March and obtained a decree to enjoin Governor Wallace from failing and refusing to protect the marchers. I was selected as one of the persons to meet with the governor at the conclusion of the march and deliver a list of grievances, including the right to vote. On that occasion, Wallace reminded me of our initial meeting over the Flake Hill cases in Eufaula.

Another major confrontation I had with the governor was during *Lee v. Macon County Board of Education*. In 1963, Governor Wallace ordered the closing of the Tuskegee Public School to prevent its integration. We subsequently obtained the statewide court orders integrating all of the public grade schools in Alabama not then already under court order, and everything under the control and supervision of the State Board of Education.

These orders were entered by a three-judge district court, which was convened for the purpose of deciding the constitutionality of certain state statutes which required the segregation of the races in public grade schools. Judge Johnson was the local resident district judge, and most of the orders that were issued, integrating these schools, were authored by Judge Johnson. It is rather interesting to note that it was Governor Wallace who closed the Tuskegee Public School, which made it possible for Judge Frank M. Johnson, Jr., to enter an order declaring the governor's acts to be unconstitutional and setting a precedent to desegregate in one lawsuit all of the state grade schools which were not already under court order. This certainly was a confrontation in the true sense of the word between Governor Wallace on the one hand, and Judge Johnson on the other. These two men were reported to be friends when they attended law school at the University of Alabama. Upon their graduation, George Wallace returned to his home county of Barbour and became involved in politics, first as a circuit judge, next as a state legislator, and then as the governor. At the pinnacle of his career, he ran as a candidate for president of the United States. On the other hand, Frank M. Johnson, Jr., returned to his home in the Free State of Winston* in north Alabama, and began to practice law. He became U. S. Attorney for the Northern District of Alabama, and then United States District Judge for the Middle District, and finally a member of the Court of Appeals for the Eleventh Circuit.

For the next two decades, these two giants would cross paths many times. George Wallace's political career guided him into becoming the governor who vowed to keep Alabama segregated "Today, tomorrow, and forever." At the same time, it was during his administration that virtually all of the state-supported institutions in this state were integrated. They were integrated by the stroke of a pen by his former schoolmate, Frank M. Johnson, Jr. As the sun sets on their two careers, it is interesting to note that in spite of the scorn, humiliation, and slander heaped upon Frank Johnson during his early years on the bench, in the twilight of his career, he has received many honors. Many of the public officials who once damned him, now consider him to be an outstanding jurist. His career on the bench is nothing short of true greatness. On the other hand, George Wallace, in the twilight years of his career, unfortunately, is remembered mostly as an ambitious obstructionist who would do anything in order to obtain his political ends. Interestingly, Judge Johnson is vigorous and alert, while Governor Wallace, sadly, is deaf, crippled and feeble.

Fate will always play its hand.

George Wallace As I Saw Him

I have had the opportunity of observing Governor George C. Wallace during what I consider to be at least three periods during his life. The first period was while he was a circuit judge, a state legislator, and his first race for governor. During that period of time he was considered a moderate, decent, fair-minded person. While in the legislature he supported Governor Jim Folsom, a

---

*When Alabama seceded from the Union in 1861, Winston County then seceded from Alabama. The fiercely independent people in that hill county owned few if any slaves and were Lincoln Republicans.

moderate. Wallace was considered one of Folsom's young reformers. Governor Folsom appointed Wallace to the board of trustees of Tuskegee Institute. When Wallace ran for governor the first time, in the race against John Patterson, he did not run as a segregationist, but as a moderate. John Patterson ran as a segregationist. It is reported that when George Wallace lost that race, he said he lost it because Patterson "out segged" him and he would never let that happen again.

The second period of George Wallace's life I call "hard core segregationist." This includes substantially the entire period that he was governor. From 1962 and his first inaugural address, his standing in the school house door, his diehard segregationist positions, and closing the public school in Tuskegee, I can think of

Ironically, when I served in the legislature, I was George Wallace's state representative; the Governor's hometown, where he always maintained his official address, was Clio, in Barbour County, in my district. Here, I am with a group of legislators and other officials as Wallace signs a bond issue for Barbour County.

no one in Alabama's history who talked more against integration and in favor of segregation of the races than George Wallace.

As a result of his election and actions, I was determined that during his administration I would intensify my efforts to "destroy everything segregated I could find." Ironically, therefore, during his tenure in office, there was actually more integration in Alabama than under any other governor. So, while Governor Wallace did not realize it and it certainly was not his intention, his anti-African American positions were contributing factors in our renewed efforts to destroy segregation.

The third part of his life was during his last administration and until the present. I was in the state legislature in the 1970s, representing Macon, Bullock and Barbour counties. Barbour County was George Wallace's home county, so I was really *his* state representative. I was a part of the inaugural festivities on Wallace's third inauguration as governor. Later I went to his office to discuss committee assignments. Notwithstanding how strongly he had been against African Americans, a substantial number of African Americans supported him in his last race for governor. He acknowledged that his views on segregation had been wrong and that he should not have done many of the things he did. When I interviewed him in preparation for this book, I became convinced that he has genuinely repented.

7

Dr. King's Most Serious Charge

The Montgomery Bus Protest had officially ended when the mandate affirming our district court victory arrived from the U.S. Supreme Court on December 20, 1956. Over the next few years the Civil Rights Movement in Montgomery still flourished. Some desegregation occurred. The buses, parks, and airport were desegregated. I was still busily engaged in many activities defending the NAACP, the Tuskegee Civic Association, and working on the *Gomillion v. Lightfoot* case. (These activities were all toward the realization of my dream of destroying segregation, but they took a back seat to the birth of our first child, Deborah, on April 2, 1957. She was a beautiful, intelligent child. In our usual Movement style, Bernice and I sent hundreds of birth announcements [see page 264] to our friends and clients.)

The Civil Rights Act of 1957 was another important milestone during this period. The U.S. Senate Sub-Committee on Constitutional Rights and the Judiciary Committee conducted hearings on the proposed act. As counsel for the Montgomery Improvement Association, I submitted a sworn statement to the committee, relating how the Bus Protest started and summarizing its development.

In September 1957, the Civil Rights Act passed. It was the first such legislation to become federal law in eighty-two years. The bill was a compromise negotiated by Senate Majority Leader Lyndon Johnson between liberals in the North and conservatives in the South. The act was just a beginning. It established a federal civil rights commission and allowed the U.S. Justice Department to file voting rights suits against boards of registrars that discriminated against African Americans.

In 1958, Dr. King's book, *Stride Toward Freedom*, was published. Recalling my activities in connection with the defense of Rosa Parks when he arrived at her trial, he stated:

> Her attorney, Fred D. Gray—the brilliant young Negro who later became the chief counsel for the protest movement— was on hand to defend her.

He also stated that after the protest ended:

> The MIA (Montgomery Improvement Association) has reduced its budget and staff, but it has broadened its focus and begun to address itself to other large areas of civic improvement. It has retained Fred Gray as full-time legal counsel to handle civil rights cases.

In January 1957, Dr. King, in conjunction with black leaders from throughout the South, formed the Southern Christian Leadership Conference (SCLC). Key Alabama African-American clergymen played active roles in the formation of SCLC, including Reverends S. S. Seay, Sr., and Ralph Abernathy of Montgomery, Joseph Lowery of Mobile, and Fred Shuttlesworth of Birmingham. The primary purpose of the SCLC was to lead the Civil Rights Movement in the South. This was particularly important because in Alabama the NAACP had been enjoined from doing business. In other Southern states, such as Mississippi, Louisiana and Georgia, similar steps had been taken to enjoin the civil rights organizations. When the Bus Protest ended, Dr. King needed a forum and an organization that would enable him to continue a civil rights movement independent of any other organization then in existence.

By 1960, Dr. King had become known internationally. This meant that he was sought after far beyond the boundaries of

Montgomery and Alabama. He had regretfully resigned the Dexter pulpit and moved to Atlanta to serve as president of the SCLC and as associate pastor of his father's church, Ebenezer Baptist Church. But before King found peace in Atlanta, white authorities in Alabama made one last desperate attempt to use the courts and legal machinery to derail the Civil Rights Movement and to smear its leader.

The Indictment and Arrest, January 1960

In January 1960, Dr. King met with representatives of the State of Alabama Revenue Department with reference to his income taxes for 1956, 1957 and 1958. Having paid all taxes that the state claimed he owed, he thought the matter was closed. You may well imagine his surprise when the police arrested him on income tax evasion charges. It was not until this arrest that Dr. King learned that a Montgomery County grand jury had indicted him in February 1960 on two counts of perjury in connection with the filing of his 1956 and 1958 Alabama income tax returns. Dr. King was not given the courtesy of being informed by the Alabama state officials of the indictment, nor was he given an opportunity to surrender himself and make bond; rather, certified copies of the indictment were sent to law enforcement officials in Atlanta, where he then lived.

To be arrested and hauled back to Montgomery on income tax evasion charges was not only embarrassing and humiliating, but it was a senseless act on the part of Alabama officials. They knew Dr. King. They knew I had represented him in many matters, and if they had informed me of the indictments, I would have notified him. They also knew he would have voluntarily returned to answer the charges.

In my opinion, the arrest was part of the plan of Governor John Patterson, or someone in his administration, to harass and intimidate African Americans in general, King in particular, and for political reasons. John Patterson had reached the governor's chair on a segregation platform. It appears that someone in his administration was responsible for the indictment and arrest of Dr. King, which appeared to have been purely for the purpose of harassment and humiliation.

Patterson had allowed deeds of harassment many times before for apparently political reasons. When he was attorney general, raids on the Tuskegee Civic Association and the confiscation of its records occurred. As attorney general, he obtained an injunction which enjoined the NAACP from operating in Alabama. He had ordered Dr. H. Council Trenholm, president of Alabama State College, to expel and suspend students who sat-in at the lunch counter at the Montgomery County Courthouse.

Dr. King's Most Serious Charge

The charge of income tax evasion was a very serious charge for Dr. King. It was a felony indictment for him, although for most persons who are charged with tax violations, it is a misdemeanor. Moreover, as far as I have been able to determine from my research, Dr. King was the first person ever indicted and tried for perjury in connection with the filing of his state income taxes. I doubt if any one has been so charged since.

This charge was also important to Dr. King because it questioned his credibility, honesty, and integrity. He was personally concerned about the effect a conviction would have on his constituents and on his ability to lead the Civil Rights Movement. For a host of reasons, King did not want this blemish on his record. Dr. King spoke to me about his apprehensions. Actually, he was more concerned about this case than any of the other cases in which he had been arrested.

I believe Alabama officials recognized that if they could get something on Dr. King to cast doubts about his credibility, then perhaps others would be less willing to follow him. Perhaps they even dreamed that this case would halt or impede the Civil Rights Movement. Obviously, many people had criticized Dr. King on a number of issues, but up to this case no official body had questioned his credibility, honest and integrity.

This action differed significantly from the case the state had filed against ninety-eight persons, including Dr. King, for the alleged violation of the Alabama Anti-Boycott Statute. It was widely believed by African Americans and whites that the ninety-eight individuals were indicted because they were participants in the Bus Protest. The indictments were simply one of many tactics devised to end the protest.

The income tax situation presented a different picture and raised new questions. The Bus Protest had ended and integration now existed, so this case had no obvious connection with a boycott or desegregation. However, the charges grew out of events which occurred during the bus boycott. A successful challenge of the accuracy of King's income tax returns for 1956 and 1958 would have been devastating. If Dr. King were convicted, this would tend to show that while leading thousands of African Americans in Alabama, and delivering his message of nonviolence around the world, Dr. King had been a dishonest man who had failed to properly report his income. A perjury conviction in connection with his Alabama state income taxes would have seriously weakened his credibility in all of the other Southern states. In my opinion, this case is probably the most important case of Dr. King's career. Therefore, for all those reasons, we had to win.

The Selection of the Defense Team

Long before this indictment, Dr. King had established a number of permanent working relationships with many lawyers and other leaders in and outside the South. In particular, two men had become very close to Dr. King; Stanley Levison, a white lawyer from New York, and Bayard Rustin, an African-American activist, also from New York. Both of them had met Dr. King shortly after his house was bombed in January of 1956. Levison, Rustin and others were involved in forming The Committee to Defend Martin Luther King and the Struggle for Freedom in the South. This committee had purchased an ad which appeared in the *New York Times* on March 29, 1960, under the heading, "Heed Their Rising Voices."

King's supporters purchased the *Times* advertisement to raise funds for his defense in the tax case. Funds were also needed to finance the student demonstrations that were then spreading across the South; the sit-in movement had begun in February 1960 when four North Carolina A&T students sought service at the white lunch counter in the Woolworth's in Greensboro, North Carolina. A portion of the ad stated: "We in the South who are struggling daily for dignity and freedom warmly endorse this appeal." Among those persons whose names were listed were the Reverends Ralph D. Abernathy and S. S. Seay, Montgomery, Fred L. Shuttlesworth, Birmingham, and J. E. Lowery, Mobile. I am sure this ad raised a substantial amount of money for the defense of Dr. King, the student sit-ins, and the struggle for freedom in the South. It later became the object of a lawsuit, *Sullivan v. New York Times*. Inasmuch as Reverends Abernathy, Shuttlesworth, Lowery and Seay were defendants in that lawsuit, I represented them. I shall write about the *Sullivan* case in greater detail later.

The Committee to Defend Martin Luther King and the Struggle for Freedom in the South, in conjunction with Dr. King, selected a team of five lawyers from three different states to represent him. The lawyers were: Hubert T. Delaney, a former judge from New York, an expert in research and appellate law; Robert Ming of Chicago, an excellent trial lawyer with substantial experience in tax law; Arthur Shores of Birmingham; Solomon Seay, Jr., of Montgomery; and myself. Robert Ming added to the team a young lawyer from his office, Chauncey Eskridge, a tax expert. All of the defense lawyers were African-American.

We were a good team. Whenever there are different personalities, there are problems that must be resolved, but all in all, we worked well together.

Each of us had assignments. My responsibilities were clear. As local counsel in Montgomery and the one who had worked closely with Dr. King throughout the Protest Movement, it was my duty to coordinate the activities and keep communication flowing between the lawyers. I had various other duties, but my primary responsibility was to maintain open communication channels.

We held many strategy conferences in Montgomery and Atlanta, as well as many telephone conferences, as we plotted Dr.

King's defense. One of the initial problems was finding an expert certified public accountant who could analyze Dr. King's returns and testify that the returns were accurately filed. We found just the expert we needed in Jesse Blayton, an African-American member of the board of trustees of Ebenezer Baptist Church. Blayton was well respected in business and accounting circles in Atlanta.

Armed with a carefully selected expert witness, the legal defense team prepared itself to raise every conceivable legal issue in this case. We realized this was a case that Dr. King had to win if he were to continue to develop as an international figure.

The Pre-Trial Motions

One of the early matters that had to be handled was the filing of a motion to permit both Judge Delaney and Robert Ming, who were not members of the Alabama bar, to practice in the Montgomery County Circuit Court. The case had been assigned to Circuit Judge Eugene Carter. You may recall that Judge Carter had earlier presided in the anti-boycott case against Dr. King. To be in accordance with the Alabama Bar Association rules, Judge Delaney and Robert Ming had to obtain recommendations from the bar commissioner of the 15th judicial circuit. The bar commissioner at that time was Thomas B. Hill, Jr. His firm had defended several persons and corporations in desegregation suits that I had filed. Attorney Hill recommended Judge Delaney and Robert Ming to practice before the Court.

Judge Delaney bore major responsibility for preparing the memoranda of law. A masterful jurist with the mannerisms of a Southern gentleman, he resolved many legal questions. Some of the issues which we raised appropriately in court concerned the systematic exclusion of Negroes from participating in the popular elections of judges; Alabama's circuit judges were and still are elected rather than appointed.

We argued that because Alabama African Americans were at the time by-and-large not permitted to register and vote, then judges so elected were constitutionally incompetent to assume and exercise jurisdiction over members of the systematically excluded class.

The issue of African-American participation in elections of judges and other officials went to the heart of segregation in Alabama. This was a novel question. We anticipated that this issue would be ignored because everyone knew that blacks had been disenfranchised. If our argument had prevailed, then no white judge in Alabama would be able to try a case involving an African American in areas where African Americans had been excluded from the electoral process, and that meant everywhere in the state. We argued that Alabama's method of judicial elections, combined with its systematic exclusion of African-American voters, was a violation of the Fourteenth Amendment. And we were morally and legally right, although we didn't expect to win the point. But we argued it anyway.

We also raised the related issue of the systematic exclusion of African Americans from Alabama juries. Actually, we raised this issue in all of our jury cases at that time, because African Americans were not serving on the juries in proportion to their numbers in the population. We challenged the composition of the grand jury that returned the indictment, the panel of petit jurors from which the jury was ultimately selected, and the twelve-member jury that actually tried the case. We proved our allegations by calling to the witness stand lawyers and judges who had tried jury cases in Alabama in which there were few or no African Americans on the jury despite large African-American populations.

Another major motion sought to transfer the trial from Montgomery County to another county which might be free of the bias and prejudice against Dr. King that existed in Montgomery County. If Dr. King were to have a fair trial, his case must be heard by jurors who were reasonably open-minded. We suspected that the newspaper accounts of the Montgomery Bus Protest from December 1, 1955, to the beginning of the trial had prejudiced most white potential jurors from Montgomery and made them incapable of delivering an impartial verdict. The motion called attention to the following which we alleged would prevent King from receiving a fair trial in Montgomery County:

1) that he was an African American, president of the Montgom-

ery Improvement Association, and had been involved in organizing and serving as spokesman for the Bus Protest which ended in the integration of buses in Montgomery; he had advocated the ending of segregation in city parks, public schools, municipal airports and other public facilities; and his views were well known in the community;

2) that he had written a book, *Stride Toward Freedom*, which depicted his involvement in the Movement; the views expressed in the book and the activities which he had been engaged in were contrary to the opinions of a majority of the whites; and white jurors would have bias and prejudice against him;

3) that the recent events which occurred in Montgomery during 1960 resulted in increased racial tension; for example, on February 25, 1960, a group of African-American students from Alabama State College went to the cafeteria located on the first floor of the Montgomery County Courthouse where only white persons had been served, they were refused service, the cafeteria was closed, and subsequently, these students had been ordered expelled by the Governor of the State or placed on probation;

4) that on February 28, 1960, in downtown Montgomery the streets were patrolled by club-wielding white men, and one of these men struck an African-American woman. There were no arrests made in this incident, but it was reported in the newspaper;

5) that on or about March 31, 1960, African Americans from the Montgomery Improvement Association, students from Alabama State College and white students from MacMurray College in Jackson, Illinois, were having lunch in a private dining room at the Regal Cafe, an African-American restaurant. While the African-American and white persons were dining, they were arrested and subsequently convicted of disorderly conduct. The accounts of these events were carried in the newspaper.

Further, we maintained in the motion that substantially all of the persons whose names were in the jury box were white, and that they believed in segregation of the races on buses, parks, schools, airport facilities and almost every phase of American life. We asserted that they also believed that segregation of facilities on account of race and color was necessary in order to preserve the "Southern way of life." This was a critical assertion, because the racial conflict and tension in Montgomery was reputed to have been generated by Dr. King as a result of his views and his active participation and efforts to eliminate racial segregation and discrimination. We argued that it was impossible for him to obtain a fair and impartial trial before a jury in Montgomery County.

I had the primary responsibility of presenting both the evidence and the arguments in support of these motions to the court. Not surprisingly, all of the pretrial motions submitted were denied.

The Trial, May 1960

On May 16, 1960, Dr. King was arraigned. We entered pleas of not guilty. Trial began May 22, 1960, and lasted four days.

The State introduced almost one thousand exhibits and its star witness was the income tax examiner who had examined Dr. King's tax returns. During his testimony, the examiner, Lloyd D. Hale, a state revenue auditor, indicated that he had talked to Dr. King after the audit. He did not find anything wrong with King's returns. When he was cross-examined by attorney Ming, he admitted that conversation, to our surprise! Of course, it was a calculated risk to ask whether he had the conversation with Dr. King. It was an even greater risk to ask him whether or not he had made those statements. However, he was an honest tax examiner. He told the truth and I think his testimony played a major role in helping to win this case.

Throughout the trial we emphasized every time we had an opportunity that this was the first time any person—white, black, green, blue, or any other color, had ever been tried in Alabama on charges of perjury relating to state tax evasion.

In presenting our case, we called Mr. R. D. Nesbitt, Sr., a deacon at Dexter Avenue Baptist Church. Nesbitt had been instrumental in getting Dr. King to accept the pastorate of that church in 1954, and had been very active in the Bus Protest. He was also the clerk of the church. He testified as to the financial transactions that Dr. King was involved in with the church and the fact that on many occasions Dr. King refused to accept an increase in pay. Nesbitt was a very good witness for us.

The legal defense team had many long hours of consultation over whether or not we would call Dr. King as a witness. In the final analysis we all felt that Dr. King would either win or lose the case for us. We had faith and confidence that Dr. King was articulate enough, familiar enough with the facts, and would be able to present himself well to the twelve white jurors. Notwithstanding the fact that he stood for integration of the races and that he believed in all of the things he was doing—we were only asking him to tell the truth. He had filed his tax return truthfully. We called him to the stand. He was great! And he was greater on cross-examination.

Of course, our star expert witness was Jesse Blanton. He was a real wizard. I don't think any of those white jurors had ever listened to a person, African-American or white, who knew as much about facts and figures and accounting as Mr. Blanton. He completely mesmerized the jurors. When he finished with all the figures, it came up to the penny of Dr. King's tax returns. Every cent was accounted for—what King had earned and what he had reported. The figures were identical.

At the conclusion of the case we moved to exclude the state's evidence, raising all the legal issues involved as to why they had not made out a *prima facie* case. Judge Carter denied the motion.

Robert Ming made the final closing argument on behalf of the defense. This had to be one of the greatest arguments that Bob Ming ever made. It was certainly one of the greatest courtroom arguments ever made in Montgomery.

The jury was spellbound and so were all of the white lawyers. The white side of the courtroom was filled with lawyers. All of the outstanding white members of the bar were there, watching and listening intensely. In carefully articulating and going through the facts and arguing the case, Ming captured the Montgomery County Bar.

While the jury was out, I overheard a conversation in which one of the old established white lawyers made the remark about Ming's closing argument, "Now you have heard the master." It was a great tribute to Bob. He was a master and he had done a masterful job.

The Verdict

After closing arguments, Judge Carter instructed the jury on the applicable law. The jury deliberated that Saturday.

Notwithstanding the work of all our witnesses and our entire team, we were joyfully surprised when the jury foreman stood up and read the verdict, "Not guilty." No one would have predicted that an all-white jury in Montgomery, Alabama, the Cradle of the Confederacy, in May 1960, in the middle of all of the sit-ins and all of the racial tension that was going on, would exonerate Martin Luther King, Jr. But it really happened.

This was the first time in my career as a lawyer on a racial case that an all-white jury returned a verdict in favor of an African American. The verdict renewed my faith in the judicial system. I felt that if in Montgomery, Alabama, a case could be tried before an all-white jury and an acquittal obtained for Dr. King, then there was hope that at some time in the not too distant future, my secret goal would be accomplished, and "everything segregated that I could find" would be destroyed.

While this tax case has not received a lot of publicity except at the time of the verdict, in my opinion, by winning this case and thus exonerating Dr. King, it completely removed from anybody's mind any questions of his credibility. It enabled him to go on to the zenith to which he was headed. It also motivated me to "keep the faith" and have confidence in our judicial system in Alabama and in Montgomery. It renewed my belief that if we kept working we would be successful.

Dr. King Moves On

This was the last major case involving Dr. King in Montgomery. His civil rights activities called him on to Atlanta, to Birmingham, to Albany, to St. Augustine, to Chicago, and ultimately to his death at the Lorraine Hotel in Memphis. I did not accompany Dr. King to Atlanta and to other cities. There were capable and competent lawyers in each city where he was to go who did an excellent job of representing him, SCLC, and the masses for whom he cared so much. My place was in Montgomery, Tuskegee, and central Alabama. The reason I went to law school was to return to Montgomery, to practice in central Alabama and to destroy segregation. However, I was always available to assist Martin. I was as close as the telephone and he called me on many occasions after he left Montgomery. I feel honored and proud that I was Dr. King's first lawyer in the Civil Rights Movement. I gave him a sound legal foundation which sustained him throughout his career. Martin was to have many other lawyers on other occasions, but I was his first.

8

Times v. Sullivan: The New Law of Libel

As mentioned earlier, when Dr. King was indicted in the tax case, some of his supporters established a committee to raise money for his defense and to support the movement generally.

To raise funds, Bayard Rustin, executive director of the newly formed Committee to Defend Martin Luther King and the Struggle for Freedom in the South, placed an advertisement in the *New York Times* on March 29, 1960. A section of the advertisement said, ". . . we in the south who are struggling daily for dignity and freedom warmly endorse this appeal . . ." The named endorsers included Alabama ministers Ralph Abernathy and S. S. Seay, Sr., of Montgomery, Joseph Lowery of Mobile, and Fred Shuttlesworth of Birmingham. They are all giants of the Movement. As a result of this advertisement, the three city commissioners of Montgomery filed separate lawsuits against the *New York Times* and against the four aforementioned individual African-American ministers, alleging that there were certain matters in the advertisement which pertained to and libeled the Montgomery City Commissioners. The first of these cases to come to trial was *Sullivan v. New York Times*. L. B. Sullivan was the police commissioner and it was his case that went all the way to the U.S. Supreme Court and resulted in the rewriting of U.S. libel law; the precedent established in the case is still good law today. The other two cases ultimately were disposed of based on the *Sullivan* outcome.

I was retained by Reverend Fred L. Shuttlesworth, in a letter dated May 10, 1960, to represent him in this matter. I received a similar letter from Reverend Abernathy, advising me that he had been served on April 19, 1960. He sent a copy of the summons and complaint and requested me to represent him in this matter. Reverends Lowery and Seay visited my office and retained me to represent them.

I had known Reverend Abernathy since my college days at Alabama State College. He was an upperclassman and a classmate of my brother Thomas, when I was a first-year student at State. Of course, I had worked with him throughout the Montgomery Bus Boycott.

A legal team was organized. Since I had represented most of the ministers in Montgomery in the Movement, I coordinated the team. My old friend and mentor Reverend Seay was the father of attorney Solomon S. Seay, Jr. It was natural that his son, who had begun his practice in my office, would be included on the defense team. Reverend Joseph Lowery lived in Mobile and wanted to have his own lawyer from Mobile, attorney Vernon Crawford, join the legal team. I had known Crawford from my college days. We were classmates at Alabama State and graduated together in 1951. As a matter of fact, Crawford had defeated me in the bid for president of our senior class. Later, he went on to Brooklyn Law School in New York, then returned to his home in Mobile and set up a practice there.

Thus, the three lawyers representing the defendant ministers had very good working relationships. So we had an easy time dividing the work among ourselves.

The three cases that were then pending were *Sullivan v. New York Times*, and two similar lawsuits brought by Montgomery Commissioners Frank W. Parks and Earl J. James; James was the mayor of Montgomery. The plaintiff in each of these cases was represented by the firm of Steiner, Crum & Baker. Roland (Rod) Nachman, Jr., was the lead counsel for the plaintiff. The Birmingham firm of Beddows, Embry & Beddows represented the *New York Times* with Eric Embry (later to sit on the Alabama Supreme Court) as lead counsel.

While Seay, Crawford, and I were retained individually by the defendant ministers, the Rustin committee, which placed the ad, promised to raise the necessary funds to pay our fees and expenses. A total fee was arranged for the team of three lawyers.

At the time the *Sullivan* case was filed, I was preparing for the trial of Dr. King's tax case. After Martin was acquitted on May 25, 1960, I had more time to work on the *New York Times* case. However, during this same period, I was also representing students at Alabama State College in the sit-in at the Montgomery County Courthouse case—*Dixon v. Alabama State Board of Education.* Also, I represented the Alabama State College students who were with the white students from MacMurray College and were arrested in the Regal Cafe for having an integrated luncheon. All of these cases were pending in various courts in Montgomery during the spring and summer of 1960.

Inaccurate Account of Events

In reviewing the newspaper advertisement, we recognized that it contained several inaccuracies. The two paragraphs in the advertisement (paragraphs three and six) which the plaintiffs claimed libeled them read as follows:

> In Montgomery, Alabama, after students sang My Country 'Tis of Thee on the State Capitol steps, their leaders were expelled from school, and truckloads of police armed with shotguns and tear-gas ringed the Alabama State College campus. When the entire student body protested to state authorities by refusing to re-register, their dining hall was padlocked in an attempt to starve them into submission.

> Again and again the Southern violators have answered Dr. King's peaceful protests with intimidation and violence. They have bombed his home almost killing his wife and child. They have assaulted his person. They have arrested him seven times—for "speeding," "loitering" and similar "offenses." And now they have charged him with

"*The growing movement of peaceful mass demonstrations by Negroes is something new in the South, something understandable.... Let Congress heed their rising voices, for they will be heard.***"**

—*New York Times editorial*
Saturday, March 19, 1960

Heed Their

Rising Voices

As the whole world knows by now, thousands of Southern Negro students are engaged in widespread non-violent demonstrations in positive affirmation of the right to live in human dignity as guaranteed by the U. S. Constitution and the Bill of Rights. In their efforts to uphold these guarantees, they are being met by an unprecedented wave of terror by those who would deny and negate that document which the whole world looks upon as setting the pattern for modern freedom....

In Orangeburg, South Carolina, when 400 students peacefully sought to buy doughnuts and coffee at lunch counters in the business district, they were forcibly ejected, tear-gassed, soaked to the skin in freezing weather with fire hoses, arrested en masse and herded into an open barbed-wire stockade to stand for hours in the bitter cold.

In Montgomery, Alabama, after students sang "My Country, 'Tis of Thee" on the State Capitol steps, their leaders were expelled from school, and truck-

loads of police armed with shotguns and tear-gas ringed the Alabama State College Campus. When the entire student body protested to state authorities by refusing to re-register, their dining hall was padlocked in an attempt to starve them into submission.

In Tallahassee, Atlanta, Nashville, Savannah, Greensboro, Memphis, Richmond, Charlotte, and a host of other cities in the South, young American teenagers, in face of the entire weight of official state apparatus and police power, have boldly stepped forth as

protagonists of democracy. Their courage and amazing restraint have inspired millions and given a new dignity to the cause of freedom.

Small wonder that the Southern violators of the Constitution fear this new, non-violent brand of freedom fighter . . . even as they fear the upwelling right-to-vote movement. Small wonder that they are determined to destroy the one man who, more than any other, symbolizes the new spirit now sweeping the South—the Rev. Dr. Martin Luther King, Jr., world-famous leader of the Montgomery Bus Protest. For it is his doctrine of non-violence which has inspired and guided the students in their widening wave of sit-ins; and it this same Dr. King who founded and is president of the Southern Christian Leadership Conference—the organization which is spearheading the surging right-to-vote movement. Under Dr. King's direction the Leadership Conference conducts Student Workshops and Seminars in the philosophy and technique of non-violent resistance.

Again and again the Southern violators have answered Dr. King's peaceful protests with intimidation and violence. They have bombed his home almost killing his wife and child. They have assaulted his person. They have arrested him seven times—for "speeding," "loitering" and similar "offenses." And now they have charged him with "perjury"—a felony under which they could imprison him for ten years. Obviously, their real purpose is to remove him physically as the leader to whom the students and millions

of others—look for guidance and support, and thereby to intimidate all leaders who may rise in the South. Their strategy is to behead this affirmative movement, and thus to demoralize Negro Americans and weaken their will to struggle. The defense of Martin Luther King, spiritual leader of the student sit-in movement, clearly, therefore, is an integral part of the total struggle for freedom in the South.

Decent-minded Americans cannot help but applaud the creative daring of the students and the quiet heroism of Dr. King. But this is one of those moments in the stormy history of Freedom when men and women of good will must do more than applaud the rising-to-glory of others. The America whose good name hangs in the balance before a watchful world, the America whose heritage of Liberty these Southern Upholders of the Constitution are defending, is our America as well as theirs . . .

We must heed their rising voices—yes—but we must add our own.

We must extend ourselves above and beyond moral support and render the material help so urgently needed by those who are taking the risks, facing jail, and even death in a glorious re-affirmation of our Constitution and its Bill of Rights.

We urge you to join hands with our fellow Americans in the South by supporting, with your dollars, this Combined Appeal for all three needs—the defense of Martin Luther King—the support of the embattled students—and the struggle for the right-to-vote.

Your Help Is Urgently Needed . . . NOW!!

Stella Adler
Raymond Pace Alexander
Harry Van Arsdale
Harry Belafonte
Julie Belafonte
Dr. Algernon Black
Marc Blitzstein
William Branch
Marlon Brando
Mrs. Ralph Bunche
Diahann Carroll

Dr. Alan Knight Chalmers
Richard Coe
Nat King Cole
Cheryl Crawford
Dorothy Dandridge
Ossie Davis
Sammy Davis, Jr.
Ruby Dee
Dr. Philip Elliott
Dr. Harry Emerson Fosdick

Anthony Franciosa
Lorraine Hansbury
Rev. Donald Harrington
Nat Hentoff
James Hicks
Mary Hinkson
Van Heflin
Langston Hughes
Morris Iushewitz
Mahalia Jackson
Mordecai Johnson

John Killens
Eartha Kitt
Rabbi Edward Klein
Hope Lange
John Lewis
Viveca Lindfors
Carl Murphy
Don Murray
John Murray
A. J. Muste
Frederick O'Neal

L. Joseph Overton
Clarence Pickett
Shad Polier
Sidney Poitier
A. Philip Randolph
John Raitt
Elmer Rice
Jackie Robinson
Mrs. Eleanor Roosevelt
Bayard Rustin
Robert Ryan

Maureen Stapleton
Frank Silvera
Hope Stevens
George Tabori
Rev. Gardner C. Taylor
Norman Thomas
Kenneth Tynan
Charles White
Shelley Winters
Max Youngstein

We in the south who are struggling daily for dignity and freedom warmly endorse this appeal

Rev. Ralph D. Abernathy
(Montgomery, Ala.)

Rev. Fred L. Shuttlesworth
(Birmingham, Ala.)

Rev. Kelley Miller Smith
(Nashville, Tenn.)

Rev. W. A. Dennis
(Chattanooga, Tenn.)

Rev. C. K. Steele
(Tallahassee, Fla.)

Rev. Matthew D. McCollum
(Orangeburg, S. C.)

Rev. William Holmes Borders
(Atlanta, Ga.)

Rev. Douglas Moore
(Durham, N. C.)

Rev. Wyatt Tee Walker
(Petersburg, Va.)

Rev. Walter L. Hamilton
(Norfolk, Va.)

I. S. Levy
(Columbia, S. C.)

Rev. Martin Luther King, Sr.
(Atlanta, Ga.)

Rev. Henry C. Bunton
(Memphis, Tenn.)

Rev. S. S. Seay, Sr.
(Montgomery, Ala.)

Rev. Samuel W. Williams
(Atlanta, Ga.)

Rev. A. L. Davis
(New Orleans, La.)

Mrs. Katie E. Whickham
(New Orleans, La.)

Rev. W. H. Hall
(Hattiesburg, Miss.)

Rev. J. E. Lowery
(Mobile, Ala.)

Rev. T. J. Jemison
(Baton Rouge, La.)

COMMITTEE TO DEFEND MARTIN LUTHER KING AND THE STRUGGLE FOR FREEDOM IN THE SOUTH
312 West 125th Street, New York 27, N. Y. UNiversity 6-1700

Chairmen: A. Philip Randolph, Dr. Gardner C. Taylor; *Chairmen of Cultural Division:* Harry Belafonte, Sidney Poitier; *Treasurer:* Nat King Cole; *Executive Director:* Bayard Rustin; *Chairmen of Church Division:* Father George B. Ford, Rev. Harry Emerson Fosdick, Rev. Thomas Kilgore, Jr., Rabbi Edward E. Klein; *Chairman of Labor Division:* Morris Iushewitz.

"perjury"—a felony under which they could imprison him for ten years.

The article was inaccurate in the following respects:

1) The students did not sing "My Country 'Tis of Thee" on the State Capitol steps. They sang the national anthem;

2) The students were not expelled after they sang on the State Capitol steps. Nine Alabama State College students were expelled and several others were placed on probation by the president of the college, Dr. H. C. Trenholm, on orders of Governor John Patterson and the State Board of Education, after the students had requested service and sat-in at a lunch counter in the Montgomery County Courthouse;

3) Truckloads of police armed with shotguns and tear gas did not ring the Alabama State College campus, however, a substantial number of armed officers was near the campus;

4) The entire student body did not protest the expulsion by refusing to register, but a substantial number of students protested by boycotting classes on a given day;

5) Dr. King had not been arrested seven times, but had been arrested four times.

There was no excuse for the inaccuracies appearing in the advertisement. A simple phone call to me from the committee would have brought forth the correct information. During this time, the committee was working with me and other lawyers in Montgomery on Dr. King's tax case. If a copy of the advertisement had been sent to me for verification, the errors probably would have been avoided. Of course, then we might not have had a major advance in the nation's libel law, and L. B. Sullivan, Rod Nachman, and Eric Embry might not have become famous. God and the law work in mysterious ways.

The fact that the advertisement did have these errors, however, raises an interesting point. Conflicts arose from time to time in Movement work. I had a few problems during the Bus Protest with some of the members of the Montgomery Improvement Association, particularly in terms of approaches. But for the most part, all went well. There were also conflicts between Northerners and Southerners. Individual personalities, work styles and approaches differed and were evident, especially in legal cases with cross-regional co-counsel situations.

From my viewpoint, there was, and apparently still is, a tendency on the part of some Northerners to believe and assert that they know what is best; and that Southerners, white or African-American, really don't have quite as much sense as Northerners. Therefore, there was a tendency by some Northerners to make decisions and take actions without being fully aware of the facts and without conferring with Southerners who were more knowledgeable about the facts. That is what happened in this case, and it is a situation which never should have occurred.

Also, the four ministers whose names were in the ad as endorsers were not contacted for their consent prior to the time their names were used. The evidence in the case further disclosed that when the advertisement was submitted originally to the *New York Times* for publication, the ministers' endorsement was not included. Apparently, this was an afterthought. As a result of the inclusion of the minister's endorsement and as a result of the inaccuracies, the libel suits were brought and a substantial amount of resources, time and effort went into defending these individual defendants.

Among the three lawyers, we made proper preparation for trial. We prepared appropriate demurrers and other legal pleadings raising many legal issues. Our clients never caused the advertisement which appeared in the *New York Times* to be published. They had not signed the advertisement, had not given their consent, nor did they have any knowledge of its existence prior to the time it was run in the *New York Times*. The case was tried in the Circuit Court of Montgomery County on November 1–4, 1960. Roland Nachman, Jr., did the closing argument for the plaintiff, Eric Embry did the closing argument for the *New York Times*, and I did the closing argument for the four ministers.

In my closing argument, I argued that the plaintiff had failed miserably to prove 1) that any of the individual ministers gave his consent to have his name placed on the advertisement; 2) that any of the ministers published or caused to be published in the *New York Times* the advertisement in question; and, 3) that any of the ministers had prior knowledge of the publication of such an advertisement or that their names would be placed in it. Further, I argued to the jury that if they examined the list of witnesses, and there were many, only one of the witnesses mentioned the name of an individual minister. And that was Sullivan, himself.

He stated that he wrote the ministers a letter and had received no response. The letter he referred to was a letter then required under Alabama libel law prior to the time a lawsuit can be filed. In order to obtain punitive damages, a letter must be written to the person who is alleged to have published the libel information requesting a retraction. In preparation for filing his suit, Sullivan had written such a letter to each of the four ministers that we represented. None had responded.

In answer to the plaintiff's argument that our clients had failed to reply to the letter of retraction, I declared that these defendants could not "retract that which they had not tracted." This phrase drew a chuckle from the judge, the jury, and the audience. I was simply saying that in view of the fact that the ministers had not published, endorsed, nor caused to be published the advertisement, then they had no power or authority to retract something that they had not published originally. Unfortunately, the jury did not agree with my argument.

The Verdict

At the conclusion of all the evidence, the jury deliberated approximately two-and-one-half hours and brought back a verdict in favor of Commissioner Sullivan for the total amount requested, five hundred thousand dollars, against all defendants.

This case was tried six months after an all-white jury in Montgomery County had acquitted Dr. King in his tax case. We had hoped that another white jury would be able to render a verdict for African-American defendants, particularly on behalf of these ministers. The evidence in the case showed absolutely no connection between the individual defendants and the publication of the offending advertisement. However, we were unable to convince the jury. As we analyzed the case after the verdict was in, we concluded that one of the reasons the jury probably returned the verdict in favor of the plaintiff was because the *New York Times* had raised an issue as to whether or not the Alabama court had jurisdiction over the *New York Times* since it was a nonresident defendant.

We concluded that the jurors wanted to make certain the Alabama defendants remained in the lawsuit so that they would be able to keep the *New York Times* in the suit; our clients had no money, but the *Times* did. We also believed that the jury was biased and prejudiced. Even though there was no evidence to support a verdict of any sort in favor of the plaintiff, a verdict was rendered for the plaintiff.

Immediately, we prepared a motion for a new trial raising all of the issues raised before, plus additional issues.

The Appeal

We perfected an appeal by giving proper notice and acknowledging ourselves security for the costs. *The New York Times* was able to file a supersedeas bond so that no levy of its assets would take place pending appeal. Our clients did not have sufficient resources to post a supersedeas appeal bond in the amount of a million dollars. They had a right to appeal but they could not suspend the right of the plaintiff to levy upon their property pending appeal. Under normal circumstances when a case like this is on appeal, the plaintiff would not levy on property, particularly when one of the defendants has posted a bond and the case is pending.

However, these were not normal circumstances. Notwithstanding my earlier optimism after Martin's tax case acquittal, this was still Alabama and this was still a civil rights case. The plaintiff in this case was so determined to punish African Americans who were identified with the Movement that his attorneys began immediately to levy on the individual property of each of these individual, relatively poor ministers. We asked the *New York Times* lawyers if they would permit the individual ministers to piggyback on the newspaper's supersedeas bond. They denied this request, saying the *New York Times* had raised the question of jurisdiction and they believed the U.S. Supreme Court would hold that the Alabama court did not have jurisdiction, but if our individual defendants were tagging on its supersedeas bond, then that would give the Alabama court jurisdiction over the *New York Times*. The *Times* executives and attorneys were probably sympathetic to our request, but for the legal reasons given they would not permit our defendants to piggyback on the company's bond.

The matter of levying on the ministers' individual property was a very serious matter. Reverend Seay's automobile was sold in Montgomery, Reverend Shuttlesworth's automobile in Birmingham was sold, and assets of Reverend Lowery in Mobile were taken. Reverend Abernathy owned an interest in some family property that he and his siblings inherited from his parents in Marengo County. His interest was sold. All of this was done as retaliation against these men for the work that they and others were doing in the Civil Rights Movement. The plaintiff did not have the human decency to wait until the appeal was over before levying on the ministers' property.

Supreme Court, Property Regained

Ultimately, the case was appealed to the United States Supreme Court. However, my work was limited to the trial of the case in the circuit court of Montgomery County, Alabama. Based on the circuit court record, the Supreme Court on March 9, 1964, entered a precedent-setting decision. It reversed the Montgomery circuit court's verdict of five hundred thousand dollars. The Court further held that:

> [T]he rule of law applied by the Alabama Courts was unconstitutionally deficient for failure to provide the safeguards of freedom of speech and of the press that are required by the First and Fourteenth Amendments in the Libel Action brought by a public official against critics of

his official conduct, and that under the proper safeguards the evidence presented in the case was unconstitutionally sufficient to support the judgment for the plaintiff.

The Court also stated:

> The constitutional guarantees require, we think, a federal rule that prohibits a public official from recovering damages for a defamatory falsehood relating to his official conduct unless he proves that the statement was made with "actual malice"—that is, with knowledge that it was false or with reckless disregard of whether it was false or not.

After the Supreme Court reversed the case, it was remanded to the Circuit Court of Montgomery County. The plaintiff was compelled to deliver to the ministers the money which the plaintiff had received from the sale of the ministers' property. I was happy to forward to my clients this money, though this did not completely restore their losses. The plaintiff never should have sold their property pending appeal.

The Importance of the Case

Little did I realize when these four ministers asked me to represent them, that this case tried in the circuit court of Montgomery County, and the issues which we raised, including the First and Fourteenth Amendments, would ultimately develop into a landmark case of libel law.

This was the first articulation by the U.S. Supreme Court of a new standard that is now well entrenched in the law. Every law student reads and briefs the case of *Times v. Sullivan*. This case *is* libel law, as it relates to public officials, and its genesis was in the raising of funds for Dr. King to defend himself against charges of perjury in connection with his Alabama income tax returns for the years 1956 and 1958. So, in a sense, this is simply another ripple that came as a direct result of the Protest in Montgomery which started on a bus on December 1, 1955.

Times v. Sullivan has been the object of many law review articles and has been cited by many courts since its decision in 1964. In *Make No Law,* a 1991 book by Anthony Lewis, it is interesting to note that Mr. Lewis quotes the remark that I mentioned earlier from my courtroom argument. Lewis writes, "In the closing argument to the jury, Gray asked, 'how could these individual defendants retract something—if you'll pardon the expression—they didn't tract?'"

Sullivan v. New York Times was a product of the civil rights movement. As I stated in an article "The Sullivan Case: A Direct Product of the Civil Rights Movement" 42 *Case Western Reserve Law Review* 1223, 1228 (1992):

> The civil rights movement and the cases which arose out of it have not only resulted in securing the rights of African Americans, but the principles developed secure rights for all Americans including other minorities, Caucasians, women, and labor. Had there been no civil rights movement and no indictment by the State of Alabama against Dr. King in his tax perjury case, there would have been no *Times v. Sullivan.* But for the movement, libel law in Alabama and in the nation would probably be very different today. The civil rights movement set the stage for *Sullivan* and served as the catalyst for the Supreme Court's historic decision protecting our First Amendment right to freedom of press. The civil rights movement gave the Supreme Court the opportunity to announce the law that exists today regarding libel. History should note the role of the civil rights movement in enhancing the rights of every American for generations to come by the legal precepts announced in *Times v. Sullivan.*

One of the justices that participated in writing the new law of libel in *Times v. Sullivan* was Justice Hugo Black, an Alabamian who at one time had been a member of the Ku Klux Klan. Later, during the Roosevelt administration, he was appointed to serve on the Supreme Court of the United States. He was also the brother-in-law of Virginia Durr, the wife of Clifford Durr, who was one of my early mentors. Justice Hugo Black, as an Alabamian, was very conservative at the beginning of his career. However, after becoming a member of the Supreme Court, he developed into one of the greatest advocates of free speech and the right to protest, which rights we were very concerned about during the Movement.

8

Sit-ins, Freedom Rides, Freedom Walks

The decade of the fifties ended with the Civil Rights Movement in full bloom. The buses and parks were integrated in Montgomery, the Civil Rights Act of 1957 had become effective, which provided for, among other things, the creation of a Civil Rights Commission and authorized the Justice Department to bring lawsuits so African Americans could vote. So far as civil rights were concerned, the sixties opened with a bang.

Perhaps encouraged by these activities, a group of students at North Carolina A&T College in Greensboro, North Carolina, decided the time was right for them to become active in the Movement. Perhaps they realized that among the key leaders of the Montgomery Bus Protest were young men not much older than themselves—Dr. King was 26, Dr. Abernathy was 29, and I was 25, to name just three examples. In any case, the A&T students wanted to make their contribution toward breaking down the walls of segregation.

On February 1, 1960, they went to the lunch counter in the F. W. Woolworth's department store in Greensboro, sat down and requested service. They were not served lunch; rather, they were served injustice. Their activities and arrests ignited student demonstrations across the nation. In almost every town with a historically black college, African-American students would go to lunch counters. There would be sit-ins and, of course, there would be arrests. As a result of these activities, the Student Non-Violent Coordinating Committee (SNCC) was founded.

Sit-in at Montgomery Courthouse, February 1960

Students on the campus of Alabama State College, following the example of the students in North Carolina, decided to go to the lunch counter at the Montgomery County Courthouse and request service. Alabama State student leaders and participants included Bernard Lee, St. John Dixon, and Joe L. Reed, later to become one of the most powerful figures in Alabama politics. Dr. Reed also received a master's degree from my alma mater, Western Reserve University, and later became executive director of the Alabama State Teacher's Association, the African-American teachers professional organization of Alabama. Reed today is a Montgomery city councilman, chairman of the board of trustees of Alabama State University, and chairman of the Alabama Democratic Conference. This conference is one of the most influential African-American political caucuses in the nation. It was this organization that later helped elect many African Americans to public office, and influenced the elections of many more sympathetic white officials in Alabama and the appointments of two African Americans as federal district judges in Alabama.

Unlike the official reactions to student sit-ins in many parts of the nation, Montgomery County officials did not arrest the students. Probably one of the reasons the students were not arrested is because the county courthouse lunch counter was under the supervision of the sheriff of Montgomery County, not under the direct supervision of the Montgomery police department. While Sheriff Mac Sim Butler, in my opinion, believed in racial segregation, he was very considerate to African Americans during the entire Bus Protest. He did not take a position that was detrimental to our cause, nor did he cause the arrest of any African Americans who participated in Bus Protest activities, unless they had been indicted by a grand jury. Instead of arresting the students, the Montgomery courthouse officials closed the lunch counter.

John Patterson, the former Alabama attorney general, who in 1956 brought action to enjoin the NAACP from doing business, was governor of the state by 1960. He won office in a highly contested 1958 race with George C. Wallace. Patterson ran a bitterly racist campaign. George Wallace, at that time and throughout the 1958 campaign, was not considered a racist but a moderate. In fact, at that time, compared to Patterson he was practically an integrationist. Immediately after the lunch counter demonstration, Governor Patterson called Dr. H. Council Trenholm, president of Alabama State College. As governor, Patterson was the ex-officio chairman of the Alabama State board of trustees and thus was Trenholm's employer. Governor Patterson told Dr. Trenholm to find out who the students were, investigate the matter in terms of finding out which faculty members were involved, and report back to him. Also, Governor Patterson ordered the immediate expulsion of all nonresident students involved in the demonstrations. Those who were residents of Alabama and involved in the incident were suspended.

St. John Dixon v. Alabama State Board of Education

The expulsion of these nine students—Bernard Lee, Marzette Watts, Howard Shipman, St. John Dixon, Edward English Jones, Joseph Peterson, James McFadden, Leon Rice, and Elroy Embry—gave rise to the case of *St. John Dixon v. Alabama State Board of Education*. I was retained by the students to get their expulsions set aside. I filed an action in federal court on July 13, 1960, on behalf of the students, recited the facts of the expulsion, and alleged that they were being denied due process and equal protection of the law in that they were expelled without a hearing and they were being deprived of the right to an education at a state-supported institution.

Attorney Derrick Bell assisted me in representing the plaintiffs. At that time, he was a staff attorney for the NAACP Legal Defense Fund. He later became a law professor at Harvard University and is the author of several books, including *And We Are Not Saved*, *Faces At The Bottom Of The Well*, and *The Permanence Of Racism*.

The defendants were the Alabama State Board of Education, its individual members, and H. Council Trenholm, as President of Alabama State College. The defendants were represented by Alabama Attorney General MacDonald Gallion; his assistants N. S. Hare and Gordon Madison; and Robert P. Bradley, Patterson's legal adviser. As you can appreciate, President Trenholm was no more interested in defending this case then we were in suing him, but he was legally responsible. The only way he could have avoided being in this case would have been to defy Governor Patterson's order to expel the students, in which case he would have been fired from his position.

This case, as were all of my federal cases during the early years, was filed in the Middle District of Alabama before Judge Frank M. Johnson, Jr. While Judge Johnson had ruled with us in *Browder v. Gayle* in desegregating the buses, he had ruled against us in *Gomillion v. Lightfoot*, the Tuskegee gerrymandering case, and he ruled against us in this one, too. In ruling against the plaintiffs on August 26, 1960, the Court stated that these students had no constitutional right to attend college and since they had no rights, the college was free to expel them without a hearing.

Judge Johnson's decision was appealed to the U.S. Court of Appeals for the Fifth Circuit on September 13, 1960. The Fifth Circuit, with Judge Richard Rives presiding, reversed Judge Johnson. The appeals court held that students attending a public institution do have a constitutional right to obtain an education at a state institution, and prior to expulsion must receive procedural due process. The court basically said that society's interest in guaranteeing that students at state colleges are treated fairly overrides whatever minor inconvenience and costs may be involved for the schools granting the due process. [See Appendix A-4.]

The defendants appealed, but the United States Supreme Court refused to review this case.

This is a landmark case that, for the first time, held that (1) a student had a constitutional right to an education at a state-supported institution, and (2) that the due process clause of the Fourteenth Amendment requires notice and an opportunity for a hearing before a student at a tax-supported institution can be expelled for misconduct. The principle established in this case has been extended to many other areas in addition to students, to require a hearing before discharge of faculty and staff at state universities and generally to require a hearing in the employment field.

This case was one of several in which I appealed Judge Johnson's ruling and was successful in getting his decision reversed. This happened in several other cases, including *NAACP v. Alabama, Gomillion v. Lightfoot,* and *A. C. Bulls v. U.S.*

Many of Judge Johnson's critics have accused him of engaging in judicial activism or making law instead of interpreting the law. In my opinion, Judge Johnson's rulings against us in *St. John Dixon vs. Alabama State Board of Education, NAACP vs. Alabama,* and *Gomillion vs. Lightfoot* clearly point out that he was not the judicial advocate or liberal judge which some people ascribed him to be. That is particularly true when you also observe his initial ruling in *Carr v. Montgomery Board of Education,* in which he applied the Alabama pupil placement law and denied Arlam Carr, Jr., the lead plaintiff in the case, the right to attend Sidney Lanier High School the first year. Judge Johnson also ruled against us in *Alabama State Teachers Association v. Alabama State Building and College Authority,* the case in which we sought to enjoin the building of Auburn University in Montgomery. When you consider Judge Johnson's opinions in these cases, they are evidence of his conservatism in the classic sense of the word. In my opinion, he interpreted the law exactly as he believed it was presently being construed by the United States Supreme Court as mandated by the Constitution. And he went no further. Therefore, he denied relief in *Dixon, Gomillion, and Alabama State Teachers Association.* In my opinion, he did so because, as he understood and interpreted the Constitution at that time, the court was without jurisdiction to grant the relief which we requested.

Regal Cafe & MacMurray College, March 1960

On March 31, 1960, several Alabama State students and members of the Montgomery Improvement Association met with touring students and a teacher from MacMurray College of Jackson, Illinois. They had lunch in the private dining room of the

Regal Cafe, a popular African-American eatery located several blocks from Alabama State College. The MacMurray College students attentively listened to personal experiences of the recent Montgomery Bus Protest from the Alabama State students. The students at this luncheon were all arrested for disorderly conduct.

The white students from MacMurray College were Theil Baumann, Charles Bradburn, Judith Ermerling, Davis C. Gibson, Bill Hatlestad, Jacqueline Desvaux, Jeanne Bergsten, R. Edwin King, Sharon Maton, Thomas W. Ramsbey, and Jeanne Walker, along with Professor and Mrs. Richard Nesmith. All of these persons were represented by attorney Clifford Durr. I represented the African Americans: Bessie Cole, Robert Earl DuBose, Jr., James Richburg, Reverend S. S. Seay, Sr., Aner Ruth Young, Elroy Embry, and Marzette Watts. Embry and Watts were also plaintiffs in *Dixon v. Alabama State Board of Education.*

This case had interesting issues. It was not a case where African Americans were requesting services in a white restaurant, and the owner of the restaurant resisted. It was an African-American restaurant in an African-American community with an African-American owner who was perfectly willing to provide food service for the integrated group. This group was orderly, and there was no disturbance whatsoever. The police somehow learned of the luncheon, came in, and arrested all present. Notwithstanding our brilliant defense, and the brilliant defense of Mr. Durr for the whites, everyone was tried in the recorder's court of Montgomery and everyone was convicted of disorderly conduct. There was no disorderly conduct. They were convicted because a mixed racial group was having lunch in a public place.

On appeal to the Montgomery County Circuit Court, Mr. Durr defended the whites before a jury. The jury exonerated all the white students, but convicted their teacher, Professor Richard Nesmith. On appeal to the Alabama Court of Appeals, he was also exonerated.

The African Americans involved were represented in the Montgomery County Circuit Court by myself with the assistance of James M. Nabritt, III, of the NAACP Defense Fund, Solomon S.

Seay, Jr., and Charles Langford. But, at the same time Mr. Durr was trying the whites with a jury, the African-American defendants were assigned a non-jury trial. The defendants challenged the right of the two sitting circuit court judges to hear the case. However, all parties agreed that Sam Rice Baker should serve as special judge. He was a member of the firm of Steiner, Crum and Baker. Roland Nachman was, or later became, a member of that firm. The City of Montgomery was represented by Horace Perry, Walter Knabe, and Rodney R. Steele. This was a city appeal, so the attorneys for the city handled the appeal, rather than having it prosecuted in circuit court by the district attorney's office. Once the initial maneuvering was over, the trial of the African Americans was recessed, and we all went into the other courtroom and listened to the jury verdict of "Not guilty" for the white students. When our case reconvened, we moved to dismiss the case against our clients on the ground that the jury had just acquitted the white students, and they were all arrested at the same time under the same circumstances. Special Judge Baker denied the motion and found our clients guilty. They ultimately were exonerated on appeal.

Again, this shows to what length the power structure in Montgomery, during this period of time, was willing to go for the purpose of maintaining segregation. Even though we lost these cases in city court and in the circuit court, we won them on appeal. It reaffirmed my personal commitment to continue to fight toward destroying everything segregated I could find.

City of Montgomery v. King and Embry, June 1960

Edwin King, white, and Elroy Embry, African-American, were among the students arrested in the Regal Cafe with the MacMurray College group. They were released on bond. When King returned to Montgomery for trial, he registered as a guest at the Jefferson Davis Hotel. He then invited his new friend Embry to have lunch at the hotel cafe. They were promptly arrested and charged with disorderly conduct for integrating the Jefferson Davis Hotel. They were convicted. This case went up to the appellate courts several times. Finally, they were exonerated.

This is another instance where a white person and an African-American person were in a public business at the invitation of a customer whose presence was desired by the business establishment. Yet, the city officials were persistent in enforcing their segregation ordinances. Of course, I was glad to represent both of them because it assisted me in obtaining my secret goal. I only regret that King and Embry did not have bigger appetites; there is no telling how much integration we could have accomplished if they had been able to visit more cafes.

Freedom Riders, May 1961

A year later, the Freedom Riders came to Montgomery, with explosive consequences.

The announced purpose of the Freedom Rides—as they came to be called—was to test whether interstate bus facilities in the South could be used free of racial discrimination. By both executive order of the Interstate Commerce Commission and by Supreme Court precedent, travelers in interstate commerce were legally entitled to use all of the facilities in bus stations, including lunch counters and seating areas, without regard to race or color. However, as a practical matter, in most of the South the officials were still enforcing segregation in bus stations.

The plan for the Freedom Rides was developed by the Congress of Racial Equality (CORE). CORE was supported by the Southern Christian Leadership Conference and the Student Non-Violent Coordinating Committee. CORE Executive Director James Farmer was the mastermind behind the plan for the Freedom Riders. His organization had conducted a similar, smaller-scale exercise as early as 1947, as a followup to the 1946 Supreme Court ruling outlawing segregated seating on interstate buses. Of course, that ruling was also still being ignored in the South in 1961. The 1947 freedom ride—though it was not called that at the time—had been limited to Maryland, Virginia, North Carolina, and West Virginia. Even there the early freedom riders ran into trouble. Farmer recounts in the book *My Soul Is Rested*, by Howell Raines, that some members of the 1947 group were arrested and spent thirty days on a North Carolina chain gang.

The 1961 campaign was planned for participants to travel by bus throughout the South, stop at stations along the way, and integrate the facilities, especially the lunch counters. The Freedom Riders were to begin in Washington, D.C., travel to Atlanta, Birmingham, Montgomery, and on to Jackson, Mississippi. The first group to arrive in Montgomery did so with no difficulty. But when another group of Freedom Riders got to Montgomery, there was a substantial amount of violence and a mini riot occurred. President John F. Kennedy mobilized the National Guard to restore order.

The Yale Group

On May 24, 1961, an integrated group, including the dean of chaplains at Yale University, arrived at the Montgomery bus station. Three African Americans and four whites purchased tickets to Jackson, Mississippi. Shortly after they left the ticket window, they seated themselves at the lunch counter. They were served. They were not disorderly. Their actions were the perfect execution of the plan for the Freedom Riders.

They were all arrested. Included in this group were Reverend Ralph D. Abernathy, John David MacGuire, Yale University Chaplain William S. Coffin, Jr., Clyde Carter, Joseph Charles Jones, George Smith, Fred Shuttlesworth, Gaylord B. Noice, Bernard S. Lee, David E. Swift, and Wyatt T. Walker. Solomon S. Seay, Jr., and I defended them in connection with their arrest at the Trailways bus station in Montgomery. They were charged with disorderly conduct and unlawful assembly pursuant to Title 14, Section 119(1) and Section 407 Code of Alabama. After the arrest and release on bond, they attended a mass meeting at First Baptist Church. I attended the mass meeting at the church.

A riot erupted during the meeting. We attempted to leave the church but Floyd Mann, the Alabama director of public safety, told us it was unsafe to leave. He protected us. This was one of the most violent situations I experienced during the Civil Rights Movement.

I was eager and determined to see what was going on outside. I moved to a window to see what there was to see. As I was looking out of a window, a rock struck me on the side of my head. It was not a serious injury but it was probably avoidable. I should have known better than to put my face in a window when it was apparent that there was an angry mob outside. My curiosity got the best of me.

As a result of the incidents which occurred in Montgomery between May 19, 1961, and May 25, 1961, I filed a suit on behalf of John R. Lewis, Paul E. Brooks, Lucretia R. Collins, Rudolph Graham, Catherine Burks, Matthew Petway, Ralph D. Abernathy, and others similarly situated against the Greyhound Corporation, Capital Motor Lines, Continental Crescent Lines, Earl James, L. B. Sullivan, Frank Parks, Goodwin J. Ruppenthal, and others. The intervenors were George Smith, Joseph Charles Jones, Wyatt T. Walker, Bernard Lee, Fred L. Shuttlesworth, Clyde Carter, William S. Coffin, John Maguire, David Swift, and Gaylord Noice. Solomon S. Seay, Jr., Charles S. Conley, and I represented the plaintiffs and the intervenors, along with Hartwell Davis, the U. S. Attorney, and John Doar from the Justice Department. The defendants were represented by Hill, Hill, Stovall & Carter, John W. Adams, Jr., Calvin M. Whitesell, MacDonald Gallion, Hill, Robison & Belser, and Jones, Murray & Stewart.

In a memorandum opinion issued by Judge Frank M. Johnson, Jr., on November 1, 1961, he clearly stated the conditions that erupted in Montgomery around the Freedom Rides.

> A serious riot occurred at the Greyhound bus station in Montgomery, Alabama, on May 20, 1961. This incident occurred after an interracial group, known as "freedom riders," arrived in Montgomery with the announced purpose of testing the bus facilities in Montgomery to determine whether the facilities could be used without any discrimination on account of race or color.
>
> There was a crowd around the bus station as the bus arrived. After the bus parked to unload its passengers, the Greyhound bus driver announced over the loudspeaker

system, "Here comes the 'freedom riders' to tame the South."

Some of the crowd then attacked the "freedom riders." General disorder broke out and during the following two hours a number of "freedom riders" and innocent Montgomery Negroes were injured by the mob. The police were not on the scene at the time the bus arrived.

On May 19, 1961, in an action brought by the Attorney General of Alabama, one of the judges of the Circuit Court of Montgomery County, Alabama, issued a broad ex parte injunction against the "freedom riders," and on May 20, 1961, the same judge issued a contempt citation against twenty of the "freedom riders"—most, if not all of whom were on the bus that arrived at the Montgomery bus station just before the riot—charging them with a willful violation of the injunction.

The Attorney General of Alabama was at the Montgomery city police station when he received information that the bus was arriving in Montgomery. He went to the bus station and "served" a copy of the state court injunction on one of the plaintiffs who had already been beaten by the members of the mob.

Limited martial law was declared in Montgomery on the night of May 21, 1961. On May 24, the "freedom riders" who had arrived on the 20th went to the Trailways bus station in Montgomery, were served at the white lunch counter, boarded a Trailways bus and departed for Jackson, Mississippi. They were accompanied by a heavy convoy of national guardsmen.

On May 25, ten individuals, including both whites and Negroes, were arrested by Montgomery County Sheriff Mac Sim Butler at the white lunch counter in the Trailways Bus Terminal in Montgomery on charges of breach of the peace and conspiracy. These arrests were made by the sheriff under specific directions from the National Guard Commander, General Graham. Prior to their arrests, some of them had purchased tickets to Jackson, Mississippi. The group was taken to and confined in the jail.

This case was filed on May 25, 1961, by seven Negro citizens, five of whom were "riders" under injunction issued by the state court. The other two Negroes are residents of Montgomery.

The plaintiffs asked for injunctive relief against racial segregation on interstate and intrastate buses and in bus terminal facilities in the State of Alabama. They also requested relief against enforcing segregation by means of signs, arrests and other forms of harassment. Finally, they asked for injunctive relief against the enforcement of the state court injunction, including contempt proceedings.

On May 26, 1961, the ten persons arrested on May 25 at the Trailways Bus Terminal were granted leave to intervene. The supplemental complaint and complaint in intervention asked the Court to enjoin the state criminal prosecutions which were then pending in Montgomery County against the intervenors."

The complaint in *Lewis v. Greyhound* asserted three legal bases for relief:

1) that the defendants were maintaining and enforcing a policy, practice and custom of segregation in buses and bus terminal facilities, and that the complained of policy, practice, custom and usage was under state law, violated the equal protection and due process clauses of the Fourteen Amendment;

(2) that they were being discriminated against in violation of Title 49 U. S. C. Section 316(d) of the Interstate Motor Carrier Transportation Act; and

(3) that the conduct of the defendants was an unreasonable burden upon interstate commerce in violation of the commerce clause of the constitution.

After a hearing, the court granted substantially all the relief requested. The court found that Greyhound and the other defendant bus companies had been maintaining and utilizing separate facilities for the use of the two races in their terminals based on race, that the enforcement of that policy not only violated the Motor Carriers Act, but also violated the Fourteenth Amendment, and it also offended the commerce clause of the Constitution. The court further held that the closing of the restaurants in contemplation of the arrival of the Freedom Riders was not justified. The court, therefore, entered an order permanently enjoining defendants from enforcing segregation in the bus terminal facilities in Montgomery. With respect to the May 24 arrest of the integrated group, including Yale chaplain William Sloane Coffin, Judge Johnson did not enjoin the criminal prosecutions, stating that while he did not condone such activities, the state court should adequately afford these persons protection in the criminal proceedings. Ultimately these criminal proceedings were appealed to the United States Supreme Court in the case of *Abernathy v. Alabama*, and all those who had been arrested were exonerated.

This decision gave a great deal of impetus to the Freedom Riders and the Civil Rights Movement. For me personally, it was another step in destroying everything segregated.

Freedom Walkers in North Alabama, April 1963

William Moore, a letter carrier from Maryland, decided to stage a personal civil rights demonstration in which he would walk from Chattanooga, Tennessee, to Jackson, Mississippi, while carrying signs urging an end to segregation. After he crossed over the state line from Tennessee into DeKalb County, Alabama, and then later into Etowah County, on April 23, 1963, he was killed by persons unknown. So that Moore's death would not have been in vain, a series of "freedom walkers" set out to retrace his steps and then continue his walk on through Alabama and into Mississippi. This action was taken to focus public attention on the problems of racial discrimination and violence against civil rights activists.

The authorities in Alabama made clear that they did not intend to allow these demonstrations along rural north Alabama highways. It was anticipated that the walkers would be arrested, and they were. In advance of the first group setting out, CORE called on me to seek the protection of the federal courts for the right to peaceably demonstrate and march on the public roads and rights of way.

About the same time the first walkers were being arrested in DeKalb County on May 3, 1963, I was filing a complaint on their behalf. DeKalb County is in northeast Alabama, over two hundred miles from Montgomery.

Those arrested were: William Walton Hanson, Jr., Samuel Curtis Shirah, Jr., Richard Lee Haley, Winston Henry Lockett, Zev Aelony, Carver Gene Neblett, Jessie Lee Harris, John Robert Zellner, Eric Weinberger, Robert Brookins Gore, Landy McNair, and James Rufus Forman. Some were white and some were African-American.

I filed the lawsuit, *John Robert Zellner v. Al Lingo, Director of Public Safety for the State of Alabama,* in federal court in Montgomery. Derrick A. Bell, Jr., and George Smith of the NAACP Legal Defense Fund assisted me in this case. The named plaintiff, Bob Zellner, was a white Montgomerian who had somehow been converted to the cause of civil rights while a student at Huntingdon College, a small Methodist-supported institution in Montgomery.

The defendants were represented by Alabama Attorney General Richmond Flowers and Assistant Attorney General Gordon Madison, with John P. Kohn and Hugh Maddox as attorneys for Al Lingo. Hugh Maddox was a former law clerk to Judge Frank Johnson, later served as legal adviser to Governor George Wallace, and is now a justice on the Alabama Supreme Court.

On May 18, after the arrests and after the authorities had gotten a state-court injunction against such marches, we amended the complaint and added more defendants. Each defendant moved to dismiss the complaint as last amended, alleging as grounds for dismissal, among other things, the court's lack of jurisdiction over the subject matter, the individual defendants, and that the court should not exercise its jurisdiction in this particular case in enjoining these criminal proceedings.

In an order dated June 19, 1963, Judge Johnson reviewed the facts of the state's interference with the marchers' peaceful and constitutional actions, asserted the court's jurisdiction over both the subject matter and the parties, and traced the decisions of the Supreme Court dealing with whether a federal court should enjoin criminal proceedings in state courts. [See Appendix A-5.] The court concluded that under the decisions of the Supreme Court it should not exercise its federal jurisdiction, and dismissed the complaint. Judge Johnson did not enjoin the criminal proceedings against the freedom walkers, because those criminal proceedings could be adequately reviewed through the state court system. That is exactly what we did. We appealed the cases through the state court system and won.

I represented the freedom walkers in the DeKalb County Court at Fort Payne, Alabama, on June 3, 1963, before the Honorable W. G. Hawkins, without a jury, under a joint complaint, charging them with breach of the peace. Before entering not guilty pleas, I filed various pleadings—challenging the constitutionality of the arrest, challenging the complaint and raising the constitutional issues we usually raised in these type cases. At the conclusion of the trial, Landy McNair and James Forman were exonerated. The other ten were convicted and fined two hundred dollars each. The case was appealed and ultimately they were exonerated by the Alabama Court of Appeals in the case of *William Walton Hanson, Jr., v. Alabama* on August 18, 1964.

Another series of individuals was arrested in Etowah County, which is south of DeKalb County. Included in those arrested in Etowah County was a white actress named Madeleine Sherwood. On June 7, 1963, she sent me a telegram which stated:

"I authorize you to represent me as defense counsel criminal action pending in Etowah County, Alabama."

I represented her along with Anna Pearl Avery, Paul E. Brooks, Wavelyn Holmes, Mary Ann Thomas, Eddie Harris, David Darling, Diane Bevel and Robert Jones in Etowah County.

When these cases were called to trial, an agreement was reached between the parties as follows:

(1) That the case of defendant Madeleine Annette

Sherwood only shall be tried, and the cases of the other defendants shall be continued from term to term pending a final determination on the merits by the highest appellate court of the case of said defendant Madeleine Annette Sherwood.

(2) That said final determination of the case of defendant Sherwood on the merits shall furnish controlling precedent for the disposition of the cases of the other defendants by the County Court of Etowah County and such disposition shall be conclusive on all of the defendants herein above named.

Since William Moore was killed in Etowah County, the spot in and around his death became a major rallying point for civil rights groups across the nation. This group, which I represented, was a small one compared to the total number arrested. Other groups were represented by Oscar Adams and U. W. Clemon, who both practiced in Birmingham. Ultimately, all the defendants were exonerated.

During this period of time, Gadsden, the county seat of Etowah, became a focal point for many civil rights demonstrations. Q. D. Adams, an African-American businessman, coordinated the civil rights activities and signed the bonds for those arrested. He is one of the unsung heroes of the Civil Rights Movement. He is still active in Gadsden, and is chairman of the Etowah County unit of the Alabama Democratic Conference. This unit is very instrumental in electing local officials in Etowah County and in electing statewide officials through the Alabama Democratic Conference.

In 1990, I received a phone call from a person who identified herself as Madeleine Sherwood. She told me that she was in Montgomery and wanted to know if I was the lawyer who represented her many years ago. She told me she was just retracing her steps in the Civil Rights Movement and wanted to talk with me if I had an opportunity. My schedule did not permit it for that day, and the next day I was scheduled to go out of town, but I told her that if she could meet me at the airport, I would come early enough so that we could spend a few moments together. She came, met me at the airport, and we talked and reminisced over what took place over twenty years before.

All the demonstration cases in Montgomery, DeKalb and Etowah Counties in which I represented both African Americans and whites in protecting their constitutional rights reflected a furtherance of my goal to destroy segregation anyplace I could find it. I represented all persons regardless of race, color, religion or previous condition of servitude. If those persons' rights were being violated, I was willing to assist. That is what I have done for the past forty years.

9

"With All Deliberate Speed"

Segregation was the order of the day when I was admitted to practice law in Alabama in September 1954. We were segregated from the cradle to the grave, from the toilet to the train, from the courtroom to the classroom.

Segregated classrooms were of special concern to African Americans because the lack of access to equal education was like a big weight around our necks, always holding us back. During slavery time, of course, it had become illegal in Alabama and elsewhere in the South to teach African Americans to read and write. This was largely because of the fear by whites of slave revolts, and it was correctly assumed that the more education a slave gained, the more difficult it would be to keep him in bondage. After slavery came "separate but equal," which was one of history's big lies. The disparity between white and African-American educational systems was huge in every respect, from the condition of facilities to teacher's salaries, from the quality of textbooks to the availability of school buses, from the existence of libraries to the length of the school year. In my home town of Montgomery, to cite just one example, there was not even a public high school open to African-American youth until after World War II. I myself, you will recall, was sent by my mother to a church school in Nashville. I then attended a completely segregated college, and had to leave Alabama to find a law school that admitted African Americans.

That African Americans gained education at all under these circumstances was remarkable, and yet the thirst for knowledge had always been enormous in our communities. We often built our own schools, sometimes with no help and sometimes with the aid of private or religious philanthropy and whatever public funding we could get. As the vestiges of slavery slowly receded, conditions gradually improved. But slowly and gradually were the keys.

Only four months before I began the practice of law, the United States Supreme Court announced its decision in the consolidated cases, *Brown v. Board of Education*. The triumph of this case was in large measure due to Thurgood Marshall, a great gentleman and a truly brilliant lawyer. Later, it would be my privilege to work with him on several cases, and my very great honor to count him as a friend. Ultimately, of course, he served with distinction on the Supreme Court, the first African American to do so.

Brown v. Board of Education quite simply declared that segregated public schools were not equal, never had been equal, and never could be equal, and thus violated the Constitution. This decision was welcomed by African Americans as if it were a second emancipation.

But there was a catch.

Having made its ruling, the Court failed to carefully and completely spell out how this tremendous change in the social order was to be implemented and enforced by the legislative and executive branches of government. Instead, the Court simply declared that public education should become integrated with "all deliberate speed." No one knew what that meant. But it gave the South years of room to evade the intent of the Court's decision.

When the Bus Protest started in Montgomery in December 1955, there was no integration whatsoever in the educational systems in Alabama. In late 1955 and throughout 1956, I was very involved in matters related to the Bus Protest. I had little time to devote to the whole issue of desegregation of schools in Alabama.

Desegregating the University of Alabama

However, the NAACP and other civil rights groups across the nation were significantly involved in litigation concerning education. They initiated lawsuits to desegregate elementary and secondary schools and higher education systems which had graduate and professional schools. Among these lawsuits was one filed in 1953 by Arthur Shores, Thurgood Marshall and other lawyers for the NAACP Legal Defense Fund, on behalf of Autherine Lucy, a young woman who wanted to attend the University of Alabama. The case, *Autherine J. Lucy v. Board of Trustees of the University of Alabama* was filed in Birmingham, in the United States District Court for the Northern District of Alabama on July 3, 1953. Autherine Lucy was ordered admitted. After her admission, she was expelled, allegedly because of certain statements she and her lawyers made with reference to certain state and school officials. Therefore, the university remained segregated.

In 1962, several civil rights groups across the state were actively seeking African Americans who were interested in enrolling in the University of Alabama, Auburn University, and other historically white state institutions. I was contacted by the NAACP Legal Defense Fund to determine whether I would represent persons who desired to attend those universities. Of course, I said yes.

James Hood of Gadsden and Vivian Malone of Mobile were interested in attending the University of Alabama. Vivian was recruited by John LeFlore, a great civil rights leader from Mobile, Alabama, who passed several years ago. The work of John LeFlore in Mobile paralleled that of E. D. Nixon in Montgomery. John LeFlore was employed by the U.S. Postal Service, and, like E. D. Nixon, was thus insulated from attacks by his employer. LeFlore High School in Mobile is named in his honor. John LeFlore was the father-in-law of the Honorable Horace Ward, the first African-American federal district judge in Georgia.

The suit was filed by Vivian J. Malone, a minor, by her mother, Bertha Malone; Sandy English; and Jimmy A. Hood, a minor, by his father, Octavia Hood, against Hubert E. Mate, dean of admissions of the University of Alabama. Joining me as attorneys for the plaintiffs were Arthur Shores, Constance Motley, and Leroy D. Clark. Representing the defendant was the law firm of Moore, Thomas, Taliaferro, Forman and Burr of Birmingham.

This case was tried before Judge H. H. Grooms. The Court

ordered Vivian Malone and James Hood admitted to the university. James Hood later withdrew for personal reasons.

This case was filed on April 15, 1963, during the first administration of Governor George C. Wallace. He had been defeated in 1958 when he ran as a relative moderate against an outspoken racist. After that loss, Wallace was reported as declaring he would never be "out-segged again." And, in this instance at least, Wallace was a man of his word.

He campaigned in 1962 on a straight segregation platform. In his inaugural speech, he uttered the infamous phrase, "Segregation now, segregation tomorrow, and segregation forever," words written for him by Asa Carter, a notorious but verbally gifted freelance white supremacist who was an "adviser" to the governor. Wallace then flew the Confederate battle flag on the dome of the state capitol. He caused the Alabama Legislature to pass numerous resolutions of nullification and interposition defying the Supreme Court and its various orders commanding an end to segregation.

How much of this was political posturing and how much was the actual philosophy of George C. Wallace, I do not know. As I mentioned earlier, Wallace was always cordial to me, and when I interviewed him for this book, he admitted that he had been wrong in many of the things he had done with respect to segregation. I felt he was making a sincere apology. Certainly, over the years, and especially as African Americans gained the vote, Wallace softened his attitude. He was elected to his fourth and final term with the support of many African Americans.

But in 1963, as the governor of Alabama, Wallace was the ex-officio chairman of the board of trustees of the University of Alabama. In his official capacity, Wallace threatened to defy U.S. District Judge H. H. Grooms's order in the Malone case. Wallace promised to personally block Vivian Malone from entering and integrating the University of Alabama.

The stage was set. There were many conferences and phone calls among Governor Wallace, U.S. Attorney General Robert Kennedy, Nicholas Katzenbach, and others with reference to the "stand in the schoolhouse door." As the television cameras rolled and the press cameras clicked, George Wallace made his stand. And then he stood aside.

Malone was admitted to the University of Alabama, thus ending the longstanding tradition of segregation in higher education in the state and at the University of Alabama. Today, the University of Alabama has one of the highest percentages of African-American student enrollment of any predominantly white Southern university. It is my hope that the University of Alabama is to remain integrated forever.

Although my primary responsibility to Vivian Malone was to get her admitted, I continued to be concerned about her while she was at the university. On July 31, 1963, I wrote to her:

> This is just a note to say that we are all proud of you for the way you have conducted yourself under such tremendous pressure. As your attorney, I am particularly proud of the fact that you have not seen fit to make public statements which would tend to embarrass you or the race. It has been our opinion all along that the fewer statements made, the better your chances will be to receive a normal education.
>
> We trust everything is going smoothly for you at the University, and would like to know how you are progressing in your studies.

She responded immediately:

> I am progressing steadily at the University. There is a lot of grind because classes are somewhat condensed during the summer sessions; however, I managed to "cook up" an A in algebra and a B in political science last session. I'm enrolled in the School of Commerce this session, and it's a rather tough department.
>
> It is my sincere hope that everything continues in the same manner as it has in the past.

Notwithstanding the Malone victory, it is ironic that twenty-one years later, I was back in court in Birmingham participating in a six-month trial, *Knight v. State of Alabama,* which alleged that vestiges of discrimination still remain in higher education in Alabama, including the University of Alabama. On December 27, 1991, U.S. District Judge Harold Murphy from Rome, Georgia, sitting specially in this case, entered a final order dealing with segregation in higher education in Alabama. Judge Murphy found that vestiges of racial discrimination still existed in Alabama, including at the University of Alabama, and he enjoined further discrimination.

The Most Segregated Institution in Alabama

The other flagship white educational institution in Alabama is Auburn University, a land grant institution located in east central Alabama across the state from the University of Alabama, which is located in Tuscaloosa in northwest Alabama.

No African Americans had attended Auburn University before January 2, 1964. The law in the field of higher education was clear for many years. As far back as 1950, with the case of *Sweatt v. Painter* in Texas and *McLaurin v. Oklahoma State Regents For Higher Education,* the Supreme Court had held that African Americans were entitled to attend graduate and professional schools at historically white universities. However, there was no such integration at Auburn University or the University of Alabama on the graduate level. Vivian Malone was enrolled at the University of Alabama in 1963 as an undergraduate.

Harold Franklin, a graduate of Alabama State College, desired a master's degree in history. He applied for admission to Auburn University and was denied admission because "he had graduated from an unaccredited college." When Franklin entered Alabama State College, it was accredited by the Southern Association of Colleges and Schools.

However, by the time of Franklin's graduation, Alabama State was not accredited. The college had lost its accreditation because the State of Alabama failed to properly fund it so it could comply with the accreditation standards. Consequently, Alabama State was deficient in several standards required by the Southern Association of Colleges and Schools. Franklin's admission to Auburn University was denied.

Harold Franklin retained me to represent him. I obtained the services of NAACP Legal Defense Fund attorneys Constance Baker Motley and Leroy Clark. A suit was filed in federal court, *Harold A. Franklin v. William V. Parker, Dean Graduate School of Auburn University, Charles W. Edwards, Registrar of Auburn University.* The defendants were represented by Sanford & Sanford of Opelika and Hill, Hill, Stovall & Carter of Montgomery.

Judge Frank M. Johnson, Jr., in an opinion dated November 5, 1963, ordering Franklin's admission, stated:

Franklin was rejected on one basis: He had not been graduated from a college that held an accredited status with the Southern Association of Colleges and Schools. Thus the State of Alabama has denied to Harold A. Franklin, a Negro—solely because he is a Negro—the opportunity to receive an undergraduate education at an accredited state college or university; at the same time, the State of Alabama afforded adequate opportunity to its white citizens to receive an undergraduate education at accredited State institutions. Now, after having done this, the State of Alabama, acting through its State operated and maintained institution Auburn University, insists that graduate education at that institution shall be open only to students who are graduates of accredited colleges or universities. On its face, and standing alone, the requirement of Auburn University concerning graduation from an accredited institution as a prerequisite to being admitted to Graduate School is unobjectionable and a reasonable rule for a college or university to adopt. However, the effect of this rule upon Harold A. Franklin—an Alabama Negro—and others in his class who may be similarly situated, is necessarily to preclude him from securing a postgraduate education at Auburn University solely because the State of Alabama discriminated against him in its undergraduate schools. Such racial discrimination on the part of the State of Alabama amounts to a clear denial of the equal protection of the laws. This is true regardless of the good motives or purposes that Auburn University may have concerning the rule in question.

After Franklin was admitted, court action was required to gain proper housing. Auburn assigned him to a dormitory. However, he was the only person assigned to a wing of a dormitory which was able to accommodate approximately one hundred students. Harold Franklin is now a professor of history at Talladega College in Talladega, Alabama.

With the *Franklin* and *Malone* decisions, the two white flagship education institutions in Alabama were desegregated. However, as you will see, winning these cases was not the end of the road; we closely monitored the continuing actions of higher education institutions in Alabama with respect to racial discrimination, especially at Auburn University.

Strain v. Philpott, Alabama Cooperative Extension Service

Auburn University was designated by the Alabama legislature as the land-grant university to receive state and federal funds for the operation of a cooperative extension service in Alabama. The Alabama Cooperative Extension Service (ACES) provides certain services for farmers in all sixty-seven Alabama counties. For many years, there was complete segregation in ACES. Willie Strain was an employee of the Extension Service. In 1971, he retained our firm to file a class action suit on his behalf and on behalf of other African-American ACES employees.

The complaint in *Willie L. Strain v. Harry M. Philpott, as President of Auburn University* alleged:

(1) that ACES has provided its services on a racially segregated and discriminatory basis;

(2) that ACES discriminates against African Americans in

hiring, promotion and in the terms and condition of employment;

(3) that ACES has maintained racially segregated 4-H and demonstration clubs;

(4) that ACES discriminated against Strain solely on the basis of race in filling the position of chairman of the Division of Information of ACES.

Assisting me in this case were Solomon S. Seay, Jr., and attorneys for the NAACP Legal Defense Fund. The defendants were represented by Sanford & Sanford of Opelika and Hill, Hill Stovall & Carter of Montgomery.

After a full hearing, the court ruled in favor of the plaintiffs. The court found that the Alabama Cooperative Extension Service is the state administrative agency for the execution and coordinaton of such services in the state of Alabama. ACES is headed by a state director, who is responsible to the president of Auburn University and its board of trustees. This position had always been filled by a white person. Prior to June 7, 1965, ACES provided and maintained a dual system of services and benefits, which was based on race. There were, in fact, two systems, one for whites and one for blacks. There were separate staffs and separate responsibilities, but the ultimate responsibility for all of the activities was with the director. This segregated program existed throughout all of the activities of ACES.

Based upon the court's findings of fact, it entered an order finding that Auburn University operated a racially discriminatory system and directed that Auburn take corrective actions toward employing, promoting, and giving African Americans an opportunity for advancement within the Cooperative Extension Service. [See Appendix A-6.]

Since 1971, on several occasions, we have petitioned the court for further relief because Auburn University continued to discriminate based on race. As recently as l990, a motion for additional relief was filed in the same case—*Strain v. Alabama Extension Service* by attorney Seay on behalf of Mr. Strain and other individuals.

Dr. James Smith, the affirmative action officer for Auburn

University, asked me to represent him in an employment discrimination action. It is remarkably ironic that a university's affirmative action officer had to take it to court over employment discrimination. Dr. Smith was permitted to intervene in the *Strain v. Alabama Extension Service* case. He alleged in the petition that Auburn University discriminated against him, in that it passed over him for promotion, filling the positions by less qualified whites.

Originally, I tried this case with Solomon Seay and others. It is interesting to note that twenty years later, in September 1991, the same case was tried again with attorney Seay. But, instead of me arguing in federal court, there was my son, Fred Jr. Fred was ten years old and attending Tuskegee Public School at the time of the original case.

My son's representation of Dr. Smith is part of my continuing battle "to destroy everything segregated I could find." I assigned Dr. Smith's case to my son after I felt he had gained sufficient experience and expertise to handle such a case. He prepared the case and worked with Dr. Smith.

Before the trial, I asked Dr. Smith, "Are you satisfied with your young lawyer?" and "How do you feel about going to court with your young lawyer?" Dr. Smith said he was satisfied.

I asked Fred the same kind of questions. I asked him, "Are you satisfied that you can adequately represent Dr. Smith." He said he was satisfied.

Both of them were satisfied. They were ready to go to court. After an evidentiary hearing, the court entered an order that the defendants had violated prior orders of the court. On June 23, 1992, the court ordered the Alabama Cooperative Extension Service to vacate the positions of assistant director of field operations and government relations and of assistant to the director—marketing relations; and to conduct a national search to fill the positions in accordance with the procedures set forth in the court's own order of twenty years earlier. Although *Franklin* integrated Auburn University over twenty-six years ago, and *Strain* integrated the Alabama Cooperative Extension Service soon thereafter, Auburn University has nevertheless been slow to integrate its student body and faculty. Many people feel that Auburn University was the most segregated institution of higher learning in Alabama.

Florence State College Desegregated, 1963

On August 20, 1963, I filed the case *Gunn v. Norton* on behalf of a young man who sought admission to Florence State College.

Wendell Gunn, his parents, and I were members of the same church—the Church of Christ. He graduated years after I did, but Wendell and I attended the same church-related school—Nashville Christian Institute in Nashville, Tennessee. After graduation Wendell wanted to return to Florence, Alabama, and attend Florence State College (now the University of North Alabama).

An excellent musician and student, Wendell Gunn enjoyed a sterling reputation among African Americans and whites in the city of Florence. The president, faculty and students of Florence State wanted Wendell to attend Florence State.

President Ethebert B. Norton wrote a letter informing Gunn that Florence State College was not authorized to admit African Americans. The letter read:

Mr. Wendell W. Gunn
Route Three
Tuscumbia, Alabama
Dear Mr. Gunn:

Upon my arrival at my office on the morning of July 30 [1963], I found on my desk a letter which had been addressed by you and apparently placed on my desk after closing hours on July 29.

This is to acknowledge your letter and your personal check on the First National Bank of Tuscumbia for $25.00 which you requested that I consider as the deposit required for the completion of an application for admission into Florence State College.

In accordance with the information which I have given to you informally in a series of conversations since July 11,

I hereby inform you that neither the Legislature of Alabama nor the State Board of Education has granted to Florence State College the authority to enroll a Negro student in this institution. I am, therefore, returning, herewith, your check for $25.00 with the information that your application is not now being processed for enrollment in September.

You will recall, I am sure, that there are two Negro colleges in Alabama under the supervision and control of the State Board of Education.

Yours sincerely,
s/E. B. Norton
President
EBN:map
Enclosure—check

This was all we needed. A lawsuit was filed in the United State District Court, Northern District of Alabama, with Judge H. H. Grooms presiding. The lawyer representing Florence State was Gordon Madison, Alabama assistant attorney general. The trial was held in the federal court building in Birmingham, Alabama. In an unprecedented desegregation trial, which took all of ten minutes, an order was entered directing Gunn's admission to Florence State. The president and other officials of the college drove Gunn from Birmingham to Florence State. He was enrolled immediately.

This was the easiest civil rights case I had the pleasure of handling. After Gunn was admitted, he related to me some of his experiences. In a December 1963 letter, he wrote:

I'm getting along fine in school, I suppose. As you know, I'm in the choir and we're having our annual Christmas concert on Sunday, Dec. 8th, at 3:30 p.m. The teachers and students treat me okay for the most part. Those who don't treat me nice, don't treat me at all. If I can hold out a while longer, I may even make the honor roll this semester...

I guess the weekend tragedy has everyone stirred up. I received an anonymous call last night, saying that someone was out to get me and I'd better stay at home. And a few minutes ago, when I was on the highway, coming home, some white fellows pulled up beside me as if they were looking for trouble. So I guess for the next few days, I'll be staying home after nightfall. No need in taking chances.

Gunn became an outstanding member of the choir and a loyal alumnus of Florence State College. He became a very influential person in President Reagan's administration with an office in the White House. Currently, he serves as vice president of Met Life in New York.

Conclusion, Colleges and Universities

Except for the University of Alabama, University of South Alabama at Mobile, Montevallo State College and Auburn University, the other state-supported institutions of higher learning which were in existence in the fifties and early sixties were under the supervision and control of the State Board of Education. These institutions were Troy State College, Livingston State College, Alabama State College, Jacksonville State College, Florence State College and Alabama A&M. These state-supported institutions of higher learning were integrated as a result of *Lee v. Macon*, which I filed on January 28, 1963, and will discuss below. I had thus filed lawsuits which resulted in the integration of all the formerly white state-supported institutions of higher learning in Alabama.

Desegregation of Elementary and Secondary Schools

On May 17, 1954, the United States Supreme Court in the case of *Brown v. Board of Education* entered an order which stated that separate elementary and secondary schools for children based on race violated the due process provision of the fourteenth amendment of the United States Constitution. It stated that in the field of education, the "separate but equal" doctrine has no legal standing. It also stated that separate schools for Negroes and whites were unconstitutional. Even though the U.S. Supreme Court decision in the case of *Brown v. Board of Education* had been on the record since 1954, there was still no elementary and secondary school integration in Alabama in 1963. These institutions continued to exist on a segregated basis just as they had existed for many years.

The African-American community in Alabama realized that the most difficult area to integrate would be the state's elementary and high schools. By the early part of the 1960s, there had been some token integration. The buses in Montgomery had been integrated in *Browder v. Gayle* (1956). The parks in Montgomery had been desegregated with *Gilmore v. Montgomery* (1959). Auburn University (1963), the University of Alabama (1963), and Florence State College (1963) had been integrated in cases that I described above. The only lawsuits that had been filed to integrate elementary and secondary schools in Alabama at that time were probably cases in Birmingham, Jefferson County and Mobile. These cases were bogged down in technicalities of one kind or another. Thus, elementary and high schools remained segregated.

The NAACP Legal Defense Fund and the NAACP spearheaded most of the litigation involving school desegregation in Alabama. The legal strategy was to select forums where there were federal district judges who would be most likely to follow the law established in *Brown v. Board of Education* and rule favorably in these cases. So, to some degree, we did do some forum shopping.

In the Middle District of Alabama, Judge Frank M. Johnson, Jr., even this early in his judicial career, had a proven record of following decisions of the Supreme Court. He did this at the expense of being socially ostracized by the white establishment and being severely and unjustly criticized by politicians, the media, and other influential white institutions and leaders, not to mention the average white citizen of that period in Alabama. During one of his earlier cases, the home of Judge Johnson's mother was bombed; it was assumed that the bombers had meant the device for him but were confused by the similarity of his father's name and went to the wrong address.

Because I practiced in the Middle District of Alabama, it was logical that the NAACP Legal Defense Fund would want my assistance with lawsuits in the district. Montgomery and central Alabama were also reasonable areas to file such lawsuits because African Americans there had made substantial gains in winning the cases to integrate buses and parks. The African-American community there was unified. It had the courage and the desire to tackle the horrendous task of integrating public schools—and so did I.

Abraham's Vineyard, Harrison Elementary

Prior to the filing of a lawsuit to integrate the elementary and secondary schools, a unique situation existed in Montgomery, Alabama. In the southern part of the city, there was a small African-American community called "Abraham's Vineyard." This community had existed for many years. There were approximately two streets in that community where African Americans resided. Whites lived in all of the residential areas that surrounded Abraham's Vineyard.

A new elementary school, Harrison Elementary, had been built adjacent to the streets where African Americans lived. The parents of these children wanted their children to attend the "new neighborhood school" instead of being bused across town to the old African-American school—Booker T. Washington Elementary School. In 1953 the parents of Abraham's Vineyard contacted E. D. Nixon. He contacted a young, white lawyer, Nesbitt Elmore, whose law books I had borrowed for the open house when I opened my law practice in 1954. Elmore was also the nephew of attorney Clifford Durr, who was a very good friend and my legal mentor. Attorney Elmore was retained to handle the case.

Elmore petitioned the school board for admission of these students. Harrison Elementary School was nearest to the homes of the African-American children, and was the neighborhood school. There was absolutely no legal rationale for denying their admission. But the petition was denied. Harrison Elementary School remained segregated. The children and the parents were disappointed and so was their lawyer, Nesbitt Elmore. This was a very interesting case and a very courageous act for a white lawyer in Montgomery. Attorney Elmore and his family were criticized severely and harassed as a result of his handling this case.

During the early sixties, the NAACP and the African-American community nationwide intensified efforts to integrate public schools. Schools were integrated in Little Rock, Arkansas; Richmond, Virginia; and other Southern cities, but not in Alabama. Ten years had passed since the decision in *Brown v. Board of Education*, and there wasn't a single African-American child in a white elementary or secondary school in the state of Alabama. In 1969, in a case I filed, *Carr v. Montgomery County Board of Education,* the United States Supreme Court described conditions of the schools in Alabama:

> The record shows that neither Montgomery County nor any other area in Alabama voluntarily took any effective steps to integrate the public schools for about 10 years after our *Brown* opinion. In fact the record makes clear that state government and its school officials attempted in every way possible to continue the dual system of racially segregated schools in defiance of our repeated unanimous holdings that such a system violated the United States Constitution.

I was retained to file a series of simultaneous cases before Judge Johnson for the purpose of finally integrating public elementary and secondary schools in Alabama. There were five lawsuits, each concerning a separate school system: *Harris v. Bullock County Board of Education*; *Franklin v. Barbour County Board of Education*; *Harris v. Crenshaw County Board of Education*; *Lee v. Macon County Board of Education*; and *Carr v. Montgomery County Board of Education*.

The cases were strikingly similar. Each was a class-action suit in which Judge Johnson appointed the United States as amicus curiae, or "friend of the court." In each case the plaintiffs were African-American parents, who filed suit on behalf of their children for the purpose of integrating the respective school system. The State of Alabama at that time had adopted many laws designed to keep African-American children from enrolling in white schools, including the adoption of a "Pupil Placement Law," which gave local school boards broad authority to assign pupils to designated schools.

Most of these cases were decided uneventfully in favor of the plaintiffs. Therefore, the elementary and high schools of Barbour, Bullock and Crenshaw counties were integrated by court orders without major incidents.

Carr v. Montgomery County Board of Education

This case was similar to the school desegregation cases filed against the Barbour, Bullock, Crenshaw and Macon counties boards of education. The case was filed on May 11, 1964. Judge Johnson appointed the United States as amicus curiae. The lead plaintiffs were Johnnie Carr and her husband, Arlam, on behalf of their son, Arlam Carr, Jr.

Mrs. Carr was one of the organizers of the bus protest. Also, she was a schoolmate of Rosa Parks. Later she was elected president of the Montgomery Improvement Association, a position she still holds. She is more than eighty years old and still going strong. The other plaintiffs in the suit were Bathsheba Thompson, John Thompson, James Thompson, and Phillip Thompson, minors, by Bishop S. Thompson, Sr., and Lois E. Thompson, their parents.

The defendants were the Montgomery County Board of Education and its members. Solomon S. Seay, Jr., my law partner, and attorneys from the NAACP Legal Defense Fund assisted me. The defendants were represented by Vaughan Hill Robison and Joseph D. Phelps, who is now an outstanding circuit judge in Montgomery County.

After a full-scale hearing, Judge Johnson entered an order on July 31, 1964, finding that the defendants operated a dual school system based on race and color and directed that the school systems in Montgomery be integrated. The court order admitted eight

African-American students out of the twenty-nine who had sought transfers to white schools.

Arlam Carr, Jr., desired to attend Sidney Lanier High School, the white high school in the city of Montgomery at that time. However, through the use of the Alabama pupil placement law, even though he was the lead plaintiff in the suit, he was not assigned to Sidney Lanier High School the first year. He remained at an African-American school. All of us were disappointed that Arlam could not attend Lanier that year. In subsequent years, Arlam was assigned to Lanier. He graduated from Lanier in 1968. Arlam Carr, Jr., is now a TV director/producer at the local NBC affiliate in Montgomery, WSFA Channel 12.

Several years after the original decision in *Carr*, the Montgomery County Board of Education had made little progress with respect to integrating its faculty. For that reason, Judge Johnson, in an order entered in 1968, provided that the board must move toward a goal under which "in each school the ratio of white to black faculty members is substantially the same as it is throughout the system." In addition, the order set forth a specific schedule for goals and numerical time-tables. Ultimately, the case was heard before the United States Supreme Court. The United States Supreme Court affirmed Judge Johnson's order and stated that his plan "promises realistically to work and promises realistically to work now."

Judge Johnson, therefore, concluded that a more specific order would be appropriate under all the circumstances to establish the minimum amount of progress that would be required for the future. To this end, his order provided that the board must move toward a goal under which "in each school the ratio of white to Negro faculty members is substantially the same as it is throughout the system." In addition, the order set forth a specific schedule. The ratio of Negro to white teachers in the assignment of substitute, student and night school teachers in each school was to be almost immediately made substantially the same as the ratio of Negro to white teachers in each of these groups for the system as a whole.

With respect to full-time teachers, a more gradual schedule was set forth. At the time, the ratio of white to Negro full-time teachers in the system as a whole was three to two. For the 1968-1969 school year, each school with fewer than twelve teachers was required to have at least two full-time teachers whose race was different from the race of the majority of the faculty at that school, and in schools with twelve or more teachers, the race of at least one out of every six faculty and staff members was required to be different from the race of the majority of the faculty and staff members at that school. The goals to be required for future years were not specified but were reserved for later decision.

About a week later Judge Johnson amended part of the original order by providing that in the 1968-1969 term, schools with less than twelve teachers would be required to have only one full-time teacher of the minority race rather than two, as he had originally required.

The Importance of the Case

The significance of this case is that for the first time the United States Supreme Court approved "quotas, goals, and numerical time-tables" as corrections for past discrimination. Many subsequent cases relied upon this decision to increase the number of African Americans not only on faculties and in student bodies, but also in many other positions, particularly in employment. The use of goals and numerical time-tables for relief in affirmative action cases can find its genesis in the *Carr* case.

Lee v. Macon County Board of Education, January 1963

The Macon County school case began similarly to the other school cases I filed in Alabama, but had some key differences. For one thing, the county population was—and is—about 85 percent African-American. For another, the county is the home of Tuskegee Institute (now Tuskegee University), founded in 1881; as we have already seen in the famous gerrymander case, there was well-organized African-American activism in the county in the form of the Tuskegee Civic Association (TCA). A third big difference was that after the case was filed and the courts ordered the Macon

County schools to integrate, the local white citizens prepared to do so without further struggle. That led to the fourth and biggest difference, the injection by Governor George C. Wallace of state politics into this local school case.

I filed the lawsuit on January 28, 1963, at the request of the TCA. However, TCA member Detroit Lee had wanted me to file such a lawsuit several years earlier, at a time when I was busy with some prior litigation. I promised Mr. Lee then that if he would wait, I would make him lead plaintiff. I identified with his anxiety and desire to file the lawsuit earlier. I had been eager myself to file a lawsuit to integrate the Montgomery buses in March 1955 after Claudette Colvin was arrested, but then had to wait nine months for Mrs. Parks to be arrested before the time was right.

So I could understand Detroit Lee's impatience and was happy to keep my promise to him when I filed *Lee v. Macon County Board of Education*. The lead plaintiffs* were Anthony T. Lee and Henry A. Lee, by Detroit Lee and Hattie M. Lee, their parents.

I was assisted by my law partner, Solomon Seay, Jr., and Constance Motley of the NAACP Legal Defense Fund. The suit was initially filed against the Macon County Board of Education, its individual members and the county superintendent of educa-tion,* just as we had done in similar cases. They were represented by Alabama Attorney General Richmond M. Flowers and his assistants, Robert P. Bradley and Gordon Madison.

---

* Additional plaintiffs were Palmer Sullins, Jr., Alan D. Sullins and Marsha Marie Sullins, by Palmer Sullins and Della D. Sullins, their parents; Gerald Warren Billes and Heloise Elaine Billes, by I. V. Billes, their father; Willie M. Jackson, Jr., by Mabel H. Jackson, his mother; Willie B. Wyatt, Jr., and Brenda J. Wyatt, by Willie B. Wyatt and Thelma A. Wyatt, their parents; Nelson N. Boggan, Jr., by Nelson Boggan, Sr., and Mamie Boggan, his parents; Willie C. Johnson, Jr., Brenda Faye Johnson and Dwight W. Johnson, by Willie C. Johnson and Ruth Johnson, their parents; and William H. Moore and Edwina M. Moore, by L. James Moore and Edna M. Moore, their parents. Additional defendants were the Macon County Board of Education; Chairman Wiley D. Ogletree; members Madison Davis, John M. Davis, Harry D. Raymon, and F. E. Guthrie; and C. A. Pruitt, Superintendent of Schools of Macon County.

These students were the desegregation pioneers in *Lee v. Macon*. From left, Robert Judkins, Shirley Chambliss, Wilma Jones, Willie B. Wyatt Jr., Janis Carter, Helois Billes, Carmen Judkins, Ellen Henderson, Anthony T. Lee, Marsha Sullins, Patricia Jones, and Harvey Jackson.

On July 16, 1963, Judge Frank Johnson, as was his practice, added the United States as a party. Judge Johnson recognized the problem of enforcement of his decrees. He wanted to be sure the U.S. government was a party to the action as the case progressed so that when he entered an order he could expect the U.S. government to enforce it. On August 22, 1963, the court ordered the defendants to desegregate. For the school term beginning September 1963, the Macon County schools began use of the Alabama Pupil Placement Law, which authorized local school boards to assign students to any school in the system.

In reality, this law was designed to delay or prevent school integration. The white residents of Macon County did not want their schools integrated. They preferred the status quo the same as did the whites of Montgomery, Bullock, Barbour, and Crenshaw counties. But even though they were reluctant, Macon County whites were prepared to accept integration.

After the court ordered Macon County schools integrated, the white and the black communities worked hard to prepare for a new school term. There were separate meetings, white citizens and black citizens—adults and students. The county was ready to abide by the court's decree.

One of the leading figures in Macon County in connection with the civil rights movement was James Allan Parker, a white businessman who was best known as the president of Alabama Exchange Bank. He was also a real estate broker, an insurance agent, and a lawyer. A vital link between the white and the African-American communities, Parker was well respected by both races. Generally, he was a stabilizing force in all segments of the county and later became a member of the Tuskegee City Council and chairman of the Macon County Commission. He was a moving force preparing the county for a peaceful integration of schools.

He was also a member of my church, the Church of Christ; later, the two of us were to be moving forces in bringing about the merger of the white and African-American congregations of the Church of Christ in Tuskegee. As a result of his work during these trying times, Parker received the National Bar Association's Gertrude

Allan Parker, of Tuskegee, with Mrs. Parker, accepts the NBA's Gertrude Rush Award in 1986.

Rush Award in 1986, when I was president of the NBA.

With the help of Mr. Parker and others, the white community was ready to receive integration of public schools on the designated day. But on September 2, 1963, the day the schools were scheduled to open, Governor George C. Wallace dispatched state troopers to Tuskegee. The troopers surrounded Tuskegee Public School and prevented its scheduled integration. The governor made various speeches on television, the radio, and in the newspapers, encouraging white parents not to send their children to the public schools. By the authority vested in him as governor and ex-officio chairman of the State Board of Education, he closed Tuskegee Public School to avoid integration.

Birth of the Private School Movement in Alabama

Governor Wallace then started a new movement. He announced the formation of a private school in Macon County to be known as "Macon Academy." He publicly solicited financial assistance from state employees and from other whites around the state. Also, he encouraged white residents to boycott the public schools in Macon County and send their children to the newly formed, private, all-white Macon Academy. As a result of the action taken by Governor Wallace in creating an atmosphere for the establishment of Macon Academy, and providing an alternative place where white parents could send their children, a private school movement began and spread like wildfire throughout Alabama and across the South. Court orders to enforce *Brown v. Board* at the local level were being handed down throughout the segregated South. White parents, in defiance of these orders, followed Governor Wallace's lead to establish, finance, and staff private, all-white "academies" as a substitute to integrated public schools. Macon Academy was one of the first such institutions. It remains segregated even until this day.

Closing of Tuskegee Public

The closing of the public school in Tuskegee was a very serious matter. After carefully reviewing the events of the day at home that evening, I concluded that if Wallace, as governor of Alabama, had the authority under state law to close down a public school to prevent integration, then he must have the authority to use that same state power to further integration in all of the public elementary and secondary schools in Alabama.

The State of Alabama had a system in which a county or city board of education theoretically had complete control over the operation and supervision of its schools. At the time there were some 119 city and/or county school boards in Alabama. Each system was considered autonomous and in order to integrate the schools, separate suits with separate plaintiffs would have to be filed against each of the separate school boards. It was for that reason that I filed separate suits against Montgomery, Bullock, Barbour, Crenshaw and Macon counties. However, since Governor Wallace had successfully exercised his state power in closing the public schools in Tuskegee, I concluded that he should be compelled to use that same power to integrate all of the school systems in Alabama which were not already then under court order.

This realization hit me like the burning bush speaking to Moses. I could not wait until the next day. About 10:30 in the evening I got on the telephone to my associates and clerical staff and told them to get to the office within the hour.

In response to the governor closing Tuskegee Public School, I wanted us to prepare an immediate motion for temporary restraining order, a motion for an order to show cause, and an amendment to the complaint in *Lee v. Macon County Board of Education*. I wanted to to file these documents as soon as possible to show Governor Wallace and the world that we were serious and we meant business.

Because Wallace had acted as he had, I saw the opportunity to do more with this one lawsuit toward accomplishing my secret goal than had been done in any other single lawsuit. I thought if we were successful there would be no need to file ninety-eight separate lawsuits and no other African-American parents would have to be subject to reprisals as a plaintiff in any other school desegregation case. There would be no more segregation in the Alabama public school systems.

In less than an hour, my entire staff was at the office and ready to work. That staff consisted of my law clerk, Edwin L. Davis; Bernice, who was my secretary in those years; and me. That was not the first time we worked all night in a crisis. Throughout the Montgomery Bus Protest, the struggle in Tuskegee which resulted in *Gomillion v. Lightfoot*, the lunch counter demonstrations, and in the time of the Freedom Riders, there was one crisis after another. Always, my staff and I—in the language of the now-deceased great civil rights lawyer David Hood of Bessemer—did what was "necessary and proper."

By morning, we were ready. We filed motions for a temporary restraining order and for an order to show cause why Governor George C. Wallace should not be made a party defendant and should not be enjoined from obstructing or preventing compliance with the court's order requiring racial integration of the schools in Macon County. Not only did we file the motions, but the governor was served the legal paperwork that same day. He was astonished at how quickly we had reacted to his closing the Tuskegee schools. Wallace appeared shaken on the six o'clock television news that evening. He must have thought we had spies in his administration because he said it would have taken days to prepare the documents. Of course, he was wrong. All it took was one hard night of work and a few hundred years of getting motivated.

On three separate occasions during the 1963-1964 school year, we petitioned the court and the court enjoined state officials from various forms of interference with the peaceful and orderly desegregation of schools in Macon County.

In February 1964, I filed, on behalf of the plaintiffs, a supplemental complaint, adding as defendants George C. Wallace as President of the Alabama State Board of Education; Austin R. Meadows, Executive Officer and Secretary of the Alabama State Board of Education; and other individual members of the State Board of Education. In our supplemental complaint, the plaintiffs requested the court:

(1) to enjoin these defendants from operating a dual school system based upon race throughout Alabama,

(2) to enter an order requiring state-wide desegregation of public schools in Alabama,

(3) to enjoin the use of state funds to perpetuate the dual school system, and

(4) to enjoin as unconstitutional the tuition grant law of the State of Alabama (Chapter 4B (sections 61(13) through 61(21), Title 52, Code of Alabama). This law had been passed at Wallace's instigation to allow diversion of tax money to segregated private schools.

After we amended the complaint, a three-judge federal court panel was convened consisting of Judge Johnson, who heard the case initially; Circuit Judge Richard T. Rives, a Montgomery native; and District Judge Hobart Grooms from Birmingham. As a result of these new parties, there were new lawyers. The law firm of Goodwyn and Smith was retained to represent the governor and the State Board of Education. T. W. Thagard was the chief attorney.

There was a full-scale hearing and the U.S. government fully participated and was a significant part of the legal team. I worked closely with the local U.S. Attorney; with John Doar, who was a Special Assistant Attorney General in the Civil Rights Division of the Justice Department, and with other U.S. government representatives. Solomon S. Seay, Jr., and NAACP Defense Fund attorneys Jack Greenberg, Charles H. Jones and Constance Baker Motley were also on my legal team.

After an oral hearing, a review of the evidence, and argument of counsel, the court on July 13, 1964, stated that Alabama maintained a dual school system based upon race and that it was the policy of Governor Wallace and the State Board of Education to promote and encourage the implementation of that racial policy in the operation of the Alabama public schools. The court also concluded that Alabama's tuition grant law was just a sham established to use state funds to pay for a white private school system. The court ordered the state not to interfere with local school systems that were trying to eliminate racial discrimination. The state was also barred from paying any tuition grant to schools that discriminated on the basis of race.

Notwithstanding this order, Governor Wallace continued to interfere with the integration of the public schools in Macon County. In September and November 1966, we filed additional supplemental complaints, again asking for a state-wide desegregation order and an injunction against the use of state funds to support a dual educational system. After a full-scale hearing, the court, on March 22, 1967, entered a sweeping order to the governor and the State Board of Education to integrate all ninety-eight school systems which were not then already under court order. The court also directed that all trade schools, junior colleges, vocational schools, and other educational institutions under the control of the State Board of Education be integrated. On the question of remedy, the court stated:

> The remedy to which these plaintiffs are constitutionally entitled must be designed to reach the limits of the defendants' activities in these several areas and must be designed to require the defendants to do what they have been unwilling to do on their own—to discharge their constitutional obligation to disestablish in each of the local county and city school systems in Alabama that are not already operating under a United States court order, the dual public school system to the extent that it is based upon race or color. In this connection, the State of Alabama and particularly the defendant state officials are under an affirmative constitutional duty to take whatever corrective action is necessary to disestablish such a system. Faculty members and staff members, facilities and activities, as well as student bodies, must be desegregated to such an extent that there no longer exists in the Alabama public school system discrimination of any sort or to any degree that is based upon race or color.
>
> This Court can conceive of no other effective way to

give the plaintiffs the relief to which they are entitled under the evidence in this case than to enter a uniform state-wide plan for school desegregation, made applicable to each local county and city system not already under court order to desegregate, and to require these defendants to implement it. Only in this way can uniform, expeditious and substantial progress be attained, and only in this way can the defendant state officials discharge the constitutional duty that was placed upon them twelve years ago in *Brown v. Board of Education*, supra.

Alabama State Teachers Association Intervened

During the course of this litigation, as was the case in other school cases, we included the Alabama State Teachers Association (ASTA) as a party-plaintiff intervenor in the lawsuit. Joe L. Reed was the executive director of ASTA, which was the African-American teachers association in the state. We felt it was very important that ASTA be made party-plaintiffs so that as the rights of parents and students were being litigated, the rights of African-American teachers, principals, coaches and administrators would also be litigated. Later when ASTA and the Alabama Education Association (AEA), the white teacher association in Alabama, merged under the auspices of the National Education Association (NEA), we substituted the NEA as party-plaintiff representing African-American teachers. This was one of the first times such school personnel were parties to this type of case. As a result of representing African-American teachers, principals, coaches, and other administrators, we were able to save the jobs of many African-American school professionals, more than in any other state.

The Importance of the Case

Ultimately, *Lee v. Macon* was appealed to the United States Supreme Court and was affirmed. This too, was a very, very important case. There are probably over three hundred different opinions which have been written on various aspects of the case.

The case was important for many reasons, including the following:

1) We integrated all of Alabama's remaining segregated public schools in this one lawsuit. This was an efficient means of dispensing justice. It was both time efficient and cost efficient. Individual students and parents did not have to file separate suits to integrate schools and be subjected to reprisals when they became plaintiffs. There were savings of hundreds of thousands of dollars in court costs.

2) The sweeping order integrated all colleges which were then under the State Board of Education without the necessity of having to file a lawsuit. The schools were Troy State College, Livingston State College, Alabama State College, Jacksonville State College, Florence State College, and Alabama A&M.

3) It merged the African-American high school athletic association and the white high school athletic association, thus leading the way for African-American athletes in high school to gain recognition for their achievements. With increased recognition, these athletes received publicity which attracted the attention of coaches from larger colleges and universities. As a result, many African-American student-athletes have gone on to become sports professionals.

4) All of the state trade schools, junior colleges, technical schools and all other colleges under the control of the State Board of Education were integrated in this order.

So this case not only had the effects indicated above, but the case is still alive and well. When there are problems existing in any of the local school systems or any problems in any of the other institutions that are under the control of the State Board of Education, there is no need for filing a new lawsuit; relief can be sought simply by going back into court under *Lee v. Macon.*

This precedent-setting case was a big win for me personally. Now I was truly on my way to "destroying everything segregated that I could find."

10

Selma Once More—the 1965 Selma March

I have related earlier how the Selma Police Department, at the time of my first case there—just twenty-two days after the beginning of the Montgomery Bus Protest in December 1955—sent me a personal message via my friend Frank Massey. Frank had ridden to Selma with me for the trial of an African-American Air Force sergeant arrested for blowing his horn at a white motorist who was sitting without moving at an intersection. While he was sitting in court watching this trial, Frank Massey himself was arrested on a bogus charge. While Frank was in jail, a Selma police officer told him to warn me, "That nigger lawyer thinks he's smart. They got a mess going on in Montgomery"— referring to the Montgomery Bus Protest—"and we're not going to have any mess in Selma." "You tell him when he cross that bridge, don't ever come back to Selma." It was some time before I returned to Selma; however, I did.

Background of the March

There were racial problems in Selma. The evidence could be seen in cases such as *Selma v. Wesley Jones* and *Alabama v. L.L. Anderson,* and numerous incidents of difficulties involving African Americans attempting to register to vote.

Registering to vote was never easy for Negroes in the South. It was especially difficult in Selma, the county seat of Dallas County, a river town in the heart of the Alabama Black Belt (that narrow region of dark, calcareous soils in central Alabama and Mississippi highly adapted to agriculture). A majority of the residents of Dallas County were and are African-American. The white officials in Selma did not want African Americans to become registered and vote.

With the assistance of John Lewis, Hosea Williams, Amelia Boynton and others, members of the Student Non-violent Coordinating Committee (SNCC) came to Selma in 1963–64 and organized a voter registration campaign. They began having mass meetings in churches and encouraging African Americans to register. They taught the importance of voting and how to complete the application for registration.

SNCC members and others active in the Civil Rights Movement wanted to spotlight the problems African Americans were having in Selma. They chose to walk the fifty miles from Selma to the state capitol in Montgomery to demonstrate the desire of Dallas County's African Americans to register to vote.

The first attempt at a Selma-to-Montgomery March was a bloody failure. The small group of demonstrators who set out were ill-prepared to make the trip, but nevertheless, they started. The group included Lewis, now a U.S. Congressman from Georgia; Williams, later to be an Atlanta City Councilman and a Dekalb County (Georgia) Commissioner; and Amelia Boynton Robinson, a businesswoman who then lived in Selma and who is now retired in Tuskegee.

I first met John Lewis during the Montgomery Bus Protest in 1955–56. A native of Troy, Pike County, Alabama, fifty miles southeast of Montgomery, John was a serious young man who talked with Dr. King, Ralph Abernathy, and me about the possibility of representing him in a suit to gain admission to segregated Troy State College. I was willing to file such a suit, but John's parents, who were born and still lived in Pike County, were somewhat reluctant. Since John was still a minor then, it would have meant the necessity of the suit being filed by them on behalf of their minor son. That suit was never filed, but I later integrated Troy State through *Lee v. Macon County Board of Education*. Then, in 1961, while he was a Nashville ministerial student, John Lewis was the sparkplug behind the Freedom Ride which ended in a bloody riot at the Greyhound bus station in Montgomery. He was the lead plaintiff in *Lewis v. Greyhound*, which arose out of that riot.

And, finally, I did represent John and others in connection with the Selma-to-Montgomery March, the beginning incident of which did as much as any single event in U.S. history to get African Americans the right to vote.

Bloody Sunday

When John Lewis, Hosea Williams, Amelia Boynton and others started across the Edmund Pettus Bridge toward Montgomery on March 7, 1965, they were met on the other side by a wall of horse-mounted state troopers and sheriff's deputies. After a brief stand-off, the demonstrators were charged by the mounted law officers. People were trampled, beaten with billy clubs, and overcome by tear gas.

On March 8, 1965, on behalf of those who were beaten back at the Edmund Pettus Bridge, I filed *Hosea Williams v. George C. Wallace* in the Montgomery federal court, for the purpose of requiring Governor Wallace and the State of Alabama to protect the marchers as they marched from Selma to Montgomery demanding the constitutional right to vote. The plaintiffs were Williams, Lewis, and Boynton. The defendants were Governor George C. Wallace, Alabama Public Safety Director Al Lingo, and Dallas County Sheriff James G. Clark. The plaintiffs were represented by Peter Hall of Birmingham; Jack Greenberg, Norman Amaker, Charles H. Jones, Jr., and James M. Nabrit, III, of the Legal Defense Fund; Solomon S. Seay, Jr., and myself. I had the primary responsibility of presenting the plaintiffs' case. Opposing counsel were Maury Smith and John Goodwin.

Judge Frank M. Johnson Jr., designated the United States of America as a party and on March 10, 1965, government lawyers filed their intervenors' complaint.

We had a hearing, and Judge Johnson granted our relief. He stated that the proposed plan to march along U.S. Highway 80

"Bloody Sunday," 1965: John Lewis is the figure near the center of this photo whose head is about to be struck by the baton of an Alabama State Trooper.

from Selma to Montgomery, for the purpose of petitioning the state government for redress of their grievances, particularly the right to vote, was reasonable and it was in exercise of the constitutional right of assembly and freedom of movement within the state of Alabama. The court provided that the march should begin no earlier than March 19, 1965, and no later than March 22, 1965. The court further held that the plaintiffs were entitled to police protection as they exercised their constitutional right to march along the highway from Selma to Montgomery. He then issued an injunction enjoining Wallace, Lingo, Clark, and all other persons acting with them from intimidating, threatening, coercing, or interfering with the proposed march.

The Hearing in New Orleans

Immediately after the hearing, Judge Johnson called the lawyers together in his office and told us that he understood that the defendants were contemplating an appeal. He had arranged for a panel of judges on the United States Court of Appeals for the Fifth

Circuit to accommodate the defendants in New Orleans that evening at 6 p.m. The judge told us about a flight going to New Orleans that afternoon. One of the defense attorneys asked if the Judge had made reservations for us. The judge said he had not, but that he understood seats were available.

Justice Department attorney John Doar and I set out for the airport to get a commercial flight to New Orleans for the hearing. The commercial flight was late, so Doar chartered a private plane. Since I was representing the plaintiffs, I went along with him. The state lawyers did not try to get a commercial plane; they used a state-owned airplane to go to New Orleans.

While in the air, Doar and I discussed the argument to be presented to the court. Once on the ground, we took a taxi to the Court of Appeals, and argued our case. The court upheld Judge Johnson's order.

Because we both had important work to do, we were eager to return to Montgomery. John Doar had to coordinate the efforts on the part of the Justice Department to be sure that proper protection was in place for the marchers. The march was scheduled to begin in the next few days and I needed to help the marchers prepare to get from Selma to Montgomery.

Meanwhile, a cold front had brought near-freezing temperatures. Doar's chartered plane had no de-icing equipment and was not suitable for travel in these conditions. By now several executive jets had flown government personnel from Washington into Montgomery's Maxwell Air Force Base in preparation for the March. Doar summoned one of those planes to New Orleans to take us back to Montgomery. (When we arrived at Maxwell Field, a motor pool sergeant was assigned to drive me to my home. Upon getting in the car, I was happily surprised to find that the driver was Sgt. Willie Thomas, the husband to my secretary, Lillian Thomas, who worked with me for many years and is now the secretary to the Honorable Myron Thompson, Chief Judge, United States District Court for the Middle District of Alabama.)

The Completion of the March

With the order in hand directing the State of Alabama and Governor George Wallace to protect the marchers, the march was free to commence. It began on schedule and proceeded without major incident over the next several days.

When the march leaders arrived in Montgomery, they came to my home to prepare for the last day of the March. Dr. King, Reverend Abernathy, Andrew Young, John Lewis, Hosea Williams and others met in my living room at 2722 West Edgemont in Montgomery to make the final plans for the last leg of the Selma-to-Montgomery march. It was really a marvelous feeling to welcome these individuals into my home to make the final plans for a historic event. All the detailed plans for the program in front of the state capitol were made in my home on the night before the final leg of the march from St. Jude's school to the capitol. This was the last of several such meetings in my home in preparation for the march.

My wife and I entertained many civil rights leaders and attorneys in our home. Substantially, all of the lawyers who came to Montgomery during the early days of the bus protest stayed in our home. African-American attorneys could not stay in white hotels. United States Supreme Court Justice Thurgood Marshall, Judge Robert Carter, Judge Constance Baker Motley and many, many others stayed in our home. We were happy to accommodate them.

I obtained the court order so that the marchers could be protected from Selma to Montgomery, but I did not do much marching—not in the streets anyway. Most of my marching was done to and from the courtroom and my office.

But, after participating in making the final plans for the march, I decided to join the marchers at the St. Jude complex, which was about a half mile from my home. I walked the last leg from St. Jude to the state capitol. When I arrived downtown at Perry Street and Dexter Avenue, a half block from my office, I was joined by Bernice. We walked the last quarter mile of the Selma-to-Montgomery march together.

Meeting with Governor Wallace

After the speeches and during a brief interlude, I was included in the group of persons who took a message to Governor Wallace. That message was to request him to use his influence so that African Americans could be registered to vote. When we entered the governor's office and the introductions began, the Governor looked at me and said, "I know Fred. We have known each other for a long time." He reminded me of the Eufaula housing cases in Flake Hill when he was the circuit judge. He asked me, "Do you remember, Fred, what you told me as we concluded those Flake Hill cases in Eufaula?" I said, "Your Excellency, I'm sure when you were circuit judge, I said so much to you during the course of that trial, but what are you referring to?" He said that I had told him when we completed that trial, that he had been "as fair to me as any judge that I had tried any case before." I did recall that. It is true. He had been fair.

We told him what our mission was and solicited his assistance so that we could obtain the right to vote. He did not promise to help, and I am sure he did not, but the meeting was cordial.

The Importance of the Case

This case is significant because a similar march attempted a week earlier was broken up by club-wielding state lawmen using cattle prods and tear-gas. The publicity of these actions and the march from Selma to Montgomery led to the enactment of the Voting Rights Act of 1965. It was very important. Tens of thousands of African Americans became voters. As a result of the passage of the Voting Rights Act, many African Americans have been elected to hundreds of offices from city councils, to state legislatures, to the U.S. Congress.

This case was also important because it compelled the officials of the State of Alabama to protect African Americans and whites as they exercised their constitutional rights to march.

Not only that, but personally it was another milestone toward obtaining my goal of "destroying everything segregated which I

In 1965, John Lewis was beaten in Selma as he tried to win the right to vote. In 1995, John Lewis is a Georgia congressman. He and I were together in Washington a few years ago at a tribute to Justice Thurgood Marshall.

could find." This step was toward destroying discrimination against African Americans in registration and voting. Of course, as African Americans gained the vote and began to share in political power, it became easier to destroy segregation in other aspects of society.

11

Sellers v. Trussell—Bullock County

The state of Alabama has a long history of discriminating against African Americans by prohibiting them from voting. The larger the African-American population in the county, the more difficult was the voter registration process. Bullock County, with a 70 percent African-American population, is a typical example of this situation. As far back as 1954, African Americans had been involved in litigation in an effort to become registered voters in Bullock County. In 1961, the United States filed a lawsuit against the state of Alabama, particularly Bullock County, so that African Americans could obtain the right to vote. The court found that there had been systematic, intentional, insidious conduct on the part of Alabama, and such conduct was a clear violation of the 15th Amendment of the Constitution.

An Illegal Act to Deny the Right to Vote

In August 1965, just as African Americans were beginning to obtain the right to vote in Bullock County, the Alabama Legislature passed Act No. 536. This act stated that the term of each member of the Bullock County Court of County Commissioners should be for six years and the incumbent member shall serve until their successors are elected and qualified. One commissioner should be elected from each of the four commissioned districts at the general election in 1968 and every six years thereafter, from the second and fourth districts at the general election in 1970, and every six years thereafter from the first and third districts. In actuality, this act extended the term of office of the incumbent white commissioners by two years. This transparent act was only a more sophisticated attempt to discriminate against African-American voters. Rather than prohibit voting by gerrymandering (*Gomillion v. Lightfoot*), passage of this act would prohibit voting by delaying an election. The election scheduled for 1967 would be delayed until 1969 and would extend the term of two incumbent white commissioners whose seats were going to be challenged by two African Americans.

On February 24, 1966, Aaron Sellers, Ben McGhee, Ed Hall, Claude T. Miller, Benjamin Jordan, and Booker T. Walker retained me for the purpose of filing a lawsuit to have this act declared unconstitutional. I filed the lawsuit in the United States District Court for the Middle District of Alabama on March 7, 1966, on behalf of Sellers, Wilborn Thomas, Hall, Paul T. Mitchell, Jordan, McGhee, and Walker. Solomon Seay, Jr., assisted me in connection with this lawsuit, along with the attorneys from the NAACP Legal Defense Fund. The defendants in the lawsuit were John C. Trussell, Jr., George E. Blue, R. C. Green, and J. R. Graham, members of the Bullock County Court of County Commissioners; Probate Judge Fred D. Main, and John Allen Crook, chairman of the Bullock County Democratic Executive Committee. They were defended by Stan B. Sikes and Maury Smith.

On March 15, 1965, acting Chief Judge John R. Brown of the Fifth U.S. Circuit Court of Appeals convened a three-judge panel of Richard T. Rives, United States Circuit Judge for the Fifth Circuit; H. H. Grooms, and Frank M. Johnson, Jr., to hear this case, which was consolidated with *U.S. v. John Allen Crook, as Chairman of the Bullock County Democratic Executive Committee.*

In an opinion written by Judge Rives and filed on April 15, 1966, the court stated:

> Act No. 536 changes the term of office of County Commissioners in Bullock County, Alabama, from four to six years. It undertakes to extend by two years the terms of the incumbent Commissioners, so that the terms of the

Commissioners representing District 2 and 4 would end in 1969, instead of 1967, and the terms of the Commissioners representing Districts 1 and 3 would end in 1971, instead of 1969. Acting pursuant to Act No. 536, the defendants are foregoing the holding of any elections for Commissioners in Bullock County in 1966.

Commissioners for Districts 2 and 4 were elected in 1962; those for Districts 1 and 3 were elected in 1964. But for the passage of Act No. 536, elections for the Democratic nominations for Commissioners for Districts 2 and 4 would take place on May 3, 1966, with a run-off, if necessary, on May 31, 1966.

Over a substantial period of time, Negroes in Bullock County were denied the right to vote on account of race, as is indicated by the following registration statistics:

Year	Voting Age Persons Registered		Population in 1960	
	W	N	W	N
1960	2266	5	2387	4450
1962	2408	886	2387	4450
1964	2727	1423	2387	4450
1966	2993	2845	2387	4450

Notwithstanding this history of discrimination against Negroes in Bullock County, the evidence introduced by the defendants has convinced this Court that Act. No. 536 was not discriminatorily motivated. On May 14, 1965, House Bill 212 was introduced in the Alabama House of Representatives, providing for a six-year term of office for County Commissioners throughout the State of Alabama, and further providing for the extension for two years of the terms of office of all incumbents who had been elected to four-year terms. That Bill died in committee. That Bill was initiated by Judge Winston Stewart, the Executive Director of the Association of County Commissioners.

Judge Stewart testified at length as to the purposes of that Bill, among others: that it was intended to keep more experienced men in office, to provide for greater incentive for qualified persons to seek the office in view of the modest pay of the office, to provide more time for the planning of county roads, and to keep the road crews from being fired so frequently by reason of the change of Commissioners. Judge Stewart testified that there was no discussion as to race before the Commissioners' Association or in any other way in the planning at Judge Stewart's request by Mr. Charles Cooper of the Alabama Legislative Reference Service.

That finding, however, does not dispose of these cases in view of the readily apparent discriminatory *effect* of Act No. 536. Act No. 536 freezes into office for an additional two years persons who were elected when Negroes were being illegally deprived of the right to vote. Under such circumstances, to freeze elective officials into office is, in effect, to freeze Negroes out of the electorate. This is forbidden by the Fifteenth Amendment.

The court went on to hold that Act No. 536 is also in conflict with Section 5 of the Voting Rights Act of 1965, in that no request had been made to have the Attorney General preclear a change in the election process. Judge Grooms concurred in the first portion of Judge Rives's opinion, but dissented in the balance. Judge Johnson concurred and stated the following:

I concur except I do not find it necessary to reach the question of the applicability of § 5 of the 1965 Voting Rights Act. I think that under the facts and circumstances of this case the Fifteenth Amendment provides a more appropriate and substantial basis upon which the issues presented must be resolved.

Nor can I concur in the finding that there was no racially discriminatory motivation in the passage of Act

536. The history of voting discrimination against Negroes over a substantial period of time in Bullock County on the part of the State of Alabama and Bullock County officials, as reflected by the evidence in this case and as judicially found to exist in *Sellers v. Wilson* . . . and in *United States v. Alabama* . . . has been systematic, intentional, invidious, and in clear violation of the Fifteenth Amendment. Any determination in this case of legislative motive must be viewed in this light. Viewing Act 536 in such light, leads me, in the absence of any reasonable explanation for its passage, to the firm conclusion that its introduction and passage was racially motivated. The explanation of the introduction of the proposed state-wide bill—which did not even get out of the House Committee—cannot serve, in the absence of some such testimony, as an explanation for the introduction and passage of local Act 536. Certainly, with this background, with the evidence in this case, and where the manifest consequences and clear effect of legislation is discriminatory, an inference of a purpose to discriminate is compelling. This is the clear teaching of *Gomillion v. Lightfoot* . . .; *Caswell v. Texas* . . .; *United States v. Alabama* . . .; and *Sims v. Baggett* . . . .

Conclusion

This is another example of the lengths to which the state of Alabama and the legislature were willing to go to deny African Americans the right to vote. As a result of this case, Benjamin Jordan and other African Americans have gone on and served as members of the county commission in Bullock County. As of 1994, a majority of the members of the county commission of Bullock County was African-American, the judge of probate was African-American, the sheriff was African-American, and there were many other African-American elected officials. This is another case in which I was able to continue to break down the walls of discrimination and to "destroy everything segregated I could find."

12

The First Vote Dilution Suit—*Smith v. Paris*

B y 1966 I was well known in Barbour County, home of Governor George Wallace, as a civil rights lawyer. I had represented African Americans in connection with the housing authority of the City of Eufaula condemning their property located on Flake Hill in 1958. I had filed the case of *Elijah Franklin v. The Barbour County Board of Education* in 1963 for the purpose of integrating the schools. I was in and out of Barbour County on legal matters almost on a weekly basis.

One of my most influential civil rights cases is one of the least known, and it began in Barbour County. This case of first impression, the first vote dilution lawsuit, had a profound effect on the American voting process. I filed the lawsuit, *Mary C. Smith v. T. W. Paris,* on May 2, 1966, in the Montgomery federal court and represented the plaintiffs along with lawyers for the NAACP Legal Defense Fund and attorney Solomon S. Seay, Jr.

The plaintiffs in the lawsuit were Mary C. Smith, Clementine Morris Gilbert, Mary Hunter, Bernice Haslam, Rosa Jordan, and Annie Ruth Davis.

Eufaula attorney Preston Clayton represented the defendants, who were Barbour County Probate Judge George E. Little and the following members of the county Democratic Executive Committee: T. W. Paris, Charles L. Weston, Robert F. Beaty, Jr., Robert H. Bennett, Floyd Peak, Fred Tew, Alfred A. Grant, Audrey K. Hollingsworth, J. D. Hinson, Rufus Lee, J. D. Gilchrist, W. D. Anderson, Will Green, Hugh Boyd, William J. Adams, Walter

Pitt Eubanks, Dan Ross, Bennett Teal, William Bush, Perry Abercrombie, and D. Pat Wilson.

Some of the plaintiffs were candidates for membership on the Barbour County Democratic Executive Committee from the "beat" in which they resided. They were candidates at the time and in the same election during which I first ran for a seat in the Alabama House of Representatives in 1966. The purpose of the suit was to have declared unconstitutional a resolution adopted by the Barbour County Democratic Executive Committee that changed the method of electing members to the committee.

The Facts

This case was submitted on June 30, 1966. The parties stipulated the facts and subsequently submitted their arguments in briefs. Judge Frank M. Johnson, Jr., in a memorandum opinion and order filed on August 22, 1966, made the following finding:

> For over thirty years, until March 17, 1966, elections of the Barbour County Democratic Executive Committee were held on a combined at-large and beat basis. Five of the twenty-one members of the committee were elected at large. The county was divided into 16 beats and the voters in each beat elected a person residing in that beat to the committee. Prior to March 1966, no Negro had ever qualified to run as a member of the committee. Moreover, prior to the passage of he 1965 Voting Rights Act, a minuscule number of eligible Negroes were actually registered to vote. This has all changed since the passage of the Act, with the result that in four of the beats in Barbour County, there is a majority of Negroes over white qualified electors. However, over the entire county, there is still a majority of white voters.
>
> By March 1, 1966, the six plaintiffs had qualified as candidates for the Executive Committee. Four of the six were candidates in beats where the majority of registered voters were Negroes.

On March 17, 1966, the Barbour County Executive Committee by resolution changed the method of electing committee members so that the 16 members previously elected by beats (or districts) were elected on an at-large basis, although each candidate is required to reside within a particular beat and, after election, represent the beat in which he resides.

The tabulation of the election returns reflects that if the election had been held under the system that had previously been in force before the resolution of March 17, 1966, three of the plaintiffs would very likely have been elected. Under the county-wide vote system established by this resolution, all plaintiffs were defeated by substantial majorities.

The Court's Decision

Based upon the stipulated facts, the court concluded:

> ... that the March 17, 1966, resolution, adopted by the Democratic Executive Committee of Barbour County, Alabama, was born of an effort to frustrate and discriminate against Negroes in the exercise of their right to vote, in violation of the Fifteenth Amendment and 42 U.S.C. section 1981.

Judge Johnson's opinion went to the heart of how any court must review a statute or a resolution. While the court does not view these statutes and resolutions in a vacuum, Judge Johnson said:

> Any statute or resolution must be viewed in the context or setting which gave rise to its enactment. Certainly a major element in the circumstances surrounding promulgation of the resolution presently under consideration, which this Court must take into account, is "the long history of racial discrimination in Alabama." *Sims v. Baggett*, 247 F. Supp. 96 (M.D. Ala. 1965). See also the discussion

and citations in *United States v. State of Alabama*, 252 F. Supp. 95 (M.D. Ala. 1965). Any determination of legislative motive or purpose, therefore, must be viewed in this light.

Focusing more specifically on the present case, we have a situation where Negroes have long been denied the right to vote and historically have not been represented by members of their race on the Barbour Democratic Executive Committee. As stated earlier, prior to the passage of the Voting Rights Act of 1965, only a small percentage of Negroes in Barbour County were registered to vote. With the passage of the Act, Negroes have registered in large numbers, and by May 3, 1966, had the voting strength to elect at least four candidates to the Executive Committee. Accompanying this increase in voter strength, there were, for the first time, Negro candidates who had qualified to run for the Executive Committee. For over thirty years the method of electing officials to this committee had remained the same until just a few weeks after all six Negro candidates had qualified. Then suddenly, the Executive Committee, with little or no debate, without taking any minutes or making any record of its meetings or discussions, and, so far as the record reflects, with little or no discussion among the members of the community, promulgated a resolution, the clear effect of which is to turn Negro majorities into minorities in certain political areas, thus, as a practical matter, eliminating the possibility of a Negro candidate winning a place on the Executive Committee. Certainly when viewed against the general background outlined above, and where the manifest consequences and clear effect of the resolution greatly diminish the effectiveness of the Negroes' right to vote, an inference of a discriminatory purpose is compelling. This is the clear teaching of *Gomillion v. Lightfoot* . . .

The Court of Appeals for the Fifth Circuit upheld Judge

Johnson's finding of unconstitutionality and ordered new elections to be held on a single-member district basis beginning in 1968.

The Significance of the First Vote Dilution Case

This case was very important for several reasons. Locally, it gave encouragement to the African-American residents of Barbour County. Now that they had the right to vote, the court would not permit a public body to diminish that right neither by resolution, ordinance, nor state statute. This case is the first case which specifically prohibited the dilution of an African-American vote. It is also interesting to note that Judge Johnson in his opinion stated that the conclusion he reached in this case was "the clear teaching of *Gomillion v. Lightfoot,*" which was one of my cases decided in 1960 by the U. S. Supreme Court. Judge Johnson's decision and the Court of Appeals decision were personal victories for me, for they continued to be stepping stones in destroying everything segregated that I could find.

13

Fred Gray the Politician

I had a front-seat view of the changing landscape of Alabama politics. As time passed, my law practice in Tuskegee was increasing, and I was seeing the results of litigation and the passage of the Civil Rights Act of 1957 and the Voting Rights Act of 1965. African Americans were now voting and beginning to hold elected offices.

The Alabama Legislature was totally devoid of African Americans. I observed in the mid-1960s that a legislative district consisting of Macon, Bullock, and Barbour counties probably could elect an African American. These were all counties where I had done a substantial amount of legal work. Many of the local county and community leaders were my clients. I knew them and they knew me. I was interested in becoming a member of the Alabama Legislature. It was not likely that the legislative districts included in Montgomery, my hometown, would elect an African American.

Barbour and Bullock County Connections

I could visualize a political base in Barbour and Bullock counties, and my satellite law practice in Macon County was prospering. I was commuting to Tuskegee twice a week, including Saturdays, where I would see an office full of clients in the morning and return to Montgomery to see an office full of clients in the afternoon. My Tuskegee clients wanted to know why I couldn't be available to them more hours a day and more days a week.

The decision to move to Tuskegee was not a hasty one. My wife and I discussed my political aspirations and the increasing demand for my legal services in Tuskegee. Bernice understood the opportunities for us were greater in Tuskegee.

We now had four children and were in need of a larger house. In anticipation of building a house, I purchased three lots in Tuskegee's Bulls subdivision. Our children, Deborah, age 9, Vanessa, age 7, Fred Jr., age 4, and Stanley, 15 months, had no problems with the decision to move. With the move to Tuskegee made in late summer of 1965 so the children would be ready for school, I prepared myself to run for the Alabama Legislature in 1966.

My First Political Campaign, 1966

It was quite a campaign. Civil rights demonstrations were occurring everywhere. I was on the campaign trail for a seat in the Alabama House of Representatives, District 31, Seat 2, consisting of Barbour, Bullock and Macon counties. I was accompanied at campaign stops throughout the district by freedom singers led by Bullock County civil rights worker Wilborn Thomas. Some of the songs were: "I ain't going to let nobody turn me around" (I ain't going to let George Wallace turn me around, I ain't going to let the KKK turn me around); "I'm walking up the freedom highway;" and "before I be a slave, I'd be buried in my grave, and go home with my Lord and be free." Some of the freedom singers were Helen Rodgers, the leader, Pearlie Mae Rodgers, Gurthie Ree Tarver, James Walker, Jewel Walker, Patricia Hill, and Olivia Tolbert. They were all from the Midway community in Bullock County.

My well-organized campaign workers included not only many African-American and white citizens from my district and across Alabama, but also Stony Cook of Atlanta, who later became a chief aide to Andrew Young; and Geraldine Williams and Kenneth McGee of Cleveland, Ohio, who had worked in the successful campaign which elected Carl Stokes as the first African-American mayor of Cleveland.

My campaign headquarters became a focal point for other

candidates and our efforts helped elect the first African-American sheriffs in Macon and Bullock counties—Lucius Amerson and H. O. "Red" Williams, respectively. Other African Americans who—for the first time since reconstruction—were running for public office in Bullock County included Rufus Huffman, for tax assessor; and Ben McGhee and Alonza Ellis, for seats on the county commission. In Barbour County, Mary Hunter, Mary C. Smith, Clementine M. Gilbert, Bernice Haslam, Rosie Jordan, and Annie R. Davis were candidates for the Democratic Executive Committee.

Interestingly, I later successfully defended Lucius Amerson on a federal charge of violating the civil rights of a prisoner. Amerson and one of his deputies were charged with kicking and beating Wilbert Dean Harris, a man who had starting shooting inside the Tuskegee jail while being arrested on a drunk driving charge. This naturally resulted in quite a struggle to subdue him. Federal prosecutors heard of this incident and decided to go after Amerson, and the matter came to trial in 1971. Personally, I thought Harris was lucky to be alive. As I told the jurors, "If he had shot up a jail in any other county in Alabama, he would have been dead." I felt that racism was involved in the decision to prosecute Amerson, and I said so during the trial. In this case, one of my co-counsels was the then-attorney general of Alabama, Bill Baxley. A flamboyant prosecutor, he was later elected lieutenant governor and narrowly lost a bid to become governor. I asked him to assist me in defending Sheriff Amerson, which he did, and in the course of the case he stated that if Amerson were convicted "you may as well disarm every law enforcement officer around here." Baxley is a fine lawyer and a good friend. He had been the youngest attorney general in the nation when he was elected at the age of twenty-eight after having already served as the elected district attorney of Houston County in southeast Alabama.

As attorney general, Bill successfully reopened the investigation and sent to prison the man who planted the 1963 bomb that killed four children in Birmingham's Sixteenth Street Baptist Church. Bill had been a law student at the University of Alabama at the time, and he later said the bombing had "sickened him" and he, even then with ambitions of becoming a prosecutor, had vowed to help bring to justice the persons responsible. A decade later, he did just that.

I actually played a role in that case, thus returning the favor Bill had shown me in the Amerson defense. His investigators had discovered a witness, a black woman then living in Detroit, who had observed the bombers near the church before the blast occurred. This witness was afraid to return to Alabama and testify. Bill tried everything to persuade her to testify but she would not be moved. Finally, Bill asked me to fly with him in the state airplane to Detroit to talk with her. I did. We talked and talked and talked. I told her how important the case was, and assured her that the resources of the State of Alabama could protect her. I talked about all my own civil rights experiences. I argued that with all the advances we as a people had made, that we now had the Attorney General of Alabama wanting to get justice in this case, and she was a vital link in the evidence, that she really should come back and testify for the prosecution. She eventually agreed, and her testimony was important. And we obtained a conviction in the case.

Now, in other cases, Bill and I have not always been on the same side, but that is the nature of the lawyering profession. In the Amerson case, I was certainly happy to be working with Bill. After an hour and five minutes of deliberation, Amerson and the deputy were acquitted by the jury. Amerson died in 1994, just a few weeks before he was to be honored for his life's accomplishments with an award at the annual Macon County Democratic Club luncheon.

However, all this came later. In 1966, while I was not the best campaigner, I was considered electable because of my broad contacts in the civil rights arena. The African-American community was very united and I was a part of that network across the three counties in the district. In addition, contributions and support were received from around the United States. My best friend, Obie Elie, of Cleveland, Ohio, a former classmate from Nashville Christian Institute, sent the able Carl Stokes aides to help in my campaign.

When the votes were tallied on May 3, 1966, the election officials announced that based on the unofficial returns I was the winner. However, all of the other African-American candidates in Bullock and Barbour counties lost. On May 6, 1966, I was featured in the *New York Times* column "Man in the News." In part, the article stated:

> By a curious twist of irony, it was the State of Alabama that helped to pay for the legal education that enabled Fred David Gray to carry on his 10-year battle against the state segregation laws. When Mr. Gray decided he wanted to become a lawyer, no Negroes were admitted to the only state-supported law school, but the state—under the "separate, but equal" doctrine—would pay the expenses of those who wished to go to out-of-state institutions.
>
> Mr. Gray went to Western Reserve Law School in Cleveland, but he "never doubted for one minute" that he would not come back to Alabama. "I wanted to be a lawyer because I felt that if there were more Negro lawyers they could do something about our situation," he recalls.
>
> **Runoff Is Indicated**
>
> Today, Mr. Gray stands an excellent chance of becoming next January one of Alabama's first Negro legislators since Reconstruction. After yesterday's Democratic primary, it was at first reported that he had won a clear majority over his two white opponents, but late returns indicated he would face a runoff election May 31. If he wins, among his constituents will be Gov. and Mrs. George C. Wallace.
>
> . . . Plunging into civil rights litigation almost immediately after completing his law training at Western Reserve, Mr. Gray was the first lawyer to Martin Luther King, Jr. in civil rights litigation. He still handles Dr. King's legal work in Alabama.
>
> **Fought Districting Case**
>
> . . . Without question his biggest case was the Tuskegee

gerrymander case of the late nineteen-fifties. When the Alabama Legislature sought to redraw the boundaries of Tuskegee County to exclude Negro voters, Mr. Gray appealed the case to the Supreme Court and won a decision that, in some measure led to the historic reapportionment decisions of later years.

Married to the former Bernice Hill of Montgomery and the father of four children, Mr. Gray is active in community affairs. He has just completed a term as president of his college alumni association. He is widely respected by white lawyers and court officials alike for his legal skills, his sense of humor and indefatigable prosecution of his cause.

"A vote for me" he states, "will place a voice, and not an echo, in the Alabama Legislature, a voice that will be unafraid to speak out for constituents' interest, a voice that will not be silenced til heard."

Victory was sweet. Everyone was jubilant. I was excited. There was a night of celebration in Atlanta with Dr. King, Andrew Young, and others from SCLC headquarters. Dr. King was very happy about my winning the primary. In 1966, winning the Democratic primary in Alabama was tantamount to winning the seat. I was about to become the first African American to have a seat in the Alabama Legislature since Reconstruction.

But I did not win. The unofficial election returns given on the night of the primary had changed. The usual procedure for tallying election votes is to count absentee ballots first. However, according to Barbour County election officers, the unofficial count did not include absentee ballots. After the absentee ballots had been counted, I was short some three hundred votes—my margin of victory had become my margin of defeat. However, I would be in the run-off election on May 31, 1966.

I remember a white businessman from the lower part of Barbour County, whom I met on the campaign trail. He told me, "Well, Fred, I think you could probably develop into a good legislator, but you are not going to win it. We have been stealing elections from each other down here for years and you can imagine what will happen to you." As it turned out, he knew his Barbour County politics.

I was disappointed personally, of course, but I was especially sad for the young freedom singers and my supporters. According to Bernice, the first words I uttered after I learned I had lost the election was, with the sound of sorrow in my voice, "And those singers, they worked so hard . . . " Bernice had worked hard, too. To this day, we believe the election was stolen from me.

I was content to wait another four years and try again. However, the consensus of African-American leaders in the three counties was that the election should be contested. I wasn't optimistic about the outcome of a challenge. However, we had discovered in each of the three counties not only irregularities in voting, but also a general pattern of conduct designed to harass, intimidate, and discourage African-American voters from going to the polls. It seemed that everything possible had been done to make sure that African-American candidates did not win the election.

Gray v. Main

My law partner, Solomon Seay, Jr., was the lead counsel in the election challenge. He was assisted by Jack Greenberg, Charles H. Jones, Jr., and Charles Stephen Ralston of the NAACP Legal Defense and Educational Fund. The case was filed as *Fred D. Gray v. Fred D. Main, in his capacity as Judge of Probate of Bullock County.* The plaintiffs were me, candidate for the Alabama House of Representatives; Henry O. Williams, candidate for sheriff of Bullock County; Rufus Huffman, candidate for tax assessor of Bullock County; Ben McGhee and Alonza Ellis, candidates for Bullock County Court of County Commissioners; and Annie Kate Anglin, Mary Marshall, A. C. Bulls, Jr., Mary E. Huffman, Nathaniel Cummings, Rosic M. Outsey, and Calvin Jackson, Jr., all of whom were voters or poll watchers in House District 31.

We sued Bullock County Probate Judge Fred D. Main; Barbour County Circuit Court Registrar James A. Teal; the Democratic Party executive committees and their chairmen in the three counties; the boards of registrars and their chairmen in the three counties; and the Alabama State Democratic Party Executive Committee, and its chairman.

The suit was filed as a class action on behalf of the plaintiffs and all other African Americans who resided in those respective counties, and whose constitutional rights to participate in the election had been violated. The basic complaint was that the plaintiffs were deprived of rights guaranteed by the fourteenth and fifteenth amendments to the Constitution of the United States. The suit was filed on June 29, 1966, challenging the manner in which the primary election was conducted on May 31, 1966, the run-off election. It sought relief in four major categories:

(1) to have the board of registrars in each county purge the registration list;

(2) to have the court enjoin the defendants from receiving, canvassing or tabulating illegally cast ballots in the May 31, 1966, primary election, and to require the respective executive committees to refrain from certifying those persons selected in that election as Democratic nominees;

(3) to have the court enjoin the defendants from failing and refusing to hold a Democratic party run-off election in Bullock County, to set aside the election as to the plaintiffs in Bullock County, to have a new election called, and to have the court set a date for a new run-off election;

(4) In the new run-off elections, to enjoin officials from inhibiting Negros in the free exercise of their right to vote. In connection with that right, the court was asked to determine: (a) whether there were more white persons qualified to vote than white persons of voting age in Bullock County, and to what extent non-resident persons were permitted to illegally vote; (b) whether names of deceased persons appeared on poll list; (c) whether white persons were permitted to cast absentee ballots illegally; (d) whether qualified Negro voters were omitted from poll list; (e) whether illiterate Negro voters were denied assistance and thus prevented from or hindered in casting their ballots; (f) whether poll watchers were excluded or harassed at various polling places; (g) whether Negro

electors were prevented from casting challenged ballots.

The essence of the complaint was that the defendants had engaged in acts, the purpose and effect of which were to dilute the voting strength of African-American voters in Barbour, Bullock and Macon counties on the basis of race. The election officials in the three counties were alleged to have permitted numerous white persons in said counties to cast illegal absentee or regular votes with the purpose of increasing the voting strength of the white community by diluting the voting strength of the African-American population in these counties. The defendant boards of registrars of the three counties and their chairmen were alleged to have failed and refused to purge the registration list of their respective counties for the purpose and with the effect of increasing the apparent ratio of whites to Negro voters in their respective counties, and providing a vehicle whereby numerous illegal votes of white persons were received and counted in primary elections.

A review of the complaint and the relief prayed for vividly discloses that if these practices existed, and we submitted that in many instances they did, this went to the core of the problem. That is, whites were still using another means of discriminating against African Americans and preventing them from voting and from electing African Americans to public office. These issues were of paramount importance. Whether the lawsuit was won or lost, the fact was that during the discovery process, all of these white elected officials were deposed, in many instances by black lawyers, and for the first time many of these irregularities which existed in these counties were made known to the public. The primary purpose of the suit was to correct the irregularities which occurred in 1966 and be sure they did not exist in future elections.

On July 5, 1966, Judge Johnson designated the United States as amicus curiae and as a party to the suit. The United States, along with the plaintiffs, worked cooperatively in developing the evidence and presenting the case for trial.

This case was subsequently assigned to Judge Virgil Pittman. Judge Pittman did not have the experience, nor was he as familiar with discrimination against African Americans in the Middle

District of Alabama as Judge Johnson. It is questionable whether the decision of this case would have been the same if it had remained with Judge Johnson. Considering all of the other cases of voter registration, voter participation and discrimination, I'm of the opinion that if Judge Johnson had continued to hear this case to its conclusion, we would have won and obtained a similar result to the one we received in *Sellers v. Trussell*.

On March 28, 1968, Judge Virgil Pittman issued a fifty-two-page opinion and order, basically against the plaintiffs and in favor of the defendants. While the court found that there had been some irregularities and some unpleasantries, it did not find that African Americans had been denied the right to vote because of their color. The court concluded that there was no racially oriented fraud of significance, or any significant racial discrimination, based on the evidence presented to the court. The court was satisfied from the evidence that there were sufficient reasons to explain why there were more white people on the voters' list than existed in the total population. The court also found some criticisms with reference to how the Bullock County Board of Registrars had purged its list, but did not find that sufficient to overturn the election. The court concluded by stating:

> In the court's judgment, this was a free election, polarized as it was by white and Negro alike. The progress made in these three counties within recent years can be viewed with high heart. All is not perfect, but having reached this level it is believed that these defendants and their successors can now look higher still, having seen this much progress, only to see that greater progress can be achieved and only seeing this opportunity, to achieve it.

The court ordered the Macon County Board of Registrars to abide by an agreement which was worked out between the plaintiffs and the defendants. The agreement included a requirement that the Board of Registrars of Macon County would prepare and publish a proper list of qualified voters, and those persons who were not legally qualified to vote in Macon County should be removed. The court also ordered that Probate Judge Fred D. Main and the Board of Registrars of Bullock County immediately begin a procedure which would purge the voters' list and change the method of assigning persons to various precincts. The court also instructed the Bullock County officials to instruct its election officials, that in all future elections:

(1) restroom facilities should not be closed and that they be made available to all persons without regard to race or color;

(2) poll watchers are to be permitted the use of writing materials, i.e., pens, pencils, and paper without restraint;

(3) the election officials at voting machines are to follow the Alabama State Statute; and

(4) illiterate voters are to be permitted assistance in voting.

As we expected, the court did not order another run-off election for the May 31 primary. However, the fact that these issues became public and that African Americans became more aware of their right to vote assisted us in preparing for the next election. The white community also realized that African Americans were there to stay in these counties, that they must be treated fairly, and that they must be permitted to participate in the electoral process without regard to race and color.

This suit also paved the way so that now in Bullock County, a majority of county elected officials are African Americans.

My Second Attempt to Win a House Seat

In 1970 the Alabama Legislature was still segregated. I ran again. From the lessons learned in the first campaign, some changes were made the second time around. Poll watching was important and necessary.

Following the Booker T. Washington saying, "Cast down your bucket where you are," the students of Tuskegee Institute were mobilized. Oscar Sykes, a talented student from East Orange, New Jersey, was selected to head the Tuskegee students and coordinate their efforts.

The students were organized and went into all three counties.

They went to Barbour County the day before the election and prepared for election day. There were students as poll watchers at each one of the polling places. Local people were afraid to be poll watchers because many worked for white people and they would not challenge anything they did. But students from Tuskegee Institute were not afraid. The students were taught how to be poll watchers, what to watch for, and what to do. They did their job well.

I remember rather well one young lady, Ernestine Washington, a student who was assigned to the Armory at Eufaula (she now owns an independent insurance agency in Griffin, Georgia). Before the polls were open, she found that several people had already voted. She immediately called the sheriff and the sheriff did not permit anyone else to vote on that machine that day.

I Won!

Johnny Ford, who became the first African-American mayor of the city of Tuskegee, was my campaign manager and assisted tremendously in helping me to win.

I was successful and was the one of the first two African-Americans to become a member of the Alabama Legislature since Reconstruction, when James Alston was the last African American to serve. Thomas Reed was the other African American who was elected on the National Democratic Party of Alabama (NDPA) ticket in 1970.

I will never forget the day after the election. A white businessman from Bullock County, who also owned property in Macon County, visited me. Early the next morning after the election, he stopped by my office and said he wanted to meet his new legislator. He said, "I'm not going to lie to you. I didn't vote for you, but I wanted to meet my new legislator. If I can be of any assistance to you in Bullock County, let me know." I thanked him for coming by and then told him there was something that he could do.

I told him about Dr. Henry Foster, an obstetrician and gynecologist, who lived in Tuskegee at that time. He operated a prenatal care program financed by the federal government. The program was based in Macon County, but funds were available to have a clinic in Bullock County. But the approval of the Medical Society of Bullock County was required before the clinic could be established. So far, Dr. Foster had not been able to obtain that approval. I told the gentleman from Bullock County that I would like him to talk with the leading white doctors in Bullock County, and seek the approval of the doctors so the program would be available in Bullock County. I assured him that the program would not interfere with the local doctors' practices. It would not take any money from their pockets because the people who would be treated at the clinic did not have money to pay a doctor. He told me he would do what he could.

A few days later he called and asked for additional information. I sent it to him, and within a very short period of time, the medical society of Bullock County approved the program. Dr. Foster opened a clinic and provided excellent medical care for many of our people in Bullock County. Dr. Foster subsequently has served as acting president of Meharry Medical College in Nashville, Tennessee.

This incident is only one example of the amazing effect the rule of law and the power of the ballot had on the behavior of white Alabamians, most of whom sincerely believed in segregation. Of course, this faith that people could change, and that conditions would change along with them, was the core principle of the strategy of non-violence that propelled the Movement. It makes you wonder what might have happened if the John Pattersons and George Wallaces of the South had used their powers of leadership to uphold the Constitution rather than to fight it.

Service in the Legislature

I took the oath of office as a state representative in a ceremony conducted at the Capitol by Circuit Judge Richard Emmett of Montgomery. Bernice and many of my well-wishers were also present.

I worked diligently in the Alabama Legislature and created a great deal of good will. As a result of my presence there, the

Bernice holds the Bible as I take the oath from Judge Dick Emmett to serve in the Alabama legislature.

legislators and the state took notice that African Americans could serve in the Alabama Legislature with distinction. As a result of work I did, I was given a press corps award, Best Orator in the Alabama House of Representatives.

I wish I could say that I was able to pass many bills during my tenure in the Alabama Legislature, but I did not. I am proud that I was one of the first persons to introduce a bill in any state legislature to have a legal holiday in honor of the life and work of Dr. Martin Luther King, Jr. Martin had been as jubilant as I when it appeared that I had won my first election in 1966. Four years later, of course, he was dead. But on March 15, 1973, I held a press conference at Dexter Avenue Baptist Church and announced that I would introduce such a bill. Mrs. Coretta Scott King, his widow and founder and president of the Martin Luther King, Jr., Center for Social Change, attended the press conference and made remarks. Mrs. King, by the way, is an Alabama native and a dynamic leader in her own right. Her strength and abilities always were evident while she and Dr. King were living in Montgomery, though she was usually in the background because she was at that

This young man, Darryl Andrews, was one of my legislative pages. Prior to the election of African-American legislators, of course, only white children got the opportunity to serve and learn in this position. Darryl, incidentally, is a cousin to my law partner, Walter McGowan. Darryl went on to become a child case officer in the Montgomery juvenile court.

time a mother of small children. Her dignity and courage inspired the world during the tragic time when her husband was murdered. Since Martin's death, she has done a tremendous job of developing the King Center, under some very strenuous and adverse conditions.

I was very proud to have her with us in Montgomery when I

(Top) In 1973 I introduced the first legislative action, a bill in the Alabama House of Representatives, calling for a legal holiday in honor of Dr King. Joining me at a press conference were the Rev. S. S. Seay, Sr., Coretta Scott King, and the Rev. A. W. Wilson. (Bottom) On the same occasion, with Rev. Seay, Mrs. A. W. Wilson, Rosa Parks, and Tuskegee Mayor Johnny Ford.

announced the bill to create a holiday in Alabama in Dr. King's memory. I introduced the bill, but it did not pass. However, it laid the foundation so that other legislators in later years would be able to pass the bill. Now all of the states and the federal government have designated a legal holiday honoring Dr. King.

§

I enjoyed my term in office and still enjoy participating in politics. However, I learned quickly that the political process is a different ballgame from the judicial process. By the end of my term, I concluded that the legislature was not a place where I could accomplish very much. It was a part-time position which required full-time service. The only way that I could keep my head above water with my law practice was to work all hours of the night when the legislature was not in session. As things turned out, the problem was solved for me.

When I was elected in 1970 from the Macon County House District, that district had two representatives—Thomas Reed also served Macon County. By 1974, a new court-ordered redistricting plan was in effect, and Tom Reed and I had to run against each other to represent House District 28. Tom won that race, and I returned my full energies to practicing law, preaching, and spending time with my family. I decided not to seek another term, or any other elective office beyond strictly local party politics, and have not regretted that decision.

Nevertheless, my election to the Alabama Legislature as one of the first two African Americans to serve in that body since Reconstruction was another victory towards my secret goal of "destroying everything segregated that I could find."

14

Fred Gray, the Preacher

During the crucial years of the Montgomery Bus Protest, some persons claimed that I only pretended to be a minister. They did not know that I was a minister of the gospel long before I became a lawyer.

Jesus Christ is and always has been the center of my life. Ever since I can remember, my mother would take me to the Holt Street Church of Christ located on the corner of South Holt Street and Columbia Avenue in Montgomery.

My father died in 1932 when I was two years old and I have no recollection of him. My mother, other family members, and his close friends have always told me that he was a very religious person. I am sure the actions of my father and the actions of my mother and the Christian life that she lived contributed greatly to my religious life. In turn, my religious life has contributed greatly toward my overall growth and development.

I obeyed the Gospel and was baptized at the age of eight, in March 1939. I was baptized under the ministry of Brother William Whittaker, then the minister of the Holt Street Church of Christ.

During my early childhood I always wanted to be a gospel preacher. My mother told of the occasion, when I was just a little boy, that I declared, "I want to be a 'zospel preacher' just like Brother Whittaker." She also told of the occasions when I would baptize cats and dogs.

As I related in an earlier chapter, I became a minister when I was twelve years of age and received my training and experience at the

Nashville Christian Institute (NCI). This was in keeping with my boyhood dream of becoming a minister and with my mother's ambition for me. NCI was a segregated boarding school operated by members of the Church of Christ. The Bible was taught daily, there were daily chapel programs, and emphasis was placed on teaching young men to become preachers.

The dean of boys, who was in charge of daily activities and living conditions, was Bonnie Matthews, from Atlanta. Brother Matthews was to have a great influence on my life. For the next four and one half years I would spend at least nine months each year under his direct supervision and control. Since my father was dead, Brother Matthews was close to a father for me, and I kept in touch with him until his death about a decade ago.

As I grew and developed at the Nashville Christian Institute, I became one of the outstanding boy preachers. Between 1944 and 1947, I accompanied the president of NCI, Brother Marshall Keeble, on fund-raising trips to Kentucky, Tennessee, Georgia, Florida, Alabama, Arkansas, Oklahoma, Texas, Louisiana, and Mississippi. These trips raised funds for the school and recruited other students. They also helped the boy preachers pay their tuition through a second offering, which was always raised after the first major offering, which was for the school.

While attending the Nashville Christian Institute, I also served as part-time minister of several congregations. I lived on campus, and would, of course, go to school during the week. On weekends, I would get a bus to a particular town, spend Saturday night there, preach on Sunday, and return to the campus on Sunday night. I served as minister of churches in Gallatin, Tennessee; Murray, Kentucky; and Bowling Green, Kentucky.

When I enrolled in NCI, I was scheduled to graduate from high school in May 1948. But I was anxious to get back home to go to Alabama State College, so I went to summer school in order to finish high school early. Through arrangements with my teachers and principal, I was able to complete my high school studies before the Thanksgiving break in 1947. I was enrolled in Alabama State College on December 1.

Back in Montgomery I attended my home church, Holt Street Church of Christ. At various times over the next three years, I was a part-time minister with several of our churches in the Montgomery area, including the Churches of Christ in Titus, LaGrande, Brundidge, and Lanett, Alabama. During this time, I was also a full-time student at Alabama State College.

During the three-year period that I attended Western Reserve University Law School in Cleveland, I served as assistant minister of the East 100th Street Church of Christ, where Brother J. S. Winston was the minister. I first met Brother Winston in 1945, in Fort Worth, Texas, when I was a boy preacher traveling with Brother Keeble. So even while I was studying for the practice of law, I continued to serve as a minister of the Gospel.

Conflict? Preacher Versus Lawyer

After I graduated from law school and came back home to begin my law practice, I served as assistant minister of the Holt Street Church of Christ in Montgomery. My friend and classmate at the Nashville Christian Institute, K. K. Mitchell, was the minister.

I was probably one of the first African Americans who was an attorney and a minister in the Church of Christ. Certainly in my home congregation in Montgomery, no one had ever heard of a preacher also being a lawyer. This created a problem for some of our members. Their experiences with lawyers were such that in many instances they considered them liars not worthy to be trusted. So I had the additional responsibility of demonstrating to my own church members that I could continue to be a preacher of the Gospel and at the same time develop into an outstanding lawyer.

This was a problem not only for members of our local congregation, but also for the African-American brotherhood in the Church of Christ. When I would return to the Nashville Christian Institute to attend seminars, some persons were rather apprehensive of my ability to be a preacher and a lawyer. This became controversial throughout the brotherhood and when I became active as the lawyer for Dr. Martin Luther King, Mrs. Rosa Parks and the Bus Protest in Montgomery, some of my churchmen had reservations.

Even Brother Marshall Keeble, the great pioneer preacher who had carried me, as a boy preacher, around with him representing the Nashville Christian Institute, probably did not understand my position. One preacher who had been a student at NCI when I was there later said to Brother Keeble about me, "Fred Gray is smart. He is involved in the Civil Rights Movement." Brother Keeble is reported to have replied, "He's too smart." I could understand Brother Keeble's position. A portion of his preaching and work in the church had been sponsored by white members of the Church of Christ. I am quite confident that it was difficult for him to understand how one of his former boy preachers would now be standing in courtrooms fighting against racial discrimination.

However, the brotherhood soon saw that even though I was a lawyer, I was still very loyal to the church and continued to perform my ministerial duties. Over the years, I have been called upon many times by our leading church leaders across the nation to preach. There is no conflict in my mind about the two professions. On the contrary, having my life centered around Christ has assisted me in all of the cases that I have handled during my practice.

In 1957, Brother Bonnie Matthews, the dean who had been my father figure at NCI, approached me about serving as minister of Newtown Church of Christ. Located in north Montgomery, Newtown was one of the most poverty-stricken areas of the city. The Newtown congregation wanted me to be their minister. They realized I was practicing law, but they did not have a minister and felt I could do a good job. When Brother Matthews asked you to do something, it was tantamount to telling you to do it. I could not say "no" to him, nor to the people of Newtown. Besides, I really did not want to say "no." While I recognized it would be a tremendous responsibility for me to carry on a full-time law practice—particularly the demanding civil rights cases—and to serve as full-time minister, I saw no conflict between the two. There was a real need in Newtown for a viable, active church. I felt that I was in a position to help and I accepted the work.

Right, the Newtown Church of Christ building when I began preaching there. Below, the dedication of the cornerstone for the new church, 1971.

When I became minister of the Newtown Church of Christ, the congregation was worshipping in a house on Ferguson Street. The average Sunday attendance was ten to fifteen, and the highest weekly offering prior to my arrival was six dollars per week.

I served as minister of the Newtown Church of Christ from 1957 until November 5, 1973. Over that time, I witnessed many moral and spiritual victories at Newtown, including an increase in membership to approximately seventy-five members, the raising of a new, modern building with seating for two hundred worshipers, the development and maintenance of a Head Start Center which served sixty underprivileged children each day, the building of an educational wing, and the establishing of a vital, vibrant bus ministry.

Programs and activities that were good for the church were good for the Newtown community. We went throughout the community with a bus we had recently purchased and brought children to church. We taught them about Christ and how to become better citizens. Many of them have developed into outstanding citizens of Montgomery, Alabama, and the nation.

One of the things I endeavored to do was to instill into the people of the Newton community, and particularly to the young people, the confidence that despite their economic condition and where they lived, they could grow and develop into what they wanted to be. From our small congregation, we were successful in producing lawyers, doctors, teachers, principals, ministers, administrators and plain good citizens.

Currently, the Newtown Church of Christ congregation is one of the leading churches in that community. It has a membership of approximately 150; their building, including the educational facility, is now completely debt free. So, I think my work with this church went a long way in making it a viable congregation in the community and in helping the individual members to grow and develop into meaningful church leaders and meaningful citizens.

Even after moving my family to Tuskegee, I continued to serve until 1973, when I resigned as minister of the Newtown congregation and became minister of the Tuskegee Institute Church of Christ. Located in a small building, the Tuskegee Institute congregation was warm and friendly, but had very few members. The church's membership was about the same size as Newtown's had been back in 1957.

ℰ

Located on South Main Street in Tuskegee was another congregation, the East End Church of Christ. This was a white congregation that had experienced a decline in membership. James Allan Parker, president of Alabama Exchange Bank, was a leader at the East End congregation.

Allan Parker and I knew each other well after numerous business transactions. He was a vital link in maintaining good community relations during the Civil Rights Movement and during the early days of desegregating the public school system in Tuskegee.

There were a few blacks at the Institute congregation and there were a few whites at the East End congregation. I discussed the importance and the need of merging the two congregations with Brother Parker. We placed in motion a plan which resulted in the two congregations merging into one. We merged on the first Sunday of November 1974 and became the Tuskegee Church of Christ. This merger was one of the first such black and white mergers in the Church of Christ and may very well have been the first in the South. Subsequent to the merger, I was appointed an elder of the congregation (a position which I still hold), along with James Allan Parker and Penniman Williams, both white.

Not only was I able to destroy segregation in government, education and transportation, but also in the church. My ministerial work has been a complement to my legal work, and the legal work has supplemented my ministerial work. They have worked hand-in-hand.

And it all started on a bus! It was a bus that took me from my mother to my education at Nashville Christian Institute and Case Western Reserve Law School. It was a church bus ministry that was important in exposing young people to a better way of life, regardless of economic background. And it was a bus that was an instrumental vehicle for change that sparked the Civil Rights Movement in America.

Though few realize it, the bus can be a wonderful vehicle of opportunity. A bus can take you from where you are, to where you want to go!

In 1992, I had the privilege of giving a guest sermon at Chicago's Monroe Street Church of Christ, a great church, which has been led for forty years by my high school friend, Robert Woods.

15

The Family

My family life began with my "Boycott Wedding" to Bernice Hill on June 17, 1956, which I discussed earlier. I also mentioned that our honeymoon was cut short because I had to get back to Alabama for an appointment with the draft board. I always had a ministerial deferment, and this was never questioned until I filed the lawsuit to integrate the Montgomery buses. The draft board then became very interested in drafting me and ordered me to take a physical examination. While the draft board was setting things in motion to draft me, I was setting in motion the appeal procedure. I had no objection to serving my country, but I did not intend to be drafted for the purpose of removing me from serving as legal counsel for the Bus Boycott.

Bernice meanwhile learned, through one of her friends who had married recently and who was expecting, that there was a policy of the draft board in Montgomery County not to draft fathers and prospective fathers. You must remember this was not during war time and there was no real need for manpower in the military, even though the draft was still active. I was able to verify that the policy did exist and that the draft board was not drafting fathers or prospective fathers. With this knowledge in hand, it became very important to Bernice and me and to the Movement that we begin our family immediately.

Several months later, Bernice suspected she was pregnant. Through some of her friends, she was referred to a white obstetrician–gynecologist. I had serious reservations about her seeing a white physician, wondering whether that person would or would not be truthful. I also discovered that this doctor was from a prominent family who was a part of the power structure in Montgomery County.

After Bernice's examination, the doctor's assistant told her that her test for pregnancy was negative, but the doctor wanted to see her again on a designated date. This seemed strange to me. If she was not pregnant, why would it be necessary for her to return?

I suggested that Bernice go to Dr. Moses Jones, an African-American physician, who was our friend, a member of the board of the Montgomery Improvement Association, and a very active civil rights leader. She went the next day and Dr. Jones advised her that she was in fact pregnant. This information was forwarded to my draft board and I used that as a means for requesting, pursuant to their own policies, that I not be drafted. The draft board was not swayed and continued with the effort to induct me. As I mentioned earlier, I was kept out of the draft by the intervention of the national director of the Selective Service. Notwithstanding, I was a prospective father.

Our first child, Deborah René Gray, was born April 2, 1957, exactly ten months after our marriage. Her birth came right in the middle of all of the activities in the aftermath of the Bus Boycott and in the middle of several other cases that we have discussed earlier. She was a very perceptive, sensitive and understanding child.

Deborah's elementary school work was done at Chisholm Elementary School in Montgomery, Alabama State Laboratory School, and Tuskegee Public. She began at Alabama Christian High School in Montgomery and completed her secondary work at Tuskegee Institute High.

She wanted to attend a small, good liberal arts college and her freshman year was spent at Macalester College in Saint Paul, Minnesota. While a student at Macalester College, she wrote a paper on the Tuskegee Syphilis Study which helped me locate participants and heirs of deceased participants in that case. The

The announcement Bernice and I sent out for Deborah's birth.

next year Deborah transferred to Loyola University in New Orleans, where she finished with a B.S. in marketing and communications. Despite transferring, she finished college in three years.

She has been employed in the communication field in several states including the following: WSFA-TV, Montgomery, Alabama; WFSU, a public television station in Tallahassee, Florida; Vanderbilt University in Nashville, Tennessee, where she produced their freshman handbook; WQXM radio station in Clearwater, Florida; and Channel 10 in St. Petersburg, Florida. She worked with several ad agencies in Los Angeles, California, and further studied at UCLA. When she became interested in beginning her own ad agency, Milton McGregor, president of Macon

County Greyhound Park, saw some of her work and asked if she would like to serve as the Atlanta-based director of marketing and sales for Macon County Greyhound Park, which position she accepted and still holds. She also holds a similar position with the new Birmingham Race Course.

Our second child, Vanessa, was born July 18, 1958. Vanessa was a highly individualistic child, not as outgoing as her older sister, but had many of her mother's characteristics. She attended Lewis Adams Elementary School in Tuskegee and graduated from Tuskegee Institute High School. She received the associate arts degree from Southwestern Christian College in Terrell, Texas, and the B.S. in office administration in 1980 from Oklahoma Christian College in Oklahoma City. She is a secretary and has been employed by the City of Tuskegee, Tuskegee University, and is a legal secretary to Walter McGowan in our law firm. She is married to Luther Taylor, an independent contractor; they produced our first grandchild, LaDrena Nichole Taylor.

After our first two children were girls, we were beginning to wonder whether we would have any sons. On September 21, 1961, Fred D. Gray, Jr., was born. Dr. Moses Jones delivered all of our children. He informed us immediately after Fred's birth that Fred was having some difficulties and would not be able to be released with his mother. Later Dr. Jones informed me that he had some very serious problems with getting Fred to breathe properly, and had some serious reservations about whether or not he would make it. But all went well, and later Fred was brought home where he grew and developed like all of the other children. He attended Lewis Adams Elementary School in Tuskegee and graduated from Alabama Christian High School in Montgomery.

I had the privilege of being the commencement speaker at his high school graduation and he gave my introduction. He graduated from Morehouse College with a degree in political science and then finished law school at Howard University. He is married to Bridgett Vassar of Seattle, Washington. They met while he was attending Morehouse, and she was attending Spelman College, from which she graduated. She is also a graduate of Jones Law

This photo of our family was made about 1966, not long after we moved to Tuskegee.

School in Montgomery and works as a law clerk in our firm. Recently Bridgett was appointed chairman of the Macon County Board of Registrars. Fred is a partner in our firm, has served as city prosecutor, and now is doing most of the legal work for the City of Tuskegee. Fred and Bridgett have given us our second grandchild, Destiny Cherelle Gray.

Our last child, Stanley Fitzgerald, was born March 22, 1964. He attended Lewis Adams Elementary School and Alabama Christian High School and finished at Tuskegee Institute High School. He was a political science major with a minor in criminal justice at the University of Alabama, and graduated from Howard University School of Law. Upon his graduation, he served as a law clerk to Judge John C. Tyson, then a judge of the Criminal Court of Appeals of Alabama. Stanley is now a member of our firm and serves as the city prosecutor for the City of Tuskegee. He is married to Lawanda Agnew from Fayette, Alabama. She received a B.S. in business from Auburn University in Montgomery and a nursing degree from Troy State University. She is a nursing administrator at an area nursing facility. Stanley and LaWanda have given us our third grandchild, Sierra Je'Von Gray. We also have a grandson, Je'Michael Agnew.

Our basic philosophy was to instill in our children several principles:

(1) to place God first in their lives and to develop into good, outstanding Christians;

(2) to develop into and be good family members, devoted to their families;

(3) to be good citizens; and,

(4) to make something out of themselves.

We never attempted to dictate the schools they should attend, but we encouraged them to complete their education and to be the very best that they could be.

Because of my work schedule and their births occurring between 1957 and 1964, during the early, crucial stage of the Civil Rights Movement, I often could not devote as much time as I would like to have devoted to them individually while they were

The grandchildren— 1993.
Je'Michael, Ladrena, Sierra and Destiny.

growing up, even though my wife, Bernice, did. We did have good quality time together. We always spent all day Sunday, including evenings, with each other in church and related activities. We always had mid-week church services and these religious activities have helped to develop them into the men and women that they are.

As I review our relationship as a family, if I had the opportunity to make a change, the one thing I would change would be to devote more time to them during their very young, formative years.

This portrait was a Christmas gift a few years ago from our children: Deborah (seated), Stanley, Vanessa and Fred, Jr.

16

A University Which Never Should Have Been Built

The racial climate in the City of Montgomery in 1966-67 was hostile. Some of the best testimony to illustrate the situation that year came twenty-four years after the fact when the noted Alabama historian J. Mills Thornton, a native white Montgomerian, testified in the case of *John F. Knight v. State of Alabama*. This was a case seeking to prove that higher education in Alabama was still segregated, despite the many court orders of the 1960s.

In his testimony on November 26, 1990, Dr. Thornton was asked to describe the atmosphere and racial conditions that existed in Montgomery at the time two legislative acts were adopted which created Auburn University at Montgomery. Montgomery, of course, already had a state-supported institution of higher learning. Alabama State College (now Alabama State University) had operated in Montgomery since 1874. The African-American residents of Montgomery raised the funds to construct many of the buildings during the early years of Alabama State's existence in Montgomery. The state of Alabama had never properly funded Alabama State— and still does not—to the same extent that it has funded the University of Alabama and Auburn University.

In 1966–67, there also were two private colleges in Montgomery, neither of which admitted African Americans. They were Huntingdon College, a Methodist-supported college, and Alabama Christian College, a Church of Christ-supported college which is now Faulkner University. The University of Alabama also had an extension in Montgomery. And Auburn University itself was only forty miles up Interstate 85. The problem was that Auburn, as we have seen already, was virtually all white, while Alabama State was virtually all black.

It was clear to the white Montgomery power structure that under court-ordered desegregation, Montgomery would soon find itself represented for the purpose of state-supported higher education by Alabama State, an African-American institution. And this would not do.

Dr. Thornton set out to explain this complicated background in his court testimony in *Knight v. Alabama*. He stated that in 1966 there was considerable racial polarization in Alabama. It was a gubernatorial election year, and at that time Alabama had a law that governors could not succeed themselves. Governor George Wallace, elected in 1962, had sought to change the state constitution so that he could succeed himself. When that failed, he decided to run his first wife, Lurleen, as a puppet candidate in his stead. Attorney General Richmond Flowers, considered a moderate, decided to run against Lurleen Wallace. As a result of the passage of the Voting Rights Act of 1965, Alabama had many new black voters, and Flowers received substantial support from the black community. He made a strong appeal for the black vote. However, when white voters saw that black voters were supporting Flowers, they became even more polarized. As a result, Lurleen Wallace won without a run-off, but most of the moderate white candidates who were running for other offices lost.

George Wallace's term as governor was to end in January 1967, when his wife was to be sworn in. In reality, George Wallace simply moved to an office in the State Capitol across the hall from the executive suite, and he continued to wield the power of state government while his wife handled ceremonial functions.

During the summer of 1966, Governor George Wallace called a special session of the legislature. In a televised speech to the legislature, he denounced Judge Frank M. Johnson, Jr., as a puppet of the U.S. Justice Department, which by inference was trying to destroy the "Southern way of life." As the governor addressed the

Professor
J. Mills
Thornton

legislature, a message flashed on the television screens below his image, urging parents to send contributions to be used to finance private schools for white children. The names and addresses of the private school foundations where these contributions could be sent were shown on television.

Thornton further testified that following the swearing-in of Wallace's wife as governor in January 1967, a great number of racial issues dominated the legislature during its regular session. One resolution called upon all public schools, black and white, to fly the Confederate flag and to play "Dixie" at all college football games and homecoming festivities in Alabama. Another resolution demanded that the U.S. Justice Department seek an indictment for treason and sedition against Stokely Carmichael of the Student Non-Violent Coordinating Committee. This was also the session of the legislature in which bills were passed creating separate boards of trustees for the four white teacher colleges in the state. It did not create separate boards for the black colleges.

And it was during this session that a bill was passed authorizing a five million dollar bond issue to create a branch of Auburn University at Montgomery. The sponsor of the bond issue bill was State Senate President Pro Tem O. J. (Joe) Goodwin, of Montgomery. He was also the principal legislative floor leader for the Wallace administration. Joe Goodwin and members of his law firm had been very active in defending cases that we had brought to integrate various facilities in Montgomery. They were the attorneys representing the state in connection with the Regal Cafe. The firm had also represented a group that, after the Supreme Court had ruled in December 1956, made a futile attempt to prolong segregation by organizing an all-white private bus line.

The African-American community opposed the creation of such an institution. We knew that such an institution would perpetuate a dual educational system based upon race. We believed that the State of Alabama should take the funds which it contemplated using to create a new college and use those funds to expand Alabama State College, so that it would become the institution that the business community envisioned. The African-American community further stated that it was not necessary to construct a new college for whites. Alabama State College could be expanded to attract white students.

Thornton concluded his testimony by stating that it was in this setting that the acts were passed to create Auburn University at Montgomery.

Suit to Prohibit Auburn University at Montgomery

In a letter on February 3, 1968, Joe Reed, then executive secretary of the Alabama State Teachers Association, asked me to file a lawsuit against the Alabama Public School and College Authority, the trustees of Auburn University, and the State of Alabama, in which we would seek to enjoin the creation of Auburn University in Montgomery. The plaintiffs were the Alabama State Teachers Association, Alvin A. Holmes and Joe L. Reed, as adult citizens of Montgomery, and William Sankey, Albert S. Harris, Jr., and Sylvester Presley, who at that time were students at Alabama State College. Mr. Reed urged me to start legal action immediately.

Solomon S. Seay, Jr., and NAACP Legal Defense Fund attorneys Jack Greenberg, Paul Brest, and Melvin Zarr helped me prepare the complaint. *Alabama State Teacher's Association v. Alabama Public School and College Authority* was filed in February 1968 in Montgomery's federal court. By then, Governor Lurleen

Wallace had died of cancer—she was already ill with the disease when she ran for office—and Lieutenant Governor Albert P. Brewer had succeeded her as governor and thus as head of the state schools. Other defendants included Ernest Stone, vice president of the authority; Robert B. Ingram, secretary of the authority; Agnes Baggett, treasurer of the authority; and E. L. Wynn, M. H. Moses, Paul S. Holley, R. C. Bamberg, Redus Collier, John W. Overton, John Pace, III, Sim A. Thomas, Roberts H. Brown, and Frank P. Samford, trustees of Auburn University; and the Board of Trustees of Auburn University. The defendants were represented by Alabama Attorney General MacDonald Gallion, his assistant Gordon Madison, James J. Carter, and Thomas D. Sanford, on behalf of the trustees of Auburn University.

We argued that the act establishing a new four-year college in Montgomery was further evidence of a legislative plan to perpetuate a dual system of education based on race. We alleged that the State of Alabama had enforced and pursued an official policy of separation of the races in public education and that pursuant to that policy, it had failed to provide adequate financial support for state-supported schools designated for use by African Americans, and particularly at Alabama State College in Montgomery.

The complaint further alleged that the purpose and effect of Act No. 403 would be to continue the state's official policy of denying the African-American citizens of Alabama a quality education, arbitrarily and capriciously denying adequate financial support to finance traditional African-American schools, while at the same time diverting available funds to a predominantly white school. And as such, the plaintiffs were denied due process and equal protection of the law under the Fourteenth Amendment to the United States Constitution.

A three-judge federal panel consisting of District Court Judges Frank M. Johnson, Jr., and Virgil Pittman, and Appeals Court Judge Walter P. Ewing was appointed and the case was set for hearing on May 2, 1968.

It is interesting to note that at the time this case was filed, the United States District Court for the Middle District of Alabama had already decided a line of cases in which the State of Alabama had consistently denied to African Americans their rights, including: *Browder v. Gayle*, which integrated the city buses in the City of Montgomery; *Lewis v. Greyhound*, which integrated the lunch counters in the bus terminals in Montgomery; *Carr v. Montgomery County Board of Education*, which integrated the public schools in Montgomery; *Smith v. YMCA*, which integrated the YMCA in Montgomery; *Gomillion v. Lightfoot*, which provided for the restoration of African Americans to city limits of the City of Tuskegee; *Sellers v. Trussell*, which prohibited the Bullock County commissioners from extending their terms to delay further the election of African Americans to county government; and *Smith v. Paris*, which prohibited the Barbour County Democratic Executive Committee from diluting the African-American vote by prohibiting them from obtaining membership on their County and the Democratic Executive Committee. I was an attorney in all of these cases.

The Importance of the Case

This was a very important case. If segregation in higher education was to end it would be necessary that white citizens understand that it is just as important for whites to enroll in historically African-American institutions as it is for African Americans to enroll in historically white institutions.

The white community was very involved and concerned about this case. The whole concept of establishing a branch of Auburn in Montgomery (AUM) began in the white community, particularly with the Chamber of Commerce.

I felt it would be advantageous to get the assistance of a lawyer in Montgomery who had some ties in the white community. At that time I had a very close working relationship with Morris Dees, who was a good, hard-working lawyer. He had asked me to assist him in *Smith v. YMCA*, the case that integrated Montgomery's citywide recreation program. I invited Morris to work with me on the AUM case. He graciously accepted and in April 1968 joined the plaintiffs' legal team. I asked Morris Dees to join in this case for several reasons. One was that he was white, and I believed he could obtain more information about the true reasons for the formation of AUM than I could.

We all worked very hard in preparing this case. We took all the necessary depositions, prepared the exhibits, properly tried the case, asked the court to take judicial notice of all of its prior action, and we were hopeful that Judge Johnson and at least one of the other members of the court would rule in our favor. I was not unmindful, however, that this was a case of first impression and that Judge Johnson, on several occasions, had ruled against my clients who were the plaintiffs in other cases of first impression.

For example, he ruled against the plaintiffs in *Gomillion v. Lightfoot,* and was reversed by the United States Supreme Court. He had ruled against the plaintiffs in *St. John Dixon v. Alabama State College,* another higher education case, which in some degree was quite similar to this case. In the *Dixon* case, Judge Johnson ruled that a student did not have a constitutional right to attend a state-supported institution and, therefore, was not entitled to procedural due process of law and could be summarily expelled from that institution. He was reversed in that case, too. So, we recognized the risk, hoped for the best, but prepared for the worst.

The Court Order Denying Relief

The worst came. On July 26, 1968, we received the bad news. In a unanimous decision authored by Judge Johnson, the court denied the request and entered judgment in favor of the defendants.

In the court's opinion, it admitted that this case was a case of first impression. That is, never before had a court been called upon to decide the issues in this case. No court, in dealing with desegregation of institutions in higher education, had gone further than ordering non-discriminatory admissions. The court then stated, "We too are reluctant at this time to go much beyond preventing discriminatory admissions."

The court acknowledged that Alabama had a dual system of higher education based on race. It further stated that this system in higher education had not been fully dismantled. However, the court disagreed with the plaintiff in terms of the scope of the court's duty to extend and impose upon institutions of higher education the same duties that it had placed upon elementary and secondary public schools with reference to desegregating their facilities.

The court saw a distinction in elementary and secondary public schools as being compulsory and free. On the other hand, institutions of higher education were neither free nor compulsive. Therefore, institutions of higher education should be governed by different standards. The court acknowledged that, at that time, there were four institutions of higher learning in Montgomery: two private, Huntington College and Alabama Christian, and two public, Alabama State College and the University of Alabama Extension Center. The Center did not offer degrees and was similar to a junior college. Alabama State was a predominantly Negro four-year liberal arts college with emphasis on teaching education.

The court further stated that the initial move to create an additional four-year state-supported institution in Montgomery was generated by the local Chamber of Commerce. A committee of the Chamber had determined that there was a need and had approached the Alabama Extension Center with reference to expanding its facilities so that it could accommodate approximately fifteen thousand students, with undergraduate majors in liberal arts, business, teaching education, as well as graduate work in education, business administration, and political science. The University of Alabama officials were not interested, due to other commitments. Auburn University was then approached and expressed an interest.

The court acknowledged our claim that the creation of an Auburn branch in Montgomery would perpetuate, rather than eliminate, the dual school system in higher education. However, the court rejected our contention, even though it admitted that Alabama State was never seriously considered for expansion into the type of facility that the Chamber of Commerce wanted.

The court concluded that, " . . . As long as the State and a particular institution are dealing with admissions, faculty and staff in good faith with basic requirements of the affirmative duties to dismantle the dual school system on the college level, to the extent that the system may be based upon racial consideration, is satisfied."

A Lost Opportunity

It is rather difficult to understand the court's rationalization in this case in light of Alabama's racial history. It is also difficult to understand how the court could have reached such a conclusion in view of the numerous cases which had been decided in the Middle District of Alabama from 1956 up until that time. The opinion is hard to square with Judge Johnson's opinions in *Sellers v. Trussell* and the *United States of America v. John Allen Crook*. Those were the cases where the legislature had arbitrarily extended the terms of the sitting white county commissioners in Bullock County, just at the point where it looked as if Bullock's 70 percent African-American population was about to take control in the county. In those cases, Judge Richard T. Rives had accepted local and state officials' explanations for the illegal term extensions. But Judge Johnson had strongly disagreed with Judge Rives, and stated:

> Nor can I concur in the finding that there was no racially discriminatory motivation in the passage of Act 536. The history of voting discrimination against Negroes over a substantial period of time in Bullock County on the part of the State of Alabama and Bullock County officials, as reflected by the evidence in this case, and as judicially found to exist in *Sellers v. Wilson* . . . has been systematic, intentional, invidious, and in clear violation of the Fifteenth Amendment. Any determination in this case of legislative motive must be viewed in this light. Viewing Act 536 in such light, leads me, in the absence of any reasonable explanation for its passage, to the firm conclusion that its introduction and passage was racially motivated. The explanation for the introduction of the pro-

posed state-wide bill—which did not even get out of the House Committee—cannot serve, in the absence of some such testimony, as an explanation for the introduction and passage of local Act 536. Certainly, with this background, with the evidence in this case, and where the manifest consequences and clear effect of legislation is discriminatory, an inference of a purpose to discriminate is compelling. This is the clear teaching of *Gomillion v. Lightfoot* . . .

Using that same logic in this case, I thought the court should have found the 1967 act creating AUM to be racially discriminatory in both intent and effect. The history of discrimination in education throughout the State of Alabama and particularly in Montgomery, as reflected by the evidence in this case, and as judicially noted in all of the cases which we cited, has been systematic, intentional, invidious, and in clear violation of the Fourteenth Amendment. Any determination in this case of legislative motive must be viewed in this light. The explanation of the Chamber of Commerce and others that Montgomery needed an institution capable of accommodating fifteen thousand students, and other excuses, should not have been credible under the facts and circumstances of this case. Such an explanation was a mere pretext.

Ultimately, this case was appealed to the U.S. Supreme Court which affirmed without an opinion. I believe the failure to grant plaintiffs' relief in this 1967-68 case made it necessary a decade and a half later for African-American plaintiffs, joined by the U.S. Justice Department, to file *Knight v. Alabama*. This 1983 case alleged that a dual system of higher learning based on race and vestiges of discrimination still existed in the State of Alabama. Judge U. W. Clemon so found on December 9, 1985. His decision was reversed on other grounds. Judge Harold Murphy of Rome, Georgia, re-tried the case in 1990 and 1991. In his order on December 27, 1991, Judge Murphy stated that there were still vestiges of discrimination in higher education in Alabama.

The Court Could Have Made History

Years and years of continued discrimination and litigation could have been avoided if the court had ruled for the plaintiffs in their lawsuit against the creation of AUM in 1968; the history of higher education in Alabama and perhaps in the nation would have been different. In 1968, the court had an opportunity to do for higher education what the Supreme Court of the United States did for elementary and secondary education in 1954 in *Brown v. Board of Education.* But, the court did not take advantage of that opportunity.

The court, in *Lee v. Macon,* integrated all public elementary and secondary schools in one court order. In that same order, the court integrated and took affirmative action, and required the State Board of Education to eliminate discrimination in junior colleges, trade schools, and all other colleges then under the control of the State Board of Education. If the court in *ASTA* had enjoined the construction of Auburn University at Montgomery in 1968, those funds could have gone toward the expansion of Alabama State University, which today would probably be one of the outstanding institutions in Alabama, with a substantial enrollment of white students. By so acting, the court could have removed the identifying mark of Alabama State University as an African-American institution. Thus, the entire pattern and course of higher education in this state could have been redirected. If the plaintiffs had been successful in that case, it would have also meant that a similar lawsuit could have been brought in Huntsville, which would have prohibited the University of Alabama from creating the University of Alabama in Huntsville, in the front door of Alabama A&M University, a historically African-American university.

When I consider all of the cases involving education that I have handled, losing *ASTA* was probably the most disappointing. Not that it was disappointing to me personally, because I gave it all I had in furtherance of my goal of destroying segregation. It was disappointing in that it has cost the State of Alabama millions of dollars in continuously perpetuating a dual system of education based on race. It has continued to deny African-American citizens their rights under the Fourteenth Amendment. It has continued to perpetuate the myth that the real way to do away with dual educational institutions in Alabama is to take African-American students and place them in historically white institutions, but never place a substantial number of white students in historically black institutions. This practice is wrong and should be stopped.

It permitted Judge Murphy to write, at least temporarily, the latest chapter in higher education in the State of Alabama. In an 840-page opinion, entered on December 27, 1991, Judge Murphy found that there are still vestiges of racial discrimination in higher education in this state and he ordered appropriate relief. His order was appealed to the Eleventh Circuit, where a portion of the court's order concerning relief was reversed and remanded. Judge Murphy set a hearing for January 1995, thus assuring that Alabama's higher education system would be litigated for yet another year. This could have been avoided if we had received a favorable decision in *ASTA* in 1968, more than twenty-five years ago.

I will tell more about the case before Judge Murphy in Chapter 20.

17

The Tuskegee Syphilis Study

On July 27, 1972, Mr. Charlie Pollard came into my office and asked me if I had been reading in the newspaper about the men who were involved in the syphilis tests for "bad blood." He said he was one of the men. He then related that a few days before, he was at a stockyard in Montgomery and a newspaper woman found him and questioned him about the Tuskegee testing program, and asked him if he knew Mrs. Rivers. He stated he did. Mrs. Eunice Rivers was the nurse who worked with the men in the study from the beginning to end. The reporter engaged him in a conversation about his involvement in a health program since back in the thirties. Mr. Pollard related in detail his involvement in the study. As a result of our discussion, I agreed to represent Mr. Pollard in a lawsuit against the government and any others we believed were legally responsible for operating and maintaining the study.

Mr. Pollard's statement confirmed the story I read on an airplane flying from Washington, D.C., to Montgomery a few days earlier. The story in *The Washington Post*, written by Jean Heller, was about a study that involved African-American males in Macon County, Alabama. The purpose of the study was to learn the effects of untreated syphilis upon male African Americans. As I read the story on the plane, I thought it was a tragedy that these poor rural men in my county had suffered such an injustice. I was not too surprised, because I had witnessed many areas wherein African Americans had been treated unjustly. This was especially

With Mr. Charlie Pollard, the lead plaintiff in the Tuskegee Syphilis Study case.

appalling because it was a life or death situation. I was shocked, however, that local African Americans and the community generally were unaware that such a study existed.

Our investigation disclosed the following with respect to what has become known as the Tuskegee Syphilis Study.

The Study, 1932–1972

In 1932, notices were issued by Dr. Smith and Nurse Rivers, announcing a new health program in Macon County. These notices were circulated throughout the county by mail and at churches and schools. Primary participation in the new program included taking blood tests. Only African Americans were given notices and only African-American males participated in the program. They were uneducated, poor, and lived in rural areas.

More than six hundred participants, divided into two groups, were involved in the study. One group had syphilis. The other group did not have syphilis and were a control group. The medical intent was to observe the effects of untreated syphilis. Both groups were given annual physical examinations. The results for the symphilitics were compared to the results for the controls.

Doctors and nurses administering the health program told the participants various things after blood tests were taken. Some of the participants were told they had bad blood. However, they did not know what bad blood meant at that time. Others were told nothing. None was ever told he had syphilis. Most knew nothing about syphilis. They were not told they were involved in a study. They never gave or were even asked to give written consent. Some were told they would receive money; others were not. Many did receive twenty-five dollars and a twenty-five-year certificate of appreciation in 1958. Some families received money for burial expenses if they would permit autopsies. This amount ranged from twenty-five to one hundred dollars, depending upon when the participant died.

Some participants were also promised free hot lunches and free transportation to be examined. The methods used to induce participation in the study are best described in an article written by Nurse Rivers and two of the physicians of the U. S. Public Health Service:

> Because of the lower educational status of a majority of the patients, such as farmers and day laborers, it was impossible to appeal to them from a purely scientific approach. Therefore, various methods were used to maintain and stimulate their interest: free medicine, except penicillin; burial assistance or insurance (the project was referred to as "Miss Rivers' Lodge"); free hot meals on the day of the examination by public health service physicians

periodically, transportation to and from the hospital, and an opportunity to stop in town on the return trip to shop or visit with friends.

All participants were given shots, a green-colored tonic and white pills. Virtually none of those interviewed knew the purpose of the shots, but assumed they were for bad blood. One participant said the shots were called 606 shots. Mr. Pollard said they were given some tonic and some pills but none of it did any good. Most believed the treatment was adequate for their medical problems.

Many participants received a spinal injection early in the program. All shots were given during the early 1930's. Many of them have forgotten the frequency of the examinations, but thought that they were examined about once a year from the inception of the program until about 1952 and then every two years.

The examination included x-rays on at least two occasions. They were made at various places, including local churches, local schools, the Veterans Administration Hospital, John Andrew Hospital, and the Macon County Health Center.

Sometime in the late forties or early fifties, there was a massive effort to get all persons in Macon County who had syphilis treated. Most of the whites and many African Americans were sent to Birmingham to receive such treatment. However, those who participated in the Tuskegee Study were not permitted to receive such treatment. Herman Shaw, one of the participants, recalls that he was included in a group of men who were taken to Birmingham for treatment. During the night before they were to be treated, a lady who was in charge of the facility where they were staying was pacing the floor. He asked her, "Ma'am, what's the matter?" She said, "There is somebody who is here that's not supposed to be here." He says, "Who is it and what's his name?" She said, "Herman Shaw." He said, "I'm Herman Shaw." She said, "You're not supposed to be here. Get up and put on your clothes."

He followed her instructions, they put him on a bus, sent him home and never treated him.

It was not until the summer of 1972 that the participants

learned through the news media that they were part of the Tuskegee Study, and many of those persons did not know that they had syphilis or that they were a part of a study.

Our Conclusions, 1972–1973

As a result of our investigation, we reached the following conclusions:

1. That the United States government violated the constitutional rights of the participants in the manner in which the study was conducted.

2. The government knew that they had syphilis and failed to treat them.

3. The Public Health Service failed to fully disclose to them that they had syphilis; that they were participating in a study; and that treatment was available for syphilis.

4. The Public Health Service led them to believe that they were being properly treated for whatever diseases they had, when in fact, they were not being treated at all.

5. The Public Health Service failed to obtain the participants' written consents to be a part of the study.

6. The Study was racially motivated and it discriminated against African Americans in that no whites were selected to participate in the Study and only recruited those who were poor, uneducated, rural and African-American.

7. That there were no rules and regulations governing the Study.

Search for Assistance

The work involved in developing this case was tremendous. I was again reminded of advice given me by my law school professor, Samuel Sonnenfield. He was also my personal adviser. He encouraged me to seek assistance of other more experienced lawyers, and be willing to share a fee with them, particularly during the early years of my practice. As I had done with civil rights cases, I tried to find someone to assist me in this case.

Finding and obtaining assistance was more difficult than I ever imagined. For almost a year, I telephoned and traveled all over the country, looking for someone to help me with this potentially historic case. I needed help in legal research and drafting pleadings and briefs and to finance the case.

Previously, with civil rights cases, I was usually able to obtain such assistance from the NAACP or the NAACP Legal Defense Fund. But both organizations are non-profit corporations, whose policies did not permit them to assist in fee-generating cases.

It was going to take a substantial amount of money to develop this case. I could not find anyone who was willing to give me assistance in my two areas of need.

With a recommendation from Jack Greenberg, Director Counsel of the NAACP Legal Defense Fund, I sought out Michael I. Sovern, then dean of Columbia Law School, and one of his professors, Harold Edgar. They assisted me with legal research.

I still had the responsibility of financing the case. I went to my local banker, James Allan Parker, president of Alabama Exchange Bank, discussed my problem, and he indicated a willingness to make a loan. It was not a loan on a contingent fee basis. No banker would have done that. I would have to pay the bank regardless of the result of the lawsuit. However, he was willing to wait until there was a resolution of the case before the loan would become due. With these two components in hand, I was now ready to file the lawsuit.

On July 24, 1973, the lawsuit was filed and amended on August 1, 1974. The plaintiffs were Charlie W. Pollard, Carter Howard, Herman Shaw, Price Johnson, and others. My law partner, Solomon Seay, Jr. assisted with the case. Cleveland Thornton, a young white lawyer from Barbour County and a member of our firm at the time, also assisted me in this case.

The defendants were the United States of America, Casper Weinberger as Secretary of the Department of Health, Education and Welfare, Dr. Ira L. Myers, State Health Officer, Dr. John R. Heller, individually, Dr. Sidney Olansky, individually, and others. The defendants were represented by William J. Baxley, then attorney general, James T. Pons, Kenneth Vines, Calvin Pryor,

Lawrence Klinger, Herman H. Hamilton, Jr., Champ Lyons, W. Michael Atchinson, and Oakley Melton, Jr.

In the complaint as finally amended we had four categories of plaintiffs: (1) living syphilitics; (2) living controls; (3) personal representatives of the estates of deceased syphilitics; and (4) personal representatives of the estates of deceased controls.

This lawsuit was to redress grievances by damages and injunctive relief in order to secure for the plaintiffs, themselves and the class they represented, protection against continued or future deprivation of their rights by the defendants.

Jurisdiction was invoked under (1) the Fourth, Fifth, Eighth, Ninth, Thirteenth and Fourteenth amendments to the U.S. Constitution; (2) the civil rights laws 42 USC Section 1981, Section 185(3), and Section 2000(D); (3) the Federal Torts Claims Act, 28 USC 2671; (4) the federal common law, and (5) the Constitution, statutes and common law of Alabama.

Discovery

One major problem in preparing the case for trial was the matter of obtaining discovery. According to the federal rules of civil procedure, after a lawsuit is filed, and prior to trial, a party may obtain any and all information which the other party has that may be relevant to the lawsuit. This is called discovery. We utilized several forms of discovery: depositions, interrogatories, request for admissions, and request for production.

Interrogatories were propounded to the known living doctors and proper officials of the Public Health Service and to the government, but many of the answers were inconclusive and the response to the motion to produce documents during the early part of the study were met with a "no records available so far as the government knew."

The plaintiffs then undertook to try and find these records. As a result of our independent efforts, I met Jim Jones, a medical researcher, who located the early records of the study, from 1931-1939, scattered through some 410 boxes in the National Archives. He literally searched through each individual box and picked out the information that was applicable to the Tuskegee Syphilis Study. Jim Jones's work was significant and made my task less difficult. He has written an excellent book about the study entitled *Bad Blood*.

The Settlement

It was only after we obtained information and made it known by appropriate pleadings and briefs that the government began to discuss the possibility of settlement.

We were successful in getting financial compensation for each of the living participants and the heirs of deceased participants in the Tuskegee Syphilis Study. In addition, the government was ordered to continue its helath care program for the living participants and widows and children of any participants who tested positively for syphilis.

While the settlement was not what I had hoped to receive for my clients, considering all of the facts and circumstances, in my opinion, it was fair and reasonable. This study started in 1932. There were a multiplicity of legal problems that would have to be resolved, if there had been a trial. If this case were discovered today under the same facts and circumstances, the value of the case would be substantially higher. When the proceeds from the settlement were paid into court, the funds were placed in an interest-bearing account. It took a number of years to locate all the participants, and after the recipients had received the principal amount there was accumulated interest to disburse. We thus had to verify again whether the participants were living or dead, and if dead, whether there were living heirs, and in all cases we had to find current addresses. This case is still pending.

Senator Edward Kennedy, Subcommittee on Health

While the case was pending, we were able to get Senator Edward Kennedy of Massachusetts interested in this study. Senator Kennedy was chairman of the Senate Subcommittee on Health. I was invited on two separate occasions to bring participants to Washington to testify about their experiences. I took four participants—Charlie Pollard, Herman Shaw, Carter Howard and Nelson Scott—to Washington and they testified. Mr. Pollard stated: "I was going to school in 1932 when they came around and gave me a blood test. They said I had bad blood . . . and they was working on it." Mr. Scott, who was recruited from his farm in 1932, stated: "I thought I was getting shots for bad blood." Asked by Senator Kennedy what he thought of the study now that he knew its real purpose, Scott said: "I don't think much of it. They were just using us for something else—for an experiment. If they had told me I would have gone to a family doctor and got treated." As a result of their testimony, Congress passed legislation which prohibits this kind of experimentation from occurring again.

Today, in order for the government, or any one else, to be involved in such studies, there must be proper protocol. There must be informed consent. The persons must know they are involved in a study, and proper safeguards must be in place so that their individual rights are protected.

In addition to the financial settlements, the government was ordered to continue to provide other benefits and a health program providing free health care for living participants and to the families of syphilitic participants, as well as free burial expenses for participants based on the standard of living at the time of their death.

Once the settlement was completed, there was a question of distributing funds. Originally, we did not know who the heirs of the deceased participants were, so we had to find them. When we began to find heirs and people realized there was money involved, it became necessary to have hearings to determine who were the legitimate heirs. The funds were finally completely distributed in 1992, except for interest payments.

Importance of the Case

This case was very important to the persons involved in it, not only for the financial remuneration which they received, the medical care, and burial expenses, but for safeguards that had been written so that other persons would not become victims of similar studies. The significance of this case was that the United States of

America, in effect, admitted to wrongdoing and was willing to compensate the aggrieved parties. This case also demonstrated that the judicial process is a viable means of rectifying wrongs perpetrated against the citizens of this country regardless of their race and economic status. The case reaffirmed the principle that prior informed consent should be obtained from individuals before they are allowed to participate in human experimentations. As a result of this, the government has re-evaluated the use of human beings and experiments and has set minimum standards in order to conduct human experimentations.

The only participants in this study were African-American. In my opinion, it would never have happened to white participants. This was another milestone toward accomplishing my goal of "destroying everything segregated which I could find."

This case is the subject matter of various television productions, theater productions, and the previously mentioned book, *Bad Blood*, by Jim Jones. The play *Miss Evers Boys* has been performed in Atlanta, Georgia, at the Alliance Theater and in Montgomery, Alabama, at the Alabama Shakespeare Festival, and other places. The television productions included a documentary produced by NOVA for PBS Television in 1993, a European production by Diverse Productions of London, England, in 1992, and a featured segment on ABC-TV's "Prime Time Live" in 1992.

18

The Judgeship That Was Not To Be

I n May of 1979, Senators Donald Stewart and Howell Heflin recommended me to President Jimmy Carter for the position of United States District Judge for the Middle District of Alabama. This is the court where I filed most of my civil rights cases. The senators acted upon recommendations of the Alabama Judicial Nominating Commission. According to the testimony at my hearings, I received the second highest number of votes of all persons under consideration by the commission. Based on the senators' recommendation, President Carter nominated me and sent my name to the United States Senate for confirmation. The nomination was referred to the Senate Judiciary Committee, where it was under consideration for a considerable period of time.

I was recommended to Senators Heflin and Stewart for the judgeship by Joe Reed, chairman of the Alabama Democratic Conference (ADC), an African-American political caucus. In the years after passage of the Voting Rights Act, the ADC became one of the most effective political caucuses in the nation. It had been instrumental in electing both Senators Heflin and Stewart, as well as in electing most of the statewide constitutional officers in the State of Alabama, including the governor.

Dr. Reed made it clear to the senators that the African-American community in Alabama wanted two African Americans named as United States District Judges. The ADC's recommendations for the nominations were State Senator U. W. Clemon of Birmingham and Fred D. Gray of Tuskegee. Senator Clemon was later confirmed and became the first African-American federal district judge to serve in the State of Alabama.

At the beginning of my confirmation hearing, I was introduced to the Senate Judiciary Committee by Senator Donald Stewart. He stated:

> Then we have Fred Gray, one of the nation's best known attorneys. He has handled a wide range of landmark cases, ranging from the famous Rosa Parks case to the syphilis lawsuit at Tuskegee. In addition to his legal career, Mr. Gray and I also served in the Alabama House of Representatives. I can say also about Fred that that experience was a good one. He handled himself in an honorable way and ably represented his people in the State House of Representatives.

Then Senator Howell Heflin said:

> I have known Fred Gray for approximately twenty years. When I went on the bench in 1971, there were two black lawyers in Alabama who were universally acclaimed to have reputations of excellence among the enlightened bar of Alabama. These were a great lawyer in Birmingham who is now in his middle seventies, Arthur Shores, and Fred Gray. He practiced before me while I was on the bench. He always did an outstanding job. From my own personal observation, I give him the rating of well-qualified.

Opposition to My Nomination

Notwithstanding those warm endorsements, I expected substantial opposition from a large segment of the white community. I had probably filed more lawsuits that had caused more institutions to be integrated in Alabama than any other lawyer. These actions were always the fulfillment of the pledge I made to myself when I was a student at Alabama State College, riding the segregated buses to and from home, school, and job—to become a lawyer and "destroy everything segregated I could find." I had always realized that accomplishing my goal would subject me to substantial criticism. After being in the trenches for twenty-five years, I understood that there were people in Alabama who would stop at nothing to keep me off the federal bench. They did attempt to sabotage my nomination, and they succeeded.

In retrospect, I feel that if I had become a federal district judge, it is quite possible that I may have been assassinated. The individuals who hated and assassinated Mrs. Viola Liuzzo and Dr. King because of the work they did, also hated me for the work I had done. I, of course, was willing to take that chance. But, as fate would have it, the judgeship was not to be.

Support from Home

There were many heartwarming experiences, which I will always cherish, as a result of those who testified in favor of my confirmation. I shall always cherish and am appreciative of the wholehearted support which I received from the white members of the bench and bar of Macon County. Particularly, I'm grateful for Circuit Judge William Byrd, who at his own expense took a train to Washington, D.C., to testify on my behalf. Also, I'm especially appreciative of attorney William Russell, a native Macon Countian, for his courage to testify about how he felt about me initially and how, as he observed my work, his views changed. He testified favorably. I am appreciative to Probate Judge Preston Hornsby, who testified on my behalf, and to his son, Andy Hornsby, who entertained us at his home while we were in Washington, D.C., and to the other persons who came to Washington, D.C., and testified. I have pointed out these particular individuals because they were white persons of good will who had the courage, faith, and confidence in me to testify on my behalf. These persons were not necessarily my best friends, but they knew me for my dedication and professionalism.

On the other hand, there was another group of my family, and close associates—Neal Pope, James Allan Parker, my staff, my secretary, Joanne Bibb—who prepared and coordinated my presentations. I had many supporters, and friends, including bus loads from Montgomery. Other persons who testified in support of my nomination included Congressman Louis Stokes of Cleveland; Congressman Parren Mitchell of Maryland; Robert Harris, president of the National Bar Association; Clarence Mitchell, Leadership Conference on Civil Rights; Coretta Scott King; Rosa Parks; James M. Nabrit, III, NAACP Legal Defense Fund; Althea Simmons, director, Washington Bureau of the NAACP and National Urban League; Probate Judge Rufus Huffman, Bullock County; William P. Mitchell, executive secretary, Tuskegee Civic Association; Tom Radney, attorney, Alexander City, Alabama; Dr. Walter Bowie, dean, School of Veterinary Medicine, Tuskegee University; Ernest C. "Sonny" Hornsby, attorney, Tallassee, Alabama, now chief justice of the Alabama Supreme Court; Harry Raymon, attorney, Tuskegee; Mayor Johnny Ford, Tuskegee; George S. Bulls, entrepreneur, Tuskegee; Otis Pinkard, Tuskegee; Elaine Jones, NAACP Legal Defense Fund, New York; Dr. Joe Reed, chairman, Alabama Democratic Conference; Mayor Richard Arrington, Birmingham; and Eric Schnapper, NAACP Legal Defense Fund. These persons testified concerning my competency to become a judge, and my integrity, honesty, and trustworthiness, among other things. There were many other persons who sent letters, statements and telegrams in support of my nomination. I remain grateful for all of them.

Morris Dees's Testimony

The greatest disappointment, which was totally unexpected, was Morris Dees's appearance and testimony in opposition to my nomination. Morris is founder, chief executive officer, and chief counsel for the Southern Poverty Law Center in Montgomery, Alabama. He and I had worked well together in both the legal arena and in politics. He grew up outside Montgomery and went to Sidney Lanier High School, which I later desegregated with the lawsuit *Carr v. Montgomery County Board of Education.*

I was practicing law in Montgomery when Morris graduated

from the University of Alabama law school and was admitted to the bar. At first, Morris did not practice law, but was a businessman specializing in direct mail marketing. He became a millionaire in business, then sold his company, and began practicing law. He handled a number of cases for the American Civil Liberties Union. We worked together on a number of cases. When I ran for the Alabama Legislature, he introduced me to Senator George McGovern, who made a substantial contribution to my campaign. Morris worked diligently with me in my campaign. After I won a seat in the Alabama House of Representatives as one of the first African Americans to serve in that body since Reconstruction, he had a reception in my honor in his home. He was the moving force behind the Alabama Civil Liberties Union presenting its Constitutional Law Award to me in 1968. It is my personal opinion that Morris, growing up in Montgomery, and later as a young businessman and lawyer, observed the work I did in breaking down legal barriers of segregation in Alabama, and wanted to use his skills to do similar work in the field of civil rights. Morris has made substantial contributions in the civil rights area. I have searched my mind since the hearings before the Senate Judiciary Committee to determine why Morris Dees, of all persons, would oppose my confirmation to the bench. I have concluded that the real reason he testified against my nomination is because of an event which occurred during the time I was co-chairman of the Alabama Black Lawyers Association, now the Alabama Lawyers Association.

While I served as co-chairman of the Alabama Black Lawyers Association, State Representative Thomas Reed was president of the Alabama State Conference of NAACP branches. In 1970, Tom and I had both been elected to the Alabama Legislature from the district comprising Macon County. In 1974, however, court-ordered single-member redistricting would take effect and Tom and I would have to run against each other in the newly drawn house district for Macon County.

Rep. Reed, as state NAACP president, asked Morris to file a lawsuit on behalf of the NAACP branches against the State of Alabama, to integrate the state troopers. Morris filed the lawsuit and represented the plaintiffs. The all-white Alabama state troopers were a potent symbol of segregation. Every African American in Alabama had vivid memories of the state troopers beating marchers in Selma in 1965, keeping African Americans out of Tuskegee schools in 1963, and similar cases. Many Alabama African Americans had even more vivid personal memories of unpleasant encounters with white state troopers over the years. In addition to the political significance of this case, I personally was eager to see such a desegregation case filed.

However, I did not expect Tom to ask me to handle the state trooper case or do any work for the NAACP while he was president, and he did not. It was not that he doubted my ability, but soon we would be running against each other for a legislative seat, and he certainly would not want to share with a rival the publicity from a high-profile case that was of great interest to African American voters.

Thus, even though from 1956 to 1966 I represented the NAACP in Alabama and assisted in taking its cases to the United States Supreme Court on four separate occasions [See Chapter 4], I was not asked to represent the NAACP in the action against the State of Alabama to integrate the state troopers. Even today, this seems ironic to me. Had it not been for the legal battles I helped win on behalf of the NAACP in the late fifties and the sixties, the NAACP would not have been in business in Alabama to file this lawsuit in the seventies. The lawsuit was precedent-setting, and it effectively integrated the Alabama state troopers. In fact, Judge Frank M. Johnson, Jr.,'s order in that case is one of the first to require affirmative action employment quotas as a way of correcting past employment discrimination. The reasoning and remedy Judge Johnson used in the state trooper case were directly descended from his precedent-setting order in *Carr v. Montgomery County Board of Education*, which was the very first case of any kind to impose numerical quotas for redress of discrimination [See Chapter 9]. Today, Alabama probably has more black state troopers than any other state in America.

Although I was not surprised that my political opponent did

not ask me to handle the state trooper case, I did expect him to ask some other African-American Alabama lawyer to be involved in some fashion. But, so far as I have been able to determine, neither Tom nor Morris solicited any African-American lawyers to assist with the state trooper case. As co-chair of the Alabama Black Lawyers Association, I wrote a letter to Tom, which was very critical of his failure to involve African-American lawyers in that lawsuit. The letter was not critical of attorney Dees, but of NAACP President Reed.

Tom apparently gave a copy of the letter to Morris, who contacted me and was very upset, and considered the letter to be a personal attack upon him. I believe that Morris never forgave me for writing that letter to Tom, and that he still considers it a personal attack upon him. I certainly had no such intention when I wrote the letter.

My relationship with Morris has not changed in the years since, notwithstanding the complimentary statements he made about me in his book, *A Season for Justice*. In an autographed copy of his book, he inscribed:

5/13/91
For Fred
   I speak very highly of you in my book because I truly believe you are a fine lawyer. I'm sorry events led me to be called in D.C. to testify. You may not believe this, but it was not personal. I hope as the years pass and as our suns set in life, we can again be close friends as we were in the cases I described.
   Best
   Morris Dees

I am sure he has a different view with reference to why he so testified. Even though I do not believe Morris's testimony was the determining factor in blocking my confirmation, I felt betrayed by one whom I considered a friend and fellow laborer in the Civil Rights Movement.

Senator Heflin's Night Call

However, the most disturbing event about my confirmation process was the manner in which Senator Heflin went about informing me that he would no longer support my nomination. We had discussions, conferences, and exchanged letters, but there was absolutely nothing said to me during that time which indicated he had any major concerns about my nomination. All of the information that came out during the hearings had been submitted to the committee and to Senator Heflin prior to the hearings. The only hint I had of trouble came from various staff members of the Senate Judiciary Committee, who asked me, continuously, whether my senators were, in fact, supporting my nomination.

These inquiries were made long before I received the "Dear John" call from Senator Heflin. On August 5, 1980, about 9:30 in the evening, I was in Dallas, Texas, attending the annual convention of the National Bar Association. Having received a page while attending a social function, I answered it and found that my wife had called. She said Senator Heflin had been trying to get me on the phone. The message was, "I should call him immediately, regardless of the time." I went to a pay telephone and dialed the number—I still remember it, 202-547-6724. Senator Heflin answered and told me curtly, "I'm unable to continue to support your nomination." Stunned, I asked why, and he said, "It would serve no useful purpose to discuss the matter further." Then he hung up.

This was devastating. I was prepared for scrutiny, interrogation by the committee, and the inevitable criticism raised by that "certain element" of the white community. I was not prepared, however, for the manner in which Senator Heflin informed me of his decision. Prior to the night of August 5, 1980, he had said nothing at all to me which indicated he might withdraw his support for nomination, or that the nomination was in jeopardy.

I returned to the Fairmont Hotel, and I was handed a slip addressed to Mr. Fred Gray, Room 1827, August 5, 1980, 9:28 p.m. "While you were out Mr. Howell Heflin, Washington, D.C. phoned, 202-547-6724. Message: "Please return my call tonight."

I have never forgotten that message slip. As a matter of fact, wherever I have traveled since August 5, 1980, whether it was to the beach, the lake, China, the Caribbean, or Africa, I have always carried that piece of paper from the Fairmont Hotel. The manner in which Senator Heflin conveyed the withdrawal of his support hit me like a storm and left my thoughts in disarray. What I had hoped would be the crowning of my legal career with the judgeship became a personal nightmare.

I wish it had been handled differently. The Senator could have called me and explained in detail the reasons why he withdrew his support, but he elected not to. Obviously, he had made up his mind and decided nothing would be gained from discussion with me. From that day to this, I have never discussed the judgeship with him.

Press Conference and Withdrawal

Life must go on. On August 8, 1980, I called a press conference at the Gomillion Building in Tuskegee. I expressed my appreciation to all those who supported my nomination, and briefly reviewed the sequence of events that began in May 1979 when Senators Heflin and Stewart recommended me to President Carter. I was candid about my disappointment as well as my beliefs about the reasons why I was opposed for the nomination. I did not withdraw my nomination, but I acknowledged that without Senator Heflin's support I could not be confirmed. I stated that I believed it was vital that an African American be appointed to the judgeship, even if that person was not me. And I said that I would withdraw my name from consideration as soon as I was sure that another African American was on the way to confirmation. My complete remarks at this press conference are in Appendix D-1.

Why, after undergoing months of investigation by the American Bar Association, the FBI, the IRS, the Judicial Nominating Committee, and trips to Washington for confirmation hearings, did I ask that my name be withdrawn? I was ranked "unqualified" by the American Bar Association, but that was neither a surprise nor a disgrace given the way the ABA obtained its ratings. By contrast, I was rated "highly" qualified by the National Bar Association. The fact that the ABA once excluded African-American lawyers was the reason the NBA had come into being. In 1980, even though much progress had been made, I took it for granted that the white, establishment lawyers I had been battling for years, when asked by the ABA about my qualifications, would give me the shoulder. U. W. Clemon was also rated "unqualified" by the ABA, and he was confirmed. I found it ironic that the ABA sent me a few years later to Liberia as an international observer on some treason trials, and then recognized me at the ABA annual convention for "outstanding" work on the association's behalf. In any event, the Judicial Nominating Committee gave me the second highest ranking of all the other nominees for the judgeship. Why, then, did I withdraw?

Essentially, I wanted to make sure that Senators Heflin and Stewart would keep their commitment to the African-American community. The commitment was that they would recommend to the President two African-American lawyers for judgeships in Alabama, and the lawyers who were recommended would be selected by the African-American community. I asked that my name be withdrawn from consideration because I wanted to be sure that another competent, African-American lawyer would be recommended by our senators, appointed by the President, confirmed by the Senate, and would sit on the bench in Montgomery.

So beginning that night, plans were put in motion that resulted in Myron Thompson being elevated to the federal bench. Many things happened in the few weeks after August 5, 1980. I contacted Ray Jenkins, the White House Assistant Press Secretary, whom I knew from his years in Montgomery as editor of the *Alabama Journal*. Mr. Jenkins was a man in whom I had faith and confidence. (After leaving the White House, he became the editorial page editor of the Baltimore *Sun*, from which he recently retired. I renewed my acquaintance with him at Mrs. Virginia Durr's ninetieth birthday celebration at Martha's Vineyard in 1993.)

I had an understanding with the White House. I was informed by the White House that my name would not be withdrawn from the Senate unless and until I so requested. My understanding was that I would not withdraw my name until such time that another African-American lawyer was recommended, had been cleared by the FBI, the American Bar Association, and the Justice Department, and had the wholehearted support of both of our senators. I did not want another African-American lawyer in Alabama to experience what I had gone through.

Two names surfaced for the judgeship—Myron Thompson and J. Mason Davis. On September 11, 1980, I received a phone call from the White House which assured me that attorney Myron Thompson had been cleared by the FBI, the American Bar Association, the Justice Department, and both of our senators had given their full-hearted support for him, and that as soon as I sent my letter of withdrawal, President Carter would forward attorney Myron Thompson's name to the Senate for confirmation. The White House had the assurance of our senators that they would work hard and move the nomination forward. If I could not become federal district judge, I could not think of a better person than Myron Thompson.

With those assurances, I wrote President Carter a letter [See Appendix D-2], withdrawing my name. I again reviewed the sequence of events, expressed my disappointment, and stated that while I still felt qualified to be confirmed, I accepted that my nomination was not to be. I explicitly declared my belief that the white power structure in Alabama had brought pressure on Senator Heflin because of my past civil rights activities. I said that I had assurances that if I did withdraw, another African American would be promptly nominated and would be confirmed.

Judge Myron Thompson

In record-breaking time, Myron Thompson became Judge Thompson. He appeared before the Senate committee for a very short period of time. I'm informed that he was taken around by Senator Heflin and introduced to the various senators (something he never did for me). Then there was a confirmation hearing that lasted a few minutes; confirmation was recommended by the committee; and he was confirmed by the Senate. The whole process from the date of my letter of withdrawal until he was sworn in was twenty-seven days. It was a record low number of days.

I was unhappy that I did not obtain the judgeship; however, I am happy that Myron Thompson became the judge. He grew up in Tuskegee. His mother, Mrs. Lillian Buford, and stepfather, Reverend K. Buford, were my friends and supported my nomination for the judgeship. I was delighted when he asked me to make remarks at his investiture ceremony. For some, this could have been a difficult task, but for me, it was delightful. Myron Thompson, in my opinion, had all of the qualifications of a judge. He was young, articulate, Ivy-League educated, possessed the proper temperament, was an excellent scholar and a good writer and had never been tarnished by the scars of the civil rights battles, though he was a beneficiary of civil rights victories. He was ideal for the position. I could think of no better person, other than myself, to occupy that judgeship.

So, I was happy to be asked to make remarks at his Investiture, and on that day in October 1980 [See Appendix D-3], I reflected on the significance of an African American striding toward a federal judgeship along a trail which had been blazed by Rosa Parks, Martin Luther King, Jr., E. D. Nixon, Joe Reed, and many other pioneers. I noted my personal confidence and pride in Judge Thompson, and I noted that he was still a young man, relatively unscarred, who had many years to climb, perhaps, higher than might be possible for one who was older and more battle-weary.

I said, "I foresee a long fruitful judicial career for Judge Thompson. Who knows, but he may become chief Judge of this court; and perhaps a few years later, he may sit on the United States Court of Appeals. Who knows, we may be here today, not merely participating in an investiture ceremony, for a district judge, but we may be witnessing the beginning of an illustrious judicial career where Judge Thompson may very well someday, hopefully in our lifetime, sit as a justice of the United States Supreme Court, and may even become the chief justice thereof. Judge Thompson, we wish you well, and I personally look forward to trying many cases before

Chief U.S. District Judge Myron J. Thompson

you." I am not a prophet, nor am I the son of a prophet, but at least one part of my prediction for Judge Myron Thompson has come true. He is now chief judge of the United States District Court for the Middle District of Alabama. Who knows but that he still may some day sit as a justice on the United States Supreme Court, or even become the chief justice, as I predicted.

Confirmation Process Should Be Changed

Prior to the confirmation hearings for Supreme Court Justice Clarence Thomas, my hearing was probably the longest hearing for any African-American nominee. While I do not agree with the positions which Mr. Justice Thomas has taken on many issues, there is one thing on which we totally agree—the process of confirmation of federal judges needs to be changed. Certainly, no job is worth the humiliation to which some federal nominees have been subjected, including me. Nominees and their families should not have to bear the pain that is inculcated by the present process. The process can be tantamount to torture. Most importantly, it often has nothing to do with getting the best judges we can find.

℃

Incidentally, as a member of the National Bar Association, I opposed Clarence Thomas's nomination to become a federal appeals court judge, the position he held before being elevated to the Supreme Court. The NBA felt that at that time, using its usual criteria, he did not have the qualifications, experience, and track record appropriate to serve at the second highest judicial level in the nation. We also anticipated—correctly as it turned out—that an African American named to a court of appeals would be in a stepping-stone position to the Supreme Court when it came time to replace Justice Thurgood Marshall. Of course, Thomas was nominated, confirmed, and did serve on the U.S. Court of Appeals for the District of Columbia Circuit. I and the NBA again opposed his nomination when President George Bush selected him to succeed Thurgood Marshall in 1991. On that occasion, I had the opportunity to state my opposition directly to him. This came about during a meeting arranged by Joe Reed, chairman of the Alabama Democratic Conference, who took a delegation of Alabamians, including me, to Washington, D.C., to meet with Thomas. We discussed the issues that were important to us, as Alabamians and as African Americans, and I explained why I opposed him. The meeting was cordial but serious.

The next time I spoke with Clarence Thomas, he was on the Supreme Court. In fact, this was at a special sitting of the Court to commemorate the life of Justice Thurgood Marshall, who had recently passed away. At the reception after the ceremony, I talked with Mr. Justice Thomas. He said he realized that we differed on many issues, but that he would like to remain in contact with me, and he invited me to visit him whenever I was in Washington. I appreciated his invitation and his sincerity.

This invitation was recently re-extended when Justice Thomas paid a visit to Tuskegee University. This was at the invitation of Tuskegee's Honda All-Star Challenge championship team, which competes in "college bowl" type events and had once met with Justice Thomas in his chambers when the team was in Washington, D.C. He said he had always wanted to visit Tuskegee University, so the team asked him to come. In the fall of 1994, he did, and he made a speech that was warmly received by the Tuskegee student body. Before that speech, my son Fred Jr., who is the president of the local bar association, convened a meeting of the local bar and presented Justice Thomas with a plaque. At this event, Mr. Justice Thomas and I spoke again, and he reminded me to visit him when I was in Washington. I will certainly do so.

I still disagree with him on many issues, although I found that we had common ground when I read his concurring opinion in

Visiting with Justice Clarence Thomas while he was in Tuskegee to give a speech, November 1994.

U.S. v. Fordice, the Mississippi higher education desegregation case. In this case, the Supreme Court found that Mississippi's historically white and historically black colleges were still treated very differently in terms of funding, operations, and racial composition of faculties and student bodies. One of the proposed remedies was simply to eliminate the historically black schools. But, said Thomas, "Although I agree that a State is not constitutionally *required* to maintain its historically black institutions as such . . . I do not understand our opinion to hold that a State is *forbidden* from doing so. It would be ironic, to say the least, if the institutions that sustained blacks during segregation were themselves destroyed in an effort to combat its vestiges." This is one of the points we are arguing in Alabama's still ongoing higher education lawsuit [see Chapter 20], and I could not agree with Justice Thomas more.

In any event, Clarence Thomas is on the Court now, and after listening to him speak to the Tuskegee students, I came away with the feeling that he really is searching for a way to find his place on the Court and to bridge the gulf that separates him on many issues from large numbers of African-American citizens. I am reminded that one of our greatest Supreme Court justices, Hugo L. Black, was once a member of the Ku Klux Klan. Yet, on the Supreme Court, he became one of the greatest champions of free speech, voting rights, and civil rights in the history of our nation. If a former KKK member can grow and develop on the Court, there is no reason that a conservative African American such as Clarence Thomas cannot in time expand his understanding of the majesty of the Supreme Court as the safeguard of rights for minorities. I believe he has the potential for that growth. And I hope I am right, because he is a young, vigorous man who is probably going to be on the Court for many years to come.

19

Post-"Judgeship"

The best way I can describe my ordeal in connection with the "judgeship" is similar to the experiences of the biblical prophet, Job. Job lost his children, his possessions, his health and friends. However, he never lost his faith. Later, Job regained more than he had initially. Job 42:12 states, " . . . So the Lord blessed the latter end of Job more than his beginning." The Lord is certainly blessing the latter part of my career.

Everything I have touched has turned to "gold" since those dreadful and disappointing days before the Senate Judiciary Committee during the summer of 1980. My opponents believed that with my name having been withdrawn as a federal district judge, that would be the end of Fred D. Gray. There were many people who believed that as a result of whatever was done to stop my confirmation, I would lose credibility with the bar, the bench, my clients, and with the nation. Everything has been to the contrary.

After all that was said and done in Washington, my law practice took a giant leap upward and outward. Many of my old clients appeared as if they were waiting until I was back in my office. And there was a steady influx of new, large cases, involving large sums of money in new areas of practice.

I also prospered outside the practice of law, and I became the recipient of a steady stream of honors and recognitions and professional affiliations.

Shortly after I requested President Carter to withdraw my nomination, I became very active in the political activities of the

National Bar Association (NBA), the largest African-American bar association in the world. It was founded in 1925 when African Americans could not become members of the American Bar Association. I had been a member since I became a lawyer, but I was never involved in the politics of NBA until 1981 when I was appointed as presidential adviser to Arnette Hubbard, the first female president of the National Bar Association. In 1984, I was named president-elect of the National Bar Association and in July 1985, I was inaugurated the forty-third president of the NBA.

During my term of office as NBA president, I was asked by the then-president of the American Bar Association (ABA), William W. Falsgraf, to go to Liberia, West Africa, as an ABA observer at a series of treason trials in 1986. The trials began in February 1986 and concluded in April 1986. I was recognized for that work at ABA's 1986 annual convention in New York.

Incidentally, William Falsgraf is also a graduate of Case Western Reserve University. So in the same year the presidents of the

One of the last public appreciation programs, in 1991, for Justice Marshall, with three past presidents of the National Bar Association: (l-r) Fred Gray, Judge Turk Thompson of Washington, D.C., and Mayor Dennis Archer of Detroit, Michigan.

Some of the past presidents of the National Bar Association, photographed in Boca Raton, Florida, at our 1993 annual convention: From left, Carl Character, Robert Harris, Dennis Archer, Arnette Hubbard, Fred Gray, Arthenia Joyner, Tom Broom, James Cobb, and James Cole. (For a complete list of all the NBA presidents who have served the organization, see page 383.)

National Bar Association and the American Bar Association were both Case Western alums. We were written up in the law school's September 1985 *In Brief* publication as "Two Bar Presidents."

Honors and Awards

I have been the recipient of numerous honors and awards, the majority of which were bestowed upon me primarily because of my work in civil rights. On May 28, 1989, the University of Massachusetts at Amherst conferred upon me my first honorary Doctor of Laws degree [See Appendix B-1]. Over the years my undergraduate alma mater, Alabama State University, has given me numerous alumni awards and on May 13, 1990, it also conferred upon me the honorary doctor of laws degree.

In 1985, Case Western Reserve University Law Alumni Association named me the Fletcher Reed Andrews Graduate of the Year. Case Western Reserve University School of Law admitted me as a member in the Society of Benchers in 1986. The Society of

Benchers is one of the university's most prestigious societies. On May 24, 1992, the university conferred upon me the doctor of laws degree [See Appendix B-2]. In February 1993, I was elected to membership on the board of trustees of Case Western Reserve University. On September 19, 1993, the CWRU Law Alumni Association awarded me the Law School Centennial Medal, a brand new award that is now the highest honor the law school bestows on one of its graduates [See Appendix B-3].

One of the honors of which I am most proud in connection with my law school came unexpectedly in 1994, when a scholarship was endowed in my name. Susie Ruth Powell, a 1973 law graduate of Case Western Reserve University, contributed $10,000 to set up the Fred D. Gray Endowment Fund for minority law students. I am deeply honored and grateful to attorney Powell for this recognition.

I have also been conferred an honorary doctor of laws degree by Southwestern Christian College in Terrell, Texas. I have served on Southwestern's board of trustees for over twenty years, the last five as chairman.

The lawyers in the Fifth Judicial Circuit, consisting of Chambers, Macon, Randolph and Tallapoosa counties, elected me their bar commissioner in 1983 (the Alabama Bar Commissioners govern the actions of attorneys). The Fifth Judicial Circuit has an outstanding bar (still predominantly white) and bench. The present judges are Howard Bryan, presiding judge, Dale Segrest, and Lewis Hamner. I enjoyed my service as a bar commissioner. It was a special pleasure during that period to work with Reggie Hamner, the executive director of the Alabama Bar Association. He was particularly helpful, and he has always invited me to become involved in various aspects of the State Bar. One of the last things Reggie did before he retired was to recommend me to become a Fellow of the American Bar Foundation. Only one-third of one percent of lawyers are elected as fellows, and I was pleased that my professional colleagues would so recognize me. The fellows basically sponsor research programs in various areas of law and the legal profession.

Some of my family and friends joined me in Washington in 1989 when the portrait (right) used in the Miller calendars was presented. Above, from left, me, Bernice, Stanley, Bernice's sister and brother-in-law, Jean and Wilmer Wilson, Elsie and Obie Elie, and my niece, Karen Gray Houston.

For more than a decade, the Miller Brewing Company has produced an annual calendar which acknowledges the work of African Americans in various professions. In 1989, I was selected as one of the twelve outstanding African-American lawyers, both living and dead. Included in that list were: Louis A. Bedford, Jr., Derrick A. Bell, Jr., Wiley A. Branton, George W. Crockett, Jr., Drew S. Days, III, Frankie Muse Freeman, Patricia Roberts Harris, A. Leon Higginbotham, Jr., Charles Hamilton Houston, Howard Moore, Jr., and Constance Baker Motley.

In 1993, for the tenth anniversary of the Miller's calendar, entitled "Excellence Has Many Faces, Gallery of Greats," the corporation selected one representative for each profession honored during the previous ten years. I was selected as the lawyer to represent "Black Civil Rights Attorneys" [See Appendix B-4].

I was featured in an article, "The Spark Behind the Spark: The Lawyer Who Helped Change America," by Darryl Tippens in the January–March 1993 edition of *Upreach* magazine, published by Highland Church of Christ, Abilene, Texas. The article examines how I have handled simultaneously the professions of law and the ministry [See Appendix B-5]. On October 22, 1993, the National Bar Association honored me by presenting me the "Wiley A. Branton Issues Symposium Award" which states: "Fred D. Gray, Esquire, Leadership on the Cutting Edge of Law For Civil Social and Economic Justice."

These are only a few of the awards and honors that I have received since the dreadful days before the Senate Judiciary Committee in 1980.

Attorney for Milton McGregor Pari-Mutuel Enterprises

During 1984, after passage of a referendum in Macon County, Alabama, which allows pari-mutuel greyhound racing, Milton McGregor called for an appointment. During our conference in my office, he informed me that he was president, treasurer, chief executive officer, and majority shareholder in Macon County Greyhound Park, Inc. He stated further that his company planned to apply for a license to own, build, and operate a pari-mutuel greyhound track in Macon County. He wanted me to represent him and his corporation. Not only did he want me to represent his company in connection with the acquisition of a license to operate a greyhound track, but if successful, I would be counsel for the corporation. I agreed. We were successful in obtaining the license. He kept all of his commitments. He is a fine person with whom to work. For several years, Macon County Greyhound Park was the number one pari-mutuel greyhound track in the country.

As of October 1994, Macon County Greyhound Park (Victoryland) has contributed approximately sixty million dollars in revenue for the Macon County Board of Education, Macon

My client Milton McGregor, center, presents a large tax check to Macon County officials (as of 1986). Far left, R. E. Corbitt, tax assessor; fifth from left, Dan Beasley, tax collector; far right, Preston Hornsby, probate judge. Victoryland vice president Willie Whitehead is standing behind.

County, Tuskegee University, the cities of Notasulga, Franklin, Shorter and Tuskegee, and other agencies located in Macon County, Alabama. With the revenue contributed to the Macon County Board of Education, a twelve million dollar comprehensive high school, Booker T. Washington High School, has been built in Tuskegee. In addition, Victoryland is responsible for over seven hundred new jobs in Macon County. It is a pleasure to represent this industry.

From 1988 to date, I have worked with Milton McGregor and his tax attorney, David Johnston of Dothan, Alabama, and the law firm of Haskell, Slaughter & Young in obtaining the ownership of the New Birmingham Race Course, a horse and greyhound racing facility in Birmingham. The facility is also one of our clients.

The Law Practice Continues to Expand

During the post-"judgeship" period from 1980 to date, my entire practice has mushroomed. I have represented people of all races and in various economic conditions. I have continued to represent corporate clients, the City of Tuskegee and all of its agencies, Tuskegee University, and Alabama State University. I have also represented plaintiffs and obtained multi-million dollar verdicts and settlements.

Due to my efforts in personal injury lawsuits against a particular railroad, it is reported that the railroad ceased doing business in Macon County and removed its railroad tracks. In 1987 when tort reform was under consideration in the Alabama Legislature, it is reported that my success in obtaining verdicts and settlements was discussed at length. In addition to success in plaintiff cases, I have also successfully defended corporations and doctors in medical

As general counsel to Tuskegee Institute in 1972, I witnessed the signing by President Luther H. Foster of a two million dollar loan for the completion of John A. Andrew Hospital on the campus. At left is Charles Allen, counsel for the Life Insurance Company of Georgia, maker of the loan. Next to me is Harold K. Logan, Tuskegee vice president for business affairs.

Mom and Bernice at the open house for my new law office on the square in Tuskegee, August 29, 1982.

THE LAW FIRM OF

GRAY, SEAY & LANGFORD

ANNOUNCES THE REMOVAL

OF ITS OFFICES

TO

108 EASTSIDE STREET

TUSKEGEE, ALABAMA

AND

INVITES YOU TO AN

OPEN HOUSE

SUNDAY, AUGUST 29, 1982
3 - 5 P.M.

malpractice cases. Throughout the flourishing of my practice, I have continued to represent African Americans whose constitutional rights have been violated and I have trained lawyers under my tutelage to do the same.

In my opinion, I would have made an excellent federal judge, but personally the best thing that ever happened to me was to have been denied the judgeship. Economically, since not receiving the judgeship, I have fared better than at any time during my life. Money has never been a primary motivator for my diligence, but it has been a by-product of the legal work I have done in an effort to serve my clients to the best of my ability.

Sons Join the Law Practice

I guess the greatest professional joy that I have received is to have my two sons return from law school and practice with me. Fred Jr. always wanted to be a lawyer and always wanted to practice with me. He graduated from Morehouse College with a B.S. in political science and then earned his law degree from Howard University School of Law. He has been practicing with the firm since 1988.

Stanley, our youngest child, did not always want to be a lawyer. As a youngster, he was interested in becoming an engineer. One day while we were in the process of remodeling the building where our Tuskegee office is located, he said, "Daddy, I would like to talk with you." We sat down and talked. He said, "It would make sense if I'd become a lawyer, wouldn't it?" I told him, "Yes, it would." He said, "Well, that's what I have decided." He was a junior in high school at that time and from that day forward he began to make preparations to become a lawyer. He is a graduate of Tuskegee Institute High School, University of Alabama, and Howard University School of Law. He was a law clerk for the Honorable John C. Tyson, Alabama Court of Criminal Appeals. He now practices with us. With the addition of Fred Jr. and Stanley, the law firm changed its name to Gray, Langford, Sapp, McGowan, Gray & Nathanson. The current members of the firm are: Fred D. Gray, Charles Langford, Ernestine S. Sapp, Walter E. McGowan, Fred

Son Stanley, left, joined me and Fred Jr. as a member of the law firm in 1990.

D. Gray, Jr., Stanley F. Gray and Allan Nathanson.

A Great Staff

One of the reasons I have been successful in most of my cases is because of an excellent staff, both legal and support.

My partner, Charles Langford is "Dean of African-American lawyers in Montgomery" in terms of length of service. He was admitted to practice in the state on April 15, 1953. He has been with me continuously since 1968. An outstanding Alabama legislator, attorney Langford served in the Alabama House of Representatives several years and is now serving his second term in the Alabama State Senate.

Attorney Ernestine Sapp has practiced law with me for over fifteen years. A graduate of Wiley College, Marshall, Texas, in 1962, she was the first African-American female to graduate from Jones Law School in Montgomery, Alabama. She is an outstanding, aggressive, excellent lawyer. Ernestine Sapp is also very active

Staff of Gray, Seay, & Langford in 1982. Standing: Fred Gray, Ernestine Sapp, Solomon S. Seay, Jr., Charles D. Langford, Edwin L. Davis and Walter McGowan. Seated: Annie L. Bailey, Joanne Bibb, Trudy Powell and Alberta Magruder.

in the National Bar Association, the Alabama Trial Lawyers Association and the Alabama State Bar.

Attorney Walter McGowan joined the firm in 1981. He had always wanted to be a lawyer and wanted to practice with me. He is a graduate of Fisk University, Temple University School of Law, and is a member of Phi Beta Kappa. I had successfully represented his mother in a personal matter at the Tuskegee Veterans Administration Hospital in 1956. Several months after that, she wrote me a letter expressing her appreciation for what I had done. She also stated that she had just given birth to a baby boy, "Walter." Little did either one of us know that her son would later practice law with me. He is one of the outstanding lawyers of the Alabama State Bar and has made substantial contributions in the development of the law firm. I consider Walter as one of my sons.

Attorney Edwin Davis initially joined me as a law clerk in 1963.

I met him while a student in law school. Thereafter he entered military service and subsequently practiced law in Florida. During the years he served as a law clerk, he assisted greatly in all of the cases that I handled during that period of time. He drafted many briefs, prepared many complaints or lawsuits and did most of the legal research. He was admitted to the Alabama State Bar in 1981. He is now an outstanding member of the bar. Attorney Davis has contributed greatly toward the growth and development of the firm. He recently retired from the firm for health reasons.

My law firm continues to expand not only in terms of numbers, but also in diversity and religion. In July 1993, Allan Nathanson became a member of our firm. He is caucasian and of the Jewish faith. He practiced law in Tuskegee for twenty-six years. He is a graduate of the University of Arizona and Tulane University. He is the son-in-law of the late Harry Raymon who practiced law in Tuskegee for a number of years. Attorney Raymon represented the defendants in *Gomillion v. Lightfoot* and also represented the Macon County Board of Education in the early stages of *Lee v. Macon*. Life is indeed a great circle.

I have the greatest support staff in the world. Annie L. Bailey, my receptionist, has been with me since 1968. Joanne Bibb, my secretary since 1968, is truly a legal assistant in every sense of the word. She has rendered valuable service in assisting me in this book. Trudy Powell, my office manager, has been with me since 1976. She helps keep us together. Alberta Magruder is attorney Ernestine Sapp's secretary and has been employed with us since 1976. Vanessa Gray-Taylor (my daughter) is attorney McGowan's secretary and has been with us since 1982. Other members of our support staff who have been recently employed are Joanne Reasor in the Montgomery office, Jeanette Whitfield, Ann Baker, and Sherri Cook. The support staff is also integrated.

The Training of Young Lawyers to Continue the Struggle

One of my greatest joys is to assist in training young lawyers and watching them grow and develop into outstanding lawyers. This has been a part of my mission. The following lawyers commenced their legal careers in private practice in my law office or practiced with me: Solomon Seay, Jr.; Alfredo Parish, who now heads a twelve-member integrated law firm in Des Moines, Iowa; Bertha Nussbaum, Seattle, Washington; Judge Aubrey Ford; Billy Carter; Calvin C. Pryor; Donald Watkins; Tyrone Means; Troy Massey; Terry Davis; Cleveland Thornton; Theron Stokes; James Wilson; Willie Turk, New Orleans, Louisiana; and Edwin L. Davis.

My work with young lawyers often brings up questions about not only the specific practice of law but the issues of history and progress and what possible impact our small individual actions can have.

Obviously, there are many unanswered questions. "What has happened to the Civil Rights Movement? Is the Civil Rights Movement dead? Are we better off now than we were in 1954, prior to the bus boycott in Montgomery? What has happened to African Americans economically? Why have the economic conditions of African Americans not kept pace with their political strength? What can be done about crime and violence? Where do we go from here?" All of these are very pertinent questions, and I don't profess to have the answers. But there are several observations that I would like to make which might shed some light on the answers and may assist this generation and future generations, as they seek answers and solutions.

There is no question, as we review where we were in 1954 when I started practicing law, and consider the case law and statutory law then and now, that African Americans and this nation as a whole have made tremendous progress. In the areas of public accommodations, education, employment, voting rights and politics, many advances are visible. We are well on our way toward developing cities, counties, states and a nation where race will not be considered, and a person is judged by the content of his character. We have not reached that point yet, and the struggle continues.

It is not sufficient for our young people—or older ones for that matter—to say that the problems which are confronting us now are so massive, difficult, and complex that there is no hope. It is true that our problems today are massive, complex and difficult. The walls of segregation and discrimination in some instances are still standing. They are more insidious and subtle than before. The area of economic discrimination is virtually untackled. Credit and employment for African Americans are far less available than they are for whites.

The young lawyers I work with know that violence is not the answer. It never has been and it never will be. And yet violence is a central issue to the American community and particularly to the African-American community.

During the fifties and sixties Dr. King preached non-violence. The Justice Department and Presidents John Kennedy and Lyndon Johnson shared that philosophy. Today President Bill Clinton has declared his intention to fight crime. We have in Attorney General Janet Reno a person of action and integrity. The House and Senate passed a major crime bill. The entire nation must join in this fight against crime and violence.

I call upon the entire community, and particularly our young lawyers, to challenge themselves to solve these problems, just as we, their elders, were able to confer, strategize with persons of good will, and find solutions. We conferred with the NAACP, NAACP Legal Defense Fund and other groups and planned strategy on how to attack the laws that were then on the books which discriminated against us based on color. This generation must do likewise. We must use the law as it has developed. We must go back to utilizing some forms of communication where those persons interested in breaking the walls will be able to meet, plan strategy, and jointly come up with some ways and means of attacking our economic problems, and all other problems which we face as a people. Many of these problems are still racial. Solutions must be found. There is a tremendous responsibility upon the young members of the bar not only to be concerned about their economic well being, but they must be dedicated and rededicated to finish the unfinished tasks of destroying discrimination and segregation wherever found. What has been written herein will assist them and others in understanding and appreciating the struggle. Also they must realize that the struggle has not ended. I challenge them to do what needs to be done until all of God's children are truly free and equal.

My plea to younger lawyers is that they will seize the opportunity to commit to the task of ending economic discrimination. This is another world of concern, and relief can be found in our Constitution and amendments. Answers may not surface easily, but this is not a job which can be accomplished alone. There is help if one will only reach out to others, work together and find solutions.

Gray's Lakeview Estates

I mentioned at the beginning of this chapter that I had also prospered outside the practice of law. Real estate is a good example. Bernice is a licensed real estate broker, and she has a passion for acquiring and developing real estate. Prior to 1979, Bernice and I had dreams of developing a new subdivision on Lake Tuskegee. We delayed plans of building a new house when it seemed possible that I could be in line for the judgeship. Then, with the judgeship behind us, we turned our energies back toward supervising the construction of our present house, and landscaping of its twenty acres.

Our house is one in a subdivision consisting of thirty-nine lots. This subdivision is developing into the most prestigious subdivision in the City of Tuskegee, overlooking Lake Tuskegee. Included in those who have built in the subdivision are: Mayor Johnny Ford; Alabama State Senator George Clay; City of Tuskegee utility board member Ora Manning; high school band director William Brassfield; insurance agent D. C. Madison; contractor Warner Marable; Tuskegee University professor Dr. Alva Bailey; Ronald Williams, assistant to the mayor; my law partner, Walter McGowan; board of education member Donna Bradford; Willie Whitehead, vice president of Macon County Greyhound Park; my sister-in-law and her husband, Jean and Wilmer Wilson; and my law partner sons, Fred and Stanley.

20

Vestiges of Discrimination

Notwithstanding the growth of my civil practice and other business and professional matters in recent years, I have continued to work on civil rights cases. In Chapter 16, I mentioned that one of my most disappointing cases was *Alabama State Teacher's Association v. Alabama Public School and College Authority,* a 1968 lawsuit filed in an attempt to block the creation of Auburn University at Montgomery.

That 1968 case had begun with a letter from Joe L. Reed, then executive director of ASTA, which was the professional association for the state's African-American teachers. By September 1990, Joe Reed was second in command of the Alabama Education Association, the previously white teachers' group into which ASTA had merged some years earlier. Joe had also become the chairman of the board of trustees of Alabama State University and, as I mentioned elsewhere, is probably the most powerful black political figure in Alabama.

This time Joe didn't write—he telephoned to discuss an education discrimination matter. He basically requested that I join as co-counsel with attorneys Solomon Seay, Terry Davis, and Armand Derfner to represent Alabama State University in the pending case, *Knight v. Alabama.* He told me that my alma mater, Alabama State University, needed me. He further stated there were only four persons he could think of who would be able to do what he wanted done in the case. Unfortunately, two of those persons were dead— Peter Hall, an outstanding civil rights lawyer from Birmingham who later became a municipal court judge in that city, and David Hood, an outstanding civil rights lawyer from Bessemer. The third person, although capable in his judgment, was not qualified because he does not have a law degree (he was speaking of himself). I was the other person he deemed capable of achieving the desired result. I told him I had never refused to do anything he asked me to do, nor had I failed to represent anyone or any institution that had a legitimate claim or defense. I was happy to represent Alabama State University.

The Lawsuit That Should Not Have Been Necessary

This case was originally filed by the Justice Department in 1983, as *United States of America v. State of Alabama.* The defendants included the governor of Alabama; the Alabama State Board of Education; the state superintendent of Education; the Alabama Commission on Higher Education; the Alabama Public School and College Authority; and the state's twelve four-year colleges and universities. The complaint alleged that the State of Alabama was maintaining vestiges of racial discrimination throughout its system of higher education. As you recall, this was the point of the 1968 lawsuit discussed in Chapter 16.

In 1984, John Knight was allowed to join this case as a class action intervenor on behalf of graduates of Alabama State University and blacks who are or will become eligible either to attend or be employed by ASU. Knight is ASU's publicity director, a former Montgomery County Commissioner, and now represents Montgomery County in the Alabama House of Representatives. Knight and a group of African-American students, alumni, faculty and administrators of ASU had instituted an earlier federal court action attacking vestiges of segregation in Montgomery area state-supported universities. That case had been in the Middle District of Alabama; this one was in the Northern District, but the issues were very similar.

A month-long trial was held in July 1985. In December 1985, Judge U. W. Clemon ruled that Alabama had failed to dismantle the vestiges of discrimination based on race in its system of higher education. He ordered the state, the governor, the Alabama Commission on Higher Education, and the Alabama Public School and College Authority to submit a remedial plan.

But the U.S. Eleventh Circuit Court of Appeals remanded the case to the District Court on the ground that Judge Clemon should have recused himself from hearing it because of his past association with some of the parties while he was a civil rights attorney and while he served in the Alabama legislature. Then, the Justice Department and the Knight plaintiffs were joined by another group of plaintiffs headed by Alease E. Sims representing graduates of Alabama A&M University. Meanwhile, following the precedent set by Judge Clemon's recusal, several other judges in the Northern District of Alabama were recused because of their relationships with various parties in the case. Finally, the matter was assigned in 1989 to Judge Harold L. Murphy of the Northern District of Georgia. The cases were consolidated for a trial which began in October 1990, and ended in April 1991, some seventy-eight courtoom days later. Thousands of exhibits and many depositions were introduced. Need I mention that many, many tax dollars were spent?

Over fifty lawyers participated in the trial, including Joe R. Whatley, Robert D. Hunter, Solomon S. Seay Jr., John C. Faulkenberry, Demetrius Newton, C. Glenn Powell, Thomas W. Thagard, Armand Derfner, Jeffrey A. Foshee, Craig M. Crenshaw, Donald V. Watkins, David R. Boyd, Stanley J. Murphy, James U. Blacksher, and Leslie M. Proll.

The major issue was whether Alabama still maintained a dual, race-based educational system of higher education. The theory of the case was that the state had never provided African Americans proper educational opportunities. Commitments that had been made during Reconstruction to Payton Finley, the African-American member of the State Board of Education—that Alabama would develop the same type of university for African Americans that the University of Alabama was for whites—were never fulfilled. Nor had the state fulfilled its commitments to African Americans during the "separate but equal" days, because Alabama

State University and Alabama A&M University were never "equal to," even though they were "separate from," the University of Alabama and Auburn University.

These cases were tried from historical, sociological, and financial points of view. We knew that Alabama's African-American institutions had never received the support and that African-American citizens in Alabama had never received a quality education similar to what the state afforded its white institutions and citizens. Thus, the plaintiffs alleged that there were still vestiges of racial discrimination in higher education in the State of Alabama.

Cases From My Past

It was a pleasure for me to represent Alabama State University in these cases. I was personally familiar with many of the witnesses and could effectively examine them on segregation and discrimination practices in this state. However, as a citizen of Alabama, it was painful to think of the work, toil, blood, sweat and tears that went into cases like *Vivian Malone v. University of Alabama*, *Franklin v. Auburn*, and *Lee v. Macon*, and realize that some twenty-five years later, the state's educational institutions still have vestiges of racial discrimination. Though my goal of destroying everything segregated had been fulfilled to some degree, I found myself—in the sunset years of my practice—involved in one of the largest desegregation cases of all times. We were retrying cases I thought we had won decades ago.

In Chapter 16, I mentioned that the 1990 testimony of Dr. J. Mills Thornton, III, had really explained what the issues were in the 1968 lawsuit against the creation of Auburn University at Montgomery. Dr. Thornton was our witness in the trial before Judge Murphy, and as I questioned him, my entire civil rights career unfolded vividly before my eyes.

Thornton was an amazing witness. He was born in Montgomery and attended its segregated public schools. He obtained his undergraduate degree from Princeton University, and went on to earn his doctoral degree at Yale University. Dr. Thornton is a noted historian of Alabama and the most noted historian of civil rights in

Alabama. Dr. Thornton testified as an expert in the fields of American history generally, Southern history more particularly, and most particularly the history of Alabama. Dr. Thornton was initially examined by James Blacksher, the attorney for the *Knight* plaintiffs, and later examined by me. Throughout his testimony were references to cases and civil rights activities in which I had participated. As he responded to our questions, I relived for a moment my own civil rights history.

He told of the role that Alabama State College played in the Montgomery Bus Protest in 1955–1956. He particularly mentioned Professor Jo Ann Robinson who worked with me very closely in organizing and planning the strategy for the bus boycott. He mentioned Rufus Lewis and E. D. Nixon. He described Rosa Parks as the heroine of the protest. He also testified with reference to the role Dr. Martin Luther King, Jr. played in the Montgomery Improvement Association, the organization that spearheaded the protest.

He related in detail the beginning and the endurance of the Montgomery Bus Boycott and the parties involved therein. He testified about the get-tough policy of the city officials in the Bus Protest and about the eighty-nine leaders of the boycott who were indicted for allegedly violating the Alabama Anti-Boycott Act of 1921. He testified with reference to the case of the *State of Alabama v. Martin Luther King, Jr.* which was tried in March 1956. I represented Dr. King and the eighty-nine leaders who were involved in that lawsuit.

Dr. Thornton also testified at length concerning the case of *NAACP v. Alabama* where Governor Patterson obtained an injunction enjoining the NAACP from transacting business in the state. I represented the NAACP. He also testified with reference to the case of *Sullivan v. New York Times* in which I represented the individual black ministers in that case.

Dr. Thornton also testified with reference to the gerrymandering act in Tuskegee which gave rise to the lawsuit of *Gomillion v. Lightfoot*. I represented the plaintiffs in *Gomillion v. Lightfoot*.

Dr. Thornton also testified with reference to the MacMurray

College students who were arrested in the Regal Cafe, and *Montgomery v. King and Embry* in which Edwin King and Elroy Embry were arrested in the Jefferson Davis Hotel for requesting service. I had represented the black persons in the Regal Cafe incident, and Embry and King in their litigation.

He described the sit-ins of the 1960s in the Montgomery County Courthouse and the subsequent expulsion of students which gave rise to the case I filed on behalf of the affected students.

Dr. Thornton testified concerning the case of *Lewis v. Greyhound*. I represented John Lewis and others in that case. He also testified with reference to the Student Non-Violent Coordinating Committee (SNCC) members who resumed William Moore's Freedom Walk. Mr. Moore was the postman who started walking from Chattanooga, Tennessee, to Jackson, Mississippi, to protest segregation and was killed in north Alabama.

Dr. Thornton's testimony moved on to education cases, beginning with *Lee v. Macon County Board of Education* which I filed in 1963. That suit, you recall, had led to a court order for the integration of Tuskegee High School, but Governor George Wallace had used state troopers to block the integration.

Thereafter, the State Board of Education had begun providing tuition grants to white students to attend nonintegrated schools. The whites had begun a boycott of the schools, of the Tuskegee School once integrated, and then the students had been moved to the new Shorter School, and the whites had begun a boycott of that.

The outcome of this was an amended version of *Lee v. Macon* in which the black plaintiffs asserted that these actions on the part of the governor and the State Board of Education indicated that there was actually a statewide unified public school system and therefore the court could issue a statewide injunction ordering the integration of all of the schools in Alabama all at once. And eventually the court did grant such an injunction.

Dr. Thornton also testified that Auburn University was desegregated as a result of the case of *Franklin v. Auburn University*. I had filed the lawsuit on behalf of Franklin in 1963.

He testified with reference to the Vivian Malone suit against the University of Alabama. We finally obtained her enrollment in that university in 1963. He also testified with reference to the case of *Carr v. Montgomery County Board of Education*. Dr. Thornton testified at length about the creation of Auburn University at Montgomery and the litigation of *Alabama State Teachers Association v. Alabama Public School and College Authority* which I filed in 1968.

It was a perplexing experience to listen to his testimony and to relive the trials of all of these cases. At one point during Dr. Thornton's testimony, the court proceedings became quite personal for me.

Dr. Thornton had been testifying at length concerning methods which white officials had used in Alabama in 1943 to prevent a black lawyer from assisting his relatives in registering to vote in Montgomery. Arthur Madison was disbarred as a result of that incident [See Chapter 3]. I solicited the following testimony from Dr. Thornton:

Q. Now, let me ask you this, Dr. Thornton, whether or not the method used here, all the way back in 1943 in terms of putting pressure on teachers and others who had sensitive positions, and the matter of using a state statute which prohibits a lawyer from representing a client without their consent, was this type of pressure used subsequent to that time?

A. Yes, it was used during the bus boycott against you. After the filing of *Browder v. Gayle*, which is the bus boycott suit filed in Federal Court, you were indicted. One of the plaintiffs, who was a woman named Jeanetta Reese, testified that you had filed a suit without her consent, and you were indicted under the same statute that Arthur Madison had been indicted under. And, I think, I presume it was the hope thereby to obtain your disbarment and thus the elimination of the legal assistance that the bus boycott was obtaining from you.

Q. Now, I think you testified earlier with respect to the Autherine Lucy case.

A. Yes.

THE COURT: Wait. Let me interrupt. How did you get out of that, Mr. Gray?

MR. GRAY: Am I permitted to tell the Court?

THE COURT: Were you ever tried?

MR. THAGARD: Judge, I wanted him to take the witness stand all morning and go under oath.

Q. Dr. Thornton, would you tell the Court, please, what finally happened to the *State of Alabama v. Fred Gray* in connection with this matter that you testified to?

A. Just before it was to come to trial, Solicitor Thetford dropped the case because it became—it was brought to his attention that the alleged criminal action of filing the suit had taken place in the Federal Courthouse and that therefore the state courts would not have jurisdiction over the action because it was in a Federal Courthouse, and so Solicitor Thetford dropped the case in State Court and referred it to the US Attorney for his consideration and the US Attorney did not prosecute.

For those readers who are interested, some other excerpts of Dr. Thornton's testimony are included in Appendix C.

In addition to the historical testimony given by Dr. Thornton, I also examined two former clients I had represented in higher education cases, Vivian Malone, University of Alabama and Harold Franklin, Auburn University.

I am not really a demonstrative individual. But you can understand that my emotions were deeply touched by these proceedings and by the weight of all that was at stake in this case concerning the education of Alabama's children—white, black, red, brown, yellow, and all shades in between. I, an African-American lawyer raised in a totally segregated society, had fought all my life against the vestiges of discrimination about which this case was being litigated. I had been barred from a law school education in my own state but I had become a lawyer anyway. And I had spent my entire legal career essentially working on the very issues which were being discussed in Judge Murphy's courtroom.

I understood, perhaps better than many, that if Alabama—the state of my birth, my home state, the state that I love with all my soul—if Alabama is ever going to realize its magnificent potential, these issues have to be resolved and the people of Alabama have to reach peace on them. Of course, my way to help reach the peace is to use the system to get rid of the impediments to peace.

Thus, I was a sympathetic listener when Judge Murphy, before court was recessed on November 15, 1990, urged the parties to settle the higher education suit over the Thanksgiving holiday. He stated that he could see where the evidence in the case was headed, and he knew this would be a long, expensive trial. He also said he knew the issues were complex and that no settlement could be reached that would completely please all the parties. However, he said, this was a case that really ought to be settled by the parties instead of by the courts. His full statement is significant, and I have included it in Appendix A-7, for readers who are interested.

When the parties failed to reach a settlement, Judge Murphy subsequently ordered a settlement conference to be held. In a statement from the bench [See Appendix A-8], he instructed the governor, the presidents of all of the state universities, the chief trustee of each of the universities, and the members of the Commission on Higher Education to appear at the settlement conference. Judge Murphy basically told us again, and in stronger language, that the parties, as representatives of the people of Alabama, should get together and work out a settlement rather than keep on spending millions of dollars in litigation.

Judge Murphy's actions here were interesting, because a common reactionary theme of political rhetoric in Alabama since the 1950s has been that federal judges have "rammed things down the throats of the people." George Wallace and numerous other state politicians made careers out of attacking the federal courts. Wallace even suggested once that Judge Frank Johnson be given "a barbed wire enema." Well, here in this case you had Judge Murphy going to extraordinary lengths to let the responsible state officials work out their problems rather than having the courts do it for them. And he ordered the highest officials themselves to attend the settlement conference so the lawyers could not claim they lacked the authority to make a final agreement. Judge Murphy warned, however, that if the Alabama officials and their lawyers did not reach an agreement, then he was certainly ready to enter an appropriate order.

This was a powerful message, but it failed to produce the result Judge Murphy had hoped for. On December 20, 1990, the appointed day of the hearing, all the parties assembled, and the judge restated the reasons for the settlement conference, then he left the courtroom and turned the negotiations over to the two senior attorneys. Attorney Tom Thagard represented Auburn University and I represented Alabama State University. For several hours we tried to reach a settlement and were unsuccessful. We presented our report to Judge Murphy, who stated that since we Alabamians did not settle the case, a federal judge from Georgia would.

On December 27, 1991, Judge Murphy entered his final order, an 850-page opinion finding that the State of Alabama maintained vestiges of racial discrimination in higher education. He ruled in pertinent part:

> In particular, the Court finds that vestiges remain within the practices of some of defendants in the following areas: faculty and administrative employment, state funding for higher education, facilities on the (HBUs)" (Historically Black Universities) "admission policies, and program duplication. To the extent that these vestiges of the formal *de jure* system impede the segregation of the state's HBUs, or limit African-American access to the predominantly white institutions. The Court had formulated a Remedial Decree designed to eliminate these practices root and branch.

The Knight plaintiffs, Alabama A&M University, and Alabama State University appealed a portion of the remedial decree, arguing that it was insufficient to completely eradicate the vestiges of racial discrimination which the court found to exist. I argued the case on behalf of Alabama State University where at this writing it is pending in the United States Court of Appeals for the Eleventh Circuit.

On February 24, 1994, the Eleventh Circuit affirmed Judge Murphy's decision that there are still vestiges of racial discrimination in higher education in Alabama. However, the court reversed and remanded for further consideration a portion of Judge Murphy's order concerning relief. The Eleventh Circuit was very complimentary of the manner in which Judge Murphy handled the case. The court stated:

> Although, as explained below, we find it necessary to reverse or vacate, and remand for reconsideration, a few isolated portions of the district court's judgment, in so doing we express nothing but the deepest respect for the manner in which the court below has handled this case. Judge Murphy's management of this complex piece of institutional reform litigation has been extraordinary. His meticulous and scholarly opinion is a model of judicial thoroughness. Writing without the benefit of Supreme Court guidance on the applicable legal standard, Judge Murphy anticipated in considerable measure the standards later set out by the Court in *Fordice*. Our ruling today reversing or vacating, and remanding for reconsideration, a few discrete elements of the court's opinion is based primarily on the legal standards announced by the Supreme Court months after the district court opinion was issued. This disposition therefore in no way reflects negatively on the district court's handling of the case. The fact that defendants do not challenge the district court's judgment at all, and that plaintiffs at this time take issue with only a few isolated rulings, bears witness to the

wisdom and fairness manifested in the court's decision.

The court then concluded:

> For the foregoing reasons, we vacate the district court's judgment with respect to the missions claim and remand to the district court for determination of whether the missions have continuing segregative effects and, if so, whether such effects can be remedied in a manner that is practicable and educationally sound. We reverse the district court's ruling that the current allocation of land grant aid between Auburn University and A & M is not a vestige of segregation and remand the land grant claim to the district court for determination of whether the funding allocation has continuing segregative effects and, if so, whether such effects can be remedied in a manner that is practicable and educationally sound. We vacate the district court's ruling that the granting of judicial relief on plaintiffs' curriculum claim is barred and remand the claim for reconsideration.

Judge Murphy set a hearing for January 1995 to consider the issue remanded by the Eleventh Circuit. Notwithstanding the trial date, Judge Murphy continued to tell the parties this case should be settled. In fact, footnote 3 on page 11 of his order entered on September 16, 1994, stated:

> The Court is convinced that courageous and reasonable leaders could settle this case. Such settlement, however, requires leaders who understand that the schools in Alabama must be desegregated, but also understand that they are not tools of social experiment; who understand that this litigation is about student choice not institutions; and who understand what may happen to some institutions, Allied and other, next year after the conclusion of the rehearing.

The Importance of the Case

The "Higher Education case," as it has come to be called, is one of the most important cases in the field of civil rights. Alabama's practice of racial discrimination predates its admission into the union. In the 1800s, it was a criminal offense in Alabama to teach blacks to read and write. As the experts testified in this case, the history of Alabama clearly demonstrates that blacks have never been treated equally in education. Beginning with the 1953 Autherine Lucy case, African-American citizens in Alabama have of necessity filed lawsuit after lawsuit to obtain equal education in this state. During the 1950s and 1960s, blacks filed and won lawsuits against discrimination in higher education.

These suits were intended to bring Alabama in compliance with the United States Constitution, and to do so the state would have to destroy segregation, "root and branch." Yet segregation thrived, roots, branch and trunk. It became necessary in 1982 to file additional suits to destroy the vestiges of discrimination in higher education. Therefore, after years of litigation and millions of dollars at taxpayers expense, Judge Murphy ruled on December 7, 1991, what we have known all along, that even in the 1990s, vestiges of racial discrimination still exist in the state of Alabama.

Judge Murphy's conclusion was the same as that reached five years earlier by Judge U. W. Clemon, the first African-American federal district judge in Alabama. Judge Murphy not only found that vestiges of discrimination still exist, he formulated a remedial decree designed to eliminate those racial practices. At the time of his order, he retained jurisdiction of this case for a ten-year period. The clock is now running on that period, but we can all hope that by the time his order expires, all vestiges of racial discrimination in higher education in Alabama will in fact be destroyed, "root and branch."

As the attorney who has filed more cases to integrate education in Alabama than anyone else, it is very disheartening and heartbreaking to know that the officials of the state of Alabama, for the most part, have never done anything more to eliminate segregation other than what the court strictly ordered. In my opinion, if Alabama is to progress and if racial discrimination is to be destroyed "root and branch" in higher education and in all areas of life in this state, there are three things that the public officials must do:

(1) recognize that racial discrimination is wrong, unconstitutional and that African Americans have been discriminated against since they began living in the state of Alabama; (2) not only acknowledge the wrong but have a determination to correct the wrong because it is the right thing to do; and (3) come forth with their own plan that will go beyond the minimum requirements of any court order to destroy racial discrimination, not only in higher education but in all aspects of American life.

When these three modest steps have been taken, and when an individual is judged on the "content of his character" and not on "the color of his skin," then the work of all those persons who have labored in the field of civil rights, and some who have died, shall not have been in vain.

Another Vestige of Discrimination

I want to mention briefly one other ongoing effort to correct past discrimination.

On May 13, 1994, I spoke on behalf of the Alabama Lawyers Association (ALA), the predominantly black bar in Alabama, before the Alabama Board of Bar Commissioners, the governing body of lawyers in the state, on a proposed consent decree in *Hoover White v. State of Alabama.*

This case had been filed by attorneys Solomon S. Seay, Jr., and Terry Davis on behalf of the Alabama Democratic Conference, the black political caucus I mentioned earlier of which Dr. Joe L. Reed is chair. The lawsuit sought to increase the number of black Alabama appellate court judges.

Alabama has three appellate courts: the Court of Civil Appeals, with five judges; the Court of Criminal Appeals, three judges; and the Supreme Court, seven justices. No black has ever served on the courts of civil or criminal appeals. In 1980, Oscar Adams, a well-known Birmingham lawyer was appointed by Governor Fob James to fill a vacancy on the Supreme Court, and Adams was subsequently elected to two full terms on the court. He thus became the first African American elected since Reconstruction to a statewide office in Alabama.

Adams retired in 1993, and Governor Jim Folsom appointed Ralph Cook, an African American lawyer who had become a circuit judge in Birmingham, to succeed him. In 1994, Justice Cook faced an election challenge from a far less qualified white candidate whose principal campaign tactic was to display pictures of himself and Cook. In the racial context of Alabama politics, that is recognized as a not-too-subtle way for a white candidate to warn unaware white voters that if they are not careful they may accidentally cast a ballot for a black. However, the tactic failed and Justice Cook became the second African American to be elected to a statewide office in Alabama in this century.

Given the history of Alabama, it seems unlikely that the racial imbalance of the appellate court judges (6 percent African American representation, compared to 25 percent African American population) will be corrected any time soon in statewide voting.

White v. Alabama raised the strategic issue that the present appellate court election process violates the Voting Rights Act because some of the seats on the Supreme Court and all of the seats on the civil appeals court have not been precleared as required by that act.

The state is represented in this action by Attorney General Jimmy Evans, and other members of his staff including special assistant attorney general Donald Watkins, who is black. The case is pending before a panel of federal judges consisting of Circuit Judge Joel Dubina, Chief District Judge Myron Thompson, and District Judge Ira DeMent. Judge Thompson is black, the others, white.

After the suit was filed, the parties, joined by the Justice Department, submitted a proposed consent decree under which the courts of civil and criminal appeals would consist of seven judges each. The additional judges would be appointed by the governor from nominations by a committee of five members to be selected as follows: one member from the Alabama Lawyers Association; one from the Alabama State Bar Association; two to be selected by counsel for the plaintiffs; and a fifth member selected by the first four.

The plan further provided an opportunity for blacks to have a minimum of two members on each of the three appellate courts, and at the same time, all of the judges on all of the appellate courts would be elected on a state-wide basis. The Justice Department had agreed conditionally to preclear this proposal if the court approved it, which in October 1994 it did, just in time to become a hot campaign issue in the November elections. White backlash against the consent decree apparently contributed to the defeat of Attorney General Jimmy Evans in that election.

The proposed consent decree had been endorsed by the chief justice of the Alabama Supreme Court, other appellate court judges, and the attorney general of Alabama, all of whom recommended to the Board of Bar Commissioners of the State of Alabama that it also endorse the proposal. However, there was opposition, and Board of Bar Commissioners initially elected to take no position. But then it became known that Judge Dubina, one of the judges hearing the case, wanted the Bar to take a position. So the Board of Bar Commissioners invited more testimony, and the president of the Alabama Lawyers Association, Deborah Walker of Birmingham, asked me to speak on behalf of the Alabama Lawyers Association.

That's how on May 13, 1994, I came to drive from my office in Tuskegee to Montgomery, a trip which I had made hundreds of times, and parked my car on Hull Street between Dexter Avenue and Washington Street. I had parked in this block many, many times, for my office for over twenty years was in the Gray Building on the southwest corner of Dexter Avenue and Hull Street. The Gray Building, incidentally, was demolished in the early 1990s to make way for Alabama's impressive new Judicial Building, but during the years I owned it, I was the only individual African American property owner on Montgomery's historic main street.

As I crossed that street to the State Bar Association building, I glanced up the hill a block eastward to the Dexter Avenue King Memorial Baptist Church.

Many thoughts ran through my mind. This is a historic block to walk. The first official meeting of the Montgomery Bus Boycott was in the basement of Dexter Avenue Baptist Church. As I looked past the church to the Capitol, I knew that at the top of the Capitol steps is a star where Jefferson Davis stood to take the oath of office as the President of the Confederacy. I stood near that same spot in 1970 to take the oath of office to become one of the first blacks elected to the Alabama Legislature since Reconstruction. And then I served in that historic Capitol building, where, incidentally, scores of resolutions and bills had been approved in the 1950s and 1960s to deny me and my fellow African American citizens of Alabama the rights and privileges of citizenship.

Also in this graceful and beautiful old building, white legislators had enacted the 1901 Alabama Constitution which disfranchised virtually all African American voters in the state, and it would take us six decades to undo that injustice. As I walked across Dexter Avenue, I remembered the feeling I had as Bernice and I were among the thousands who marched up that same street in 1965 culminating the Selma-to-Montgomery March. which was led by Dr. King and others. At the end of that march, I was included in the group that went in to formally present our petition to George Wallace asking him, as governor, to help Alabama's blacks obtain the right to vote.

These thoughts were on my mind as I crossed the street to the Alabama State Bar Building, and I began to wonder, what shall I tell these fifty lawyers from across Alabama, all white except one? These fifty determined the fate of lawyers in this state, and set the pace for lawyers and the impression that the nation receives from Alabama lawyers. I had served as a bar commissioner; in fact, I was the first black in Alabama history to do so. Now I felt an awesome responsibility to impress upon the sitting commissioners to look favorably upon a proposed consent decree that could have profound effect upon decisions to be rendered by the appellate courts of this state, not only affecting the rights of African Americans, but affecting the rights of every person, firm, and corporation that will have matters litigated before the appellate courts.

This was indeed an awesome responsibility. It is one thing to argue a case before a single judge or even a panel of justices of the highest court. But what does a black Alabama lawyer, born in poverty in Montgomery, say to fifty lawyers who have come from every corner of Alabama? What can one say to persuade them to reach a decision that will have a positive effect upon the state?

As I entered the meeting room, only two African Americans were present. Of course, I knew that would be the case. One was Commissioner J. Mason Davis, who had come from a prestigious middle-class African-American family in Birmingham, was former secretary to the Alabama Democratic Party, law professor at the University of Alabama, and now a member of one of the largest predominantly white law firms in Birmingham. The other was Terry Davis, an attorney for the plaintiffs. We were the only persons of color. There were three white women, who were also members of the Board of Bar Commissioners. The balance of the members were Caucasians, and they represented the cream of the crop because these lawyers had been selected by lawyers all over the state, from each of the judicial circuits to represent those on the Board of Bar Commissioners.

Secretary Reginald T. Hamner called the roll, the minutes were adopted, and the first order of business was the matter of discussing the proposed consent decree. State Bar President James Seales called upon Attorney General Jimmy Evans who explained that he had carefully reviewed the law and the facts of the case, and was thoroughly convinced that the consent decree was in the best interests of Alabama. Deputy Attorney General Marc Givhan discussed specifics of the proposed decree and answered questions.

President Seales then introduced me as a former member of the Board of Bar Commissioners, and indicated that I would be speaking on behalf of the Alabama Lawyers Association. I greeted the president and members of the Bar Commission and told them that it was good to be back home. I then stated four reasons why the proposed decree should be approved:

1. The goal of its remedial provisions is to correct past and present effects of racial discrimination which keep African Americans from being elected to the appellate courts of Alabama. The provisions are flexible but meaningful and are intended to enhance racial diversity in the membership of these courts, which is in the best interest of the state.

2. The Constitution and laws of the United States mandate that minorities be able to freely exercise their choice in the selection of elected officials, including judges. The 1965 Voting Rights Act prohibits any form of election which has a direct adverse effect on the choice of minorities in voting. When it comes to the election of appellate judges in Alabama, the substance of the proposed decree gives African Americans the greatest possible participation. It permits African Americans to have a voice in the selection of at least two black lawyers on each of our appellate courts, and at the same time it retains African Americans' rights to share equally in the choice of all of the other members on the court. This does not mean that African Americans must elect African Americans for these seats. I believe that when a person is doing a good job, whether white or black, he or she should be retained. However, it gave to African Americans a major voice in the selection process.

3. Our experiences have taught us that single-member districts have given us the greatest results in city, county, school board, legislative, and congressional elections. On the other hand, we feel it is very important that African Americans not give up their right of participation in deciding all of the members on the appellate courts, and that can only be done by maintaining the at-large election. At the same time, we want to be sure that there is an opportunity for a minimum of two African Americans on each of these courts. This proposed settlement gives us the best opportunity to correct the imbalances of the past.

4. In addition, it is significant that the court itself and the other parties in the lawsuit have voluntarily agreed on this resolution of the problem. They recognize that the old system does not meet constitutional mandates, and that to litigate the issue is not the best

resolution. The Alabama Lawyers Association believes that this is the spirit in which residents and public officials of this state should begin to resolve our problems. We should be willing to voluntarily reach an agreement without waiting on the court to mandate the result. For too long in this state, our officials have only done what federal courts have mandated in connection with the protection of rights for African Americans. We are elated that we have appellate court judges and public officials in this state who recognize the problem, and who voluntarily agreed on a solution. We hope the resolution of this issue will serve as a model so that when we have other problems, and there are others, the proper officials and the parties will recognize the problems, recognize there is a need for solutions, and then sit down and solve the problems.

At the conclusion of my presentation, I was warmly received by the members of the Board of Bar Commissioners. Commissioner J. Mason Davis spoke passionately in support of the proposal. And Commissioner John P. Oliver, II, also spoke out forcefully for it. John Oliver, a white lawyer from Dadeville, is the commissioner from the 5th Judicial Circuit. Not only does Oliver hold the seat I held as a bar commissioner, but he is the commissioner who represents me and my law firm. His support meant a lot to me, personally. After some discussion and maneuvering, the commissioners ultimately endorsed in principle the concept of the consent decree. And, as I mentioned, the federal court accepted the consent decree.

The action taken by the State Bar was indeed historic. Never before, can I recall, has the governing body of the State Bar Association taken an affirmative action in asking the court to end blatant discrimination in anything. This resolution had the following impact:

First, it supported a statewide system of at-large election of appellate court justices which provides diversity and increased opportunity for minority participation.

Second, it supports in principle the concept of settlement in *White v. Bennett*. This is a far cry from the Board of Bar Commissioners that once adopted resolutions that prohibited blacks from participating in the process; in earlier times, the Bar Commission-ers had been the leading behind-the-scenes force opposing the rights of African Americans. Their 1994 resolution, regardless of what ultimately happens to the case, goes a long way toward setting the right tone for the resolution of issues for this state. And for it to come from the lawyers who govern lawyers is a tremendous symbolic step.

There is another great dynamic involved in this action. Let's look at the parties.

Alabama Attorney General Jimmy Evans took a bold position in agreeing to the consent decree. This is a far cry from earlier attorney generals like John Patterson and others who filed suits to enjoin the NAACP from doing business in Alabama and did everything possible to stop African Americans from obtaining their rights. The suit is being supported by the Alabama Democratic Conference, headed by Joe Reed. I had represented Joe and other students when they were expelled from Alabama State College in 1960 for a sit-in at the snack bar in the Montgomery County courthouse. Reed has developed into probably the greatest political leader in Alabama, black or white.

Plaintiffs' attorneys Solomon S. Seay, Jr., and Terry Davis both began their legal practice in my office. Donald Watkins, special counsel for the State of Alabama in this action, at one time, was the special assistant to University of Alabama President David Matthews. I recruited him from Dr. Matthews's office to come to our office and practice law. He received his basic introduction to civil rights litigation with my law firm, Gray, Seay, and Langford.

I have had the opportunity of working with and helping to train and develop these outstanding lawyers. It is indeed a good experi-ence to have worked with lawyers who are doing an outstanding job in the civil rights field, helping to change the landscape of this country. This too, I believe, is one of my legacies as a result of my practice in this state during the last forty years.

Arthur D. Shores

Clifford J. Durr

Frank M. Johnson, Jr.

George C. Wallace

21

Four Men Who Affected My Legal Career

There are four men who played major roles in the development of my legal career. Each is a Southerner, an Alabamian and a lawyer. Attorney Arthur D. Shores, Attorney Clifford J. Durr, Judge Frank M. Johnson, Jr., and Governor George C. Wallace each served a unique and significant function in connection with my career, and each contributed differently in helping to eradicate segregation in Alabama. Surprisingly, three are white.

Arthur D. Shores is the dean of African-American lawyers in Alabama. He was practicing law before I was a member of the bar. He was handling civil rights cases all over Alabama before I went to law school. He was my mentor.

When I considered going to law school, I thought about Arthur Shores, an African-American lawyer who was doing the things I wanted to do. I thought to myself, if Arthur Shores could be a civil rights lawyer, so can I.

Not only did he sign an affidavit so I could take the bar examination, but he assisted me in getting other affidavits. When I became a lawyer, during the early years of my practice, I would always invite him to assist me in most of my early civil rights cases. He would be with me in the courtroom and assist in any capacity requested. He never tried to take over my cases, but he gave me the courage and support that any young lawyer needs in the courtroom during his/her early formative years. Arthur was always there for me. But for him, I may not have had the courage to continue.

When I was president of the National Bar Association (NBA), in 1985, I initiated the NBA Hall of Fame primarily to honor Arthur Shores and other pioneer African-American lawyers like him. He was one of the first initiated into the NBA Hall of Fame. He has received many honors for his work in the civil rights field. He recently retired. However, he continues his practice in Birmingham with his daughter Helen in charge.

Clifford J. Durr served as my adviser on a daily basis during the formative years of my career, beginning when I opened my office in 1954. He assisted and advised me generally in the development of my practice, and specifically concerning civil rights litigation. He also assisted in research and drafting pleadings. He rendered valuable assistance to me in representing the plaintiff in my first wrongful death case. Without Clifford Durr during those early years, my career likely would have had a slower start.

During his lifetime, there was no official recognition of his work in the city of his birth, Montgomery. However, on March 1, 1992, he was so honored posthumously. On that date, Auburn University at Montgomery (AUM) inaugurated the Cifford J. Durr Lecture Series, a series of lectures in which nationally recognized speakers address issues concerning constitutional protection of civil liberties. A resolution was adopted by the City Council of the City of Montgomery recognizing his work. The speakers for the occasion were Mrs. Lyndon B. Johnson, the widow of President Lyndon B. Johnson; Tom Johnson, president of CNN; and Fred Gray. Invited to speak on "Clifford J. Durr: The Attorney," I stated among other things, "It is appropriate that this university recognize an outstanding Alabamian for the outstanding contributions which he has made in the field of civil liberties to this nation, to this state and to this city . . . . In the real sense of the word, Clifford Durr has been a silent partner in my law practice from day one."

Virginia Durr, his widow, was honored by her family and friends at Martha's Vineyard on the occasion of her ninetieth birthday. On August 7, 1993, my wife and I attended and presented her with a plaque which states, SIT LONG, TALK MUCH. To know Virginia Durr is to know that she talks much and at her age, she sits for long periods of time.

Judge Frank M. Johnson, Jr., became Federal District Judge for the Middle District of Alabama on November 7, 1955. That was 24 days before Mrs. Rosa Parks refused to give up her seat to a white man on a city bus in Montgomery, and eighty-seven days before I filed *Browder v. Gayle*, which integrated the buses in Montgomery. All of the civil rights cases that I filed in the Middle District of Alabama were decided by him or with his participation. Many of these cases were precedent setting cases. He is a man of courage, intestinal fortitude, who interpreted the Constitution in such a manner that it ended segregation in all areas of life in Alabama. But for Judge Johnson's rulings, the realization of the Civil Rights Movement may have been delayed several years if not decades. But for Judge Johnson's rulings, my career likely would not have blossomed so radiantly, or certainly not as early as it did. Even more significantly, his rulings created a new way of life for many Americans.

Judge Johnson is the recipient of many honors, awards, and degrees. On May 22, 1992, the Federal Courthouse in Montgomery was named the Frank M. Johnson Jr. Federal Building and United States Courthouse. He was honored by the American Bar Association at its convention in August 1993, when he was awarded the Thurgood Marshall Freedom Award.

Governor George C. Wallace is included with the four men for a different reason. Governor Wallace's position on the race issue was not designed to assist African Americans in achieving their constitutional rights. He displayed no regard for the Constitution of the United States or the Constitution of the State of Alabama. His primary concerns were political. He was determined to do whatever he considered to be politically expedient, regardless of the adverse effect it had on others.

I saw Governor Wallace on television during his inaugural address on January 14, 1963, when he stated "I draw the line in the dust and toss the gauntlet before the feet of tyranny . . . and I say segregation now . . . segregation tomorrow . . . and segregation forever." These burning words of Governor Wallace motivated me to accomplish my goal of destroying everything segregated I could find as soon as possible. I was determined that during his tenure in office, I would do everything I could to destroy everything segregated I could find.

The fight was on. I filed many of the cases discussed in this book when he was governor. In many instances, he was named as a defendant and was enjoined from maintaining segregation. Thus his declaration—"segregation now, segregation tomorrow and segregation forever"—was defeated.

Of course, I also remember that when I first met George Corley Wallace he was a fair and reasonable circuit judge of Barbour and Bullock counties. Only later did he develop into one of the greatest racists in this nation's history. Many of the cases I filed and many of the decisions that were rendered were a result of his racial stands. So in a true sense, he really helped the Movement.

During the last part of his life, he has indicated that his earlier positions on race were wrong, and that he is sorry about them, and I think he has made amends. It is interesting to note that he won re-election to his final term as governor with the overwhelming support of Alabama's black voters, who preferred a repentant Democratic George Wallace over his Republican opponent.

In a personal sense, these four men affected my career. In a larger and more significant sense, they affected the lives of many people across the nation and around the world.

22

The Many Faces of Power

In addition to the four men named in the previous chapter, I had the privilege over my legal career to work with and against some of the most powerful individuals in Alabama and the nation, who shaped the political and social landscape from 1955 onward. I remember them well, and I am always struck by how they variously held, sought, reflected, and were affected by power—sometimes legal, sometimes spiritual, sometimes physical, and sometimes moral.

Beginning with the Montgomery Bus Boycott, we had on the one hand the mayor and commissioners, the bus company officials, and, for the most part, the entire white population who advocated segregation. They had the power, and they were determined to maintain the status quo, beginning with segregated bus seating.

On the other hand, after the first mass meeting on December 5, 1955, the forty thousand African Americans in Montgomery realized that they had the power. Power they never knew they had. Power they had never used before. They also had and were developing strong, powerful leaders.

E. D. Nixon had been a leader for many years and had done much in Alabama and particularly in Montgomery to advance the cause of African Americans. He truly can be called the Father of the Modern Civil Rights Movement. It is tragic that he died of a broken heart because he felt that he was never given proper credit for the groundbreaking work he did. I personally feel he laid the foundation on which Martin King was able to stand.

As the boycott progressed and as Dr. King became a viable force in Montgomery and Alabama, because of his ability to speak and his remarkable presence, he became a national leader. No other single African American in this century possessed the power and influence of Dr. King. In fact, as a direct result of what transpired in Montgomery, Dr. King perhaps achieved more power and notoriety than any other single person in the history of this nation, white or black. During his short lifetime Martin utilized that power to help get passed the Civil Rights acts of 1957 and 1963 and the Voting Rights Act of 1965, and he was able to get President Lyndon Baines Johnson, a fellow Southerner no less, to sign these acts into law and to publicly proclaim, in a speech to the nation, the anthem of the Movement, "We shall overcome."

The Montgomery Movement also produced another humble, compassionate leader in the person of Mrs. Rosa Parks. She never sought publicity, honor or fame. Yet her simple act of courage inspired others around the world. Many do not know that her actions made it very difficult for her to obtain employment in Montgomery. Consequently, after the boycott ended, she moved to Detroit, where for many years she worked in the office of Congressman John Conyers. She now stands as a heroine and as the Mother of the Modern Civil Rights Movement.

During the early years of my practice, particularly during the bus protest, I was able to develop a close working relationship with the most outstanding ministers in Montgomery. Such giants in religion as A. W. Wilson, pastor of Holt Street Baptist Church; Roy Bennett, president of the Ministerial Alliance; E. N. French, pastor of Hillard Chapel A. M. E. Zion Church; W. J. Powell, pastor of Old Ship A.M.E. Zion Church; H. H. Hubbard, pastor of Bethel Baptist Church; Ralph D. Abernathy, pastor of First Baptist Church; A. W. Murphy, pastor of Oak Street A.M.E. Zion Church; Felix James, pastor of Hall Street Baptist Church; and many, many more. I represented all the ninety-eight who were indicted along with Dr. King for boycotting. These were great individuals. They possessed substantial power which they used in encouraging the members of their churches to support the boycott and its leaders, including me as the attorney for the protest.

In addition to the religious leaders, we had the support of the African American business community, including P. M. Blair, who at one time was considered the "black mayor of Montgomery"; R. B. Binion, insurance executive; W. E. Lee, funeral director; D. Caffey, a businessman; Frank L. Taylor; Dr. Moses Jones, Exalted Ruler of the Elks; and Eddie Lee Posey, Elks president and the owner of the parking lot in downtown Montgomery which was the hub of the alternative transporation system we established. They gave the Movement economic power.

Then the Movement had women power. In addition to Rosa Parks and Jo Ann Robinson, we had all the educated women of the community, including the members of the Federated Women's Clubs; Mrs. A. W. West; Coretta Scott King; Mrs. R. T. Adair; Jimmie Lowe; Cora McHaney; and Johnnie Carr. And then there were the plain foot soldiers of the Movement, including strong women such as Lottie Green Varner, Alberta James, Zecozy Williams, and so many more.

So what we had in Montgomery, really, was the joining of forces of every possible segment of the African American community. Each time the established white leadership would do something, instead of stopping the Movement, it cemented it. So this tremendous amount of power that African Americans demonstrated in Montgomery is the driving force that brought about all of the other civil rights activities that later developed. From the Civil Rights Act of 1957 to the Voting Rights Act of 1965, it all started with the power that African Americans corralled in Montgomery, Alabama. This power was a pattern not only for the U.S. Civil Rights Movement, but it continues to motivate people around the world including China, Germany, Russia, and South Africa.

As I reflect on the mistakes that were made by the white leaders of the City of Montgomery, the greatest must be their underestimation of the leadership and the power of Montgomery's black leaders. The established white leadership failed to realize the pent-up power that black persons possessed. And they never thought that their refusal to give in to our three meager original demands would have resulted in the breaking down of the walls of segregation in Montgomery, Alabama, and the nation. It was a blessing in disguise that the white leaders reacted as they did. I hate to think where we would be with civil rights if they had done differently.

Dr. King utilized the power that he obtained to advocate great causes, including his campaign against the Vietnam War. He was not always successful, but his power opened doors so he could talk to governors, presidents, and heads of state around the globe. His example has enabled other African-American leaders to obtain and use power.

One of his chief lieutenants, Andy Young, later became a congressman, ambassador to the United Nations, and mayor of Atlanta. Jesse Jackson, who was one of Martin's young disciples, observed the way he used power. He is able to use it now. John Lewis is another example. I represented John when he was a student and a Freedom Rider in *Lewis v. Greyhound* during the turbulent sixties. I have watched him grow and develop, and he is now a congressman from Georgia. I represented Joe Reed and the other students who were expelled or suspended from Alabama State College. Since that time, Dr. Reed has grown and developed into one of the most powerful political individuals in Alabama. Not only does he serve as a city councilman in Montgomery, chairman of the board of trustees of Alabama State University, and associate director of the Alabama Education Association, but he is also chairman of the Alabama Democratic Conference, probably the most powerful African-American political group in the nation. The ADC in recent years has had a hand in the election of most white and black politicians in Alabama, and the appointment of two black federal judges.

This is a tremendous amount of power, and I have observed Dr. Reed in the exercise of that power. He has never done it for personal gain, but he has always used it for African Americans so that we may continue to break down the walls of segregation and the economic barriers which keep the races apart.

For the most part, the power mentioned above in connection with Dr. King and other civil rights leaders was exercised as social and political power. I personally always tried to draw from a different power, that of the law. Of course, one would not have worked without the other. The power of the Movement created a climate for the evolution of the law. And the power of the law protected the Movement and brought the actual final successes that we won.

In taking on and winning civil rights cases, my greatest asset was that I was always privileged to obtain as co-counsel outstanding legal minds. These were such attorneys as Thurgood Marshall; Arthur Shores; Jack Greenberg; Herbert O. Reid; Howard Law School professors; Robert Carter, then general counsel for the NAACP; Orzell Billingsley and Peter Hall, associates of Arthur Shores in Birmingham; Charles Langford, dean of Montgomery black lawyers and later my law partner; and Solomon S. Seay, Jr., another law partner.

During my professional career, I also observed power on the other side. I sat across the counsel table on numerous occasions from Alabama's great legal minds. Some I especially remember are Jack Crenshaw, who represented the Montgomery City Lines; Eugene Loe, who prosecuted Mrs. Parks in city court; Judge John Scott, Sr., who presided over her trial; Walter Knabe, one of the city attorneys; Drayton and Herman Hamilton, who represented the city in *Browder v. Gayle*; William Thetford, who prosecuted us in the anti-boycott case; Attorney General John Patterson, who brought the suit against the Tuskegee Civic Association and outlawed the NAACP in Alabama; assistant attorney general Gordon Madison; Harry Raymon of Tuskegee; James J. Carter; Maury Smith; Tom Thagard; Joe Goodwin; Roland Nachman; and Joseph Phelps, now a circuit judge in Montgomery.

These lawyers were well prepared and they tried their cases well. However, they lost 90 percent of these civil rights cases. They lost and we were victorious because we were trailblazers and were carefully working on precedents that had been laid by lawyers such as Charles Hamilton Houston and Thurgood Marshall. We also had right and the march of history on our side.

No one wields power like judges, and over forty years I have tried cases before justices of the peace in rural Alabama and justices of the Supreme Court in Washington, D.C. I have always received from judges the utmost respect, and felt that I was as respected as any other member of the court. On the other hand, I have always conducted myself before all these judges in a respectful manner. These judges often differed substantially with me on the facts and the law, and disagreed with my cause of ending segregation. Nevertheless, they listened, they were respectful, and in most instances they ruled against me and I appealed, and in many cases ultimately won. These judges possessed a great deal of power and they had a great deal of discretion. In most instances, the state court judges particularly ruled against me, and their discretion was almost always against me. But I never took it personally. I would always try cases before all of these judges as if the case was going to the Supreme Court, and many times it was. I can recall only one state circuit court judge who ruled for us in a major civil rights case, Judge Will O. Walton in the suit Attorney General Patterson brought against the Tuskegee Civic Association.

I remember rather well that during the early years of my practice, we were never able to get a civil rights case decided on its merit. There was always some reason for the court to dismiss the case so there would never be a clearcut ruling on the constitutional issue so that we could appeal that issue to the Supreme Court. The opposition correctly feared that if we could get to the Supreme Court we would win the constitutional question.

There was at least one notable exception to the general trend of the state appellate courts to rule against us. In the Regal Cafe cases (*DuBose v. Montgomery*), the Alabama Court of Appeals reversed the convictions in the Montgomery Circuit Court, and a similar reversal occurred in the related *King and Embry v. Montgomery*.

However, I have watched the appellate courts in Alabama in recent years, particularly the Alabama Supreme Court. In my opinion, we now have a court that demonstrates respect for the constitution and laws of not only the State of Alabama but also the United States of America. I feel very comfortable in appearing before our appellate courts and arguing state law questions or federal constitutional issues, and I feel that the courts will rule on the issues in accordance with the law, regardless of the parties and regardless of race, creed or national origin. I believe the work we did in breaking down the barriers of racial segregation, and by African Americans becoming voters and influencing the election of our appellate judges, played a major role.

I have seen several of Alabama's appellate judges change their positions from staunch segregationists to individuals who will rule on matters without regard to race. John Patterson, now an excellent judge of the Alabama Court of Criminal Appeals, is an example. In several events in this book, I have described the actions of John Patterson against African Americans while he was attorney general and governor. But he has acknowledged that he was wrong on many of his views and that many of them were for political reasons. His opinions on the court demonstrate that he is sensitive to the rights of African Americans.

I am of course grateful for the tolerance and understanding which has been extended to me personally and which has permitted my professional success. I am even more grateful for the unusual opportunities that success has given me to enjoy intellectual contact with the finest representatives of the white race. Too few African Americans have been granted that opportunity.

Power has been utilized in the Movement to change society from total segregation to one which is becoming ever more just. We are not there yet, but we are moving in that direction. I believe that the success of the legal cases that I have been involved in speaks well for democracy and for the Constitution. It shows that one can use the system, abide by its rules and regulations, and change society. When we look at today's landscape, we see that most of our public accommodations are desegregated.

However, one of the most disheartening observations I have made over the years is that most of the persons who made up what we called the white power structure have never gone beyond doing exactly what the courts have ordered.

I hope the time will come that elected and appointed officials would treat African Americans fairly, equally, and go beyond the letter of the law to bring about change not because a court ordered them to, but because it's the right thing to do.

This is particularly needed in the whole area of higher education and most importantly in the area of economic freedom. There is no logical reason why there should be such economic disparity as exists in this nation between blacks and whites. There is no reason for the disparity between an African American teenager having a job and a white teenager having one. Yet, in almost every instance, the white child will receive a job more quickly than the black child.

There is an obligation upon all of us, black and white, to work in the area of economic freedom and economic security and use the law and use political power to bring about a change of this economic condition.

Tuskegee University President Dr. Benjamin Payton, left, and I greeted Governor Jim Folsom at the 1994 Macon County Democratic Club annual luncheon, held at the Tuskegee University Kellogg Conference Center.

Epilogue

I wrote this book primarily to record my work as a lawyer during one of the most crucial periods in the history of this nation, from 1954 to the present. I did not dream that my secret ambition to "destroy everything segregated I could find" would be so challenging and fulfilling. My world has been saturated by law—first, by the law of God which has directed my life, and second, by the law of the land (the United States Constitution and its amendments) which have been my tools to tear down the walls of segregation and discrimination. The challenge at times appeared insurmountable. There were times when I grew weary and discouraged, but not once did I lose my determination.

I have had the privilege of filing many precedent-setting lawsuits and representing many outstanding persons who were instrumental in changing the conditions in this country from a completely segregated society based on race and color, to a society in which, in the language of Dr. King, a person may be "judged not by the color of his skin, but by the content of his character." My life has been enriched by the people and great personalities whom I have met as clients, defendants, plaintiffs, judges, witnesses, co-counsel, opposing counsel, jurors, public officials, and plain citizens. There are many books written about the Civil Rights Movement and its many facets. Very few of these books have been written by lawyers and particularly by lawyers who have been in the "eye of the storm." Not only have I had the privilege of being in the "eye of the storm", but I have been a part of the eye and a part of the storm. It was incumbent upon me to write this book pointing out my exact role in the Civil Rights Movement as it has unfolded.

In the final analysis, it was the lawsuits which really changed conditions in the South and in this nation. The demonstrations were important in getting mass participation and public attention. However, it was the courts' decisions that made the law, created and interpreted the law that gave the rights which made it possible for all Americans to enjoy these rights and privileges which were written in our Constitution and the Amendments thereto many, many years ago. The courts could not have made the ruling without lawsuits being filed to request the relief. It was my role and the role of the attorneys who worked with me, as attorneys for the plaintiffs, to file these lawsuits and at other times, to defend those who were unconstitutionally prosecuted.

The mere filing of these lawsuits in and of themselves would not have gotten the desired result. The presence of Judge Frank M. Johnson, Jr., as judge of the United States District Court of the Middle District of Alabama at the time these major suits were filed

I have always enjoyed my work, and I am not ready to retire. However, I do like to relax, and sometimes I even get the "evidence" to prove it. I caught these catfish off the pier at our cabin on Lake Martin north of Montgomery.

made the difference. He was courageous and possessed the tenacity to review each case that came before him as if it were the only case on his docket. He interpreted the Constitution of the United States of America as a living document to be used to correct the ills of the day. The courts' decisions ultimately changed the landscape of Alabama and the nation.

When one reviews the various cases that I filed, beginning with *Browder v. Gayle* which integrated the buses; *Gomillion v. Lightfoot*, which replaced African Americans into the city limits of the City of Tuskegee and laid the foundation for the precedent of the whole concept of one man, one vote; *NAACP v. Alabama*, which permitted civil rights organizations to assert the rights of their members; numerous education cases, which now assure African-American students a non-discriminatory education regardless of the level of their education, in a non-discriminatory manner, which was the first vote dilution case filed in the state of Alabama involving African-American membership on the Barbour County Democratic Executive Committee; *St. John Dixon v. Alabama State*, which held that students had a constitutional right to an education in a state supported institution and that they cannot be expelled without due process of law; *Lee v. Macon*, which desegregated ninety-nine public systems in the State of Alabama and desegregated all institutions then under the control of the Alabama State Board of Education; *Williams v. Wallace*, which ordered the governor of the State of Alabama to protect the marchers as they marched from Selma to Montgomery, which resulted in the passage of the Voting Rights Act; *Pollard v. United States*, which prohibited the United States Government from continuing to refuse to treat African Americans who had been used in a human experiment, and all of the companion cases which I have handled, we must conclude that we have made progress. These cases demonstrate conclusively that today this country is not the same country that it was when I returned to Alabama in 1954 and found everything segregated.

I have been deeply blessed to be a part of the change. Looking back over the first forty years of a dual career in the ministry and the law, I feel that I have succeeded within the limits of my own powers, opportunities, and ambitions.

Looking forward to the next forty, I intend to keep trying to be a part of the solution and not a part of the many problems facing our world today. I also intend to live well, laugh often, love much, and keep the respect of intelligent people. I intend to enjoy my children, spoil my grandchildren, catch more fish, and take Bernice to the Gulf of Mexico more often.

Above all, I pledge to do my best to live a Christian life as a benediction to those I have loved and who have loved me, and to those who have inspired me and in some cases given their very lives so that I could do my part in "destroying everything segregated I could find."

May God bless America, my home, sweet home! And may God bless you.

Table of Cases

*Fred Gray was counsel of record
**Fred Gray was a defendant
***Fred Gray was a plaintiff

*Gomillion v. Lightfoot, 364 U.S. 339, 81 S. Ct. 125, 167 F. Supp. 405, 270 F. 2d 594 (1960).

Gaines v. Canada, ex rel., 305 U.S. 337 (1938).

*City of Montgomery v. Rosa Parks, 36 Ala. App. 681, 92 So. 2d 683 (1957).

*Pollard, et al. v. United States of America, Middle District of Ala., Case No. 4126-N (1975). 384 F. Supp. 304.

*Aurelia A. Browder et.al, v. W. A. Gayle et.al., 142 Fed. Supp. 707, aff'd 77 S. Ct. 145, 352 U.S. 903 (1956)

Brown v. Board of Education, 349 U.S. 294 (1955).

Plessy v. Ferguson, 16 S. Ct. 1138 (1896).

**State of Alabama v. Fred D. Gray, In the Circuit Court of Montgomery County, Case No. GJ202 (1956).

**City of Montgomery v. Fred Gray, In the Recorder's Court of the City of Montgomery (1956).

*State of Alabama v. Martin Luther King, Jr. (Boycott Case). It is reported in the Court of Civil Appeals of Ala. Sup. (1957-1959).

Thornhill v. Alabama, 310 U.S. 88, 60 S. Ct. 736, 84 L.Ed 1093.

*The City of Montgomery vs. Montgomery Improvement Association, et.al., In the Circuit Court of Montgomery County, In Equity, Case No. 31075 (1956).

*City Of Selma v. Wesley Jones, Jr., In the Recorders Court of the City of Selma (December, 1955).

*State of Alabama v. L. L. Anderson, 39 Ala. App. 380, 101 So. 2d 96 (1958); 40 Ala. App. 509, 120 So. 2d 397; 270 Ala. 575, 120 So. 2d 414 (1960); 366 U.S. 208, 81 S. Ct. 1050 (1961).

*NAACP v. Alabama, ex rel. John Patterson, Attorney General, 78 S. Ct.

1163357 U. S. 449 (1958).

*NAACP v. Alabama, ex rel. John Patterson, 79 S. Ct. 1 1001, 360 U.S. 220 (1959) reh. den 80 S. Ct. 43, 161 U.S. 856.

*NAACP v. MacDonald Gallion, Attorney General of Alabama, et al., 82 S. Ct. 4, 368 U.S. 16 (1961).

*NAACP v. Alabama ex rel. Richmond M. Flowers, Attorney General, 84 S. Ct. 1302, 377 U.S. S. Ct. 288 (1964).

*State of Alabama ex rel. John Patterson, Attorney General of Alabama v. Tuskegee Civic Association, In the Circuit Court of Macon County, In Equity, Case No. 2157 (1956).

Colegrove v. Green, 328 U.S. 549 (1946).

Baker v. Carr, 369 U.S. 186, 82 S. Ct. 691, U.S. Tenn., March 26, 1962.

*Housing Authority of the City of Eufaula vs. Oscar Bovier, et al.,
Circuit Court of Barbour County, 1958.

*State of Alabama v. Martin Luther King, Jr., (Tax Case) 1960.

*Sullivan v. New York Times. (New York Times vs. Sullivan) 84 S. Ct. 710, 376 U.S. 254, 11 L.Ed 2d 686, 95 AL R. 2d 1412, motion denied 84 S. Ct. 1130, 376 U.S. 967, 12 L.Ed. 2d 83 (1960).

*William P. Mitchell, et al. v. Edgar Johnson, et al., 250 F. Supp. 117 (1966).

Thomas v. Diversified Contractors, Inc., 551 So. 2d 343 1989 appealed after remanded, 578 So. 2d 1954 (1991).

Edmonson v. Leesville Concrete Company, 111 S.C. 2077 (1991).

Baston v. Kentucky, 476 U.S. 79 (1986).

*James H.M. Henderson, et al. v. ASCS, Macon County, Alabama, et al. 392 F. 2d 531 (1969); 317 F. Supp. 430 (1970).

*State v. Eddie Lee Jordan, February - March, 1957, Circuit Court of Bullock County (1957).

Gilmore v. City of Montgomery, 473 F. 2d 832, cert. den., 94 S. Ct. 215, 414 U.S. 907, 38 L.Ed. 2d 76 (1963).

*Stephen Tate, et al., v. The City of Eufaula, et al., 165 F. Supp. 303 (1958).

*Lee v. Macon County Board of Education., 221 F. Supp. 297 (1963), 231 F. Supp. 743 (1964); 429 F.2d 1218; 448 F.2d 746, appeal after remand 455 F. 2d 978; 453 F. 2d 524; 453 F. 2d 1104; 482 F. 2d 1253, appeal after remand 498 F. 2d 1090; 221 F. Supp 297, supplemented 231 F. Supp. 743; 253 F. Supp 727; 267 458 aff. Wallace v. U. S. 88 S. Ct. 415.

*Wallace v. U. S. 88 S. Ct. 415, 389 U.S. 215 (1967).

*Franklin v. The Barbour County Board of Education, 259 F. Supp. 545, (1966).

*Dixon, et al. v. The Alabama State Board of Education. 186 F. Supp. 945; 294

F. 2d 150 (1960) Cert. den. 82 S. Ct. 368 (1961), 368 U.S. 930, 7 L.Ed. 2d 193.

A.C. Bulls v. U.S., 356 F. 2d 619 (1966).

Carr V. Montgomery Board of Education, 89 S. Ct. 1972, 395 U.S. 225 (1969).

Alabama State Teachers's Association, et al., v. Alabama Public School and College Authority, (ASTA), 289 F. Supp. 784 (M. D. Ala. 1986). Aff'd Curian 393 U.S. 400 (1969).

City of Montgomery v. King and Embry. 168 King So. 2d 30 (1964), 41 Ala. App. 260, 42 Ala. App. 462, 140 So. 2d 292 (1962).

Abnernathy v. Alabama, 380 U.S. 447, 85 S. Ct. 1101 (1963).

Lewis, et al., v. S.E. Greyhound, Inc., 199 F. Supp. 210 (1961).

John Robert Zellner, et al., v. Al Lingo, Director of Public Safety for the State of Alabama. 218 F. Supp. 513, aff. 334 F. 2d 620, (1963).

William Walton Hanson, Jr., et al., v. The State of Alabama, et al. 42 Ala. App. 409, 166 So. 2d 886, (1964).

State of Alabama v. Madeline Sherwood, Case No. 1204 Circuit Court of Etowah Ct. (1963).

Autherine J. Lucy v. Board of Trustees of the University of Alabama, et al. 213 F. 2d 846, (1954).

Vivian Malone v. University of Alabama, Ala. Cr. App., 358 So. 2d 490, cert. den. Ex parte, State ex cel, 358 So. 2d, 494 (1978).

Knight, et al., v. State of Alabama, et al., 628 F. Supp 1137, 828 F2d 1532, 787 F. Supp 1030, 14 F 3d 1534 (1994).

Sweatt v. Painter, 339 U.S. 629 (1950).

McLaurin v. Oklahoma State Regents For Higher Education. 339 U.S. 637 (1950).

Harold A. Franklin v. William V. Parker, Dean, Graduate School of Auburn University, Charles W. Edwards, Registrar of Auburn University, et al., 223 F. Supp. 724, mod. 331 F. 2d 84 (1963).

Willie L. Strain, et al., v. Harry M. Philpott, as President of Auburn University, et al., 331 F. Supp. 83 (1971).

Wendell Wilkie Gunn, a minor by Mollie Gunn, his mother and next friend, v. Ethebert B. Norton, President of Florence State College and Chester M. Arethart, Registrar of Florence State College. CA-63-418, U.S. Northern Dist. of Alabama (1963).

Harris v. The Bullock County Board of Education, 232 F. Supp. 959 (1964).

Harris v. Crenshaw County Board of Education, 259 F. Supp. 167 (1966).

Williams v. Wallace, 240 F. Supp. 100 (1965).

*Sellers v. Trussell, 253 F. Supp. 915 (M.D. Ala. 1966).

United States of America v. John Allen Crook, as Chairman of the Bullock County Democratic Executive Committee, 240 F. Supp. 100 607 F. 2d 670, Reh. den. 609 F. 2d 1009, 253 F. Supp. 915 (1965).

Sellers v. Wilson, 123 F. Supp. 917 (1954).

United States v. Alabama, 61 S. Ct. 1011, 313 U.S. 274, 85 L.Ed. 1387, U.S. 125-27. (1941)

Caswell v. Texas, 339 U.S. 282 (1950).

U.S. v. Alabama, 304 F. 2d 583 (5th Cir. 1962).

*Mary C. Smith, et al., v. T. W. Paris, et al., 386 F. 2d 979, 257 F. Supp. 901, (1966).

U.S. v. State of Alabama, 252 F. Supp. 95 (M.D. Ala. 1965).

*Smith v. YMCA, 316 F. Supp. 899, Modified 462 F. 2d 634, (1970).

Hoover White, et al. v. The State of Alabama, et al., CA 94-T-94-N, U. S. District Court For The Middle District, Northern Division.

***Fred D. Gray, et al., v. Fred D. Main, in his capacity as Judge of Probate of Bullock County, et al., 291 F. Supp. 998, 309 F. Supp. 207.

Lane v. Wilson, 307 U.S. 268, 275, 59 S.Ct. 872, 876, 83 L.Ed. 1281 (1939).

Reynolds v. Sims, 84 S. Ct. 1362, 377 U.S. 533, 12 L. Ed 2d 506, reh. den. 85 S. Ct. 12, 379 U.S. 870; 13 L. Ed 2d 76 (1963).

*Robert E. DuBose, Jr. v. The City of Montgomery, 41 Ala. App. 233, 127 So 2d 845 (1961).

Richard Nesmith v. The City of Montgomery, rev. rem. on authority of DuBose v. City of Montgomery, 41 Ala. App. 233, 127 So 2d 845 (1961).

Edwards, et al., v. South Carolina, 372 U.S. 229. (1963)

Wright, et al., v. State of Georgia, 83 S. Ct. 1240 83 S. Ct. 1240 (1963).

Peterson, et al., v. City of Greenville, South Carolina, 83 S. Ct. 1119 83 S. Ct. 1133 (1963). Reversed by 83 S. Ct. 1119.

Lombard, et al., v. State of Louisiana, 83 S. Ct. 1122 (1963).

Douglas v. City of Jeannette, 63 S. Ct. 660, (1943) 63 S. Ct. 877 (1943) 63 S. Ct. 1170 (1943) 63 S. Ct. 882 (1943).

Steffanelli v. Minard, 72 S. Ct. 802 (May 1951), 72 S. Ct. 118 (1951).

Cleary v. Bolger, 82 Ct. 602 (196), 83 S. Ct. 18 (1962), 83 S. Ct. 385 (1963).

Hutchins v. United States Industries, Inc., 428 F. 2d 303, 310 (5th Cir. 1970).

Local 50, Asbestos Workers v. Vogler, 407 F. 2d 1047, 1052 (5th Cir. 1969).

Cooper v. Aaron, 358 U.S. 1, 15-17 (1958).

Sims v. Baggett, 247 F. Supp. 96. 109 (M.D. Ala. 1965).

U. S. v. Fordice, 112 S. Ct. 2727 (1992).

APPENDIX A

Selected Judicial Orders

A-1. November 14, 1960, U.S. Supreme Court decision by Mr. Justice Frankfurter, in *Gomillion v. Lightfoot*

At this stage of the litigation we are not concerned with the truth of the allegations, that is, the ability of the petitioners to sustain their allegations by proof. The sole question is whether the allegations entitle them to make good on their claim that they are being denied rights under the United States Constitution. The complaint, charging that Act 140 is a device to disenfranchise Negro citizens, alleges the following facts: Prior to Act 140 the City of Tuskegee was square in shape; the Act transformed it into a strangely irregular twenty-eight sided figure as indicated in the diagram appended to this opinion. The essential inevitable effect of this redefinition of Tuskegee's boundaries is to remove from the city all, save four or five, of its 400 Negro voters while not removing a single white voter or resident. The result of the Act is to deprive the Negro petitioners discriminatorily of the benefits of residence in Tuskegee, including inter alia, the right to vote in municipal elections. These allegations, if proven, would abundantly establish that Act 140 was not an ordinary geographic redistricting measure even within familiar abuses of gerrymandering. If these allegations upon a trial remained uncontradicted or unqualified, the conclusion would be irresistible, tantamount for all practical purposes to a mathematical demonstration, that the legislation is solely concerned with segregating white and colored voters by fencing Negro citizens out of town so as to deprive them of their pre-existing municipal vote...

"The [Fifteenth] Amendment nullifies sophisticated as well as simple-minded modes of discrimination." *Lane v. Wilson*, 307 U.S. 268, 275, 59 S.Ct. 872, 876, 83 L.Ed. 1281...

The petitioners here complain that affirmative legislative action deprives them of their votes and the consequent advantages that the ballot affords. When a legislature thus singles out a readily isolated segment of a racial minority for special discriminatory treatment, it violates the Fifteenth Amendment. In no case involving unequal weight in voting distribution that has come before the Court did the decision sanction a differentiation on racial lines whereby approval was given to unequivocal withdrawal of the vote solely from colored citizens. Apart from all else, these considerations lift this controversy out of the so-called "political" arena and into the conventional sphere of constitutional litigation ...

A statute which is alleged to have worked unconstitutional deprivations of petitioners' rights is not immune to attack simply because the mechanism employed by the legislature is a redefinition of municipal boundaries. According to the allegations here made, the Alabama Legislature has not merely redrawn the Tuskegee city limits with incidental inconvenience to the petitioners; it is more accurate to say that it has deprived the petitioners of the municipal franchise and consequent rights and to that end it has incidentally changed the city's boundaries. While in form this is merely an act redefining metes and bounds, if the allegations are established, the inescapable human effect of this essay in geometry and geography is to despoil colored citizens, and only colored citizens, of their heretofore enjoyed voting rights. This was not *Colegrove v. Green*.

364 U.S. 339, 81 S.Ct. 125, 167 F. Supp, 270 F.2d 594 (1960).

A-2. Judge Johnson's order in *Gomillion v. Lightfoot*

Since, as stated by the Supreme Court upon its review of this case, these allegations concerning the effect of the geographic redistricting measure remain uncontradicted, the conclusion is—as far as this Court is concerned—irresistible, "tantamount for all practical purposes to a mathematical demonstration," that the Legislature of the State of Alabama in enacting Act. No. 140 was solely connected with segregating white and colored voters by putting the Negro citizens out of the municipal limits so as to deprive them of their municipal vote. Therefore, when a legislature singles out an isolated segment of a racial group and imposes upon that group discriminatory treatment because of its color, which discriminatory treatment deprives said group and the members thereof of its right to vote, then the action of said legislature violates the Fifteenth Amendment and exceeds the scope of relevant limitations imposed by the United States Constitution. In such instances, when a state—whether the action be by the chief executive, the legislature, or any of the state officers acting within the scope of their authority as such—exercises power "wholly within the domain of state interest, it is insulated form judicial review. But such insulation is not carried over when state power is used as an instrument for circumventing a federally protected right." In the latter instances, as was so aptly stated by the Supreme Court in *Lane v. Wilson*, 307 U.S. 268, 275, "The [Fifteenth] Amendment nullifies sophisticated as well as simple-minded modes of discrimination."

. . . It necessarily follows that said Act must be declared unconstitutional and that each of said defendants, his agents, and/or successor in office, should be permanently enjoined from enforcing or executing said Act against these plaintiffs and those similarly situated.

> (Judge Johnson's Order of February 15, 1961, after the Supreme Court reversed and remanded the case.)

A-3. *Henderson v. Macon County* decision

Conduct on the part of government officials which results in disparate treatment toward members of a particular race must be subjected to the "most rigid scrutiny." Having carefully reviewed the evidence, this Court finds that defendants have failed to demonstrate any compelling interest or legitimate overriding purpose independent of invidious racial discrimination to justify the nomination of such a disproportionate number of black candidates. The evidence clearly reflects that defendants purpose in nominating a plethora of Negro candidates was to prevent the election of Negroes to membership on the community and county committees. The effect of defendants' discriminatory conduct was to deny Negro candidates the opportunity to compete for office on an equal basis with white candidates.

The nomination by defendants of an inordinate number of Negro candidates also resulted in the dilution of the voting strength of the Negro majority in Macon County. While "[t] he principles rationally extrapolated from the voting rights cases derive content from the concrete situation that gave rise to them," *Sims v. Baggett*, 247 F.Supp. 96, 109 (M.D. Ala. 1965), one principle of universal application is that a qualified voter has a constitutional right to vote in elections without having his vote wrongfully denied, debased, or diluted. The importance of an unrestricted and meaningful exercise of the franchise has been emphasized by the Supreme Court on numerous occasions. In *Reynolds v. Sims*, 377 U. S. 533, the Supreme Court stressed that:

> The right to vote freely for the candidate of one's choice is of the essence of a democratic society, and any restrictions on that right strike at the heart of representative government. And the right of suffrage can be denied by a debasement or dilution of the weight of a citizen's vote just as effectively as by wholly prohibiting the free exercise of the franchise.

.....defendants have failed to produce any acceptable evidence to justify the conduct—the nomination of such a disproportionate number of black candidates—which gave rise to that dilution. Thus, "[w]hile [recognizing that] the Fifth Amendment contains no equal protection clause," this Court concludes that defendants' conduct was "so unjustifiable as to be violative of due process."

192 F.2d 531 (1969); 317 F.Supp. 430 (1970).

A-4. Fifth Circuit opinion in *St. John Dixon v. Alabama State Board of Education*

...It is not enough to say, as did the district court in the present case, "The right to attend a public college or university is not in and of itself a constitutional right." ...That argument was emphatically answered by the Supreme Court in the *Cafeteria and Restaurant Workers Union* case, *supra*, when it said that the question of whether "...summarily denying Rachel Brawner access to the site of her former employment violated the require-ments of the Due Process Clause of the Fifth Amendment...cannot be answered by easy assertion that, because she had no constitutional right to be there in the first place, she was not deprived of liberty or property by the Superintendent's action. 'One may not have a constitutional right to go to Baghdad, but the Government may not prohibit one from going there unless by means consonant with due process of law.'" As in that case, so here, it is necessary to consider "the nature both of the private interest which has been impaired and the governmental power which has been exercised..".

There was no offer to prove that other colleges are open to the plaintiffs. If so, the plaintiffs would nonetheless be injured by the interruption of their course of studies in midterm. It is most unlikely that a public college would accept a student expelled from another public college of the same state. Indeed, expulsion may well prejudice the student in completing his educa-tion at any other institution. Surely no one can question that the right to remain at the college in which the plaintiffs were students in good standing is an interest of extremely great value.

. . . Nevertheless, the rudiments of an adversary proceeding may be preserved without encroaching upon the interests of the college. In the instant case, the student should be given names of the witnesses against him and an oral or written report on the facts to which each witness testifies. He should also be given the opportunity to present to the Board, or at least to an administrative official of the college, his own defense against the charges and to produce either oral testimony or written affidavits of witnesses in his behalf. If the hearing is not before the Board directly, the results and findings of the hearing should be presented in a report open to the student's inspection. If these rudimentary elements of fair play are followed in a case of misconduct of this particular type, we feel that the requirements of due process of law will have been fulfilled.

The judgment of the district court is reversed and the cause is remanded for further proceedings consistent with this opinion.

186 F.Supp. 945; 294 F.2d 150 (1960) Cert. den. 82 S.Ct. 386 (1961); 368 U.S. 930, 7 L.Ed.2d 193.

A-5. Judge Johnson's order in *Zellner v. Lingo*, 1963

A study of the complaint reflects that the plaintiffs had planned a "freedom walk" through the State of Alabama as a memorial to one William Moore, who was shot and killed recently on a similar walk. On May 18, 1963, the plaintiffs filed an amendment and supplemental complaint, adding additional defendants and making additional averments. The amended and supplemental complaint reflects that on Friday, May 3, 1963 (at or about the time the original complaint was filed in this Court), the plaintiffs, while walking two abreast at approximately 15 feet apart, along U. S. Highway 11 to DeKalb County, Alabama, and while carrying signs protesting racial segregation, were arrested by the defendant Lingo and those acting under his direction and control; that plaintiffs were immediately thereafter incarcerated in the DeKalb County Jail at Fort Payne, Alabama, and charged with conduct calculated to provoke a breach of the peace under §119(1), Title 14, of the Alabama Code. The amended and supplemental complaint further reflects that, while plaintiffs were incarcerated on this breach of peace charge, at the instigation of the Attorney General for the State of Alabama and other attorneys, herein made defendants, acting for the Governor for the State of Alabama, the Circuit Court of DeKalb County, Alabama, without prior notice to plaintiffs and without an opportunity for them to be heard, issued a temporary injunction wherein said plaintiffs were, insofar as DeKalb County is concerned, enjoined from participating in the "freedom walk" demonstration. The plaintiffs, in their amended and supplemental complaint, ask[ed] this Court to issue an injunction against the defendants, forbidding them from continuing to act under color of law of the State of Alabama in such a manner as to interfere with their right to walk peacefully through the State of Alabama and enjoining them from continuing to imprison and prosecute plaintiffs for their having exercised their constitutional right to walk peacefully through the State of Alabama and, generally, enjoining the defendants and those acting in concert with them from prosecuting plaintiffs "and others similarly situated" for violations of the criminal laws of the State of Alabama on account of plaintiffs' exercising their constitutional rights.

218 F.Supp. 513, aff. 334 F.2d 620, 1963.

A-6. Judge Johnson's opinion in *Strain v. Philpott*

Finally, the Court concludes that there is absolutely no valid justification whatsoever for the various discriminatory practices engaged in by the defendants. . . . there is no valid legal reason for the state to assign its Negro employees to the counties which have traditionally had Negro offices and to assign these employees to subject matter areas dealing primarily with low-income farming. Therefore, such conduct of the defendants is unconstitutional.

Under such circumstances as exist in this case, the courts have the authority and the duty not only to order an end to discriminatory practices, but also to correct and eliminate the present effects of past discrimination. *Hutchins v. United States Industries, Inc.*, 428 F. 2d 303, 310 (5th Cir. 1970), *Local 50, Asbestos Workers v. Vogler*, 407 F. 2d 1047, 1052 (5th Cir. 1969).

The racial discrimination in this case has so permeated the employment practices and services distribution of the defendants that this Court finds it necessary to enter a detailed and specific decree which will not only prohibit discrimination but which will also prescribe procedures designed to prevent discrimination in the future and to correct the effects of past discrimination. A decree will be entered accordingly.

331 F.Supp. 83 (1971).

A-7. November 15, 1990, statement of U.S. District Judge Harold Murphy to the parties in *Knight v. Alabama*

THE COURT: In a moment we'll recess, Before we recess, let me say something to counsel in the case. We have finished the third week of this trial and admittedly we haven't gone five days a week, but when we have been here we have worked long days. And the Court appreciates the diligence of counsel and the Court appreciates the fine lawyers that are handling this case and I say that very sincerely, I'm impressed with all the lawyers in this case and the parties are very fortunate to have the kind of representation that they have.

From what I have thus far heard and from the cross examination that I've heard, I have a pretty good sense of where this case is going insofar as the evidence that's going to be presented to the Court is concerned. It's apparent that it's not going to be a short case.

There is not any guarantee that any particular side or any particular party in this case is going to ultimately prevail. Decisions of the few Courts who have touched on the problems in this case mean that if the case is not resolved between the parties, it may well go on for a long, long time. The case is already quite old. And I'm quite aware that counsel and the parties in this case have made real efforts to try to settle it.

But as a Court, and I speak from the standpoint of settlement, as a Court, I do not see any reason why this case could not be settled between the parties within the present framework of the educational system in Alabama as to state universities and colleges.

I do not see how it can be settled on a basis that would make any party to the case happy, really, because the case is so complex, issues are so broad and so complex that it is hard for me to see how as many parties in the case could agree on a settlement that would make anybody particularly happy.

But it's the kind of case that ought to be settled, and I'm not the first one who's told you this I know. It's the kind of case that ought to be settled in the interest of the students, and the people, and the state of Alabama.

All of you and your clients could perform a great service for this state if you could settle this case and get to the business of education rather than litigation. And I know the schools are still operating, I well know that, but I also know this is quite time consuming. I know how hard all of you have worked and you are working, I have seen all of these stacks of files, and I know how important this case is to the plaintiffs, to the government, and to all the defendants, all of the defendants.

And I'm not at this point giving anybody a lecture, not at all. I think that to settle this case it will take substantial amounts of leadership on the part of the lawyers handling this case, and I have seen the kind of leadership among the lawyers her in this courtroom that could settle the case.

But if you're going to settle the case, the lawyers, you lawyers are the ones who know the issues in the case and you lawyers are the ones who know the problems in the case. And you can't ever settle it unless you tell your clients what they ought to do.

If you are trying to handle the case and settle the case based on what your clients say you can do, then you won't ever get this case settled.

But all of you know as well as I do that the responsibility of a lawyer is to tell his client what he ought to do, encourage him to do it, and let him know why he or she or it should do it, and then ultimately, of course, do what your client let you do. But a lawyer abdicates his responsibility and her responsibility if they do not really let their clients know what ought to be done about a case.

Having said that, let me say again that I'm not lecturing anybody. I'm just letting you know that I'm aware of the seriousness of this case, as I hope you already know. And I'm also fully aware of what a mammoth job it would be to resolve the case. The age of the case hasn't helped it all, but I'm aware that I have a Bar of considerable ability here trying the case and lawyers that I have come to respect.

As the coach, I just want to give you a pep talk, because you have got about a week or a little more than a week that you all could try to resolve something. I don't know that it's at all possible, but let me suggest to you that you shouldn't give up. A bad settlement is a lot better than a good trial, especially when you don't know how you're going to come out.

And so having had the little say the Court wanted to tell you, we'll stand in recess.

628 F.Supp 1137, 828 F.2d 1532, 787 F.Supp 1030, 14 F.3d 1534 (1994).

A-8. December 11, 1990, bench order of U.S. District Judge Harold Murphy in *Knight v. Alabama*

The Court has been concerned for some time at the lack of movement in this case toward resolution of a case that is important to the people of Alabama and particularly the young people, the future of Alabama, insofar as education is concerned.

Portions of this case were filed in 1981, if I remember correctly, and the case has had massive size since 1983. It has cost the state of Alabama millions and millions of dollars that could have been spent in educating its youth. And I think it's the responsibility of this Court, as a responsible Court, to make one last effort to get this case resolved between citizens of Alabama, rather than to have your differences resolved by one United States District Judge, whose decision will be reviewed, but whose ultimate decision will get considerable deference in the Appellate Courts.

So I'm going to make one last effort, and if after that effort, the leadership in Alabama is unable to resolve this issue, then this Court will continue its responsibility and will resolve it for you.

So the Order the Court is entering is as follows: Pursuant to the Court's authority under Rule 16 of the Federal Rules of Civil Procedure and the Court's inherent authority as Presiding Judge in this case, a settlement conference is scheduled in this case for ten o'clock a.m. on Thursday, December 20th, 1990, in this courtroom on the 7th floor of the United States Courthouse in Birmingham, Alabama.

The Court expects and directs that there be present at the conference with counsel at least one individual on behalf of each active party to this case with plenary and absolute authority to settle all issues in this case. If settlement requires the approval of a committee on behalf of any party, then the Court directs that such committee be present or that someone be present with absolute authority to act for such committee.

The Court directs that there be present at this settlement conference the Chief Executive Officer of each institution of higher education who is an active party to this case. The Court further directs there also be present at such conference the Honorable Guy Hunt, Governor of Alabama; the Chief Executive Officer or Officers of the Alabama Commission on Higher Education; and the Alabama Public School and College Authority; the Hon. Wayne Teague, State School Superintendent or State Superintendent of Education; and an individual or individuals authorized to act on behalf of the Alabama State Board of Education.

Any defendant not actively participating in this trial shall have present at such conference a representative or representatives with absolute authority in the premises, else such absent party shall be bound by any action taken as a result of such conference to the extent the Court can enforce such action.

The Court will not hear any witnesses on December the 20th, 1990, as it is expected that the efforts of counsel will be otherwise engaged.

The Court expects counsel for the respective parties to have comprehensive settlement proposals prepared for submission and discussion on that date.

The Court is not attempting and will not coerce a settlement in this case. This case is, however, so massive that any settlement requires the presence of these people and their wisdom and their leadership.

The Court will initially preside at the conference, but will not participate in any manner in settlement discussions as to any terms and conditions. Inasmuch as the Court is trying this case without intervention of a jury, it will not allow itself to be informed of any settlement proposals, of course, until such settlement is ready for submission to the Court for its approval, should the parties be able to reach a settlement.

Should any of your clients desire not to attend the conference as directed by the Court, I suggest that you call their attention to Rule 11 of the Federal Rules of Civil Procedure and 28 USC, United States Code, Section 1927. I would suggest to you that you inform your respective clients that this will be more than a fifteen minute lecture from the Court. The Court will not hesitate to embarrass any individual who fails to appear as directed by the Court and the Court will not hesitate to use its authority to require that this settlement conference be held.

Should the Court's efforts fail, as I have previously indicated to you, and should your efforts fail, which I know will be done in good faith, then, as I have previously indicated to you, the Court will recommence the trial of this case at nine o'clock a.m. on the first Monday of the new year.

The Court directs that this oral Order be transcribed by the court reporter and filed with the Clerk of the Court and that the clerk immediately forward a copy thereof to all parties in this litigation.

628 F.Supp 1137, 828 F.2d 1532, 787 F.Supp 1030, 14 F.3d 1534 (1994).

Appendix B

Excerpts of Citations and Honors

B-1. From the May 28, 1989, citation of the University of Massachusetts at Amherst conferral of the honorary Doctor of Laws degree:

The many laurels already accorded you for your historic and effective work for civil rights cannot begin to equal the approbation you are owed by an insufficiently grateful nation. Behind the scenes and before the bar, in the Alabama legislature and as special assistant to that state's Attorney General, you have been a pivotal figure in our country's slow swing toward real human equality. We honor you as a powerful partisan of justice and a zealot in the cause of freedom.

B-2. From the May 24, 1992, citation of the Case Western Reserve University conferral of the Doctor of Laws Degree:

IN A SOCIETY willing to grant fleeting fame for relatively minor accomplishments, you played a key role in a defining event for an entire generation of Americans when, only a year after graduation from law school, you served as defense attorney in the celebrated case of *City of Montgomery vs. Rosa Parks*. Before then, your life illustrated the triumph of intelligence and courage over adversity. Beginning with that case, your career reads like a history of the civil rights movement....

The intervening years have seen progress toward your goal of dislodging segregation and discrimination, bringing you legal challenges that may be less well known but no less complicated than the charges against Mrs. Parks. Your law practice has included considerable work in educational desegregation, which has frequently made you the target of harassment by opponents of civil rights. Your accomplishments have been recognized widely, including by your election as president of the National Bar Association, an organization for minority lawyers.

B-3. From the September 19, 1993, citation accompanying the Law School Centennial Medal, awarded by the Case Western Reserve University Law Alumni Association:

Fred Gray earned his bachelor's degree in 1951 at Alabama State University (the black "equivalent" of the University of Alabama), but the state had no "equivalent" law school and instead sent him north. Armed with a CWRU law degree, he returned to Montgomery in 1954 and almost immediately began to challenge Southern segregation. A list of his significant cases, beginning with *City of Montgomery v. Rosa Parks*, and including *M. L. King, Jr. v. State of Alabama*, and *Gomillion v. Lightfoot*, reads like a history of the civil rights movement.

B-4. From the inscription to the 1993 the tenth anniversary edition of the Miller Brewing Company calendar, "Excellence Has Many Faces, Gallery of Greats":

Attorney Fred D. Gray was initiated quickly into the civil rights movement in 1954, when Rosa Parks asked him to represent her. The case seemed simple enough: Mrs. Rosa Parks had been arrested for refusing to give up her seat on a Montgomery, Ala., city bus to a white man. But her arrest sparked the flame of protest that swept first throughout the South and later to many other parts of the nation. While the history books have recorded the name of Rosa Parks and the other "super stars" of the civil rights movement, there is no mention of Fred D. Gray—or of many civil rights attorneys who toiled behind the scene....

While others marched, boycotted and resisted, the civil rights attorneys were creatively using the system to overturn discriminatory laws and practices. They devised the legal strategy that struck down unjust doctrines such as "separate but equal." And they kept the front-line soldiers on the battle field, rather than in jail cells....

They were heard. They did change the world...

B-5. From "The Spark Behind the Spark: The Lawyer Who Helped Change America," by Darryl Tippens:

January–March 1993 edition of *Upreach* magazine, published by Highland Church of Christ, Abilene, Texas. The article examines how I have handled simultaneously the professions of law and the ministry.

Great numbers of Americans remember Rosa Parks, that Montgomery bus rider who on December 1, 1955, sparked the Civil Rights revolution that changed America. Prompted by "her personal sense of dignity and self-respect [and] by the accumulated indignities of days gone by and the boundless aspiration of generations yet unborn" (in the words of Martin Luther King, Jr.), Rosa Parks resisted the racism of her day, and she made a lasting difference.

Why was this one instance of resistance to evil so remarkably effective?

The answer, in part, lies in the host of talented friends who stood beside and behind Rosa Parks. One of them was Fred D. Gray—friend, counselor, minister, civil rights advocate, and attorney. Most of all, though, Fred D. Gray was-and is-a disciple of Jesus Christ.

The article ends with the following words:

When people remember the great Civil Rights movement, they usually recall leaders like Martin Luther King, Jr., Ralph Abernathy, or Julian Bond. They visualize the Montgomery Bus Boycott or the 1963 March on Washington. But they should also remember the spark behind the spark, the preacher-turned-lawyer named Fred Gray who still works tirelessly in the courts today, just as he did four decades ago, proving to the world that seeking God and seeking justice by imitating Jesus Christ are a single enterprise:

Let justice roll down like waters, and
righteousness like an everflowing
stream....Sow for yourselves righteousness;
reap steadfast love...for it is time to seek the
Lord, that he may come and rain righteousness on you.
Amos 5:12; Hosea 10:12

Appendix C

Selected Excerpts from Testimony of Expert Witness J. Mills Thornton, III, in *Knight v. Alabama*, 1990

Q. What about Mr. Gray?

A. Mr. Gray was an undergraduate at Alabama State before attending law school in Cleveland, Ohio.

Q. In Cleveland, Ohio?

A. That's where he attended law school, yes. Mr. Gray, I might add, was an honors graduate of Alabama State.

Q. Still is. But he was the lawyer in the *Browder versus Gayle* case?

A. Yes.

Q. That finally brought a resolution to the bus boycott?

A. Yes. In fact, of course he was an attorney in all of the legal proceedings that grew out of the Montgomery bus boycott of which there were quite a number, not merely Federal Court suits against segregation in the buses, but the state court proceedings to try the boycotters for violation of the Alabama Anti Boycott Act of 1921. The *NAACP versus Alabama* brought by Attorney General Patterson that I mentioned before, and then in the fall of 1956, a different proceeding by the city of Montgomery to enjoin the operation of the car pool that the Montgomery Improvement Association used to transport blacks so that they wouldn't have to ride the buses. All of those cases grew out of the Montgomery bus boycott and in all of those cases Fred Gray was an attorney.

. . .

Q. Was Alabama State also a factor in the Montgomery sit-in's of 1960?

A. Yes. In fact, Alabama State was the sole factor, thirty-five students from Alabama State College who went to the Montgomery County Courthouse towards the end of February of 1960 and sought services at the snack bar in the basement of the Montgomery County Courthouse, and that's the beginning of the sit-in crisis in Montgomery.

[Dr. Thornton also testified with reference to the gerrymandering act in Tuskegee which gave rise to the lawsuit of *Gomillion v.*

Lightfoot:]

A And then the following year in 1957, a boycott began in Tuskegee, just to the east of Montgomery, against the merchants of the downtown, merchants of Tuskegee, in retaliation for a bill that was introduced in the legislature by the state senator from Macon County, Sam Englehart, which redrew the boundaries of the city of Tuskegee to exclude essentially all black residents so that the town became for all practical purposes an all white city.

Q. Were you—Are you familiar with the general racial composition of Macon County at that time, white/black, percentages?

A. Yes it's overwhelmingly black. In fact, I think it may have been 80 percent black. It's certainly overwhelmingly black....

Q. And was there a municipal election coming up relatively soon which —

A. Yes. That right. By the time of the redrawing of the boundaries in Tuskegee, enough blacks had been registered so that it was very clear that blacks were going to play a very significant role in the upcoming municipal election, and that is unquestionably the proximate cause of the redrawing of the boundaries. It excluded all of those blacks who had become registered voters from participating in the municipal election.

Q. Did it exclude any whites?

A. No, it excluded no whites. It did leave one or two blacks within the city limits, but for all practical purposes, all blacks had been eliminated.

Q. And that Act gave rise to what action on the part of the black community?

A. Well, the black community had always had an organization or had for many, many years had an organization called the Tuskegee Civic Association, the TCA, and the TCA called a boycott of downtown merchants in an effort to bring pressure to bear to repeal this act, initially not to pass the act, and then to repeal the act....

Q. All right. Now, you mentioned the fact that a boycott started of merchants. What else, if anything, occurred after the boycott started?

A. Well, Attorney General Patterson, using the pattern of the indictment of the black leaders in Montgomery the preceding spring for violation of the Anti Boycott Act attempted to use the Anti Boycott Act to halt the boycott that had started in Tuskegee. He initially, he and his first Assistant Attorney General, McDonald Gallion, raided the Tuskegee Civic Association offices, seized all of the records and then brought suit in Circuit Court in Macon County seeking an injunction against the boycott to forbid the boycott on the grounds that boycott was violating the Anti Boycott Act.

Q. And what else did that passage of the act give rise to or what else did the black community do?

A. Well, eventually, of course, the black community filed suit in Federal

Court to have the act declared unconstitutional that had redrawn the boundaries of Tuskegee and so the boycott proceeded along with the legal challenge, and of course, both legal challenges, both Patterson's in State Court and the black challenge in Federal Court.

What happened on the State Court was simply that because the state was unable to show that the Tuskegee Civic Association had been responsible for any of the actions of intimidation that enforced the boycott, therefore Judge Will Walton, who was the Circuit Judge presiding, ruled that none of the evidence of harassment was admissible because there had been no connection made to the defendant and therefore that there was no case and therefore he refused to grant the injunction.

And then in the Federal Court suit, what happened is that though Judge Johnson, Judge Frank Johnson decided that—refused to rule that the law was constitutional, on appeal to the U.S. Supreme Court, the U.S. Supreme Court in the case of *Gomillion versus Lightfoot* reversed Judge Johnson and ruled that the law was indeed unconstitutional.

Appendix D

National Bar Association Presidents

1994	H. T. Smith	Miami, Florida
1993	Paulette Brown	Newark, New Jersey
1992	Allen J. Webster	Los Angeles, California
1991	Sharon McPhail	Detroit, Michigan
1990	Algenita Scott Davis	Houston, Texas
1989	*Thomas A Duckenfield	Washington, D.C.
1988	James O. Cole	Oakland, California
1987	Walter L. Sutton, Jr.	Dallas, Texas
1986	Thomas J. Broome	Oakland, California
1985	Fred D. Gray	Tuskegee, Alabama
1984	Arthenia L. Joyner	Tampa, Florida
1983	Hon. Dennis W. Archer	Detroit, Michigan
1982	Warren Hope Dawson	Tampa, Florida
1981	Arnette R. Hubbard	Chicago, Illinois
1980	William A. Borders, Jr.	Washington, D.C.
1979	Robert L. Harris	Oakland, California
1978	Junius W. Williams	Newark, New Jersey
1977	Mark T. McDonald	Houston, Texas
1976	Hon. Carl J. Character	Shaker Heights, Illinois
1975	W. George Allen	Ft. Lauderdale, Florida
1974	Charles Howard	Baltimore, Maryland
1973	Archie Weston	Chicago, Illinois
1972	O.T. Wells	New York, New York
1971	James W. Cobb	Washington, D.C.
1970	*Hon. Edward F. Bell	Detroit, Michigan

1969	Hon. William E. Petersen	Chicago, Illinois
1968	Charles Waugh	Muskegon Heights, Illinois
1967	*Hon. Billy Jones	East St. Louis, Illinois
1966	Hon. Revius O. Ortique	New Orleans, Louisiana
1965–66	*Theodore Coggs	Milwaukee, Wisconsin
1963–64	*Robert Lillard	Nashville, Tennessee
1961–62	Elmer C. Jackson	Kansas City, Kansas
1959–60	Hon. Willam S. Thompson	Washington, D.C.
1957–58	*Hon. Richard Atkinson	Washington, D.C.
1955–56	*Hon. Richard Atkinson	Washington, D.C.
1954	Harold Bledsoe	Detroit, MI
1953	*W. Harold Flowers, Sr.	Pine Bluff, Arkansas
1951–52	*Hon. Scovel Richardson	New York, New York
1949–48	*James R. Booker	Little Rock, Arkansas
1947–48	*Thurman L. Dodson	Washington, D.C.
1945–46	*Earl B. Dickerson	Chicago, Illinois
1943–44	*Charles W. Anderson	Louisville, Kentucky
1941–42	*Euclid Louis Taylor	Chicago, Illinois
1939–40	*Sidney R. Redmond	St. Louis, Missouri
1937–38	*William L. Houston	Washington, D.C.
1935–36	*George W. Lawrence	Chicago, Illinois
1933–34	*Eugene W. Rhodes	Baltimore, Maryland
1931–32	*Jesse S. Heslip	Toledo, Ohio
1929–30	*Raymond P. Alexander	Washington, D.C.
1928	*C. Francis Stradford	Chicago, Illinois
1927	*Homer G. Philips	St. Louis, Missouri
1926	*Charles Calloway	Kansas City, Missouri
1925	*George H. Woodson	Des Moines, Iowa

*Deceased

Appendix E

Relating to the Federal Judgeship, 1979–1980

E-1, Remarks of Fred D. Gray at Press Conference, August 8, 1980

First, I would like to express my appreciation and thanks for all of those who have assisted me in connection with my nomination to become a Federal District Judge. I am appreciative to President Carter, Senators Stewart and Heflin, the National Bar Association, the Alabama Black Lawyers Association, Tuskegee Institute, Mrs. Coretta Scott King, Joe Reed, Mayor Ford, Mayor Arrington, Messers Parker, Pinkard, Mitchell & Bulls, Attorneys Russell and Raymon, Judges Byrd, Hornsby and Huffman and all of the other witnesses who went to Washington and testified for me, including the two bus loads, and persons who went by plane in support of my nomination. I am appreciative to my law partners, Messers Seay and Langford, Mrs. Bibb, my Office Manager and members of my staff who have worked so hard during the last 18 months. Last, but not least, I am appreciative to my lovely wife, Bernice, and my children, Deborah, Vanessa, Fred, Jr. and Stanley; for they have suffered more than anyone else during what we had hoped would be a wonderful experience, but what has developed into an ordeal. Most of all, I am thankful to God who has given us all the strength to overcome.

In May of 1979, Senators Stewart and Heflin recommended me to the President for the position of United States District Judge for the Middle District of Alabama. The Senators acted upon recommendations of the Alabama Judicial Nominating Commission of Alabama, and according to testimony at my hearing, I received the second highest number of votes of any person under consideration by the Commission.

Based on the Senators' recommendation, President Carter nominated me and sent my name to the United States Senate for confirmation. The nomination was referred to the Senate Judiciary Committee where it is under consideration.

Immediately following my nomination, allegations and charges were made against me in the news media, particularly the Birmingham papers, a TV station in Montgomery and more recently the Tuskegee News. These allegations questioned my integrity as well as my competency as a lawyer. These allegations had the sole purpose of attempting to block my confirmation as a United States District Judge and were spurred by my well-known past and present efforts to secure full freedom and equality for Black persons in this state and throughout this nation.

I have answered fully and completely each of the charges. I was supported in my nomination by Blacks and whites from across this state and nation who know me best, and who are best able to attest to my integrity, my honesty, my legal competency and temperament.

As I met and successfully explained and defended each charge, new and even more groundless charges were contrived by persons who would go to any length to prevent my confirmation because of my background in civil rights litigation.

With full knowledge of the baselessness of the charges, my opposition sought to sabotage my confirmation by either creating delaying circumstances or by developing an atmosphere designed to lend itself to a conclusion that where there is a lot of smoke, there must be some fire.

I appeared before the Senate Judiciary Committee on May 19, 20, 21, 22, 28, 30 and July 2. Every aspect of my public and private life has been thoroughly scrutinized. Every business transaction which I have entered into has been investigated. I have been subjected to more investigations and hearings than any other nominee for a Federal District Judgeship in the history of this Country.

Senator Max Baucus, who chaired the Committee, said at the conclusion of the hearings:

"Mr. Gray, my hat is off to you. You have sat here a lot. I do not know any other nominee who has gone through quite as exhaustive a hearing as you have. For one reason or another, partly because of the charges that have been raised, the Committee has gone through your background in the 25 years that you have been practicing law more than any other nominee. That's due, in part, to the issues raised prior to the hearing, issues raised by the American Bar Association. You have conducted yourself in a very, very proper manner for which you and the State of Alabama can be very proud."

I am well pleased with the record made at my hearings. All of the allegations and charges were proven to be false and untrue. Anyone objectively reading that record will conclude that it completely exonerates me of the allegations and charges, and that I am well qualified to serve as a District

Judge. I am saddened to know that Senator Heflin, for whom I have a great deal of respect, has decided to withdraw his support of my nomination. While the Senator, on several occasions expressed to me his doubts that there were sufficient votes in the Committee for my confirmation, it was Wednesday of this week, for the first time, that he informed me he could no longer support my confirmation.

For 25 years I have practiced law in this state. I have handled many civil rights cases which include: desegregating the buses in Montgomery; desegregating the University of Alabama, Auburn University and Florence State College; and desegregating over 100 public school systems in this state. I have represented the National Association for the Advancement of Colored People, the Tuskegee Civic Association, the Montgomery Improvement Association, Dr. Martin Luther King, Jr., Mrs. Rosa Parks, Rev. Ralph Abernathy, Dr. Charles Gomillion with the Tuskegee gerrymander case and many, many more.

A substantial segment of power structure of Alabama has never approved the role which I played in attempting to change Alabama from a segregated state to one of equal opportunity. They have never forgotten that I am a lawyer, more so that anyone else, who substantially desegregated this state. It is this segment of the power structure, motivated by racism, that created, manufactured and orchestrated the climate which has placed my nomination in jeopardy. They would rather have any person, white or black, male or female, young or old, experienced or inexperienced, to be Federal District Judge in Montgomery, the cradle of the confederacy—rather than Fred Gray. It appears that they have been successful.

I have been asked to step aside. I have been told that with Senator Heflin's withdrawal of support I will not be confirmed. That is probably true. I have been advised that if I step aside immediately the process can be expedited and that a Black can be confirmed as a United States District Judge for the Middle District of Alabama before this session of Congress ends. I would like to believe that can be done. However, looking at the four District Judges that have been recently appointed in Alabama and the two most recent United States Court of Appeals Judges for the Fifth Circuit from Alabama, the process from recommendation to confirmation has taken substantially longer than 60 days. Time is not now, nor has it ever been the ally of the Black man in this Country.

There has never been a Black Federal District Judge in the Middle District of Alabama. The Court that has done more to integrate this nation than any other Court, should itself be integrated. I will gladly step aside if the Black people of Alabama can be assured that a Black lawyer, acceptable to the Black community, will be confirmed during this session of Congress.

If our Senators, both of them, and White House can give this assurance to Black people of Alabama, I will step aside as soon as such assurance is made.

In making this offer of withdrawal of my nomination, I am fully cognizant that the decade of the 80's is not the proper period in the history of this country to continue to experiment with racism. I take this action with some comfort in the knowledge that "those who pioneer, seldom settle."

August 8, 1980
Tuskegee, Alabama

E-2, Letter to President Carter

September 12, 1980
Honorable James E. Carter
President of the United States
The White House
Washington, D.C. 20500
Dear Mr. President:

I appreciate the faith and confidence that you expressed in nominating me to become a United States District Judge for the Middle District of Alabama.

Shortly after you submitted my nomination to the Senate for confirmation, numerous allegations appeared in the media which questioned my integrity and my competency as a lawyer. These allegations had the sole purpose of attempting to block my confirmation and were prompted by my well known past and present efforts to secure full freedom and equality for Black persons in Alabama and throughout this nation. As each charge surfaced, I promptly furnished responses to Senator Heflin as well as the staff of the Senate Judiciary Committee.

I appeared before the Senate Judiciary Committee on May 19, 20, 21, 22, 28, 30 and July 2. I also submitted to the Minority members of the Committee answers to some 69 questions submitted to me by them.

I am well pleased with the record made at my hearings. All of the allegations and charges were proven to be false and untrue. Anyone objectively reading that record will conclude that it completely exonerates me of the allegations and charges, and that I am well qualified to serve as a District Judge.

Every aspect of my public and private life has been thoroughly scrutinized. Every business transaction which I have entered into has been investigated. I have been subject to more investigations and hearings than any other nominee for a Federal District Judgeship in the history of this Country.

On Tuesday, August 5, 1980, at approximately 9:30 p.m., while I was attending a National Bar Association Annual Convention in Dallas, Texas, I received a phone call from Senator Heflin. He then informed me, for the first time, that he was unable to continue to support my nomination. I inquired as to his reasons but he refused an explanation saying that it would serve no useful purpose to discuss the matter further—he had made up his mind.

At no time prior to Tuesday, August 5, 1980, did Senator Heflin ever express to me his inability to continue to support my nomination. I had numerous conversations with the Senator and he had expressed that he was concerned that we did not have the number of votes needed for confirmation in the Senate Committee. We informed the Senator that my supporters were actively supplying to the members of the Committee all the facts and circumstances which they needed to act favorably upon my nomination.

In my opinion, I believe that the white power structure of Alabama brought pressure to bear upon Senator Heflin and told him that they did not want Fred Gray to be District Judge; and that if they must have a Black they would rather have a black who did not have my civil rights record. I am enclosing a copy of my statement to the press concerning this matter.

I understand that Senator Heflin has written to Senator Edward M. Kennedy, Chairman of the Senate Committee on the Judiciary, and stated that he was withdrawing his support for my confirmation and requested that "my blue slip be returned to me." As I understand the "blue slip" procedure, Senator Heflin has in effect vetoed my nomination and under the usual rules of courtesy, the members of the Committee will not vote favorably upon my confirmation under these circumstances.

I have been informed that if I request you to withdraw my name from consideration, another Black will be nominated and possibly confirmed before the current session of Congress ends. I further understand that Attorneys Myron Thompson and J. Mason Davis are currently being investigated by the FBI and American Bar Association for this position. While I feel that I am competent to serve as a Federal District Judge and that my record before the Committee so substantiates, under the facts and circumstances set out in this letter, I am requesting that you withdraw my name from nomination as a United States District Judge.

Again, may I express appreciation for your consideration and confidence in me.

Very truly yours,
Fred D. Gray
FDG:b
Enclosure

E-3, Remarks of Fred D. Gray at the Investiture of the Honorable Myron J. Thompson, October 9, 1980

May it please the Court, other members of the Judiciary, the Honorable Thompson, ladies and gentlemen. It is with both pride and satisfaction that I share in this historic occasion. Pride—because a talented, young Black attorney today assumes important responsibilities as a United States District Judge. Satisfaction—because so many Blacks, including but not limited to, Mrs. Rosa Parks, Martin Luther King, Jr., E.D. Nixon, Joe Reed and others have paved the way to make this occasion possible.

When it became apparent that I would not serve as a federal district judge, I immediately began to think about another person I would like to see so serve. My personal choice, I am happy to say, is Judge Myron Thompson. Not only is he my choice, but he is the choice of the Black leadership of this State, the United States Senate and the President. What would have been a pinnacle for a Black, 49 year old, battle-scarred civil rights lawyer, is merely a stepping stone for a Black 33-year-old, talented Yale educated lawyer.

Judge Myron Thompson is probably the only District Judge appointed in recent years who did not actively seek the judgeship, the Black community solicited him. It has been said with respect to greatness: "Some men are born great, some acquire greatness and still others have greatness thrust upon them." In the case of Judge Thompson, greatness has been thrust upon him in the form of an opportunity to serve as Federal District Judge.

Those of us who were closely involved in the Civil Rights Movement, certainly envisioned the time when men would be given responsibilities in all areas of public life in accordance with their ability and not because of the color of their skin. Since those days—as witnessed here—Blacks have made great strides. We still see in so many ways, however, that the ideals and principles of this great democracy are in many areas unfulfilled; that equal justice under the law is not yet fully ours. So, this is a momentous occasion, for Judge Thompson, a man of honesty, integrity, tremendous ability, a lawyer's lawyer now assumes the responsibility of assisting in fulfilling these ideals.

We note the importance of this occasion for another reason. Through the years, we as Black Americans have been stifled in our career goals. Why? Because in the few instances when we are appointed to top level positions, it is late in life. We have had to claw our way up the rungs so hard that we are already tired before we are recognized for what we can do. Not so with Myron Thompson. His appointment comes early in life. He is young, energetic, talented and has lots of time to grow further in stature.

Sixty days ago few persons in this room would have given Judge Thompson a ghost of a chance of becoming a federal district judge. But he has been appointed. I foresee a long fruitful judicial career for Judge Thompson. Who knows, but he may become Chief Judge of this Court; and perhaps a few years later, he may sit on the United States Court of Appeals. Who knows, we may be here today, not merely participating in an investiture ceremony, for a District Judge, but we may be witnessing the beginning of an illustrious judicial career where Judge Thompson may very well someday, hopefully in our life time, sit as a Justice of the United States Supreme Court, and may even become The Chief Justice thereof.

Judge Thompson, we wish you well, and I personally look forward to trying many cases before you.

Thank you.

Sources of Photographs and Illustrations

Unless noted below, all photographs and illustrations were provided by the author.

Page 7, Frank H. Lee; 11, James Ladd; 65, Ebony Magazine; 113, Lawrence Sims, nephew of Dr. Gomillion; 210, Tuskegee University archives; 263, Charles Thompson; 270, Hawkins Studio; 280, Frank H. Lee; 307, Thomas Martin; 311, Arthur Freeman; 317, Tuskegee University Archives; 318, Frank H. Lee; 322, Frank H. Lee; 351, top left—Arthur Shores, top right—Mrs. Virginia Durr, bottom left—Frank Sikora; 359, Walter Scott.

Grateful appreciation is expressed to the above-named providers of illustrations for this book.

Index

Hill, Robison & Belser 182
Hill, Thomas B., Jr. 154
Hillard Chapel A. M. E. Zion Church 350
Hinkle, Alvin 11
Hinson, J. D. 232
Hitchcock, Jimmy 71
Hodnett, O. L. 118
Hoffman, Aaron 83
Holley, Paul S. 273
Hollingsworth, Audrey K. 232
Holmes, Alvin A. 272
Holmes, Booker T. 83
Holmes, Clarence 20
Holmes, Reverend 135
Holmes, Wavelyn 187
Holt Street Baptist Church 83, 88, 350
    site of 1st mass meeting, 57–58
Holt Street Church of Christ 8, 77, 88–89,
    254, 256
Hood, David 29, 54, 214, 324
Hood, James 143, 192
Hood, Octavia 192
Hooks, Lonnie 130
Hornsby, Andy 293
Hornsby, Ernest C. "Sonny" 294
Hornsby, Marjorie 130
Hornsby, Preston 118, 293, 313
Houston, Charles Hamilton 77, 311, 353
Houston, Karen Gray 311
Houston, Marguerite 104
Howard, Carter 286, 289
Howard Law School 77
Howard, Ralph O. 130
Hubbard, Arnette 308, 309
Hubbard, H. H. 83, 350
Huddleston, Charles 118
Huddleston, Lovie 11
Huffman, Mary E. 243
Huffman, Rufus 239, 243, 294
Hunter, John D. 102
Hunter, Mary 232, 239
Hunter, Robert D. 325
Huntingdon College 186, 269

I

Ingram, Robert B. 273
Interstate Commerce Commission 180

J

Jackson, Calvin, Jr. 243
Jackson, James 112
Jackson, Jesse 352
Jackson, Mabel H. 209
Jackson, Mattie 23
Jackson, Satiree 113
Jackson, Thomas O. 22
Jackson, Willie M., Jr. 209
Jacksonville State College 202, 218
James, Alberta 351
James, Alberta Judkins 83

James, Collier 11
James, Earl 162, 182
James, Felix 350
James, Fob 337
James J. Carter 273
Jefferson Davis Hotel 179
Jenkins, Ray 300
Jim Crow 74, 91
John A. Andrew Hospital 284, 314
John Green 83
Johnson, Brenda Faye 209
Johnson, Dwight W. 209
Johnson, Edgar 126
Johnson, Frank M., Jr. 62, 80, 96, 176–
    177, 203
    as influence on Fred Gray, 347
    as seen by Fred Gray, 177
    historical significance of, 358
    in ASTA v. Alabama Public School and
        College Autho 273–280
    in Browder v. Gayle, 73, 90
    in Carr v. Montgomery, 206–208
    in Franklin v. Parker, 196–197
    in Gomillion v. Lightfoot, 119, 122
    in Gray v. Main, 245–246
    in Lee v. Macon, 210
    in Lewis v. Greyhound, 182–185
    in Mitchell v. Johnson, 126–127
    in Sellers v. Trussell, 228, 230–231
    in Selma March case, 221–226
    in Smith v. Paris, 233–236
    in Tate v. Eufaula, 137–138
    in Zellner v. Lingo, 186
    relationship with George Wallace, 144–
        145, 270
Johnson, Geraldine 11
Johnson, H. H. 83
Johnson, Lyndon 149, 321, 350
Johnson, Mentha H. 83
Johnson, Mrs. Lyndon 346
Johnson, Price 286
Johnson, Robert 83
Johnson, Ruth 209
Johnson, Sutton 10
Johnson, Tom (of CNN) 346
Johnson, William H. 83
Johnson, Willie C. 209
Johnson, Willie C., Jr. 209
Johnston, David 313
Johnston, Reed, Jr. 130
Jones, Charles H., Jr. 215, 221, 243
Jones, David 11
Jones, Edward English 175
Jones, Elaine 294
Jones, Jim 287, 290
Jones, Joseph Charles 181, 182
Jones Law School 26
Jones, Moses William 83, 85, 263, 265,
    351
Jones, Nettie B. 118